# Houghton Mifflin
# Reading

# Traditions

**Senior Authors**
J. David Cooper
John J. Pikulski

**Authors**
Kathryn Au
David J. Chard
Gilbert Garcia
Claude Goldenberg
Phyllis Hunter
Marjorie Y. Lipson
Shane Templeton
Sheila Valencia
MaryEllen Vogt

**Consultants**
Linda H. Butler
Linnea C. Ehri
Carla Ford

 **HOUGHTON MIFFLIN**

**BOSTON**

Acknowledgments begin on page 719.

Printed in the U.S.A.

ISBN: 0-618-24149-3

2 3 4 5 6 7 8 9 VH 09 08 07 06 05 04

# Traditions

# Theme 1

# Journeys

Theme Wrap-Up
## Check Your Progress

# MYSTERIES

**Fiction**

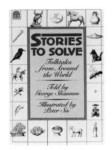

**Fiction**

# American Stories

# American Stories

**Theme Wrap-Up**
## Check Your Progress

# Theme 3

# That's Amazing!

**Fantasy**

**Fairy Tale**

**Theme Wrap-Up**

## Check Your Progress

# Theme 4

# Problem Solvers

**Theme Wrap-Up**

# Check Your Progress

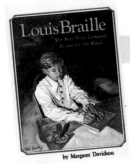

# HEROES

# HEROES

16

# Focus on Genre

# POURQUOI TALES

**Folktale**

**Folktale**

**Folktale**

# Theme 6

# Nature
## *Friend and Foe*

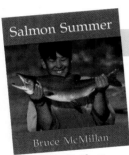

**Theme Wrap-Up**
## Check Your Progress

# 1

## Journeys

A journey of a
thousand miles
must begin with
a single step.

— *Lao-tzu*
*(604–531 B.C.E.)*

# Journeys

## with Allen Say

Welcome! Are you ready for the first step on your theme journey? Here is a letter for you from *Journeys* author Allen Say.

MR. ALLEN SAY
2934
Street.

AIR M

BaHaMas

No. 1631

**Passport**

IMPORTANT

The person to whom this passport is issued must sign his name on page three immediately on its receipt. The passport is NOT VALID unless it has been signed.

The bearer should also fill in blanks below as indicated.

Bearer's address in the United States

foreign address

Consulate General

of

The United States of America

Dear Reader,

I remember reading somewhere that the best part of a journey is going home. Whoever said that was talking about homesickness. But my mother used to say, "Let your dear child journey." It's an old Japanese saying.

I didn't get to go on my first big trip by myself. My mother and my little sister came along, and we never went home afterwards. We were running away from the city because bombs were falling there. Our house burned to the ground.

When World War II ended, we went to live in a harbor town in Kyushu, the south island of Japan. It was a beautiful place with mountains all around, and the sea was full of small islands. My father had found a job there. I went to my fourth grammar school and I was still in the first grade. One day I saw an American soldier doing tricks with his bicycle. I had never seen anything like it.

Then my parents were divorced, and I was sent to Tokyo. The day I left, I stared at the mountains and the harbor and the islands in the sea. I wished I had a camera.

Well, I've been on a journey ever since. It's the Big Journey. And I've kept my eyes wide open. It's only natural that I became a photographer.

But when I grew older, I wanted to do more than take pictures. I wanted to tell stories — of people I met and places I visited. So I wrote about the bicycle man and drew the harbor town from memory. Forty years later I again saw the mountains and the harbor and the islands in the sea. They were just as I had remembered them, and once again, for a moment, I was a young boy.

Do I get homesick? Of course. But the journey is so interesting that I don't think about it very much. It's exciting to know that I'm going to see something new just over the next hill.

And you, dear reader, are already on the Big Journey of your own, so keep your eyes wide open!

Sincerely,

*Allen Say*

# Take a Journey...

When you think of a journey, what comes to mind?  Compare Allen Say's ideas with your own. What do you think he means by the "Big Journey"?

As you read this theme, think about what makes each selection a journey.  How does each one change your ideas about journeys?

Now you're ready!  It's time to travel by train, plane, ship, and even dogsled as you set out to read *Journeys*.

To learn about the authors in this theme, visit Education Place.  **www.eduplace.com/kids**

# Background and Vocabulary

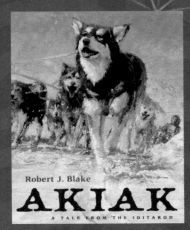

*Akiak*

Robert J. Blake
# AKIAK
A TALE FROM THE IDITAROD

**Read to find the meanings of these words.**

*e* ● Glossary

blizzards
checkpoints
courageous
experienced
musher
rugged

# Running THE IDITAROD

Every March teams of sled dogs run the world-famous Iditarod race. The course covers more than 1,000 miles of **rugged** Alaskan trails. Teams of up to sixteen dogs pull a sled carrying their **musher**, or driver, who works closely with the **experienced** lead dog.

Because it can be dangerous, the Iditarod has many rules to make sure the teams reach the end of the race safely. Racers, both animal and human, are required to rest often as well as to sign in at many **checkpoints** along the way.

In the story you are going to read, one special racer struggles to overcome the odds and to make the most of her last chance at an Iditarod victory.

**MUSHER**

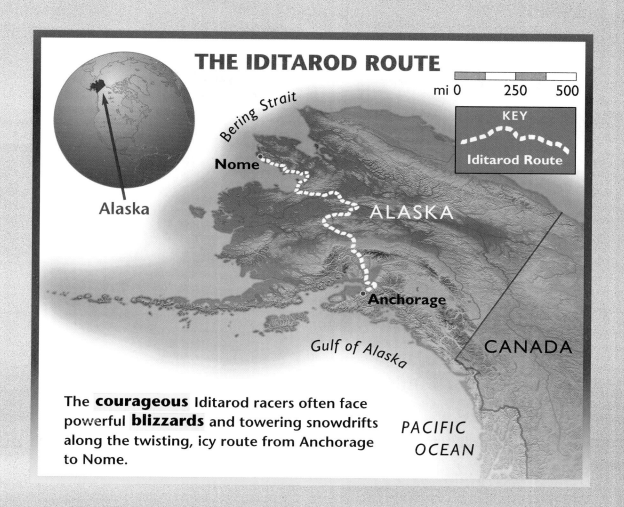

# THE IDITAROD ROUTE

Bering Strait

Nome

Alaska

ALASKA

Anchorage

Gulf of Alaska

CANADA

PACIFIC OCEAN

mi 0    250    500

KEY
Iditarod Route

The **courageous** Iditarod racers often face powerful **blizzards** and towering snowdrifts along the twisting, icy route from Anchorage to Nome.

**LEAD DOG**

# MEET THE AUTHOR AND ILLUSTRATOR

# ROBERT BLAKE

As a young boy growing up in New Jersey, Robert Blake always loved to draw. He recalls the time he drew a mural on the hallway wall. This drawing was "not artistically appreciated" by his parents, he says.

Blake enjoys traveling to get ideas for his stories. For *Akiak,* he journeyed to Alaska to watch the famous Iditarod race. To research some of his other books, he has traveled to places as far away as Ireland and has sailed the coast of New England.

Blake says that he hopes to paint in every state in the nation and in every country in the world. But in the meantime, he lives in New Jersey with his wife and son. He continues to paint in his studio, which is located in a barn.

**Other books by Robert Blake:**
*Spray, The Perfect Spot, Dog*

To find out more about Robert Blake, visit Education Place. **www.eduplace.com/kids**

Robert J. Blake

# AKIAK

A TALE FROM THE IDITAROD

## Strategy Focus

*Akiak* is divided into sections describing different days of the Iditarod race. As you read, stop every few pages to **summarize** each day's events.

## DAY ONE

Akiak knew it.  The other dogs knew it, too.

Some had run it many times and others had never run it at all.  But not a dog wanted to be left behind.

It was Iditarod Race Day.  1,151 miles of wind, snow, and rugged trail lay ahead, from Anchorage to Nome.  Akiak had led the team through seven races and knew the trail better than any dog.  She had brought them in fifth, third, and second, but had never won.  She was ten years old now.  This was her last chance.  Now, they must win now.

Crack!  The race was under way.  One by one, fifty-eight teams took off for Nome.

## DAY TWO

"Come on, old girl, show 'em how," Mick called.  "Haw!"

Mick worked the sixteen-dog team through Akiak, calling "Haw!" when she needed the dogs to turn left, and "Gee!" to go right.  Mick was the musher, but the team followed the lead dog.  The team followed Akiak.

Through steep climbs and dangerous descents, icy waters and confusing trails, Akiak always found the safest and fastest way.  She never got lost.

# DAY THREE

Akiak and Squinty, Big Boy and Flinty, Roscoe and the rest of the team pounded across the snow for three days. The dogs were ready to break out, but Mick held them back. There was a right time — but not yet.

High in the Alaskan range they caught up to Willy Ketcham in third place. It was his team that had beaten them by just one minute last year. Following the rules, Willy pulled over and allowed Mick's team to pass.

"That old dog will never make it!" he laughed at Akiak across the biting wind.

"She'll be waiting for you at Nome!" Mick vowed.

## Day Four

High in the Kuskokwim Mountains they passed Tall Tim Broonzy's team and moved into second place. Just after Takotna, Mick's team made its move. They raced by Whistlin' Perry's team to take over first place.

Ketcham made his move, too. His team clung to Mick's like a shadow.

Akiak and her team now had to break trail through deep snow. It was tough going. By the Ophir checkpoint, Akiak was limping. The deep snow had jammed up one of her pawpads and made it sore. Mick tended to her as Ketcham raced by and took first place from them.

"You can't run on that paw, old girl," Mick said to her. "With a day's rest it will heal, but the team can't wait here a day. We've got to go on without you. You'll be flown home."

Roscoe took Akiak's place at lead.

## Day Five

By morning most of the other dog teams had passed through the Ophir checkpoint. The wind was building and the pilot was in a hurry to leave. Akiak tore at the leash as the volunteer brought her to the airplane.

"Get that dog in," the pilot hollered. "I want to get out of here before the storm hits!"

Akiak jumped and pulled and snapped. All she wanted was to get back on the trail. To run. To win. Then all at once, the wind gusted, the plane shifted, and Akiak twisted out of the handler's grip. By the time they turned around she was gone.

## Day Six

Akiak ran while the storm became a blizzard. She knew that Mick and the team were somewhere ahead of her. The wind took away the scent and the snow took away the trail, but still she knew the way. She ran and she ran, until the blizzard became a whiteout. Then she could run no more. While Mick and the team took refuge in Galena, seven hours ahead, Akiak burrowed into a snowdrift to wait out the storm.

In the morning the mound of snow came alive, and out pushed Akiak.

## Day Seven

Word had gone out that Akiak was loose. Trail volunteers knew that an experienced lead dog would stick to the trail. They knew she'd have to come through Unalakleet.

She did. Six hours after Mick and the team had left, Akiak padded softly, cautiously, into the checkpoint. Her ears alert, her wet nose sniffed the air. The team had been there, she could tell.

Suddenly, cabin doors flew open. Five volunteers fanned out and tried to grab her. Akiak zigged around their every zag and took off down the trail.

"Call ahead to Shaktoolik!" a man shouted.

41

# DAY EIGHT

At Shaktoolik, Mick dropped two more dogs and raced out, still six hours ahead of Akiak.

Hungry now — it had been two days since she had eaten — Akiak pounded over the packed trail. For thirst, she drank out of the streams, the ice broken through by the sled teams.

She struggled into Shaktoolik in the late afternoon. Three men spotted her and chased her right into the community hall, where some mushers were sleeping. Tables overturned and coffee went flying. Then one musher opened the back door and she escaped.

"Go find them, girl," he whispered.

At Koyuk, Akiak raided the mushers' discard pile for food. No one came after her. At Elim, people put food out for her. Almost everybody was rooting for Akiak to catch her team.

## Day Nine

Mick rushed into White Mountain twenty-two minutes behind Ketcham. Here the teams had to take an eight-hour layover to rest before the final dash for Nome. Mick dropped Big Boy and put young Comet in his place. The team was down to eight dogs with seventy-seven miles to go.

Akiak pushed on. When her team left White Mountain at 6 P.M., Akiak was running through Golovin, just two hours behind. A crowd lined the trail to watch her run through the town.

# DAY TEN

Screaming winds threw bitter cold at the team as they fought their way along the coast. Then, halfway to the checkpoint called Safety, they came upon a maze of snowmobile tracks. The lead dogs lost the trail.

Mick squinted through the snow, looking for a sign.

There. Going right. She recognized Ketcham's trail.

"Gee!" she called. Gee — go right.

But the dogs wouldn't go. They wandered about, tangling up the lines. Mick straightened them out and worked the team up the hill. At the top they stopped short. Something was blocking the trail.

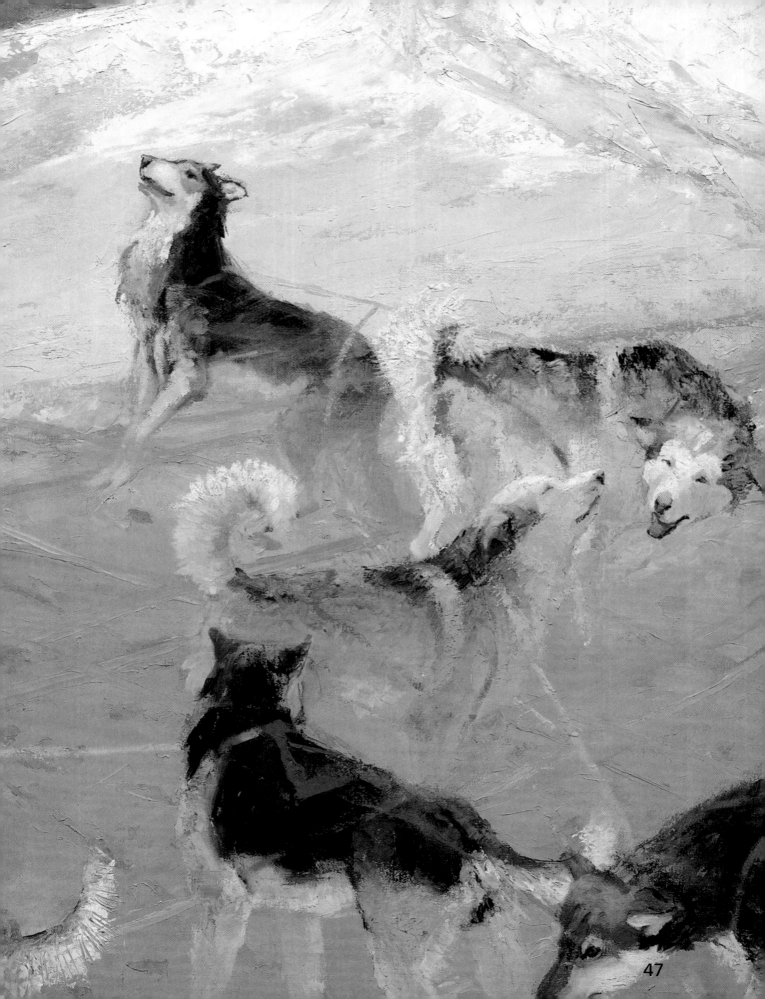

47

"Akiak!" Mick called.

She ran to her usual spot at the harness, waiting to be hooked in.

"Sorry, old girl." Mick hugged her. "Rules say I can't put you back in harness. Get in the sled."

But instead, Akiak circled the lead dogs, pushing them and barking.

"What is it, girl?" Mick asked.

Akiak ran back down the hill.

Mick laughed. Ketcham's team had taken the wrong trail! She turned her team around and rushed them down to Akiak, who jumped into the sled.

"Take us to Nome!" Mick called to her.

Mick first heard the noise a mile outside of Nome. At first she wasn't sure what it was. It grew so loud that she couldn't hear the dogs. It was a roar, or a rumble — she was so tired after ten days of mushing she couldn't tell which. Then she saw the crowd and she heard their cheers. People had come from everywhere to see the courageous dog that had run the Iditarod trail alone.

As sure as if she had been in the lead position, Akiak won the Iditarod Race.

"Nothing was going to stop this dog from winning," Mick told the crowd. Akiak knew it.

The other dogs knew it, too.

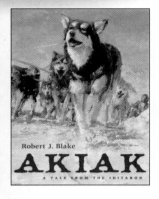

# Think About the Selection

**1.** How do you think Mick feels when she sends Akiak home on Day Four? Would you have made the same decision?

**2.** What qualities make Akiak such a good lead dog? Do you think her age is an advantage or a disadvantage? Give reasons for your answer.

**3.** The author tells the story in an unusual way: by breaking it down into days. Why do you think he chose to do that?

**4.** One man helps Akiak by opening a door for her. Why do you think he did that?

**5.** Did Akiak *really* win the race? Give reasons for your answer.

**6.** **Connecting/Comparing** Why is this particular journey so important to Akiak and Mick?

# Write a Victory Speech

After the race, Mick receives an award for winning the Iditarod. Write a speech that she might give on this special occasion. Remember, Mick didn't win the race alone, so be sure to give credit to all those who lent a helping hand — or paw — along the way.

**Tips**

- To get started, brainstorm reasons why Mick and Akiak were so eager to win.
- Include some exciting highlights of the race.

# Make a Poster About Sled Dogs

Huskies have been used as sled dogs for hundreds of years. Why do you think people choose huskies to run the Iditarod and not poodles? Make a poster that includes facts and illustrations telling why huskies are the best dogs for sled-racing. Be sure to check the Social Studies Link on pages 54–57.

# Have a Panel Discussion

According to an Iditarod rule, once Akiak drops out of the race she cannot re-enter it. In a group, hold a panel discussion to share your views on the importance and fairness of that rule. Before the discussion, review the story and decide whether you are for or against the rule.

> **Tips**
>
> - To get started, list both the good and bad points of the rule.
> - A moderator should make sure everyone gets to speak.
> - Keep an open mind! You may change your opinion during the discussion.

**Internet**

# Go on a Web Field Trip

Connect to Education Place to learn more about the Iditarod and Alaska.

**www.eduplace.com/kids**

**Skill:  How to Read a Magazine Article**

❶ **Preview** the article to see what it is about.

❷ **Look** at the headings to see how the article is organized.

❸ **Read** the main part of the article first. Then read other special sections, such as captions and boxes.

# GO, TEAM, GO!

*by Judith E. Rinard*

**Eager dog teams streak through an icy wilderness with passengers and sleds in tow.**

## WILD ride, WILD place, WILD animals!

Sounds like another wild weekend for Alexandra Smith and her brother, Skye. Alexandra, 14, and Skye, 10, are mushers, or sled dog drivers.  On weekends and holidays they help parents Diane and Richard Smith run dogsled trips for the family business.

Diane Smith harnesses a
dog team in Alberta, Canada.

They guide the sleds through remote wild country near
the Rocky Mountains, some 60 miles from their hometown
of Rocky Mountain House, in Alberta, in Canada (see map).
Wild animals such as moose sometimes watch as they speed by.

Downhill sledding feels like a fast descent on a roller coaster. To gain speed and momentum, mushers often "pedal," or push with one foot. "You feel the wind in your face," says Alexandra. "I love it."

Alexandra and Skye also train and care for the 38 purebred Siberian huskies that pull the sleds. Daily they give the dogs food, water, and exercise. They also give them lots of attention by talking to them and brushing and petting them. Alexandra says that when a dog gets too old to pull a sled, it becomes an "old friend."

**RARING TO PULL**

King scrambles to get into a truck as Alexandra lifts him up. "He's pretty bouncy," she says. "All the dogs get really excited about going to the trail."

**ICY DRINK**

Skye and his dad drill a hole through ice to get water. The dogs will drink first.

"HIKE" = Go

"WHOA" = Stop

"GEE" = Turn right

"HAW" = Turn left

**PILES OF SUPPLIES**
Skye pulls a rope tight to hold food, clothing, and gear in place on his sled.

**BACK TO BASICS**
Skye washes in a basin of lake water heated by wood stove in a cabin at base camp. It might be in the wild, but it's still home, so Alexandra sweeps snow to avoid tracking it in.

Dogsledding season for the Smiths runs from mid-November to mid-April. To get ready for a trip, the family loads hundreds of pounds of gear and 24 dogs into a truck. They drive to the trailhead. From there they take their clients on dogsled runs. A trip might last one hour or as long as ten days. They use voice commands to communicate with the dogs. (See bubble on opposite page.)

In the wild the dogs can sense if someone is hurt and needs aid. "They do their best to help," says Alexandra. "They're always there for us."

# DOGS ON THE RUN

 Many a husky has both a brown eye and a blue eye.

 A Siberian husky has two coats of warm fur and tough padded feet for running on ice and snow.

 At night a husky's nose goes dry — to keep it from icing up in subzero temperatures.

 Rex, a white Eskimo dog, is the only dog to cross both Antarctica and the Arctic Ocean. He traveled with his owner, explorer Will Steger.

# A Personal Narrative

A personal narrative is a true story about something that happened to the writer. Use this student's writing as a model when you write a personal narrative of your own.

A good **title** shows the reader what the narrative is about.

A good **beginning** catches the reader's interest.

## A Special Day at the Beach

"Whoopee!" I cried. We were going to the beach near our hotel. I couldn't sit still for a moment. But when my grandmother told me to simmer down, I definitely did. After I quickly ate my homemade pancakes, I questioned Grandma, "Can we go out on the beach now?" She said we could. So I got my flip flop sandals on and quickly ran to the beach.

I couldn't wait. I was squirting out the suntan lotion very quickly. After I finally blobbed it on, I did cartwheels on the sand. Then I had a great idea. My brother and I could cover me up with sand. We hurriedly got to work. Before you could say, "Let's play in the sand," we were finished. My mom wanted to take my picture, so I had to wait forever for her to get the camera ready. Finally, click went the camera. Then I got myself unburied, and off I ran to the water, scattering sand all around me. After my swim, I grabbed a kite and off it swirled into the light blue sky.

At about 3 o'clock I was splashing in the ocean again. For about a half an hour I surfed the waves. A little while after that I had fun going under water with my goggles on. The sun glimmered on the clear water. What a beautiful sight!

Why did we have to go eat? I guess we were all hungry, so we piled into the car and drove off. Soon we came to a seafood restaurant that was packed with people. I had shrimp and French fries. The ice cream I had for dessert melted in my hands.

When we got back to the hotel, I looked over at the beach. I saw a beautiful sunset that faded quickly. I couldn't wait to go back again the next day.

**Details** told in time-order bring the story to life.

The **ending** should tie the narrative together.

## Meet the Author

Ashley A.
**Grade:** four
**State:** North Carolina
**Hobbies:** drawing, writing, and reading
**What she'd like to be when she grows up:** a writer, an illustrator, or a veterinarian

# Background and Vocabulary

**Grandfather's Journey**

## Read to find the meanings of these words.

*e* ● Glossary

bewildered

homeland

longed

marveled

reminded

surrounded

# Far Away from Home

Have you ever traveled to another town, city, or country? If you have, perhaps you felt **bewildered** by new foods, different kinds of transportation, or even a language you didn't understand. You may have been **surrounded** by unfamiliar sights, sounds, or smells. But other things may have **reminded** you of home and made you homesick. In *Grandfather's Journey*, you will read about a man who traveled from Japan to the United States one hundred years ago.

The Asakusa temple in Tokyo, Japan, late 1800s

**Tokyo, Japan**

Young women in a Japanese garden, early 1900s

People riding a trolley in San Francisco, late 1800s

At that time, a Japanese traveler might have **longed** for his **homeland** where many people still wore traditional robes called *kimonos*, rather than the hats and overcoats that were popular in the United States.  But he also might have **marveled** at this big, new country, which was so different from the small island country of Japan.

Market Street in San Francisco, late 1800s

**San Francisco, United States**

# Grandfather's Journey

ALLEN SAY

★ **Strategy Focus**

This is the story of a journey the author's grandfather made. Pause at different points in the story and **predict** what Grandfather will do next.

My grandfather was a young man when he left his home in Japan and went to see the world.

He wore European clothes for the first time and began his journey on a steamship. The Pacific Ocean astonished him.

For three weeks he did not see land. When land finally appeared it was the New World.

He explored North America by train and riverboat, and often walked for days on end.

Deserts with rocks like enormous sculptures amazed him.

The endless farm fields reminded him of the ocean he had crossed.

Huge cities of factories and tall buildings bewildered and yet excited him.

He marveled at the towering mountains and rivers as
clear as the sky.

He met many people along the way. He shook hands
with black men and white men, with yellow men and red men.

The more he traveled, the more he longed to see new
places, and never thought of returning home.

Of all the places he visited, he liked California best.
He loved the strong sunlight there, the Sierra Mountains,
the lonely seacoast.

After a time, he returned to his village in Japan to marry his childhood sweetheart. Then he brought his bride to the new country.

They made their home by the San Francisco Bay and had a baby girl.

As his daughter grew, my grandfather began to think about his own childhood. He thought about his old friends.

He remembered the mountains and rivers of his home. He surrounded himself with songbirds, but he could not forget.

Finally, when his daughter was nearly grown, he could wait no more. He took his family and returned to his homeland.

Once again he saw the mountains and rivers of his childhood.

They were just as he had remembered them.

Once again he exchanged stories and laughed with his old friends.

But the village was not a place for a daughter from San Francisco.

So my grandfather bought a house in a large city nearby.

There, the young woman fell in love, married, and sometime later I was born.

When I was a small boy, my favorite weekend was a visit to my grandfather's house. He told me many stories about California.

He raised warblers and silvereyes, but he could not forget the mountains and rivers of California. So he planned a trip.

But a war began. Bombs fell from the sky and scattered
our lives like leaves in a storm.

When the war ended, there was nothing left of the city
and of the house where my grandparents had lived.

So they returned to the village where they had been
children.

But my grandfather never kept another songbird.

The last time I saw him, my grandfather said that he longed to see California one more time. He never did.

And when I was nearly grown, I left home and went to see California for myself.

After a time, I came to love the land my grandfather had loved, and I stayed on and on until I had a daughter of my own.

But I also miss the mountains and rivers of my childhood. I miss my old friends. So I return now and then, when I cannot still the longing in my heart.

The funny thing is, the moment I am in one country, I am homesick for the other.

I think I know my grandfather now. I miss him very much.

## Meet the Author and Illustrator

# Allen Say

*"My favorite painting in Grandfather's Journey is the picture of myself as the F.O.B. (Fresh Off the Boat), standing in the sun-drenched, empty parking lot. I love that painting."*

### FACT FILE

❖ Allen Say was born in Yokohama, Japan, on August 28, 1937.

❖ At the age of six, he wanted to be a cartoonist. When he was twelve, he went to work as an assistant to a well-known cartoonist.

❖ When he was sixteen, he moved to Southern California with his father.

❖ After high school, he went back to Japan, but soon he returned to the United States. He worked for many years as a photographer before he started to illustrate and write books.

❖ When he starts a new book, he paints all the pictures first and then he writes the story. It took him two years to complete *Grandfather's Journey*.

❖ His favorite hobby is fly-fishing.

### OTHER BOOKS:

*Tea with Milk, Tree of Cranes, The Bicycle Man, The Lost Lake, A River Dream*

Internet

If you want to find out more about Allen Say, visit Education Place. **www.eduplace.com/kids**

## Think About the Selection

1. Why was Allen Say's grandfather so impressed by what he saw on his first trip to North America?

2. If you were seeing North America for the first time, what do you think would impress you the most? Why?

3. Why do you think Grandfather kept songbirds in North America and in Japan? Why did he stop after the war?

4. How are the journeys that Allen Say and his grandfather take similar? How are they different?

5. Why do you think Allen Say wanted to tell the story of his grandfather's journey?

6. **Connecting/Comparing** How do the settings in *Grandfather's Journey* and *Akiak* play an important part in each journey? Be sure to give examples.

## Write a Travel Brochure

Allen Say's grandfather traveled to many parts of the United States. Pick one of the places he visited and see what the author says about it. Write a travel brochure describing that place and why it's worth a visit. Then illustrate the brochure with your own pictures.

**Tips**

- Use a word web to help you plan your writing.
- Look at the illustrations to find more details to include.
- Begin place names with capital letters.

## Social Studies

# Plan Your Own Journey

Find a map of the United States and pick four places you want to visit. Make a copy of the map, and then draw the best route for the journey, starting from your hometown. Remember to label every place you will visit.

**Bonus** Use the scale of miles on the map to measure how long your journey would be in both miles and kilometers.

## Viewing

# Compare Illustrations

Allen Say says that his favorite illustration in *Grandfather's Journey* is the one of himself as a young man in California. Which is your favorite illustration? What do you like about it and why? Get together with a classmate and compare your choices and why you like them.

## Internet

# Post a Review

What did you think of *Grandfather's Journey*? Write a review. Be sure to give examples to support your opinions. Post your review on Education Place.

**www.eduplace.com/kids**

**Skill: How to Read a Haiku**

❶ **Read** the haiku aloud.

❷ **Use** the punctuation marks to help you follow the rhythm of the poem. **Read** the haiku aloud again.

❸ Try to **picture** what is happening in the haiku.

❹ **Think** about what feeling the writer of the haiku expresses.

# Haiku:
# *Just a Moment!*

Have you ever stopped to watch ants walking in a line? A haiku is a very short, three-line poem that tries to capture that kind of moment. Haiku were invented in Japan more than three hundred years ago.

Traditional haiku in the Japanese language always had five syllables in the first line, seven in the second line, and five in the third line. Modern haiku don't always follow the traditional rules. But they are still usually made of three short lines. And they still try to capture a single moment.

## Traditional Haiku
### *from Japan*

Summer sky
clear after rain —
ants on parade.
Shiki, 1867–1902


May rains!
Now frogs are swimming
At my door.
Sanpū, 1647–1732

# Modern Haiku
## *in English*

firefly  there
not  there
there
M. L. Bittle-DeLapa

Even in summer,
bees have to work in their orange-
and-black striped sweaters
Myra Cohn Livingston

Frog's shadow
reaches the rock
before the frog.
Virginia Brady Young

79

**FINDING THE TITANIC**

by Robert D. Ballard, discoverer of the *Titanic*

**Finding the Titanic**

Read to find the meanings of these words.

*e* ⚬ Glossary

hull

iceberg

shipwrecks

survivors

unsinkable

voyage

wreckage

# Return to the Titanic

For hundreds of years people have been fascinated by **shipwrecks**. The most famous shipwreck of them all is the *Titanic*. It rests more than two miles below the surface of the cold Atlantic Ocean.

Many undersea explorers search for shipwrecks. Some dream of discovering sunken treasure. Others want to learn what the **wreckage** can tell about the past. That's because a sunken ship is like an underwater museum, frozen in time.

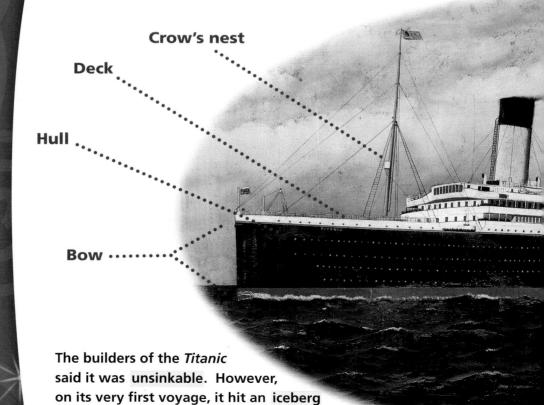

Crow's nest

Deck

Hull

Bow

The builders of the *Titanic* said it was **unsinkable**. However, on its very first voyage, it hit an **iceberg** that tore a hole in the ship's **hull**.

It was once impossible to find some of the deepest wrecks. Scientists lacked the technology — that is, until recently. Dr. Robert Ballard is a scientist who uses modern submarines and robots to locate and photograph shipwrecks. In 1985, he became the first to find the *Titanic*.

Read on to meet one of the **survivors** of the *Titanic* disaster and to learn about her dramatic rescue. You'll also join Ballard on his exciting **voyage** of discovery.

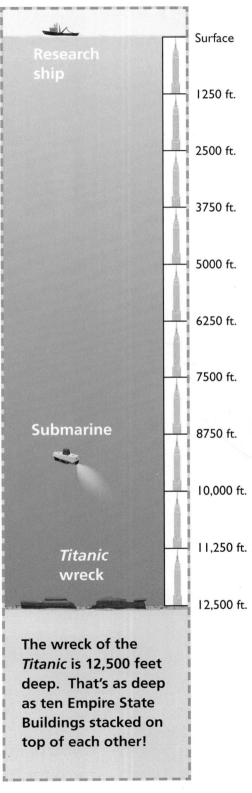

Research ship

Surface

1250 ft.

2500 ft.

3750 ft.

5000 ft.

6250 ft.

7500 ft.

**Stern**

Submarine

8750 ft.

10,000 ft.

11,250 ft.

*Titanic* wreck

12,500 ft.

The wreck of the *Titanic* is 12,500 feet deep. That's as deep as ten Empire State Buildings stacked on top of each other!

# FINDING THE
# TITANIC

### by Robert D. Ballard,
### discoverer of the *Titanic*

## Strategy Focus

As you read about the *Titanic* disaster and the search for the wreck, **monitor** your understanding. **Clarify** by rereading or by reading ahead.

# CHAPTER ONE

## August 25, 1985

I went to the control center of our ship. "Have you seen anything yet?" I asked my team. I looked at the video screen. Nothing had appeared.

We were searching for the *Titanic* — the most famous of all shipwrecks. The *Titanic* was once the largest ship in the world. It had grand rooms. It seemed like a floating palace. Some people even said the ship was unsinkable.

But on its first voyage in April 1912, the *Titanic* hit an iceberg and sank. It was carrying over two thousand people. Many of them died when the ship went down.

I had dreamed of finding the *Titanic* since I was a boy. No one had seen it in almost seventy-five years. It lay two and a half miles down on the bottom of the Atlantic Ocean. This is far deeper than any diver can go.

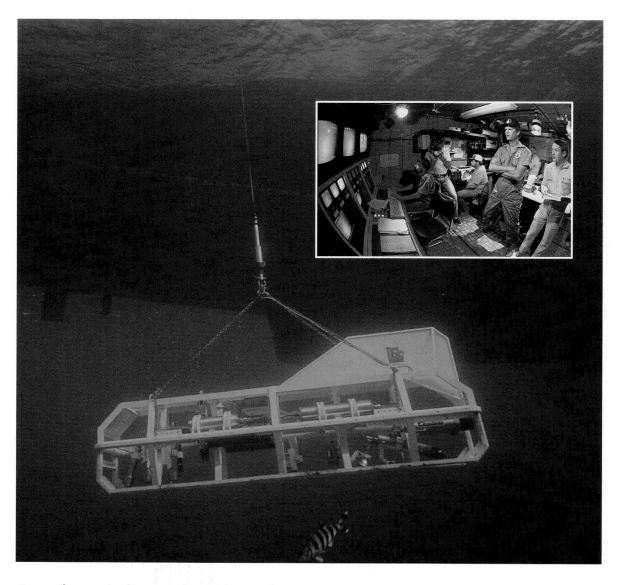

From the control center, I could see what *Argo* saw.

We built an underwater sled, *Argo,* to search for the ship. This sled took moving video pictures as it was pulled along just above the ocean floor. We watched these moving pictures on our ship's video screen.

We began our search where the *Titanic*'s lifeboats had been found by a rescue ship. For days we pulled *Argo* along above the ocean bottom. Nothing appeared on our video screen but mud. I wondered if the ship had been buried by an underwater mudslide.

I kept my eyes on the screen. But I thought about the people who survived the shipwreck. They told stories that will never be forgotten.

# CHAPTER TWO

## April 10, 1912

"It's so big!" cried twelve-year-old Ruth Becker. The huge black hull of the *Titanic* sat in the docks at Southampton, England.

The Becker family had been living in India. But now Ruth's brother was ill. Mrs. Becker decided to take her children back to America. So Mrs. Becker, Ruth, four-year-old Marion, and two-year-old Richard had sailed from India to England. Now they would board the *Titanic* for the trip to New York.

Ruth could hardly wait to get on the beautiful new ship. Yellow letters on the bow proudly spelled out the name: TITANIC. The *Titanic* was the largest ship afloat. It had nine decks and it was as tall as an eleven-story building. You could walk for miles along its decks and passageways.

The Beckers boarded the *Titanic,* and a steward helped them find their cabin.

"This is just like a hotel room!" Ruth said.

Before the ship set sail, Ruth decided to explore. She climbed up the Grand Staircase. Gold-plated light fixtures hung from the ceiling. Sunlight shone through a big glass dome overhead.

Ruth found the rooms of the wealthy first-class passengers. One of the doors was open. Ruth peeked inside. This room was bigger than her whole cabin. It was fancier, too.

Ruth stepped into an elevator near the Grand Staircase. She went down as far as it would go. She discovered a swimming pool and steam baths.

The hallways in the lower decks of the *Titanic* were crowded. Families carried large trunks and suitcases. Ruth heard many different languages. These were the third-class passengers. Many of them were hoping to make new lives for themselves in America.

A loud whistle sounded. Ruth hurried back to her cabin. It was noon — sailing time. She and her family went onto the boat deck.

Hundreds of passengers cheered as the *Titanic* pulled away from the dock. They waved to their friends on shore. There were

Sitting Room

Grand Staircase

even small boats waiting in the water. These boats were filled with people who wanted to see the biggest ship in the world set sail.

For the first few days of the voyage the weather was clear and the ocean was calm. The Beckers ate their meals in the second-class dining room. They sat at long tables with many other passengers.

On Sunday afternoon it became very cold. Ruth sat with her mother and some of the other passengers in the lounge.

"We're making good speed," one man said. "We might even arrive in New York early — if we don't run into ice."

"So I hear," said Mrs. Becker.

"I wouldn't mind seeing an iceberg, though," he continued. "I'm told they're quite a sight."

Deck

Parisian Café

# CHAPTER THREE

## April 15, 1912 — 12:30 A.M.

"Ruth, Ruth, wake up!"

*Where am I?* Ruth wondered. She rubbed her eyes. Then she remembered. She was on board the *Titanic.* But why did her mother sound so frightened?

"Get out of bed and put coats on the children," her mother continued. "The ship has hit an iceberg! We're supposed to go up to the deck."

Now Ruth was wide awake. She got out of bed and quickly dressed Marion and Richard. The Beckers left their cabin. In their hurry, they forgot their life belts.

The family joined a group of passengers waiting to be led up to the boat deck. Some of them were fully dressed. Others, like Ruth and her mother, had coats over their nightclothes.

"It sounded just like the ship ran into gravel," one woman said.

Everyone wanted to know more about what had happened. Had the iceberg made a big hole? How serious was the damage? Was water flowing into the ship?

A crewman arrived and took the passengers to the lifeboats. "Women and children first!" people shouted.

Someone lifted Marion and Richard into lifeboat No. 11. "That's all for this boat," an officer said.

"Oh, please let me go with my children!" Mrs. Becker cried. A seaman helped her into the lifeboat. But Ruth was left behind!

"Ruth!" her mother screamed. "Get in another boat!"

Ruth walked over to the next boat. "May I get in?" she asked an officer. He lifted her into lifeboat No. 13. It was so crowded that Ruth had to stand up.

"Lower away!" the officer shouted. The boat dropped jerkily

toward the sea. Ruth looked up at hundreds of passengers still on board the *Titanic*. There were not enough lifeboats for all of them.

Ruth's boat reached the water safely. But no one knew what to do or where to go. The passengers on board asked one of the crew to be their captain.

"Row toward those lights in the distance," he ordered. "They might be the lights of a ship that could pick us up."

Ruth looked back at the *Titanic*. Rockets went up from the ship sending bursts of stars into the sky. They were distress signals calling any nearby ships to come and help.

The bow of the *Titanic* was sinking. Ruth looked at the people still on board. They were trying to move back toward the stern. The ship's lights went out. Suddenly there was a loud noise like thunder. The *Titanic* broke apart. Ruth watched people leap into the sea.

The bow disappeared under the water. For a minute the stern stood straight up in the ocean. It looked like a huge whale. Then the *Titanic* dove beneath the waves.

# CHAPTER FOUR

## April 15, 1912 — 3:00 A.M.

"The sea will be covered with ships tomorrow," said a crewman in Ruth's boat. "They will race from all over to find us."

The lifeboats from the *Titanic* drifted on the calm, cold ocean. The survivors tried to keep the boats together by calling out to one another in the dark.

Ruth heard a rocket. In the distance she spotted a faint green light. Could it be a rescue ship? Everyone in the boat who had a

scrap of paper lit a match to it. They held these "torches" up high in the air. Maybe someone would see them.

The passengers at the oars rowed toward the lights. As they drew closer, they could see that the lights came from a large ship.

The ocean became rough. Ruth was drenched by the cold, splashing water.

Finally the lifeboat pulled alongside the rescue ship. Crewmen on board lowered a swing down to the boat. Ruth's hands were too numb to grasp the ropes. Someone had to tie her into the swing. The crew pulled her up the side of the ship. Its solid deck felt good beneath her feet.

Ruth went up to the ship's open deck. Most of the lifeboats had come in, but there was no sign of her family.

Then Ruth felt a tap on her shoulder. "Are you Ruth Becker?" a woman said. "Your mother has been looking for you!" She led Ruth to the second-class dining room.

Mrs. Becker, Marion, and Richard threw their arms around her. Ruth's eyes filled with tears of relief.

The crew of the rescue ship, the *Carpathia*, searched the sea for several hours. But no more survivors were found.

Several days later, the *Carpathia* arrived in New York City harbor. Thousands of people waited in pouring rain to greet the survivors. Ruth heard cries of joy from the people who had found their loved ones. But many others looked sad as they searched for family and friends who had drowned.

**Some of the *Titanic*'s passengers prepare to board the rescue ship from their lifeboat.**

# CHAPTER FIVE

## August 31, 1985

Almost seventy-five years had passed since the *Titanic* sank. And now my team and I searched for the wreck. As each day went by, I wanted to find the lost ship more than ever. Our time was running out. We hadn't seen a single sign of the wreck. We sometimes wondered if the *Titanic* really did lie on the ocean floor.

Late one night, Stu Harris pointed to the video screen. "There's something." The sleepy crew looked at the screen. They could see pictures of man-made objects.

"Bingo!" Stu yelled. *Argo's* cameras picked up a huge boiler on the ocean floor. Boilers burned coal to drive a ship's engines. This one had to belong to the *Titanic*!

Soon we saw pieces of railing and other wreckage. At last my dream was about to come true. The *Titanic* must lie nearby. Everyone was shaking hands and slapping one another on the back.

Someone noticed that it was 2 A.M., close to the time that the *Titanic* had sunk. We were excited, but we felt sad, too. We held a few moments of silence in memory of those who had sailed on the great ship so long ago.

Our first video run over the wreckage with *Argo* was risky. We weren't sure where the main part of the ship was. I was afraid that *Argo* might crash into it. All of a sudden, the huge side of the ship appeared. The *Titanic* was sitting upright on the ocean floor!

Over the next few days we made some important discoveries. The ship had broken in two sections. We saw large holes in the deck of the bow section where the funnels had once stood.

But at the end of our trip many mysteries still remained. What did the ship look like inside? Where was the hole made by the iceberg? And what lay scattered on the ocean floor around the wreck? Only another visit to the *Titanic* would tell us what we wanted to know.

# CHAPTER SIX

## July 13, 1986

A year later we were ready to explore the *Titanic* from *Alvin,* our three-man submarine. I took off my shoes and climbed in.

We were squeezed inside *Alvin's* tiny cabin. Soon we began our long fall to the ocean bottom. As we went down, it became colder and darker inside the little submarine.

When *Alvin* reached the bottom, I peered out my window. Where was the *Titanic?* We could only see a short distance in the darkness of the deep ocean.

The pilot turned *Alvin,* and we glided along the ocean floor. I stared out the window. The bottom looked very strange. It seemed to slope sharply upward. My heart beat faster.

Suddenly an enormous black wall of steel loomed in front of us. It was the *Titanic!*

The next day we explored the bow section of the ship. The bottom part of the bow was buried in mud. But I could see the large anchors still hanging in place.

We rose slowly up the ship's side. To my surprise, the glass in many of the portholes was not broken. I searched for the yellow letters spelling out the name TITANIC. But they were covered with rust.

*Alvin* began to move over the forward deck of the ship. Its wooden planks had been eaten away by millions of tiny sea worms.

We passed over the bridge of the ship. From here the captain and his officers had steered the *Titanic.*

We headed toward the Grand Staircase. Its big glass dome was gone. This would be the perfect place for our small robot, *Jason Junior,* to go inside the ship. Then we could take close-up pictures.

The next morning we landed *Alvin* near the opening to the Grand Staircase. At last *Jason Junior,* or *JJ,* would see inside.

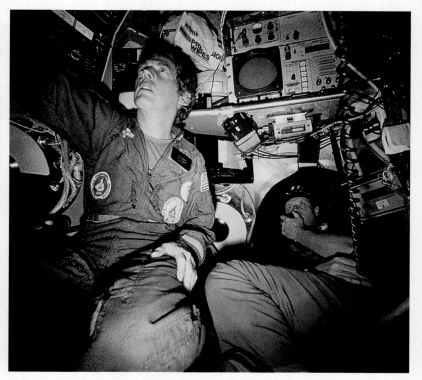

*Alvin* is lowered into the water.

We work inside *Alvin* on our way to the ocean bottom.

One of the *Titanic*'s boilers lying on the ocean floor.

This is how the huge boilers looked before they were placed in the ship.

*JJ*'s pilot slowly guided our robot out of its little garage on the front of *Alvin*. *JJ* floated over the hole in the deck where the staircase had once been. The little robot went down into the ship and we lost sight of it. We watched the video screen inside our submarine to see what *JJ* was looking at.

A room appeared on the screen. "Look at that chandelier," *JJ*'s pilot exclaimed. It was one of the light fixtures which had lit Ruth Becker's way up the Grand Staircase. The metal part of the light was still bright and shiny.

We explored most of the great wreck over the next few days. *JJ* took a close-up look at the crow's nest. From here the lookout had spotted the iceberg seconds before it hit the ship. We looked near the bow for the hole made by the iceberg. But it was covered with mud.

I wondered what might lie on the ocean floor between the two parts of the wreck. When the *Titanic* broke in two, thousands of objects fell out. We found many of them still lying where they had fallen. It was like visiting a huge underwater museum.

There were pots and pans, cups and saucers, boots, bathtubs, suitcases, and even a safe with a shiny brass handle.

Before we left the *Titanic* we placed two metal plaques on its decks. The one on the stern section is in memory of all the passengers who lost their lives. The plaque on the bow section asks anyone else who visits the *Titanic* to leave it in peace.

TITANIC
DISASTER
GREAT LOSS
OF LIFE
EVENING NEWS

◀ *JJ* takes a close-up look at one of the *Titanic*'s anchors.

# Epilogue

I was sorry when our trips to the *Titanic* were finished. But I was proud of what we had done. We found the ship. And we took many beautiful pictures of it. People all over the world would be able to "visit" the wreck when they saw *JJ*'s pictures. They would think about the people who had sailed on the *Titanic* — those who had lost their lives as well as the survivors.

Ruth Becker and her family had been lucky. Ruth grew up to become a teacher. She married and had three children. Like many *Titanic* survivors, Ruth wouldn't talk about the sinking. Her children didn't even know she had been on the ship.

She finally began to talk about her experience toward the end of her life. When she was eighty-five years old, Ruth saw pictures of the wreck on the ocean floor. When Ruth was ninety, she went on her first sea voyage since the *Titanic*. She died later that year.

After our trip, another group of people went down to the *Titanic*. They brought up many things from the wreck — the ship's telephone and the bell from the crow's nest, some china, a leather bag full of jewelry and money, and hundreds of other objects.

I was very sad when I heard this. The *Titanic* should be left in peace as a monument to those who lost their lives on that cold, starry night so long ago.

**Our search ship, the *Knorr***

# Robert D. Ballard

*"I loved Captain Nemo in Jules Verne's 20,000 Leagues Under the Sea. Here was a person who built his own submarine. . . . He explored beneath the sea. . . . I always had this dream of being inside his ship, the Nautilus."*

Robert Ballard has realized his dream of becoming a deep-sea explorer like the hero of *20,000 Leagues Under the Sea*. Today, Ballard works as a marine scientist (a scientist who explores and studies the ocean).

Ballard has explored underwater mountains, underwater volcanoes, and shipwrecks. Since finding the *Titanic* in 1985, Ballard has continued to search the world's oceans. In 1999, he discovered two ancient ships that sank off the coast of Israel nearly 2,750 years ago!

Ballard started the Jason Project, a program that allows students to go on science expeditions all around the world, on sea and on land. "I think all kids are born explorers," Ballard says. "All kids are born scientists. All kids ask, 'Why?'"

**OTHER BOOKS:**

*Ghost Lines: Exploring the World's Greatest Lost Ships*
*The Lost Wreck of the Isis*

To learn more about Robert Ballard, visit Education Place.
**www.eduplace.com/kids**

# Responding

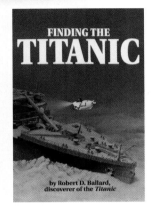

## Think About the Selection

1. Why do you think Robert Ballard was so determined to find the *Titanic*?

2. What conditions made the *Titanic* especially hard to find?

3. In this selection, Ballard tells two stories that take place at different times. How does he keep the two stories separate?

4. How would you feel if you were on the *Titanic* like Ruth, or if you were with Ballard's crew? Explain.

5. Why do you think people are still fascinated today by the *Titanic*?

6. **Connecting/Comparing** Both Ruth Becker and Grandfather in *Grandfather's Journey* took trips that changed their lives. Compare how they felt as they looked back on their journeys.

## Write a Journal Entry

How might Ruth Becker have described the disaster on the *Titanic*? Write a journal entry telling what happened from Ruth's point of view.

**Tips**

- To begin, go back to the selection to find key events.
- Write in Ruth's voice using the pronoun *I*.
- Remember to include details about Ruth's feelings.

## Science

# Organize an Inventory

Robert Ballard found the *Titanic* with the help of special cameras, ships, submarines, and other technology. Make an inventory chart of the equipment Ballard used. Next to each item, describe what it is and what it does.

| Equipment | What is it? | What does it do? |
|---|---|---|
| The <u>Knorr</u> | Search ship | Carries tools and crew across ocean |

## Listening and Speaking

# Role-Play a News Conference

In a small group, role-play a news conference with Robert Ballard. A volunteer can play Ballard, and others can be reporters. Discuss Ballard's expedition and how he located the *Titanic*.

Internet

# Take an Online Poll

Should the *Titanic* be left on the ocean floor, or should it be brought to the surface for scientific study? Give your opinion in an Education Place online poll.

**www.eduplace.com/kids**

# ICEBERG RIGHT AHEAD!

## These Trackers Work to Prevent *Titanic: The Sequel*

### by Gail Skroback Hennessey

**"ICEBERGS BELOW!"** These words electrify the crew flying 8,000 feet above the frigid North Atlantic Ocean. Taking the aircraft down close to the bergs, Commander Steven Sielbeck gazes out at huge mountains of ice. It's an awesome sight that few people ever see.

Commander Sielbeck is an "ice pick." That's what people call ice watchers for the International Ice Patrol (IIP). The IIP tracks icebergs that drift into North Atlantic shipping lanes each spring and summer. The group warns ships so they can steer clear of these huge blocks of ice that move through the ocean.

What can a berg do to a ship? "Titanic" damage! In 1912, *Titanic* was the biggest ship in the world. People thought nothing could sink it. But on its first voyage, something did. *Titanic* ran into a huge iceberg and quickly sank. Of the 2,224 people on board, more than 1,500 died.

The sinking of *Titanic* frightened people who sailed between Europe and North America. Shippers realized a patrol was needed to locate icebergs and warn ships to steer clear of them. Two years after *Titanic* sank, the IIP was started.

Today, 17 countries support the IIP. They've gotten their money's worth over the years. According to Sielbeck, "Since we have been doing the job, nobody who followed our safety information has lost his life."

INTERNATIONAL ICE PATROL

# Iceberg Alley

The icebergs that endanger North Atlantic shipping lanes form when chunks of glaciers break off from Greenland. Currents move the icebergs about 2,500 miles toward the Grand Banks, off Newfoundland, Canada. That's where the busiest shipping lane in the world is located. The IIP calls the area where the icebergs travel "Iceberg Alley." "It's like a constant conveyor belt of icebergs," Sielbeck told *Contact Kids*. Many bergs melt before reaching this area. But in 1998, about 1,300 icebergs were spotted by the IIP.

Part of the U.S. Coast Guard, the IIP has 14 staff people. But this small group does a big job. To make sure they find every berg, the IIP patrols an area nearly one-half million square miles. That's about twice the size of Texas.

The IIP crews use radar to spot icebergs. But they also use their eyes. That's because smaller bergs, called "growlers" or "bergy bits," aren't as easy to detect by radar.

Ice picks like Sielbeck track icebergs and record their position, size, and shape. They also drop special buoys into the water. These devices record ocean temperature and sea current flow.

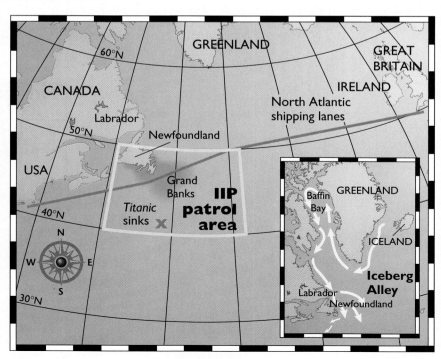

**The area between Greenland and Labrador, Canada, is known as "Iceberg Alley." Most icebergs flow into North Atlantic shipping lanes through here.**

All this information is fed into computers located at IIP headquarters in Groton, CT. The computers predict how much the bergs will melt and in what direction they'll drift. Every day, this information is sent by radio and the Internet to shippers. For the 2,000 ships that sail the North Atlantic every year, the IIP is a real lifesaver.

## Bergs Are Cool!

Saving lives can be risky business. "The Grand Banks of Newfoundland has some of the worst weather in the world," explains Sielbeck. More than half the time it's foggy. Storms can bring lightning and high winds. Sometimes ice forms on the airplane's wings. Flying in these conditions is ultra-dangerous.

But for Sielbeck, seeing icebergs up close and personal makes it all worthwhile. "Imagine seeing a chunk of ice the size of the Texas Astrodome drifting in the ocean!" he says. "You never get tired of looking at them."

## The Life and Death of an ICEBERG

**1** An iceberg we see today began its life as a flake of snow falling on land. Over years — sometimes centuries — the snow crushes snowflakes beneath it, packing down the snow.

**2** Year after year, the layers of snow melt and refreeze until they form layers of ice thousands of feet thick. The pressure of newer snow causes older layers of ice to move over land. The moving ice is called a glacier.

**3** The glacier slowly moves forward until it reaches the sea. Then ocean tides cause chunks of the glacier to break off, or calve. When the chunk falls into the water, an iceberg is born.

**4** Ocean currents carry the berg south. Greenland produces thousands of bergs a year. But only about one percent reach the Atlantic. Most melt after six months. So icebergs usually end up as ice cubes!

# Background and Vocabulary

LAURA INGALLS WILDER
### By the Shores of Silver Lake

ILLUSTRATED BY GARTH WILLIAMS

**By the Shores of Silver Lake**

**Read to find the meanings of these words.**

*e • Glossary*

conductor
depot
jolting
lurching
platform
satchels

# ALL ABOARD!

Wouldn't it be exciting to take a ride on the newest, fastest kind of transportation around? In the 1870s, that would have been a train. Railroads finally linked the east and west coasts of the United States in 1869. Settlers heading west to start new farms often took a train for part of their journey.

Trains of the 1870s were pulled by locomotives, which puffed clouds of smoke out of their smokestacks. People who wanted to take the train waited on the **platform** with their **satchels** or other luggage. Once they boarded the train, a **conductor** punched special holes in their tickets. Then travelers had a bumpy, **lurching**, **jolting** ride at an alarming twenty miles per hour!

To see what an 1870s train ride was like, read about the Ingalls family's first train trip in a story from *By the Shores of Silver Lake*.

This advertisement promises Union Pacific passengers a speedy and comfortable trip.

This Illinois Central Railroad poster shows a train at the **depot** and a map of railroad routes of the 1880s. Older forms of transportation appear in the corners.

LAURA INGALLS WILDER

# By the Shores of Silver Lake

ILLUSTRATED BY GARTH WILLIAMS

## Strategy Focus

Laura and her family are going on their first train trip. As you read, think of **questions** about what they see and think during their train ride.

*The Ingalls family is leaving their farm on Plum Creek and heading west. They have been sick with scarlet fever — Mary so severely that she has gone blind. Now they are well enough to travel. Pa has gone ahead to work for the railroad and to claim a homestead, a piece of land given by the government to settlers willing to farm it. Ma, Mary, Laura, Carrie, and baby Grace are taking the train to meet him.*

# Riding in the Cars

When the time came, Laura could hardly believe it was real. The weeks and months had been endless, and now suddenly they were gone. Plum Creek, and the house, and all the slopes and fields she knew so well, were gone; she would never see them again. The last crowded days of packing, cleaning, scrubbing, washing, and ironing, and the last minute flurry of bathing and dressing were over. Clean and starched and dressed-up, in the morning of a weekday, they sat in a row on the bench in the waiting room while Ma bought the tickets.

In an hour they would be riding on the railroad cars.

The two satchels stood on the sunny platform outside the waiting-room door. Laura kept an eye on them, and on Grace, as Ma had told her to. Grace sat still in her little starched white lawn dress and bonnet, her feet in small new shoes sticking straight out. At the ticket window, Ma carefully counted money out of her pocketbook.

Traveling on the train cost money. They had not paid anything to travel in the wagon, and this was a beautiful morning to be riding in the wagon along new roads. It was a September day and small clouds were hurrying in the sky. All the girls were in school now; they would see the train go roaring by and know that Laura was riding in it. Trains went faster than horses can run. They went so terribly fast that often they were wrecked. You never knew what might happen to you on a train.

Ma put the tickets inside her mother-of-pearl pocketbook and carefully snapped shut its little steel clasps. She looked so nice in her dark delaine dress with white lace collar and cuffs. Her hat was black straw with a narrow turned-up brim and a white spray of lilies-of-the-valley standing up at one side of the crown. She sat down and took Grace on her lap.

Now there was nothing to do but wait. They had come an hour early to be sure not to miss the train.

Laura smoothed her dress. It was brown calico sprinkled with small red flowers. Her hair hung down her back in long, brown braids, and a red ribbon bow tied their ends together. There was a red ribbon around the crown of her hat too.

Mary's dress was gray calico with sprays of blue flowers. Her wide-brimmed straw hat had a blue ribbon on it. And under the hat, her poor short hair was held back from her face by a blue ribbon tied around her head. Her lovely blue eyes did not see anything. But she said, "Don't fidget, Carrie, you'll muss your dress."

Laura craned to look at Carrie, sitting beyond Mary. Carrie was small and thin in pink calico, with pink ribbons on her brown braids and her hat. She flushed miserably because Mary found fault with her, and Laura was going to say, "You come over by me, Carrie, and fidget all you want to!"

Just then Mary's face lighted up with joy and she said, "Ma, Laura's fidgeting, too! I can tell she is, without seeing!"

"So she is, Mary," Ma said, and Mary smiled in satisfaction.

Laura was ashamed that in her thoughts she had been cross with Mary. She did not say anything. She got up and she was passing in front of Ma without saying a word. Ma had to remind her, "Say 'Excuse me,' Laura."

"Excuse me, Ma. Excuse me, Mary," Laura said politely, and she sat down beside Carrie. Carrie felt safer when she was between Laura and Mary. Carrie was really afraid of going on a train. Of course she would never say that she was frightened, but Laura knew.

"Ma," Carrie asked timidly, "Pa will surely meet us, won't he?"

"He is coming to meet us," Ma said. "He has to drive in from the camp, and it will take him all day. We are going to wait for him in Tracy."

"Will he — will he get there before night, Ma?" Carrie asked. Ma said she hoped so.

You cannot tell what may happen when you go traveling on a train. It is not like starting out all together in a wagon. So Laura said bravely, "Maybe Pa's got our homestead picked out, already. You guess what it's like, Carrie, and then I'll guess."

They could not talk very well, because all the time they were waiting, and listening for the train. At long, long last, Mary said she thought she heard it. Then Laura heard a faint, faraway hum. Her heart beat so fast that she could hardly listen to Ma.

Ma lifted Grace on her arm, and with her other hand she took tight hold of Carrie's. She said, "Laura, you come behind me with Mary. Be careful, now!"

The train was coming, louder. They stood by the satchels on the platform and saw it coming. Laura did not know how they could get the satchels on the train. Ma's hands were full, and Laura had to hold on to Mary. The engine's round front window glared in the sunshine like a huge eye. The smokestack flared upward to a wide top, and black smoke rolled up from it. A sudden streak of white shot up through the smoke, then the whistle screamed a long wild scream. The roaring thing came rushing straight at them all, swelling bigger and bigger, enormous, shaking everything with noise.

Then the worst was over. It had not hit them; it was roaring by them on thick big wheels. Bumps and crashes ran along the freight cars and flat cars and they stopped moving. The train was there, and they had to get into it.

"Laura!" Ma said sharply. "You and Mary be careful!"

"Yes, Ma, we are," said Laura. She guided Mary anxiously, one step at a time, across the boards of the platform, behind Ma's skirt. When the skirt stopped, Laura stopped Mary.

They had come to the last car at the end of the train. Steps went up into it, and a strange man in a dark suit and a cap helped Ma climb up them with Grace in her arms.

"Oopsy-daisy!" he said, swinging Carrie up beside Ma. Then he said, "Them your satchels, ma'am?"

"Yes, please," Ma said. "Come, Laura and Mary."

"Who is he, Ma?" Carrie asked, while Laura helped Mary up the steps. They were crowded in a small place. The man came pushing cheerfully past them, with the satchels, and shouldered open the door of the car.

They followed him between two rows of red velvet seats full of people. The sides of the car were almost solidly made of windows; the car was almost as light as outdoors, and chunks of sunshine slanted across the people and the red velvet.

Ma sat down on one velvet seat and plumped Grace on her lap. She told Carrie to sit beside her. She said, "Laura, you and Mary sit in this seat ahead of me."

Laura guided Mary in, and they sat down. The velvet seat was springy. Laura wanted to bounce on it, but she must behave properly. She whispered, "Mary, the seats are red velvet!"

"I see," Mary said, stroking the seat with her fingertips. "What's that in front of us?"

"It's the high back of the seat in front, and it's red velvet too," Laura told her.

The engine whistled, and they both jumped. The train was getting ready to go. Laura knelt up in the seat to see Ma. Ma looked calm and so pretty in her dark dress with its white lace collar and the sweet tiny white flowers on her hat.

"What is it, Laura?" Ma asked.

Laura asked, "Who was that man?"

"The brakeman," Ma said. "Now sit down and — "

The train jerked, jolting her backward. Laura's chin bumped hard on the seat back, and her hat slid on her head. Again the train jerked, not so badly this time, and then it began to shiver and the depot moved.

"It's going!" Carrie cried out.

The shivering grew faster and louder, the depot slid backward, and under the car the wheels began to beat time. A rub-a-dubdub, a rub-a-dubdub, the wheels went, faster and faster. The lumberyard and the back of the church and the front of the schoolhouse went by, and that was the last of that town.

The whole car swayed now, in time to the clackety-clacking underneath it, and the black smoke blew by in melting rolls. A telegraph wire swooped up and down beyond the window. It did not really swoop, but it seemed to swoop because it sagged between the poles. It was fastened to green glass knobs that glittered in the sunshine and went dark when the smoke rolled above them. Beyond the wire, grasslands and fields and scattered farmhouses and barns went by.

They went so fast that Laura could not really look at them before they were gone. In one hour that train would go twenty miles — as far as the horses traveled in a whole day.

The door opened, and a tall man came in. He wore a blue coat with brass buttons, and a cap, with CONDUCTOR in letters across its front. At every seat he stopped and took tickets. He punched round holes in the tickets with a small machine in his hand. Ma gave him three tickets. Carrie and Grace were so little that they could ride on the train without paying.

The Conductor went on, and Laura said low, "Oh, Mary! so many shining brass buttons on his coat, and it says CONDUCTOR right across the front of his cap!"

"And he is tall," Mary said. "His voice is high up."

Laura tried to tell her how fast the telegraph poles were going by. She said, "The wire sags down between them and swoops up again," and she counted them. "One — oop! two — oop! three! That's how fast they're going."

"I can tell it's fast, I can feel it," Mary said happily.

On that dreadful morning when Mary could not see even sunshine full in her eyes, Pa had said that Laura must see for her. He had said, "Your two eyes are quick enough, and your tongue, if you will use them for Mary." And Laura had promised. So she tried to be eyes for Mary, and it was seldom that Mary need ask her, "See out loud for me, Laura, please."

"Both sides of the car are windows, close together," Laura said now. "Every window is one big sheet of glass, and even the strips of wood between the windows shine like glass, they are so polished."

"Yes, I see," and Mary felt over the glass and touched the shining wood with her fingertips.

"The sunshine comes slanting in the south windows, in wide stripes over the red velvet seats and the people. Corners of sunshine fall on the floor, and keep reaching out and going back. Up above the windows the shiny wood curves in from the walls on both sides, and all along the middle of the ceiling there's a higher place. It has little walls of tiny, long, low windows, and you can see blue sky outside them. But outside the big windows, on both sides, the country is going by. The stubble fields are yellow, and haystacks are by the barns, and little trees are yellow and red in clumps around the houses.

"Now I will see the people," Laura went on murmuring. "In front of us is a head with a bald spot on top and side whiskers. He is reading a newspaper. He doesn't look out of the windows at all. Farther ahead are two young men with their hats on. They are holding a big white map and looking at it and talking about it. I guess they're going to look for a homestead too. Their hands are rough and callused so they're good workers. And farther ahead there's a woman with bright yellow hair and, oh, Mary! the brightest red velvet hat with pink roses — "

Just then someone went by, and Laura looked up. She went on, "A thin man with bristly eyebrows and long mustaches and an Adam's apple just went by. He can't walk straight, the train's going so fast. I wonder what — Oh, Mary! He's turning a little handle on the wall at the end of the car, and water's coming out!

"The water's pouring right into a tin cup. Now he's drinking it. His Adam's apple bobs. He's filling the cup again. He just turns the handle, and the water comes right out. How do you suppose it — Mary! He's set that cup on a little shelf. Now he's coming back."

After the man had gone by, Laura made up her mind. She asked Ma if she could get a drink of water, and Ma said she might. So she started out.

She could not walk straight. The lurching car made her sway and grab at the seat backs all the way. But she got to the end of the car and looked at the shining handle and spout, and the little shelf under them that held the bright tin cup. She turned the handle just a little, and water came out of the spout. She turned the handle back, and the water stopped. Under the cup there was a little hole, put there to carry away any water that spilled. Laura had never seen anything so fascinating. It was all so neat, and so marvelous, that she wanted to fill the cup again and again. But that would waste the water. So after she drank, she only filled the cup part way, in order not to spill it, and she carried it very carefully to Ma.

Carrie drank, and Grace. They did not want any more, and Ma and Mary were not thirsty. So Laura carried the cup back to its place. All the time the train was rushing on and the country rushing back, and the car swaying, but this time Laura did not touch one seat that she passed. She could walk almost as well as the Conductor. Surely nobody suspected that she had never been on a train before.

Then a boy came walking along the aisle, with a basket on his arm. He stopped and showed it to everyone, and some people took things out of it and gave him money. When he reached Laura, she saw that the basket was full of boxes of candy and of long sticks of white chewing gum. The boy showed them to Ma and said, "Nice fresh candy, ma'am? Chewing gum?"

Ma shook her head, but the boy opened a box and showed the colored candy. Carrie's breath made an eager sound before she knew it.

The boy shook the box a little, not quite spilling the candy out. It was beautiful Christmas candy, red pieces and yellow pieces and some striped red-and-white. The boy said, "Only ten cents, ma'am, one dime."

Laura, and Carrie too, knew they could not have that candy. They were only looking at it. Suddenly Ma opened her purse and counted out a nickel and five pennies into the boy's hand. She took the box and gave it to Carrie.

When the boy had gone on, Ma said, excusing herself for spending so much, "After all, we must celebrate our first train ride."

Grace was asleep, and Ma said that babies should not eat candy. Ma took only a small piece. Then Carrie came into the seat with Laura and Mary and divided the rest. Each had two pieces. They meant to eat one and save the other for next day, but some time after the first pieces were gone, Laura decided to taste her second one. Then Carrie tasted hers, and finally Mary gave in. They licked those pieces all away, little by little.

They were still licking their fingers when the engine whistled long and loud. Then the car went more slowly, and slowly the backs of shanties went backward outside it. All the people began to gather their things together and put on their hats, and then there was an awful jolting crash, and the train stopped. It was noon, and they had reached Tracy.

*To follow the Ingalls family's adventures in the wilderness and to find out how they help to start a brand-new town, read more of* By the Shores of Silver Lake. *At first, Laura continues "seeing out loud" for Mary. But later in the* Little House *series of books, Mary goes to a school for the blind where she learns many skills that make her more independent.*

# Meet the Author

**Laura Ingalls Wilder**

Laura Ingalls Wilder was born on a farm in the "big woods" of Wisconsin in 1867. The Ingalls family moved west several times before settling in the prairie town of De Smet, South Dakota, where *By the Shores of Silver Lake* takes place. Wilder's first book, *Little House in the Big Woods*, was published when Wilder was sixty-five years old. It became one of eight *Little House* books based on her life. Wilder lived to be ninety. The little girl who had journeyed west by covered wagon went on to ride in a car and fly in an airplane!

# Meet the Illustrator

**Doris Ettlinger**

Doris Ettlinger lives in New Jersey with her husband, two children, a dog, and a guinea pig. She has illustrated many stories by Laura Ingalls Wilder. Before Ettlinger illustrates a story, she makes little pictures of the scenes she wants to draw. "Ideas come to me as I move my pencil around," she says. She uses watercolor paints and colored pencils in the finished illustration.

**Internet**

To find out more about Laura Ingalls Wilder and Doris Ettlinger, visit Education Place. **www.eduplace.com/kids**

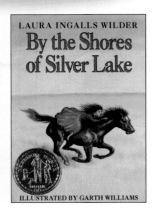

## Think About the Selection

1. What makes this train ride special for Laura and her family?

2. How can you tell that Ma is nervous about the family's trip?

3. How do you think Laura and Mary feel about each other? What clues does the story give?

4. Laura "sees out loud" for Mary, but Mary also notices things on her own. Give examples of how Mary observes her surroundings.

5. If you were traveling during Laura's time, would you rather go by horse and wagon, or by train? Why?

6. **Connecting/Comparing** Laura is excited and nervous before her train trip. Compare her feelings with the way another character in this theme feels at the beginning of a journey.

## Write a Description

Laura describes the train in great detail so that Mary can see it in her mind. Use a similar method to write a description of your classroom for someone who has never seen it.

**Tips**

- Describe what you see, hear, smell, and touch.
- Use vivid words such as *shining* and *enormous*.
- Use location words such as *in front of*, *behind*, and *next to*.

128

# Compare the Speed of Trains

In Laura's time, trains were the fastest way to travel. Today, some trains can go 186 miles per hour. Look in the selection to find out how many miles Laura's train traveled in one hour. In miles per hour, how much faster are today's trains?

**Bonus** Suppose one day's travel is eight hours. Make a bar graph showing how many miles a horse, a train from Laura's time, and a modern train would travel in eight hours.

## Art

# Draw a Landscape

The train to Tracy passes through towns and countryside. Go back to the selection and pick your favorite description of what Laura sees outside the train window. Draw a picture using Laura's details.

**Internet**

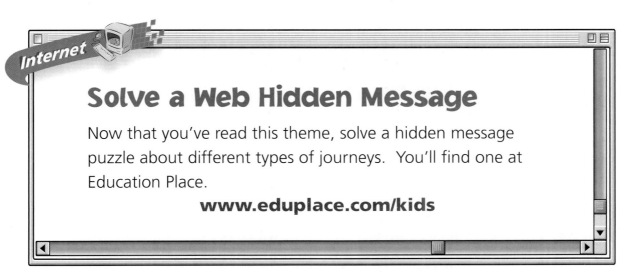

# Solve a Web Hidden Message

Now that you've read this theme, solve a hidden message puzzle about different types of journeys. You'll find one at Education Place.

**www.eduplace.com/kids**

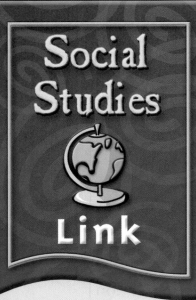

# Finding Her Way

## by Karen Crowe

Cortney Osolinski is hurrying to get ready for school. She checks the time by feeling the raised dots on her watch. To

choose her outfit, she feels the texture of the clothes in her dresser and pulls out a soft ribbed shirt. Cortney, 13, has special ways of getting ready in the morning because she can't see.

Cortney has been blind since birth, but being blind hasn't kept this New Jersey girl from doing things that other girls her age do. She's just developed different ways to do them. We spent a day with Cortney to learn how she uses other senses and skills to find her way through her world.

After dressing, Cortney heads downstairs to the kitchen. She can see blurry, light- and dark-colored shapes as she walks, but she can't tell what those shapes are. So Cortney has memorized the layout of every room in her house. She knows where the furniture, windows, and doors are.

Downstairs, Cortney chooses her breakfast by reading the bumpy Braille labels that she makes for the cereal boxes. Braille is a code of small, raised dots that can be read by touch. Here is how Cortney spells her name in Braille:

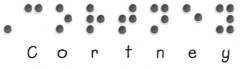

C  o  r  t  n  e  y

7:45 A.M.

After giving her mom and dog goodbye hugs, Cortney grabs her backpack and white cane and heads for the bus stop at the end of her street.

To get to the bus stop, Cortney taps the ground with her cane to find where the grass meets the road. She uses the street's edge as her guide to the corner.

"Hi, Cortney!" her friends call out. She knows the bus stop is just ahead.

131

**8:25 A.M.**

Cortney weaves through the busy hallways at her school. As she walks, she swings her cane back and forth in front of her to detect objects in her path. Cortney has taught the kids at school that her cane is her eyes, and that it's *supposed* to bump into things — even people — so that she doesn't!

**9:15 A.M.**

When Cortney's teacher asks the class to write sentences using their spelling words, Cortney turns to her Braille writer. It's like a typewriter, but it has only six keys — one for each dot in the Braille system. Cortney presses different keys to make the correct combination of dots for each letter. The machine creates a Braille page for Cortney and a printed copy for her teacher.

**12:44 P.M.**

At lunchtime, kids in Cortney's class tell her what foods are on the menu as they go through the line. "I can always tell when it's pizza day by the smell. That's my favorite lunch!" Cortney says.

She's also learning some tricks for keeping track of paper money: Cortney keeps $1 bills flat, folds $5 bills in half lengthwise, folds $10 bills in half widthwise, and folds $20 bills in quarters. If a coin is dropped, she can identify whether it's a penny, nickel, dime, or quarter just by the sound.

## 3:48 P.M.

Cortney's friend Christina Gountas often visits after school. Christina is also blind. Sometimes they draw together using thin strips of sticky wax. They can feel the shapes they make on paper.

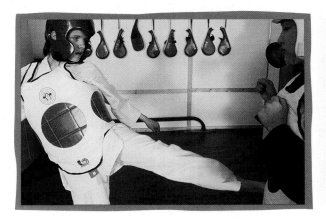

## 6:25 P.M.

Cortney has been taking Tae Kwon Do classes for three years. Instead of watching her teacher demonstrate moves, she learned to kick, punch, and flip people by feeling her teacher's arm or body position, then copying it herself.

## 9:30 P.M.

Cortney climbs into bed, taking along a Braille version of the novel *Jurassic Park*. She says that books help her see the world.

# CORTNEY'S TIPS FOR KIDS

☐ 1. Please don't say "Guess who I am," or expect me to know you by your voice. This will embarrass me if I don't know. When greeting me, say your name, like "Hi Cort, it's A. J., what's up?" In group situations, say my name first when addressing me. Then I'll know you're talking to me.

☐ 2. Please don't move my body — for example, turn me for directions or place my hands on something. Spoken directions are much more helpful and considerate.

☐ 3. My cane is used for what I can't see with my eyes. I keep it with me ALL the time. Please don't move it without me knowing.

☐ 4. Don't think that I'm "amazing" because I read Braille or can find my way using a cane. I'm just an ordinary person who is blind. You or anyone could do it, if you were taught the skills.

133

# Check Your Progress

Your theme journey has taken you from the mountains of Alaska to the open prairies of the 1800s. Take this time to review how far you've come — and travel a little farther. You'll discuss the theme, read and compare two more selections, and polish your test-taking skills.

Take a moment to review Allen Say's letter on pages 23–24. What new thoughts or feelings do you have about his ideas after reading the theme so far?

Now you will read about two different, more unusual kinds of journeys. As you read, ask yourself why these two particular journeys go so well together. Think about how they differ from the other journeys in the theme. Don't unpack your bags just yet. It's time for more *Journeys*. . . .

# Read and Compare

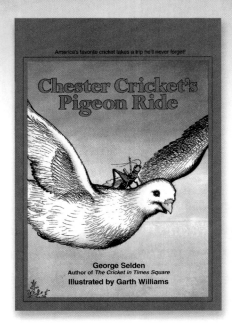

The first selection is about a cricket's amazing journey through New York City, riding on a pigeon.

**Try these strategies:**
Predict and Infer
Monitor and Clarify

The second selection is a true story about a girl who makes an incredible trip to visit her grand-mother — as a package!

**Try these strategies:**
Question
Summarize

**Strategies in Action**  *Remember to use all your reading strategies while you read.*

# Chester Cricket's Pigeon Ride

by George Selden
illustrated by Garth Williams

*Chester Cricket lives a quiet life in a meadow in the Connecticut country-side. Life becomes more exciting for Chester when he comes to live in New York City, under a sidewalk grating in the Times Square subway station. There, Chester meets Tucker, a mouse, and Harry, a cat. Things get even more exciting when Chester meets a pigeon named Lulu. As this excerpt begins, Chester and Lulu have flown to the television antenna tower at the top of the Empire State Building.*

Chester felt as if not only a city but the entire world was down there where he could look at it. He almost couldn't see the people. "My gosh!" he thought. "They look just like bugs." And he had to laugh at that: like bugs — perhaps crickets — moving up and down the sidewalks. And the cars, the buses, the yellow taxis, all jittered along like miniatures. He felt that kind of spinning sensation inside his head that had made him dizzy on the way up. But he refused to close his eyes. It was too much of an adventure for that.

"Lulu, my foot," said Chester, "you're stepping on it. Could you please —"

"Ooo, I'm sorry," the pigeon apologized. She lifted her claw.

And just at that moment, two bad things happened. The first was, Chester caught sight of an airplane swooping low to land at LaGuardia Airport across the East River. The dip of it made his dizziness worse. And the second — worse yet — a sudden gust of wind sprang up, as if a hand gave them both a push. Lulu almost fell off the Empire State.

Lulu *almost* fell off — but Chester *did*! In an instant his legs and feelers were torn away from the pigeon's leg, and before he could say, "Old Meadow, farewell!" he was tumbling down through the air. One moment the city appeared above him — that meant that he was upside down; then under him — he was right side up; then everything slid from side to side.

He worked his wings, tried to hold them stiff to steady himself — no use, no use! The gleeful wind was playing with him. It was rolling him, throwing him back and forth, up and down, as a cork is tossed in the surf of a storm. And minute by minute, when he faced that way, the cricket caught glimpses of the floors of the Empire State Building plunging upward as he plunged down.

Despite his panic, his mind took a wink of time off to think: "Well, *this* is something that can't have happened to many crickets before!" (He was right, too — it hadn't. And just at that moment Chester wished that it wasn't happening to *him*.)

He guessed, when New York was in the right place again, that he was almost halfway down. The people were looking more and more like people — he heard the cars' engines — and the street and the sidewalk looked *awfully* hard! Then —

*Whump!* He landed on something both hard and soft. It was hard inside, all muscles and bones, but soft on the surface — feathers!

"Grab on!" a familiar voice shouted. "Tight! Tighter! That's it."

Chester gladly did as he was told.

"*Whooooey!*" Lulu breathed a sigh of relief. "Thought I'd never find you. Been around this building at least ten times."

Chester wanted to say, "Thank you, Lulu," but he was so thankful he couldn't get one word out till they'd reached a level where the air was friendly and gently buoyed them up.

But before he could even open his mouth, the pigeon — all ready for another adventure — asked eagerly, "Where now, Chester C.?"

"I guess I better go back to the drainpipe, Lulu. I'm kind of tired."

"Aw, no — !" complained Lulu, who'd been having fun.

"You know, I'm really not all that used to getting blown off the Empire State Building — "

"Oh, all right," said the pigeon. "But first there's one thing you *gotta* see!"

Flying just below the level of turbulent air — good pilot that she was — Lulu headed south, with Chester clinging to the back of her neck. He felt much safer up there, and her wings didn't block out as much of the

view as they'd thought. He wanted to ask where they were going, but he sensed from the strength and regularity of her wingbeats that it was to be a rather long flight. And the wind was against them too, which made the flying more difficult. Chester held his peace, and watched the city slip beneath them.

They reached the Battery, which is that part of lower New York where a cluster of skyscrapers rise up like a grove of steel trees. But Lulu didn't stop there.

With a gasp and an even tighter hold on her feathers, Chester realized that they'd flown right over the end of Manhattan. There was dark churning water below them. And this was no tame little lake, like the one in Central Park. It was the great deep wide bay that made New York such a mighty harbor. But Lulu showed no sign whatsoever of slowing. Her wings, like beautiful trustworthy machines, pumped on and on and on and on.

At last, Chester saw where the pigeon was heading. On a little island off to the right, Chester made out the form of a very big lady. Her right hand was holding something up. Of course it was the Statue of Liberty, but Chester had no way of knowing that. In the Old Meadow in Connecticut he never had gone to school — at least not to a school where the pupils used books. His teacher back there had been Nature herself.

Lulu landed at the base of the statue, puffing and panting to get back her breath. She told him a little bit about the lady — a gift from the country of France, it was, and very precious to America — but she hadn't flown him all that way just to give him a history lesson.

"Hop on again, Chester C.!" she commanded — and up they flew to the torch that the lady was holding. Lulu found a perch on the north side of it, so the wind from the south wouldn't bother them.

"Now, just look around!" said Lulu proudly, as if all of New York belonged to her. "And don't anybody ever tell *this* pigeon that there's a more beautiful sight in the world."

Chester did as he was told. He first peered behind. There was Staten Island. And off to the left, New Jersey. To the right, quite a long way away, was Brooklyn. And back across the black water, with a dome of light glowing over it, the heart of the city — Manhattan.

And bridges! Bridges everywhere — all pricked out with tiny lights on their cables — that joined the island to the lands all round.

"Oh, wow! We're in luck!" exclaimed Lulu. With a flick of her wing, she gestured down. Almost right below them, it seemed, an ocean liner was gliding by, its rigging, like the bridges, strung with hundreds of silver bulbs.

An airplane passed over them. And even *it* had lights on its wings!

Through his eyes, Chester's heart became flooded with wonder. "It's like — it's like a dream of a city, at night."

"You wait till I fly you back," said the pigeon. "You'll see how that dream can turn real."

The wind, which had been a hindrance before, was a help now. Lulu coasted almost all the way back to Manhattan, only lifting a wing now and then to keep them on an even keel. But once or twice, just for the fun of it, she tilted her wings without warning. They zoomed up, fast — then dipped down, faster — a roller coaster in the empty air.

And all the while, the dream city drew nearer. It seemed to Chester like some huge spiderweb. The streets were the strands, all hung with multicolored lights. "Oh, Lulu, it's — I don't know — it's — "

"Hush!" said the pigeon. "Just look and enjoy." They were flying amid the buildings now. "Enjoy, and remember."

Chester Cricket could not contain himself. He gave a chirp — not a song, just one chirp — but that single chirp said, "I love this! *I love it!*"

Then there was Times Square, erupting with colors. Chester pointed out the grating he'd come through — and Lulu landed next to it.

"How *can* I ever thank you?" said Chester.

"Don't bother, Chester C. Just glad to meet someone who loves New York as much as I do. And come on over to Bryant Park again. I'll be there — one branch or another. Night, Cricket."

"Night, Lulu."

She fluttered away.

Chester bounded through the grate and hopped as fast as he could toward the drainpipe. He hoped that Tucker and Harry were back. Tonight he *really* had an adventure to tell them!

# The Parcel Post Kid

by Michael O. Tunnell   illustrated by Renee Graef

On a cold February morning in 1914, Leonard Mochel arrived for work. He was a railroad postal clerk and rode in the mail car that traveled between Grangeville and Lewiston, Idaho. But on this particular morning, he had more than his lunch with him. Accompanying him was his five-year-old cousin, Charlotte May Pierstorff.

When the postmaster saw May and her small traveling bag, he thought that Leonard was going to buy her a train ticket. Imagine his surprise when Leonard announced that he wanted to mail May to her grandmother in Lewiston!

May's train fare would have cost $1.55, a lot of money in those days. But May's parents had discovered that she could be mailed for only 53 cents — if the post office would accept May as a package. Leonard thought it was a crazy idea, but he agreed to try.

Charlotte May Pierstorff

Train crossing trestle no. 31,
Lewiston to Grangeville

We would never think of mailing a human being today, but things were different in 1914. For one thing, sending heavy packages by mail was something new, so who could guess what might be allowed? And in 1914, mail was carried in rolling post offices instead of in the bellies of airplanes or the backs of trucks. Postal clerks like Leonard Mochel would sort mail while trains traveled between towns. If May were mailed, she would have her cousin Leonard's company as well as a safe and comfortable place to ride.

When the postmaster checked his book of rules, he found several things that he could not mail. No poisons. No insects. No reptiles. Nothing that smelled strongly. According to Leonard, the postmaster had a few funny things to say that morning. Maybe he sniffed May, laughed, and declared that she passed the smell test.

Live animals were also forbidden, but the postmaster found that it was all right to send baby chicks by parcel post. So he classified May as a baby chick, weighed her in at 48 1/2 pounds (which may have included her small suitcase), and attached 53 cents in postage to her bag. As well as being "stamped," May was also "addressed":

*Deliver to Mrs. C. G. Vennigerholz*
*1156 Twelfth Avenue*
*Lewiston, Idaho*

Leonard helped May into the mail car, and at 7:00 A.M., the train chugged out of the station.

Thus began the winding, seventy-seven-mile trip through the mountains to Lewiston. The train crawled through dark tunnels and over tall wooden trestles that stretched across the deep canyons. As it jolted and swayed over the tracks, May began to get dizzy. She hurried to the door to get some fresh air. Immediately Harry Morris, the conductor, spotted her and demanded to see May's ticket. When Leonard explained that May was actually a parcel and showed him the 53 cents in stamps, Mr. Morris laughed. "I've seen everything now!" he said. He was certain May's adventure would make a terrific story for the newspapers.

Traveling about nineteen miles an hour, the train finally reached Lewiston at 11:00 A.M. Leonard turned the Lewiston mail — including May — over to a clerk in the post office. Then he promptly "received" May from the clerk and delivered her to her grandmother. Grandma Mary was flabbergasted when May appeared on her doorstep. No one had told her that her granddaughter was coming to visit, and delivery by mail was an extra shock!

Meanwhile, Harry Morris wasted no time in reporting May's adventure to the newspaper. *The Gem State Banner* printed a story with the headline "Send Girl Aged 4 by Parcel Post." Even though the paper got May's age wrong, it managed to stir up trouble.

Two days later, another headline appeared in a paper from nearby Spokane, Washington: "Illegal to Send Child by Mail." Post office inspectors had gotten wind of May's story, and Leonard's job was on the line. The rule banning live animals from the mail excludes children, too, said the inspectors. And because May had been mailed, people were now asking to mail other live animals. Why, one man wanted to send his dog to Spokane!

In the end, Leonard kept his job, partly because May's parents agreed to pay half the train fare. But never again was anyone mailed by parcel post.

# Think and Compare

The Parcel Post Kid
by Michael O. Tunnel

1. Which journey do you think meant more to the main characters afterwards — Chester's or May's? Explain. How are the journeys alike and different?

2. How do you know that May's journey really happened? Give examples.

3. Chester was amazed by the new things he saw during his journey. Which theme character has the most in common with Chester in this way? Explain.

4. Which journey in this theme seems most like May's journey? In what ways are the journeys alike and different?

5. Which journey in this theme do you think is the most adventurous? Explain. Give examples from the selection.

**Strategies in Action** How did using the reading strategies help you during this theme?

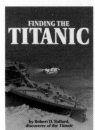

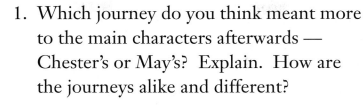

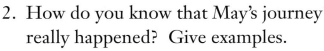

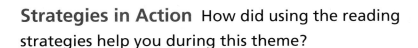

## Describing

# Write a Character Sketch

Choose one character from the theme. Write a character sketch that describes that character to someone who hasn't read the selection.

**Tips**

- Look for details in the story and the illustrations.
- Tell what makes the character special.
- Explain why the character's journey is important to him or her.

## Choosing the Best Answer

In order to answer a multiple-choice test question, you have to decide what is the best answer. A test about *Chester Cricket's Pigeon Ride* might have this question.

---

**Read the question. Fill in the circle for the best answer in the answer row at the bottom of the page.**

1. After Chester's fall, what does Lulu want to show him?

   **A** the Empire State Building

   **B** the Old Meadow

   **C** the torch of the Statue of Liberty

   **D** the view from the Statue of Liberty's torch

   | ANSWER ROW 1 | Ⓐ Ⓑ Ⓒ ● |
   |---|---|

---

 **Understand the question.**

Find the key words. Use them to understand what you need to do.

> I think the key words are *After Chester's fall* and *show*. I need to find out what sight Lulu wanted Chester to see *after* his fall.

**② Look back at the selection.**

Think about where to find the answer. You may need to look in more than one place. Skim the selection, using the key words.

> I have to find the part of the story that is *after Chester's fall.* That part starts on page 134D. I need to look ahead from there.

**③ Narrow the choices. Then choose the best answer.**

Find the choices that are clearly wrong. Have a good reason for choosing an answer. Guess only if you have to.

> **A** and **B** are wrong because Chester was at those places *before* his fall. Lulu flies to the Statue of Liberty's torch so that Chester can see the city's sights. So **D** is correct.

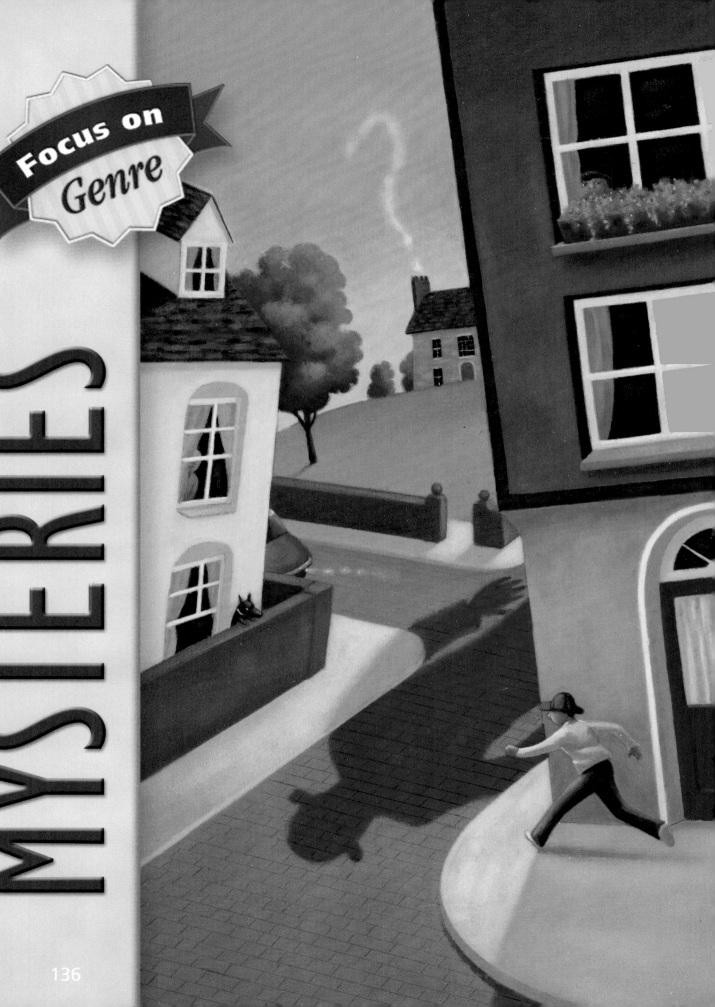

MYSTERIES

# HERE'S A PUZZLE TO SOLVE!

What kind of writing is full of **suspense**, contains a **crime**, a **detective** who's trying to figure it out, **clues** to point the way, **suspects** who might have done it . . . and finally, the

## SOLUTION?

If you said it's a **mystery** — you're right!

**Turn the key and read on!**

## CONTENTS

137

# The Case of the
# EARTHENWARE PIG

*by Donald J. Sobol*

"The cops are after me!"

The words came out of a blur. Something that looked like Charlie Stewart in fast motion sped through the Brown Detective Agency and disappeared into the tool closet.

Encyclopedia glanced up and down the street.

"There isn't a policeman in sight," he announced. "You gave them the slip."

The news failed to cheer Charlie. Opening the closet door a crack, he moaned, "I'm a wanted man!"

"Wanted for what?" asked Encyclopedia.

"How should I know?" said Charlie. "Five minutes ago I was walking down Locust Street. I came to the outdoor telephone booth at the corner of Locust and Beech, and there stood Bugs Meany and Officer Carlson. Bugs pointed at me and hollered, 'Arrest that kid!' I got scared and ran."

Charlie tiptoed out of the tool closet.

"I think this has something to do with my tooth collection," he said.

139

Charlie's tooth collection was the pride of Idaville. No boy anywhere in the state had collected more interesting uppers and lowers than Charlie. He kept them in a flowered cookie jar.

"Bugs owns an earthenware teapot shaped like a pig," Charlie continued thoughtfully. "He wanted to trade it for my tooth collection. I don't drink tea. So I told him no soap."

"What could Bugs want with your tooth collection?" asked Encyclopedia.

"Bugs was going to string the teeth behind the Tiger clubhouse," answered Charlie. "If anybody tried to sneak up on the clubhouse from the rear, he'd trip over the string. The string would shake, and the teeth would start chattering and warn the Tigers."

"Wow, dental detectors!" exclaimed Encyclopedia. "Pretty neat. I have to hand it to Bugs —"

Encyclopedia's voice trailed off. A police car had pulled into the Brown driveway. Bugs Meany hopped out, followed by Officer Carlson.

"I told you we'd find the little thief here!" sang Bugs. "I always knew this detective business was just a cover for a den of crooks!"

Officer Carlson motioned Bugs to be quiet. Then he said to Charlie, "Why were you walking on Locust Street about five minutes ago?"

"I got a telephone call to come there," replied Charlie. "A boy's voice asked me to meet him at the telephone booth right away. He said he had two grizzly bear teeth to sell. He wouldn't give his name."

"Yah, yah, yah!" jeered Bugs. "You were on your way to buy grizzly bear teeth! So how come the second you saw Officer Carlson you made like a drum and beat it?"

"B-because y-you hollered for him to arrest me," Charlie said. "I got plain scared."

"Stop it, you two," said Officer Carlson. "Bugs says you stole an earthenware teapot shaped like a pig, Charlie. Did you?"

"I did not!" said Charlie. And looking hard at Bugs he added, "I don't like pigs!"

As Bugs turned a lovely shade of purple, Officer Carlson held up his hand. "Let's all go to Bugs's house and try to find out what really happened."

Walking toward the police car, Charlie slipped Encyclopedia twenty-five cents. "I'll need you," he whispered. "I've never been in trouble with the police before."

At his house, Bugs stopped in the entrance hall.

"My folks have gone for the day," he said. He pointed to the staircase on his left. "I'd just come home when Charlie raced down the stairs. He had my teapot pig under his arm. I chased him out the front door, but he got away."

"Why couldn't you catch him?" inquired Encyclopedia. "You're bigger, older, and faster."

"Why?" said Bugs. "I'll tell you why, Mr. Brains. I obey the law. There was a green light over at Locust Street, and I don't cross against the green. I'm no jaywalker!"

"He's lying like a tiger skin," muttered Charlie.

Officer Carlson said, "Let's say Charlie did cross against the light and got away. What did you do next, Bugs?"

"I went straight to the telephone booth on the corner and called the police station," said Bugs. "I waited there till you arrived."

"You told me," said Officer Carlson, "that the cabinet in which you keep the teapot pig is always locked. You said the thief removed the hinges of the cabinet door to get inside it."

"Yeah," said Bugs. "It was a slick job. Charlie sure knew what he was doing." He led the way upstairs to his room.

The cabinet stood in a corner. The glass door, lifted off its hinges, was leaning against the wall.

"There," said Bugs. "Just like I said."

"But Charlie wasn't carrying the teapot pig when we saw him coming toward the telephone booth," pointed out Officer Carlson.

"He had plenty of time to hide it," said Bugs. "Then he tried to bluff you with that nutty story about buying grizzly bear teeth at the telephone booth. He had his alibi all ready!"

Officer Carlson regarded Charlie sternly. "I better call your parents," he said.

"Aw, I don't want him sent to prison or nothing," said Bugs. "I'm the kind that's always ready to forgive and forget. Charlie's been after me for weeks to swap my teapot pig for his tooth collection. I'll tell you what. If he's so crazy for my teapot, he can keep it. I'll take his crumby old tooth collection in trade."

"You won't take anything of Charlie's," said Encyclopedia. "He never stole your teapot pig!"

WHAT MADE ENCYCLOPEDIA SO SURE?

Turn to page 146 for the solution to the Case of the Earthenware Pig.

# The Sticks of TRUTH

### Retold by George Shannon

ONG AGO IN INDIA judges traveled from village to village. One day a judge stopped at an inn to rest, but the innkeeper was very upset. Someone had just that day stolen his daughter's gold ring. The judge told him not to worry and had all the guests gather so that he could question them. When he could not figure out from their answers who the thief was, the judge decided to use some old magic. He told them all he was going to have to use the sticks of truth.

"These are magic sticks," he explained, "that will catch the thief."

He gave each guest a stick to keep under the bed during the night.

"The stick belonging to the thief will grow two inches during the night. At breakfast we will all compare sticks and the longest stick will be the thief's."

The next morning the judge had all the guests come by his table and hold their sticks

up next to his to see if they had grown. But one after another all were the same. None of them had grown any longer. Then suddenly the judge called, "This is the thief! Her stick is shorter than all the rest."

Once caught, the woman confessed and the ring was returned. But all the guests were confused about the sticks of truth. The judge had said the longest stick would be the thief's, but instead it had been the shortest stick.

Why?

For the solution, turn to page 147.

145

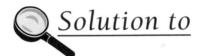 *Solution to*

# THE CASE OF THE EARTHENWARE PIG

According to his own story, Bugs chased Charlie out of the house. Furthermore, he did not go upstairs to his room where the cabinet was until he brought back Officer Carlson, Charlie, and Encyclopedia.

Yet he knew how the cabinet had been opened!

He could not have known whether the lock had been forced, or the glass door broken, or the hinges removed — unless he had been the "thief" himself!

When Encyclopedia pointed out his mistake, Bugs confessed. He had tried to make it look as if Charlie were the thief in order to get Charlie's tooth collection.

The Tiger leader admitted he had been the boy who had lured Charlie to the telephone booth with the offer of selling him grizzly bear teeth. He had wanted Charlie to tell a story so unbelievable that Officer Carlson would think Charlie was guilty.

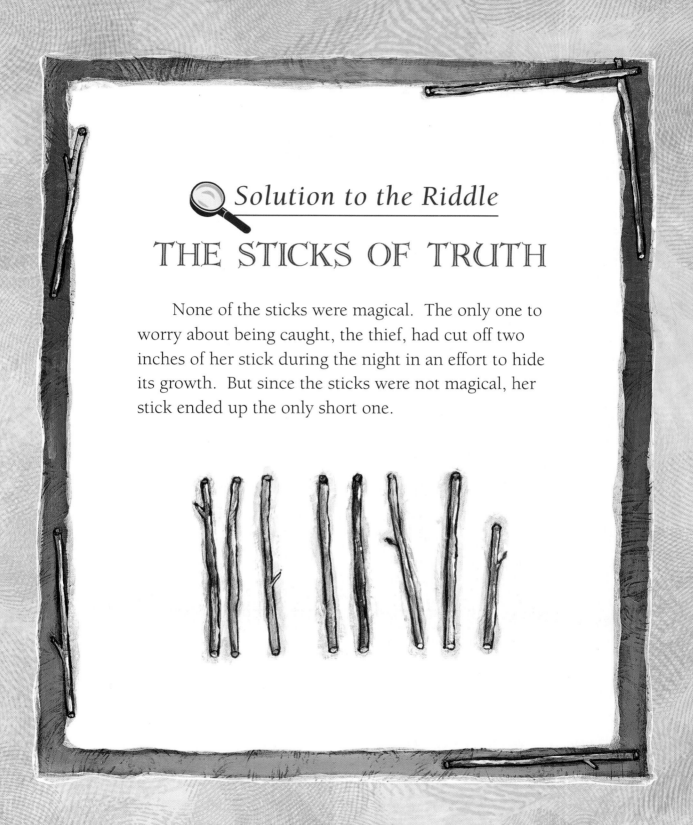

## Solution to the Riddle

# THE STICKS OF TRUTH

None of the sticks were magical. The only one to worry about being caught, the thief, had cut off two inches of her stick during the night in an effort to hide its growth. But since the sticks were not magical, her stick ended up the only short one.

# *Think About the* MYSTERIES

1. Which elements of a mystery do the two selections have in common? What is the biggest difference between the two stories?

2. In what ways is the judge like Encyclopedia Brown? In what ways is he different?

3. In the first selection, how does the author make you think that Charlie could be guilty? Give examples from the story.

4. Explain which of the two mysteries you enjoyed better and why. Which one was more of a challenge for you to solve?

5. If Encyclopedia Brown could discuss detective work with the judge, what qualities might they agree are needed to be a good detective?

**Internet**

## Complete a Web Crossword Puzzle

Grab your magnifying glass and put on your private detective hat! Follow the clues and solve our online mystery crossword puzzle.

**www.eduplace.com/kids**

**Creating**

# Write a Mystery

Now it's your turn to be a mystery writer. Start with the "crime." Decide what happened, who did it, and why. Then think of other suspects. Now create a detective character. Figure out how the detective will solve the case. Finally, write the whole story. Be sure to focus on solving the crime!

**Tips**

- To get started, make a chart of the elements of your mystery story.
- Be sure to create clues that lead to each of the suspects.
- Keep the reader in suspense — don't give away all the clues at once.

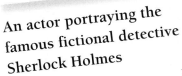

An actor portraying the famous fictional detective Sherlock Holmes

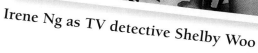

Irene Ng as TV detective Shelby Woo

149

# American Stories

### This Land Is Your Land

This land is your land,
this land is my land,
from California
to the New York Island,
from the redwood forest
to the Gulf Stream waters,
This land was made
for you and me.

— *Woody Guthrie*
*from the song*

# American Stories

## with Valerie Flournoy

Dear Reader,

My children's books are my own personal "American Stories." They are based on childhood memories of people, places, and times in my life that have shaped me into the person I am today. When I was writing *Tanya's Reunion*, I had two special people in mind, and one particular place — my Aunt Kay's farm.

We visited the farm when I was eight years old. The trip in our old green station wagon seemed to take forever. When we arrived, my brothers, sisters, and I were disappointed.

There was no white picket fence, no horses, no indoor plumbing, and no television. But we soon fell in love with the place. In the stream alongside the pasture, we discovered frogs. When the sun shone too hot, we had the cool shelter of the barn. After dark, we had plenty of moonlight, the star-filled night sky, and hundreds of flickering fireflies.

*Tanya's Reunion* was written with two beloved relatives in mind: my Great Aunt Lucy Wricks and my father, Payton Isaac Flournoy, Sr. Aunt Lucy taught school for forty years. Her annual Thanksgiving dinner brought together the entire family. There was always a place at the table for the neighbor or friend who needed a hot meal and some fellowship with friends.

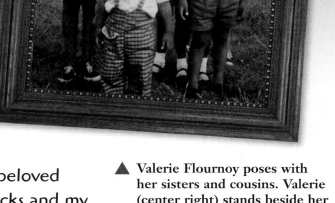

▲ Valerie Flournoy poses with her sisters and cousins. Valerie (center right) stands beside her twin sister Vanesa (center left).

▼ A farm similar to the one Valerie Flournoy describes in *Tanya's Reunion*

Because of her service to friends, family, and community, Aunt Lu (pictured below) was the person my dad most admired. Dad (pictured above) was a police officer from 1950 to 1976. For most of that time, he was Chief of Police of my hometown, Palmyra, New Jersey. But to family and friends, he was just "TeeWee" — a regular guy quick to laugh and joke, who devoted time to his community and loved listening to jazz trumpeter Louis Armstrong, reading books, and cooking his favorite barbecue.

How did I get from Aunt Lucy and Dad to *Tanya's Reunion*? This story is a memory of a time when Aunt Lucy and Dad were alive and living life to the fullest. This story is a memory of some of the happiest times of my life. It is a memory of events that inspired a book — my own American Story. Perhaps there's a certain person, place, or time in *your* life that always makes you smile when you think of it? Perhaps you already have a special memory . . . a personal story . . . your special American Story that will remain with you forever, too!

Happy reading always,

*Valerie Flournoy*

# So Many Stories to Tell...

Valerie Flournoy explains that, for her, American Stories are made up of special people and places from her own life. Who and what would you include in *your* American Story?

As you read each selection below, ask yourself what ingredients help to make it an American Story. There are people to meet, places to see, and best of all, stories to be shared — *American Stories.*

**Internet**

To learn about the authors in this theme, visit Education Place. **www.eduplace.com/kids**

# Background and Vocabulary

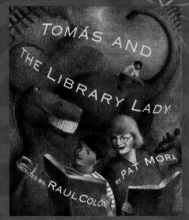

**Tomás and the Library Lady**

**Read to find the meanings of these words.**

*e* ● Glossary

borrow
check out
eager
storyteller

# TOMÁS RIVERA
## READER AND WRITER

Do you borrow books from a library? Imagine having a big library, a book award, and even an elementary school named after you! That is what happened to Tomás Rivera, who, as a boy, helped his family pick crops in Texas and the Midwest. Tomás was an eager reader and a great storyteller. When he grew up, he wrote stories, poems, and a book. He also became a teacher and head of a university. Tomás Rivera even traveled around the world to talk about Mexican American writers in the United States. Read *Tomás and the Library Lady* to see how Tomás got his start when he was a boy.

# TOMÁS RIVERA
## A SCHOOL, AN AWARD, A LIBRARY

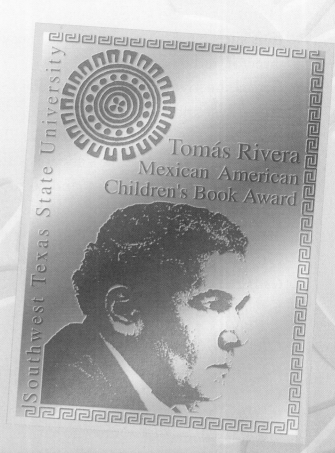

**AN ELEMENTARY SCHOOL**
Because of Tomás Rivera's accomplish-
ments, this elementary school in
Denton, Texas, was named after him.

**A BOOK AWARD**
This official seal goes on
books that win the Tomás
Rivera Mexican American
Children's Book Award.

**A LIBRARY**
The Tomás Rivera Library in Riverside, California. Maybe one
day you'll check out books from the library named after Tomás!

# Meet the AUTHOR

**Where she was born:** El Paso, Texas

**Home:** Edgewood, Kentucky

**Jobs she's had:** English teacher, museum director, radio show host

**Places she loves:** the deserts of the U. S. Southwest and northern Mexico

**Languages she speaks:** English and Spanish

**Why she writes:** She says she loves the way words can move, entertain, and comfort people, and make them laugh.

**Interesting fact:** *Tomás and the Library Lady* won the Tomás Rivera Mexican American Children's Book Award in 1997.

**Other books:** *This Big Sky; The Race of Toad and Deer; Confetti: Poems for Children*

*Pat Mora*

# Meet the ILLUSTRATOR

*Raul Colón*

**Where he was born:** Puerto Rico

**Where he lives now:** New City, New York

**How to say his name:** Rah-OOL Coh-LONE

**Things he likes to do:** listen to all kinds of music, play the guitar

**Languages he speaks:** English and Spanish

**Other books he has illustrated:** *Always My Dad* by Sharon Dennis Wyeth; *A Band of Angels* by Deborah Hopkinson

To find out more about Pat Mora and Raul Colón, visit Education Place. **www.eduplace.com/kids**

# Selection 1

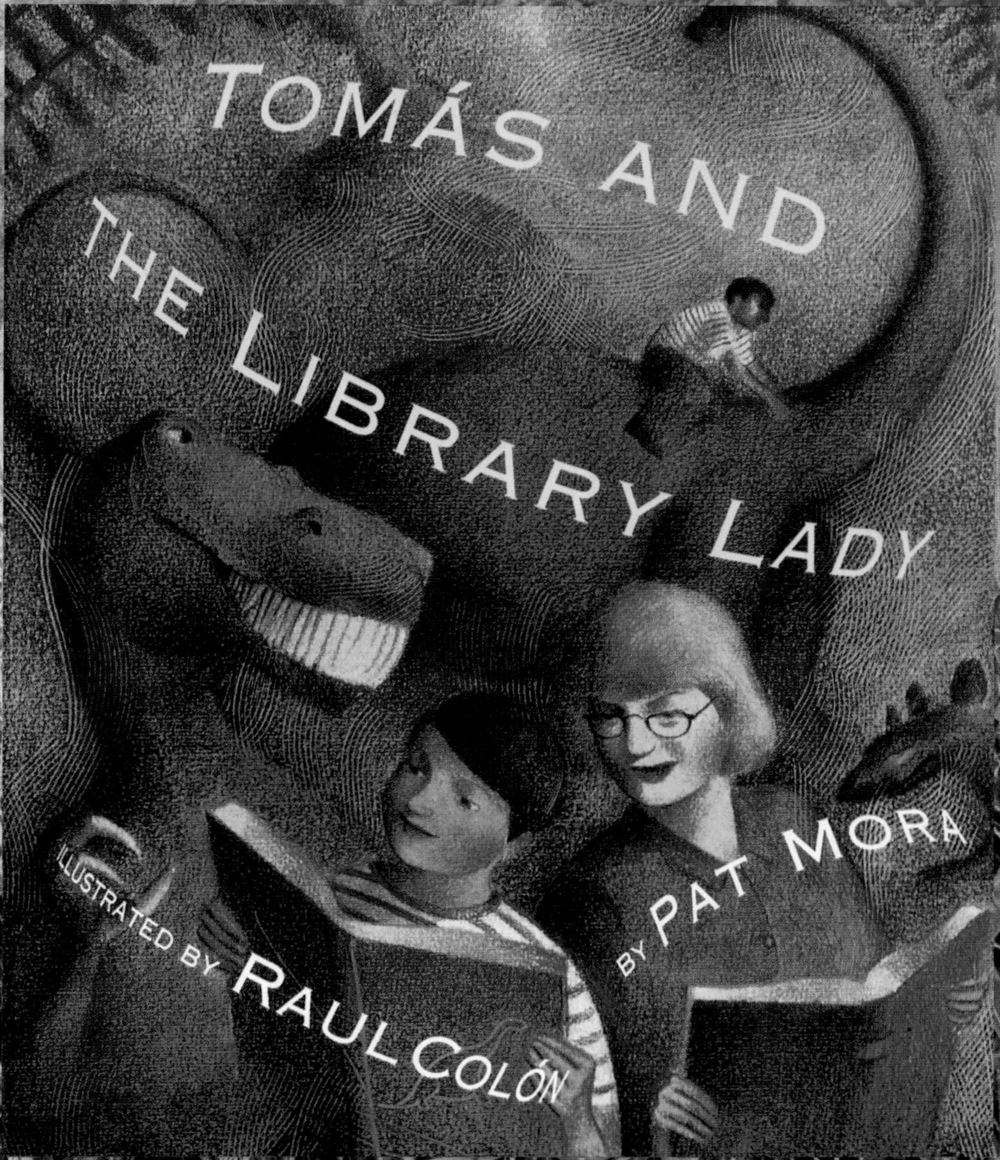

TOMÁS AND THE LIBRARY LADY
BY PAT MORA
ILLUSTRATED BY RAUL COLÓN


## Strategy Focus

You know that Tomás Rivera grew up to be a well-known writer and educator. What do you **predict** this story will tell about Tomás?

It was midnight. The light of the full moon followed the tired old car. Tomás was tired too. Hot and tired. He missed his own bed, in his own house in Texas.

Tomás was on his way to Iowa again with his family. His mother and father were farm workers. They picked fruit and vegetables for Texas farmers in the winter and for Iowa farmers in the summer. Year after year they bump-bumped along in their rusty old car. "Mamá," whispered Tomás, "if I had a glass of cold water, I would drink it in large gulps. I would suck the ice. I would pour the last drops of water on my face."

Tomás was glad when the car finally stopped. He helped his grandfather, Papá Grande, climb down. Tomás said, *"Buenas noches"* — "Good night" — to Papá, Mamá, Papá Grande, and to his little brother, Enrique. He curled up on the cot in the small house that his family shared with the other workers.

Early the next morning Mamá and Papá went out to pick corn in the green fields. All day they worked in the hot sun. Tomás and Enrique carried water to them. Then the boys played with a ball Mamá had sewn from an old teddy bear.

When they got hot, they sat under a tree with Papá Grande. "Tell us the story about the man in the forest," said Tomás.

Tomás liked to listen to Papá Grande tell stories in Spanish. Papá Grande was the best storyteller in the family.

"*En un tiempo pasado*," Papá Grande began. "Once upon a time . . . on a windy night a man was riding a horse through a forest. The wind was howling, *whooooooooo,* and the leaves were blowing, *whish, whish* . . .

"All of a sudden something grabbed the man. He couldn't move. He was too scared to look around. All night long he wanted to ride away. But he couldn't.

"How the wind howled, *whoooooooooo.* How the leaves blew. How his teeth chattered!

"Finally the sun came up. Slowly the man turned around. And who do you think was holding him?"

Tomás smiled and said, "A thorny tree."

Papá Grande laughed. "Tomás, you know all my stories," he said. "There are many more in the library. You are big enough to go by yourself. Then you can teach us new stories."

The next morning Tomás walked downtown. He looked at the big library. Its tall windows were like eyes glaring at him. Tomás walked around and around the big building. He saw children coming out carrying books. Slowly he started climbing up, up the steps. He counted them to himself in Spanish. *Uno, dos, tres, cuatro* . . . His mouth felt full of cotton.

Tomás stood in front of the library doors.  He pressed his nose against the glass and peeked in.  The library was huge!

A hand tapped his shoulder.  Tomás jumped.  A tall lady looked down at him.  "It's a hot day," she said.  "Come inside and have a drink of water.  What's your name?" she asked.

"Tomás," he said.

"Come, Tomás," she said.

Inside it was cool.  Tomás had never seen so many books. The lady watched him.  "Come," she said again, leading him

to a drinking fountain. "First some water. Then I will bring books to this table for you. What would you like to read about?"

"Tigers. Dinosaurs," said Tomás.

Tomás drank the cold water. He looked at the tall ceiling. He looked at all the books around the room. He watched the lady take some books from the shelves and bring them to the table. "This chair is for you, Tomás," she said. Tomás sat down. Then very carefully he took a book from the pile and opened it.

Tomás saw dinosaurs bending their long necks to lap shiny water. He heard the cries of a wild snakebird. He felt the warm neck of the dinosaur as he held on tight for a ride. Tomás forgot about the library lady. He forgot about Iowa and Texas.

"Tomás, Tomás," said the library lady softly. Tomás looked around. The library was empty. The sun was setting.

The library lady looked at Tomás for a long time. She said, "Tomás, would you like to borrow two library books? I will check them out in my name."

Tomás walked out of the library carrying his books. He ran home, eager to show the new stories to his family.

Papá Grande looked at the library books. "Read to me," he said to Tomás. First Tomás showed him the pictures. He pointed to the tiger. "*¡Qué tigre tan grande!*" Tomás said first in Spanish and then in English, "What a big tiger!"

"Read to me in English," said Papá Grande. Tomás read about tiger eyes shining brightly in the jungle at night. He roared like a huge tiger. Papá, Mamá, and Enrique laughed. They came and sat near him to hear his story.

Some days Tomás went with his parents to the town dump. They looked for pieces of iron to sell. Enrique looked for toys. Tomás looked for books. He would put the books in the sun to bake away the smell.

All summer, whenever he could, Tomás went to the library. The library lady would say, "First a drink of water and then some new books, Tomás."

On quiet days the library lady said, "Come to my desk and read to me, Tomás." Then she would say, "Please teach me some new words in Spanish."

Tomás would smile. He liked being the teacher. The library lady pointed to a book. "Book is *libro*," said Tomás.

"*Libro*," said the library lady.

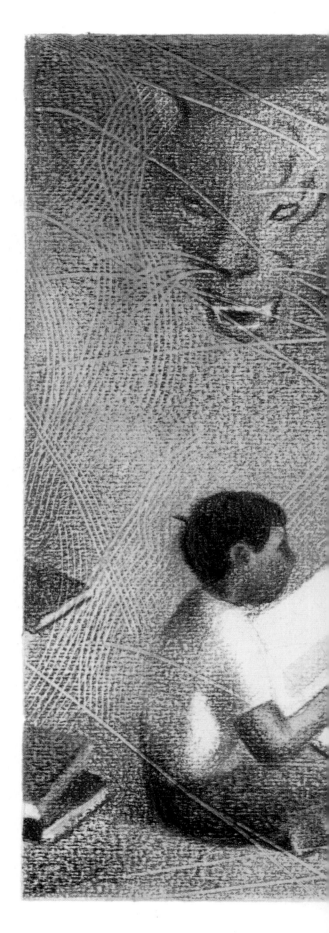

"*Pájaro,*" said Tomás, flapping his arms.

The library lady laughed. "Bird," she said.

On days when the library was busy, Tomás read to himself. He'd look at the pictures for a long time. He smelled the smoke at an Indian camp. He rode a black horse across a hot, dusty desert. And in the evenings he would read the stories to Mamá, Papá, Papá Grande, and Enrique.

One August afternoon Tomás brought Papá Grande to the library.

The library lady said, *"Buenas tardes, señor."* Tomás smiled. He had taught the library lady how to say "Good afternoon, sir" in Spanish.

"*Buenas tardes, señora,*" Papá Grande replied.

Softly Tomás said, "I have a sad word to teach you today. The word is *adiós.* It means good-bye."

Tomás was going back to Texas. He would miss this quiet place, the cool water, the many books. He would miss the library lady.

"My mother sent this to thank you," said Tomás, handing her a small package. "It is *pan dulce,* sweet bread. My mother makes the best *pan dulce* in Texas."

The library lady said, "How nice. How very nice. *Gracias,* Tomás. Thank you." She gave Tomás a big hug.

That night, bumping along again in the tired old car, Tomás held a shiny new book, a present from the library lady. Papá Grande smiled and said, "More stories for the new storyteller."

Tomás closed his eyes. He saw the dinosaurs drinking cool water long ago. He heard the cry of the wild snakebird. He felt the warm neck of the dinosaur as he held on tight for a bumpy ride.

175

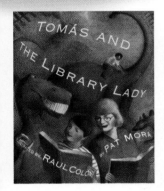

## THINK ABOUT THE SELECTION

**1.** How do you think Tomás feels when he first sees the library? Give examples from the story to support your opinion.

**2.** Before Tomás meets the library lady, his grandfather is the family storyteller. Why does this change after Tomás starts visiting the library?

**3.** How would you describe the library lady? What kind of person is she?

**4.** What do you think Tomás enjoys most about reading books? Tell about *your* favorite book and what you enjoy most about it.

**5.** Tomás and the library lady become friends. What do you think they learn from each other?

**6.** **Connecting/Comparing** Tomás Rivera grew up to be a successful educator and writer. Why do you think the author of this book chose to write about this time in Tomás Rivera's life?

### Expressing

## WRITE A THANK-YOU NOTE

Write a note from Tomás thanking the library lady for her help. Include how Tomás felt about the way she treated him and why his visits to the library were so important. Include a greeting, a closing, and a signature.

**Tips**

- Make a list of words that describe Tomás's feelings.
- Use details from the story to explain why Tomás had those particular feelings.

## Math

### FIND DISTANCE TRAVELED

Tomás's family traveled between two states every summer. Use a map of the United States to find the capitals of those states. Then measure the distance between the two cities. Use the scale of miles on the map to figure out the length of their round trip.

## Vocabulary

### MAKE A SPANISH PHRASE BOOK

Copy the Spanish words and phrases you find in the story. Next to each one, write its English translation. Make a colorful cover and put together your Spanish-English phrase book. Be sure to put a title on the cover.

**Bonus** Look for connections between the Spanish words and words you know in English. For example, *libro* (book) is related to *library*. You might want to use a Spanish-English dictionary to find more examples.

### Internet

### E-MAIL A FRIEND

What did you like most about *Tomás and the Library Lady*? Would you recommend this book to a friend? Write an e-mail to tell a friend about the story and what you thought of it.

**Skill: How to Read a Social Studies Article**

*Before you read . . .*

**1** **Read** the title, headings, and captions.

**2** **Look at** the pictures or photos.

**3** **Predict** what you will learn in the article.

*While you read . . .*

**1** **Identify** the time and place the article tells about.

**2** **Identify** the main idea of each paragraph.

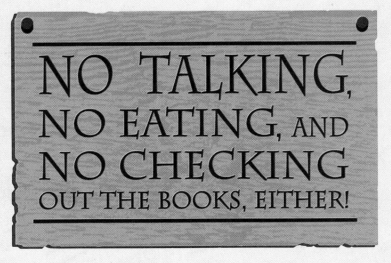

# NO TALKING, NO EATING, AND NO CHECKING OUT THE BOOKS, EITHER!

*by Gwen Diehn*

If you think the rules in your school library are strict (all those due dates, overdue fines, and no talking or snacking), imagine how you would have felt in the medieval library at Hereford Cathedral in England. In this library the books were actually chained to the shelves!

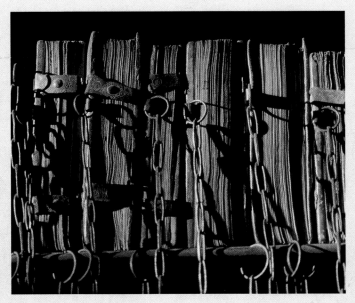

*Chained books at the Hereford Cathedral library*

If you wanted to read one of them, the librarian had to help you lift the book, chain and all, down to a kind of table below the shelf. There you could sit (without talking or eating!) on a wooden bench that looked like a church pew and browse through the book. But you absolutely could not check it out or even carry it across the room. In those days, books were such rare and precious objects that in many libraries they were chained up so they wouldn't be stolen.

*A wooden bookcase with attached table for reading the chained books*

*Part of an ancient Egyptian papyrus scroll with an illustration and hieroglyphs [HI-ruh-gliffs], the ancient Egyptian form of writing*

*A Babylonian clay tablet "book"*

If you think it's hard to find a book on a certain topic in your school library, imagine trying to find a particular book in the ancient Egyptian library in the city of Alexandria. This library had about 400,000 papyrus scrolls and no cataloging system until years after it opened! In fact, finding a particular scroll was such a horrendous job that librarians were driven to invent the first library cataloging system.

And if you sometimes get tired of lugging your books back and forth to the library, be glad they aren't made of clay tablets, as were the books of the ancient Babylonians. The very first libraries that we know of were giant storehouses in Babylonia and Egypt full of clay tablets and papyrus scrolls containing written records.

# Record-Breaking Books

*The smallest published book in the world*

The *Guinness Book of Records* has listed a book that measures 1/25 by 1/25 of an inch! The pages are so small that they can be turned only with a needle! The book contains the children's story, *Old King Cole*, and was published in 1985 by The Gleniffer Press in Scotland.

The *Guinness Book* has listed some other record holders:

- The oldest handwritten book found in one piece is a book of psalms discovered at Beni Suef in Egypt. The book is about 1600 years old.

- The oldest mechanically printed book is the Dharani scroll, found in South Korea in 1966. The scroll was printed from carved wooden blocks, and is at least 1200 years old.

- And finally, the most overdue library book ever returned in the United States was a book on diseases checked out in 1823 from the University of Cincinnati Medical Library. It was returned December 7, 1968 by the borrower's great-grandson. The fine was $2,264, but the library said "Never mind!"

# A Description

A description is a picture in words that helps the reader see, hear, taste, smell, and feel what you're writing about. Use this student's writing as a model when you write a description of your own.

# Tabby the Tabby Cat

Good **opening sentences** tell what the description is about.

**Exact, vivid** words create a mental image in the reader's mind.

It is helpful to put the **details** in time order, spatial order, or order of importance.

My cat Tabby is a small tabby cat. I found her one summer sitting on the steps in my back yard. She was skinny, so I fed her some cat food. I asked my parents if I could keep the poor little thing, and they said, "No, it might have fleas!" So I just kept feeding her, and petting and scratching her behind the ear. I kept begging my parents so much they finally gave in. I could keep her! I quickly thought of a name for her. First I chose Tigger, then Tinkerbell, and finally Tabby!

Tabby has bright green eyes that glow at night. She has spots and stripes. She is black, gray, white, brown, orange, and copper. Her fur is soft and fluffy. She is as fast as a road runner, well, almost, all right, not even close, but she's pretty fast. Tabby is also nice, lovable, pretty, smart, and she's mine.

**Sense words** help your reader picture what you are describing.

A good **ending** wraps up the description.

Tabby

## Meet the Author

Molly D.
**Grade:** four
**State:** New Jersey
**Hobbies:** taking care of Tabby, playing soccer and softball
**What she'd like to be when she grows up:** a veterinarian

**Tanya's Reunion**

TANYA'S REUNION
• sequel to *The Patchwork Quilt* •
by VALERIE FLOURNOY
pictures by JERRY PINKNEY

### Read to find the meanings of these words.

*e* ● Glossary

arrangements

gatherings

homestead

pitches in

reunions

satisfaction

# Family Reunions

Family **reunions** are **gatherings** of family members. They can be as small as two cousins meeting for the first time in years or as large as hundreds of relatives from many generations. And they take place just about anywhere. Some families meet at the old **homestead** where family members have lived for years, while others might go to a local park or hotel.

To organize a big reunion, everyone **pitches in** to
help with the **arrangements**. Relatives may be coming
from other states — or even from other countries! It's
a lot of work, but the **satisfaction** of bringing the family
together makes it worthwhile. Read *Tanya's Reunion* to
see how one family gets ready for their gathering.

# Meet the Author

**Home:** Palmyra, New Jersey

**Birthday:** April 17

**Family fact:** She has a twin sister, Vanessa, who is also a writer.

**Why she writes:** She loves to take one little thought or idea and stretch it into a story everyone can enjoy.

**Other books:** *The Patchwork Quilt, Celie and the Harvest Fiddler, The Twins Strike Back*

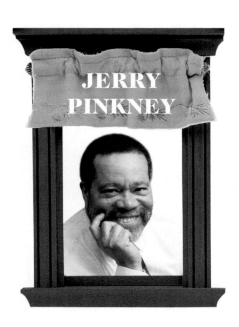

# Meet the Illustrator

**When he started drawing:** at age four or five

**Family facts:** He has illustrated several books written by his wife, Gloria Jean. Their son, Brian, is an author and an illustrator too.

**How he illustrates books:** Often he asks people to dress up as characters and act out the story. Then he uses photos of them to help him draw.

**Other books he has illustrated:** *The Patchwork Quilt* by Valerie Flournoy; *John Henry* by Julius Lester; *The Sunday Outing* by Gloria Jean Pinkney

If you want to find out more about Valerie Flournoy and Jerry Pinkney, visit Education Place.

**www.eduplace.com/kids**

186

# TANYA'S REUNION

- sequel to *The Patchwork Quilt* -

by VALERIE FLOURNOY

pictures by JERRY PINKNEY

Tanya is going to a family reunion. As you read the story, **evaluate** how the author helps you understand what Tanya is feeling.

188

It was Saturday. Baking day. One of Grandma's special days. Tanya had just popped the last spoonful of bread pudding made that morning into her mouth when Grandma announced, "Got a card from Aunt Kay and Uncle John today. They've invited me to the farm before all the family arrives for the big reunion. And I've decided to go."

A silence fell across the dinner table. Neither Tanya nor her brothers, Ted and Jim, could remember their grandmother going *anywhere* without the rest of the family.

"Aren't *we* going to the farm and reunion too?" Tanya asked. She had been looking forward to the big family event and her first trip to a farm ever since the announcement had arrived.

"Yes, Tanya. We're still going," Papa reassured her.

"We can *all* go to the farm together *after* the boy's football summer camp is over," Mama suggested, glancing toward Papa.

Grandma sucked her teeth and sighed. "Now, what's all the fuss? My baby sister asked me to come home early. I suspect she needs help working out all the sleeping arrangements and finding just the right spot for all the history people will be bringing with them."

Tanya remembered Mama and Grandma talking about the plan to have as many items that were once part of the homestead . . . the farm . . . returned for the biggest family gathering ever!

"But, Mother," said Mama, "You were sick not too long ago. Do you really think this trip is wise?"

Tanya watched Grandma reach out and touch Mama's hand.

"That was then, honey, and this is now, and I'm just fine. So I'm gonna go while I'm able," the old woman said firmly. "Besides, if you're so worried about me, you can always send Tanya along to see I stay out of trouble."

A trip with Grandma! Just the two of them. Tanya couldn't believe her ears.

"*May* I go with Grandma to the farm?" she pleaded excitedly.

Mama looked from Tanya to Papa to Grandma.

"Ted and Jim *are* going to football camp," Papa gently reminded Mama. "And we *will* be joining them shortly."

Grandma pulled a letter from her apron pocket. "I think Kay mentioned some of *her* grandchildren would be visiting early too. So Tanya will have someone to play with."

Mama looked from Grandma to Papa to Tanya again. "All right," she finally agreed. "You can go."

Tanya couldn't hide the pride she felt when she saw the surprised looks on Ted's and Jim's faces.

"We've had some special days on that old farm," Grandma said with satisfaction. "And so will Tanya. You'll see."

The sun rose slowly in the morning sky as Tanya watched all her familiar places vanish behind her. Past her schoolyard and the park. Past row after row of houses and traffic lights.

And still they traveled on and on. They stopped only to switch from one bus to another. Tanya listened while Grandma spoke about "going home" to the great land of Virginia that "borned four of the first five Presidents of these United States."

And still they traveled on and on. Until the bright sunny sky grew cloudy and gray and the highway turned into never-ending dirt roads that seemed to disappear into the fields and trees, down into the "hollers," the valleys below. Tanya could barely keep her eyes open.

And still they traveled on and on . . . until finally the bus crawled to a stop.

Grandma shook Tanya gently. "We're here, Tanya honey, wake up." Tanya rubbed her eyes awake. "We're home."

Standing on the last step of the bus, Tanya spied a car, trailing clouds of dust, coming toward them. In the distance were a farmhouse and barn.

"I've been sitting for the past eight . . . nine hours," Grandma told Uncle John, who'd come to get them, "so I think I'll just let these old limbs take me the rest of the way."

Tanya watched Grandma walk slowly but steadily up the familiar roadway.

"Memories die hard," Uncle John whispered to Tanya.

Tanya wasn't certain what her great-uncle meant. She only knew that if Grandma was going to walk, she would walk too. And she raced to the old woman's side.

"Take care, honey," Grandma said. "August weather down here's meant to be eased on through, not run through."

Tanya looked up at Grandma as she stared off into the distance, a faraway look in her eyes. What Tanya saw didn't look like the pictures in her schoolbooks or magazines or the pictures in her head.

There wasn't a horse in sight and the farmhouse was just a faded memory of its original color. Tanya noticed clouds of dust floating about her ankles, turning her white socks and sneakers a grayish-brown color.

"Just open your heart to it," Grandma said. "Can't you feel the place welcomin' ya?"

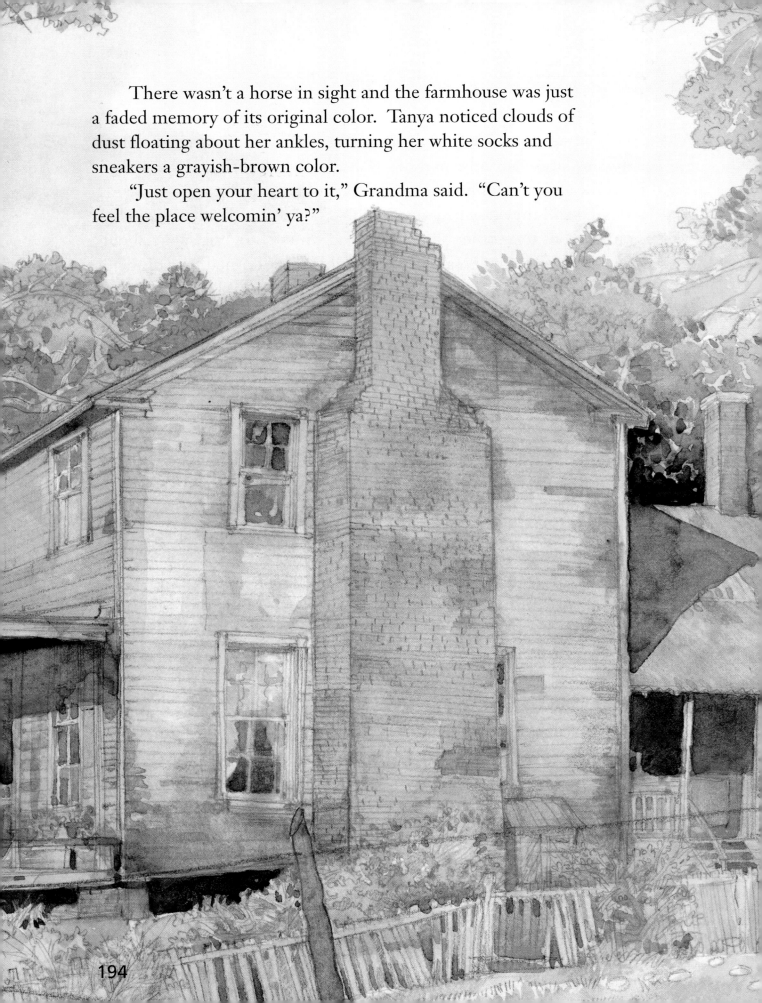

Tanya didn't feel anything but hot and tired and disappointed. The farm wasn't what she expected. No, it wasn't what she expected at all.

A dog's bark drew Tanya's gaze back to the farmhouse. Stepping off the porch, a large dog at her side, was Grandma's baby sister, Kay.

"Watchin' you walk up that road, Rose Buchanan," Aunt Kay began, then gave Grandma a hug.

"Yes, on summer days like this it's as if time were standing still just a bit," Grandma finished for her.

Aunt Kay turned to her great-niece, smothering her in a welcoming hug full of warmth and softness that reminded Tanya of Grandma.

A summer breeze suddenly blew across the land, pushing the scattered gray clouds together. Tanya felt raindrops.

"Looks like it's comin' up a cloud," Uncle John said, hurrying the women onto the back porch and into the house. "I think it's *finally* gonna rain!"

Tanya was swept into the house by the laughing, talking grown-ups. Inside the kitchen Tanya met her cousin Celeste and her children, baby Adam and seven-year-old Keisha. The room was filled with wonderful aromas that made Tanya's mouth water — until she noticed the fly strip hanging above the kitchen table.

197

When Tanya went to bed that night, she was miserable. She barely touched her supper, until Uncle John thought to remove the fly strip dangling overhead. She missed her own room. She missed Mama and Papa, even Ted and Jim. Cousin Keisha and baby Adam were nice. But he was too small to really play with, and Keisha refused to leave her mother's side all night.

Grandma helped Aunt Kay tuck the children in. "What happened to our special days, Grandma?" whispered Tanya.

"Seems to me our first one went just fine," said Grandma. "The land needed the rain and it's finally gettin' it. Makes today kinda special, don't you think?"

Tanya sighed. "I wanna go home," she murmured into her pillow.

*Cockle-doodle-do!* The rooster's morning wake-up call startled cousin Keisha out of her sound sleep, and she cried until her mother came to take her into her room with the baby.

From the bed by the window, Tanya leaned against the windowsill looking over the empty farmyard. The sky was slate gray, but the air was fresh and clean and a gentle breeze swept through the window. It was also Saturday. Baking day, Tanya remembered before drifting back to sleep.

A single raindrop plopped on Tanya's face . . . then another . . . and another, until she awoke and closed the window. By the time she finished dressing, the rain sounded like a thunderous drumroll along the rooftop.

Hurrying down the staircase, Tanya stopped at the room Aunt Kay had called her sitting parlor. The room she chose to hold the family's memories. Several quilts — including Grandma's — with different colors and designs were draped across the sofa or hanging from the walls. Crocheted tablecloths and napkins, baptismal gowns and baby blankets, and a rocking chair and baby crib were also in place. There were various pots and pans, blacksmithing and gardening tools, candle molds and a few toys. Even a broom that couples jumped over when they married during slavery times. Every item was clearly and neatly labeled by its owner.

"Ahhh! Here's my northern niece. Ready for breakfast?" asked Uncle John.

"Yes! Ready!" Tanya said, turning from the doorway.

It rained through breakfast. It rained through checkers with cousin Celeste and four games of dominoes with Uncle John and Keisha. It rained through Adam's crying and Keisha's temper tantrum when Tanya hid all too well while playing hide-and-seek. It rained all morning long.

"Grandma," Tanya finally called. "Grandma, where are you?"

"In here," Grandma answered.

Tanya found Grandma, Aunt Kay, and cousin Celeste in the kitchen surrounded by boxes and lists about sleeping arrangements and who would cook what for the big reunion.

"Grandma, aren't we gonna bake today?" Tanya asked.

Grandma looked up from her lists. "Oh my," she murmured.

Tanya sighed unhappily and Grandma put her arm around her granddaughter's shoulder, leading her out the back door. The rain fell in a straight, steady stream, like a curtain separating the porch from the barnyard beyond.

Grandma patted the place behind her on the swing and Tanya slid into a familiar spot under her grandmother's arm.

"I'm sorry, Tanya honey. I guess I just plumb forgot what day this was." The old woman sighed, then laughed. "And I guess no number of stories can make you see this place through these old eyes."

"Did you *really* like living on this farm, Grandma?" Tanya asked. "Weren't you *ever* lonely?"

Grandma laughed again. "No, Tanya, I wasn't lonely. Back then, this whole farmyard: the barn, the pasture, fields, and orchard beyond" — she stretched out her arm — "this place was filled with activity. We had the land and the land had us. We worked over it, tilled and planted it. Then harvested it when it was ready. In turn the land gave us water, food, clothing, and a roof over our heads."

"If you weren't lonely, Grandma, why did you leave?" Tanya persisted.

206

Grandma looked out over the land, remembering. "It was after the Second World War. My Isaac — your grandpa Franklin — and many other people thought we'd find better opportunities, better jobs closer to the cities up north. And we did. But we still kept the land and paid taxes on it. Sometimes let other people pay to work it, 'til Kay and John came back. But this will always be home."

Tanya and Grandma rocked slowly, silently, looking out across the rain-soaked land.

"Grandma, when you look far away . . . out there . . . what do you see?"

Grandma's eyes glowed. "I see your aunts and uncles and cousins when they lived on the farm. I see *my* father's father and his Indian bride. They built this farm so many, many years ago."

"And do you see Grandpa?" Tanya asked quietly.

"My, yes, Tanya. Your grandpa's always with me. But here on the farm he's 'specially close," the old woman answered.

The steady rain began to taper off. Grandma gave Tanya's shoulder a squeeze. "Now you, and Keisha and Adam, are a part of this farm, child," she said. "Family gatherings of this size can't happen without lists and planning and work. Everybody just pitches in and does the best they can. I know you will too."

When Grandma and Tanya returned to the kitchen, the room was in an uproar. Adam was crying loudly. The phone was ringing and the delivery man was at the door. Aunt Kay was searching for her handbag.

Grandma laughed. "Looks like we're needed."

Cousin Celeste took Adam while Grandma handled the delivery man. Tanya answered the phone and with Keisha's help found the missing box of diapers. All was calm when Aunt Kay returned with her handbag.

"Aunt Kay, may Keisha and I visit Uncle John in the barn?" Tanya asked.

"I'm sure he'll like the company," Aunt Kay said. "Just put on these old boots before you go."

Tanya and Keisha pulled on the boots and off they marched. The girls watched as Uncle John finished milking the cow. Then with his consent, Tanya sprinkled chicken feed on the ground. While the chickens ate, she and Keisha collected their eggs. After that the girls explored the barn, and when they grew tired, they climbed into the hayloft to rest.

The sun shone bright and hot when the threesome left the barn. "Weather can be right funny down here," Uncle John chuckled.

"John!" Grandma called through the screened window. "We could use some apples."

Uncle John handed each girl her own basket before pointing them in the direction of the orchard.

"Race ya!" Keisha squealed, and away she ran.

Keisha reached the orchard first. Tanya wasn't far behind when she saw something lying on the ground. She picked it up, brushed it off, and put it in the bottom of her basket before she began to pick apples.

The day slipped into dusk when the family finally sat down to supper. They had homemade apple pie for dessert — Tanya had shown Keisha how to roll the dough for the crust — topped with homemade ice cream.

Only when the last bite of pie was gone did Tanya bring out what she had found that afternoon: a piece of the fence that had once separated the farmyard from the orchard. Carved in the wood were the initials

R. B.
+
I. F.

Rose Buchanan and Isaac Franklin.

"This is *your* history, isn't it, Grandma? Yours and Grandpa's."

"Oh yes, child. A special memory of your grandpa and me," said Grandma, beaming. "We'll put it in the parlor for everyone to share."

That night Uncle John placed sleeping bags on the porch so Tanya and Keisha could pretend they were camping out. Tanya had never seen so many fireflies or heard so many crickets.

"Doesn't the farmyard *ever* get quiet?" Tanya asked Grandma, who was rocking beside her.

"Those are just night sounds, honey," Grandma said, breathing in the hot, humid night air. "Telling us all is well."

And it was.

# Think About the Selection

**1.** Describe the relationship between Tanya and her grandmother. How do you think they feel about each other?

**2.** How does Tanya's opinion of the farm change during the time she spends there?

**3.** Aunt Kay gathers special family items to display at the reunion. What might these objects add to the reunion?

**4.** If your family had a reunion like Tanya's, what object would you want to share? What would you say about it?

**5.** Why is Tanya excited to find the piece of fence with her grandmother's initials? Why is her grandmother excited too?

**6.** **Connecting/Comparing** Both Tanya and Tomás from *Tomás and the Library Lady* visit new places. What do they learn from their experiences in those places?

Narrating

# Write a Story

Long ago, R. B. and I. F. carved their initials into a fence post. Write a story about this day. Be sure that your story fits with all you know about Rose Buchanan and Isaac Franklin.

**Tips**

- To get started, list words that show how the characters look, talk, and move.
- Use descriptive words to create a colorful story, such as *rain-soaked* or *beaming*.

## Social Studies
# Make a Diagram

Tanya learns her way around the farm as the family prepares for the reunion. Use information from the story and your own imagination to make a diagram of the farmhouse and its surroundings. Include the following places on your diagram:

farmhouse
farmyard
barn
orchard
fence

## Listening and Speaking
# Conduct an Interview

Tanya's grandmother talks about what it was like when she was growing up. Interview an adult about what it was like when he or she was your age. It's a good idea to write down your questions before you do the interview.

**Tips**

- Take notes or use a tape recorder.
- Ask more questions if you are confused about something the person tells you.

# Post a Review

Write a review of *Tanya's Reunion*. Tell what you liked or didn't like about it. Post your review on Education Place.

**www.eduplace.com/kids**

*Internet*

**Skill: How to Read Instructions**

❶ **Read** the title of the activity.

❷ **Read** the instructions once, all the way through.

❸ **Think** about how to do each of the steps.

❹ **Stop** when you have difficulty understanding a step. **Reread** the instructions starting from the last step you understood.

# Fun and Games

## FOR FAMILY GATHERINGS

by Adrienne Anderson

### CHARIOT RELAY

This is the same as any running relay, except that two, three, or four players hook arms and run together. They round a given point and, on returning to their line, they touch off the next members of their team. This may be made very interesting and spectacular if some of the players, acting as horses, pull a driver around on a piece of cardboard or tarp or other suitable substitute for a chariot.

214

## NATIONS

Players are arranged in several small groups of equal size, each bearing the name of a nation and each nation having a circle drawn for its home base (flour can be used to draw a circle or just use an old shirt to designate home base). The leader throws a ball against the side of a building or tree, or if there is nothing against which to throw, she may toss it up. As it bounces back or comes down, she calls the name of a nation. The players of that nation rush for the ball and then run for their home base, trying not to be caught by the other players. Those caught join the nation by whom they were caught. The game is up when one nation has caught all the others.

## KNEE WALK

Each participant sits back on heels and grasps insteps with hands. In this position, he tilts forward to his knees, keeping feet off the floor, and hitches forward on his knees, using first one knee, then the other. Object: to walk on knees 10 feet without losing balance or grip on insteps.

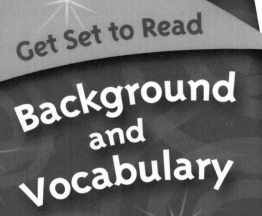

## Background and Vocabulary

# BOSS OF THE PLAINS

### THE HAT THAT WON THE WEST

by Laurie Carlson
pictures by Holly Meade

**Boss of the Plains**

**Read to find the meanings of these words.**

*e* ● Glossary

adventurers

determined

frontier

gear

opportunity

pioneers

settlers

# GO WEST!

**IN THE 1850S,** America was a country on the move. Many Americans were packing up and heading west, eager to start new lives. These **pioneers** were all traveling to lands very different from the ones they had known back east.

Some were **adventurers** who were **determined** to follow dreams of striking it rich in newly discovered goldfields. Others were excited by the **opportunity** to set up farms on the wide and windy plains.

**Frontier** life was challenging for **settlers**. New climates and new kinds of work required new **gear**. Clothing worn by Easterners in big cities often did not make sense in the wide open spaces of the West.

**Pioneers often traveled together in long wagon trains.**

**This family has stopped for a rest on a Utah trail.**

One example of this new, Western style of dress is the cowboy hat. In *Boss of the Plains* you will discover how this one-of-a-kind hat won the hearts — and heads — of the American West.

# Meet the Author

Laurie Carlson may not have grown up in the Wild West of the 1850s, but *her* west was still pretty wild. She was born and raised in the rugged gold-mining country of California's Sierra Nevada mountains. When Carlson was a young girl, rattlesnakes were a common sight near her home. But she remembers that it was her "ornery milk cow" that once made her run for her life!

These days, Carlson and her family have taken to wearing cowboy hats themselves. She thinks that Stetson hats "reflect the spirit of the West." Carlson adds that when she wears a Stetson hat, she feels as if she stands taller and straighter and finds that she looks people "right in the eye."

# Meet the Illustrator

Holly Meade says that it is the "pleasure and challenge of the process" of creating art that made her decide to become an artist. For her illustrations in *Boss of the Plains*, Meade started by researching the Old West. Then she did sketches "again and again and again." Finally, using cut paper, paint, and pencils, she began the final art.

Meade's art in *Hush!* by Minfong Ho received a Caldecott Honor — one of the highest honors for an illustrator of children's books.

Are you interested in learning more about Laurie Carlson and Holly Meade? If so, check out Education Place.
**www.eduplace.com/kids**

# BOSS of the PLAINS

## THE HAT THAT WON THE WEST

by
Laurie Carlson

pictures by
Holly Meade

## Strategy Focus

This biography tells how the Boss of the Plains hat was invented and became a success. Stop at different points in the story to **summarize** key events.

219

**At first, settlers and travelers** in the American West wore whatever hats they had worn back home: knit caps, wool derbies, or straw sombreros. Some wore old sea captain's caps; others wore army hats, calico sunbonnets, homburgs, slouch hats, or even silk high hats.

Everyone wore some kind of hat, though, because the weather was likely to be either burning sunshine, drenching rain, whipping wind, or swirling snow. A hat was important protection.

One hat would come along that was particularly well suited to frontier life. This is the true story of that amazing hat — the hat that won the West.

In the 1840s, while explorers pushed on through new territory and pioneers tamed the mountains and plains of the West, twelve-year-old John Batterson Stetson sat on a high wooden stool, working along with his father and his eleven brothers and sisters in the family's tiny, damp hatmaker's shop in Orange, New Jersey.

The Stetsons made hats the same way hatters had done it for years: by pressing felt, made from wet fur and wool, over a wooden form to shape it.

John sat at the worktable and dreamed of the West he'd heard customers and neighbors talk about.

Out west there were clear skies, roaming buffalo, and the promise of adventure. Everyone seemed to be going there. Everyone except hatmakers.

It wasn't until years later, when the dampness and steam of the shop had weakened his lungs and he became sick with tuberculosis, that John Stetson decided to go west himself. If he wanted to see the West, he couldn't wait. So he headed to the town where the West began: St. Joseph, Missouri, the jumping-off point where people bought gear and supplies for their journey to the goldfields.

It was 1859, and St. Joe's streets were bustling and crammed with wagons, mules, pack dogs, and adventurers bound for the frontier.

Determined to start a new life in St. Joe, John looked around for some way to make his mark. It was only when he met up with a group of travelers heading to Colorado Territory that opportunity presented itself.

"Why not come to Pikes Peak with us?" they asked. "There's gold there, and fortunes to be made."

That was all John Stetson needed to hear.

It was a 750-mile trip, and the long days of walking in the dry prairie air soon improved John's health. Before long his legs grew strong and he hardly ever coughed.

One night the Pikes Peakers huddled around their campfire.

"Sure wish we had a snug tent," one of the travelers commented. "Maybe we could make one out of the rabbit skins we've been saving."

"Won't work," someone else replied. "The skins will shrink up and get hard unless they're properly tanned."

John Stetson smiled. "Fur can be made into cloth without tanning," he announced.

"Can't be done!" the others scoffed.

But John knew that it could. He'd been making hats that way for years. So he spread out a blanket and gathered the dried rabbit pelts, along with a hatchet, a canteen of water, and a hickory sapling. He put the kettle on to boil.

He carefully shaved the fur from the first hide and piled it in the center of the blanket.

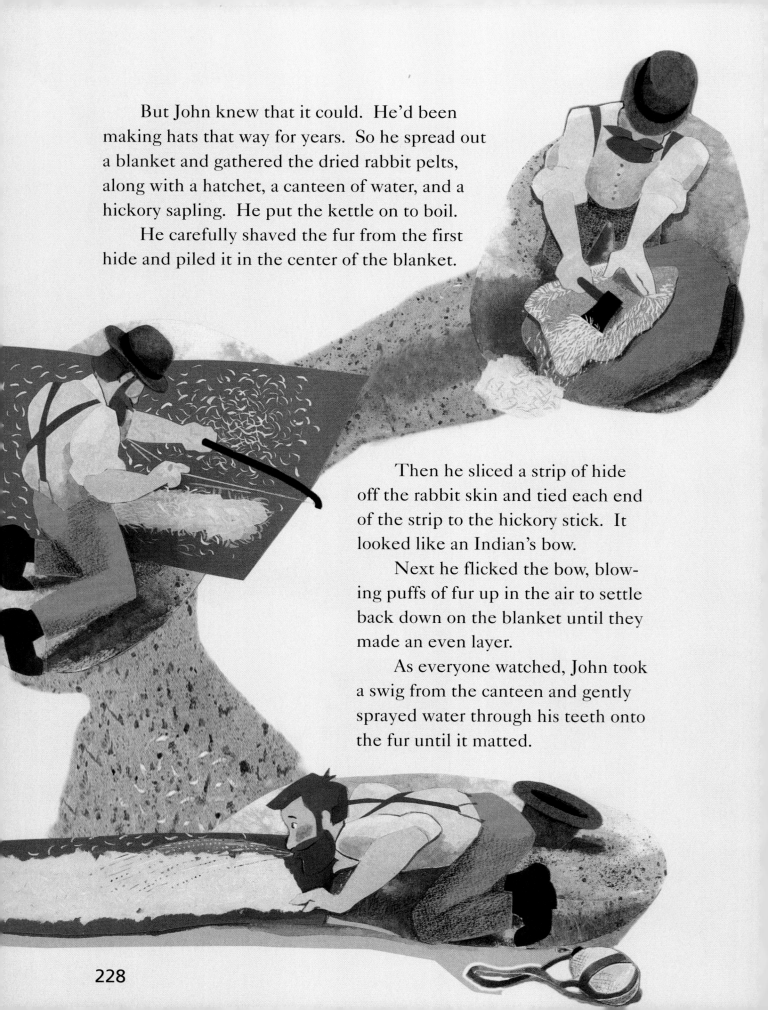

Then he sliced a strip of hide off the rabbit skin and tied each end of the strip to the hickory stick. It looked like an Indian's bow.

Next he flicked the bow, blowing puffs of fur up in the air to settle back down on the blanket until they made an even layer.

As everyone watched, John took a swig from the canteen and gently sprayed water through his teeth onto the fur until it matted.

With a gleam in his eye, he carefully lifted the corner of the fur; it came up off the blanket in one piece. Then he walked to the campfire and dipped the piece of matted fur in and out of the boiling water until it shrank into a little blanket.

"Felt!" he proclaimed. "Thick, warm, and stronger than a piece of cloth." It had worked!

Soon John and his friends were sleeping warm and snug in a new felt tent.

Over a month later, the Pikes Peakers reached the gold hills of Colorado. They eagerly went from diggings to diggings, trying their luck.

The scorching sun blistered John's face, and the whipping wind blinded him. The short brim of his derby hat, so stylish back in New Jersey, gave him no protection at all.

Before long John decided to make a better hat for himself. "Big and picturesque," he declared, and set to work, using the same technique he'd used to make his tent. It felt good to be making a hat again.

At first the other miners teased John about his funny hat. It certainly was different from the hats back home and the ones they wore. It had a wide brim and a tall crown and was made of thick fur felt. But it worked. The brim kept the sun out of John's eyes and the rain off his back. And when it got dirty, the tough felt could be brushed or thumped to knock the dust off.

One day a horseman rode into camp. When he saw John's unusual hat, his eyes lit up with excitement.

To everyone's amazement, he reached into his pocket, pulled out a five-dollar gold piece, and offered to buy the hat right off John's head!

Delighted, John pocketed the coin. Back in New Jersey, even the finest hat sold for just two dollars. He grinned and waved as the stranger rode out of camp wearing his distinctive hat.

Pickings in the Colorado goldfields were slim, and after a year of digging, John had little money to show for it. But he still had a trade and talent. He decided to move to Philadelphia to do the one thing he really knew how to do: make hats.

At first he made the styles that were most popular back east, but so did all the other hatters. John wanted to make something unique, something special — a hat that everyone would notice. He even made up styles of his own and wore the hats to drum up orders, but no one in the city was interested.

John Stetson was determined to succeed. He remembered the horseman out west who had thought that his high-crowned, wide-brimmed hat was just right. Maybe other Westerners would like it, too — bullwhackers, who drove oxen; mule skinners, who led mule teams; and drovers, who herded cattle or sheep. He'd make a hat for the wranglers and cowboys of the West. And he knew just what he'd name his new hat: Boss of the Plains.

John spent what little money he had left from mining gold on materials for sample hats. He made them all the same: of light tan felt, with a wide brim, a high crown, and a plain band. He packed sample hats and order forms in special boxes and sent one to every clothing store and hat dealer in the West. Then he waited.

Two weeks passed. Nothing happened. John sat in his empty shop thinking about the gamble he had taken. Had he wasted his time and all his money? Had he been foolish to think anyone would buy his unusual hats?

But then, all at once, orders began pouring in. Each day's mail brought more. People wanted the hats. In fact they wanted them right away, and they had stuffed money into the envelopes to make sure they got them quickly.

John used the money to buy supplies and began turning out hats as fast as he could. Out west, cowboys tossed away their knit caps, sombreros, and derbies. In no time, John B. Stetson's Boss of the Plains became the most popular hat west of the Mississippi.

SAMMIS AND Co DRY GOODS

BOSS of the PLAINS SOLD HERE

Even though the Boss of the Plains cost a cowboy a whole month's wages, it was worth it.

It shielded a cowpoke's eyes from blinding sun and caught the rain before it trickled down his back.

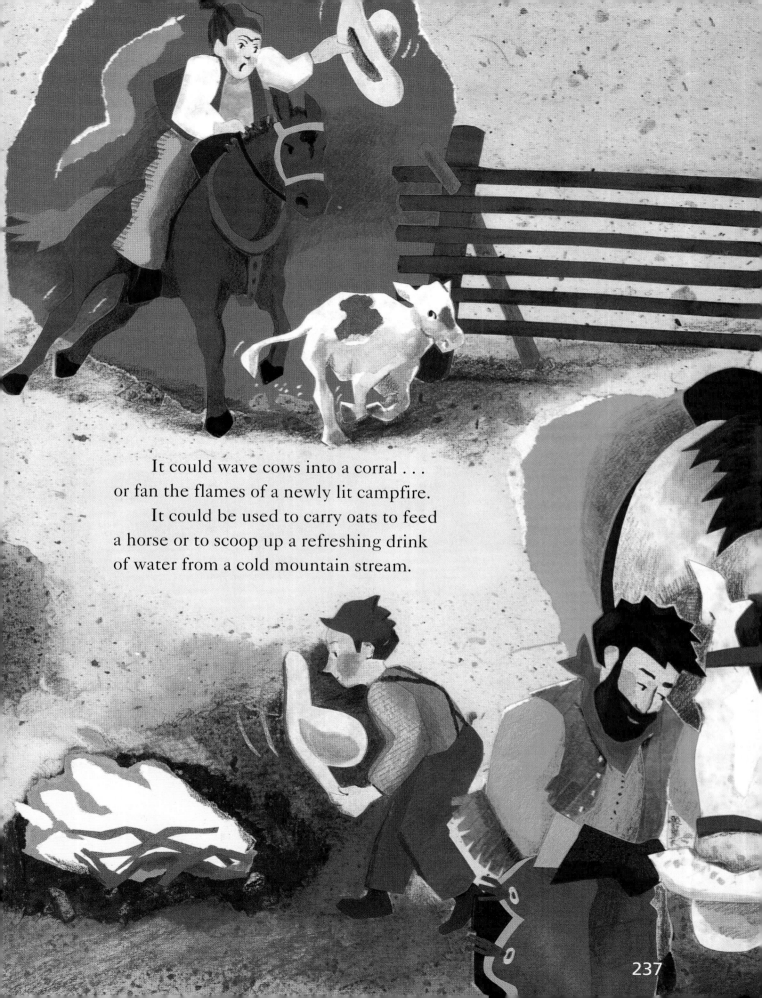

It could wave cows into a corral . . .
or fan the flames of a newly lit campfire.
    It could be used to carry oats to feed
a horse or to scoop up a refreshing drink
of water from a cold mountain stream.

It could impress a lady at the Saturday night dance . . . or come in handy when the sweetest huckleberries were ready to be picked.

It was the perfect decoy when a cowboy was in trouble . . . and made a soft cushion for a cowboy's head at the end of a hard day.

238

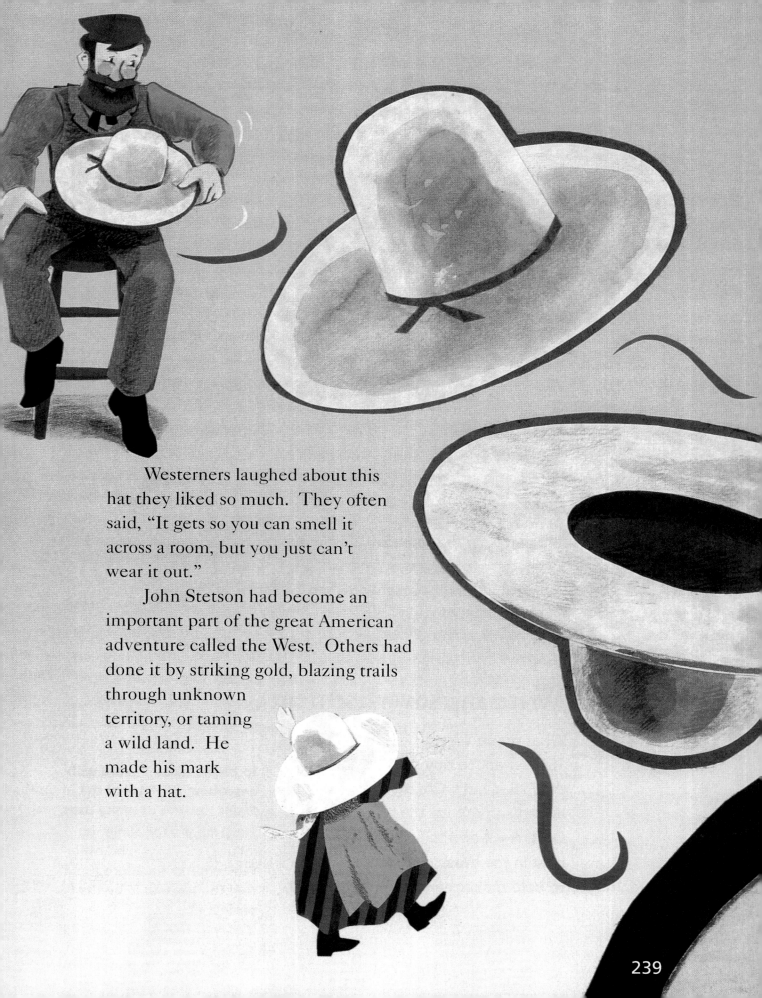

Westerners laughed about this hat they liked so much. They often said, "It gets so you can smell it across a room, but you just can't wear it out."

John Stetson had become an important part of the great American adventure called the West. Others had done it by striking gold, blazing trails through unknown territory, or taming a wild land. He made his mark with a hat.

# Think About the Selection

**1.** How did John Stetson's poor health change his life?

**2.** What character traits made John Stetson a good inventor? What made him a good businessman? Give examples.

**3.** What were some of John Stetson's failures? What do you think he learned from them?

**4.** Why do you think John Stetson named his hat Boss of the Plains? What would *you* have named it?

**5.** The Boss of the Plains hat is still being made today. Why do you think it was a success in the Old West? Why do you think it's still popular?

**6.** **Connecting/Comparing** John Stetson and Tomás Rivera used their imaginations in different ways. How is imagination important to each of them?

# Write an Advertisement

What made Westerners of the 1860s want to buy the Boss of the Plains hat? Create an advertisement for the hat. Describe it and tell why it is the best in the West. Use illustrations to help make the sale.

### Tips

- **To begin, make a word web describing the Boss of the Plains hat and its many uses.**
- **Remember your audience: miners, cowboys, and other Westerners. Convince them that the hat would be the perfect fit.**

## Science
# Make a Mineral Chart

When John Stetson went west, he hoped to strike it rich mining for gold. There are many other valuable minerals that can be found underground. Make a chart of the minerals gold, silver, copper, and diamonds. Use a dictionary or the encyclopedia to find information about them.

| Mineral | Physical Properties | Where Found | Uses |
|---------|--------------------|-----------| -----|
| gold | shiny, soft, yellow | | |
| silver | | | |
| copper | | | |
| diamonds | | | |

## Viewing
# Picture the Old West

With a small group, look carefully at the illustrations in the story. Then discuss other pictures you've seen of the Old West in movies, on television, or in books. How are they similar to Holly Meade's illustrations? How are they different? What do you think the Old West was *really* like?

*Internet*

# Complete a Web Crossword Puzzle

How well do you know the people and places in *Boss of the Plains*? Test yourself by completing the crossword puzzle that you can print from Education Place.

**www.eduplace.com/kids**

**Skill:  How to Read Song Lyrics**

❶ Identify the **verses** in the song.

❷ Identify the **chorus**, which is repeated after each verse.

❸ Skim the **lyrics**, or words of the song, before singing.

❹ First sing the lyrics printed with the music.  Then sing the rest of the verses and the chorus to the same tune.

# Cowboy Songs

**Back in the Old West,** long before headphones and portable CD players, cowboys who wanted to hear a song had to sing it themselves.  Songs were such a big part of Western life that a ranch would often have its very own song.  Cowboys would even trade songs so that they could keep up with the latest tunes.

A cowboy's work could get mighty lonesome out under those big, starry, Western skies, and a song was often the perfect cure.  Out on a long cattle drive, the "dogies," or calves, might get jittery and threaten to stampede.  A soothing tune could be just the thing to calm them down.  And, of course, no campfire would be complete without a sing-along at the end of a long and dusty day.

# Home on the Range

1. Oh, give me a home where the buf-fa-lo roam, Where the deer and the an-te-lope play,____ Where sel-dom is heard a dis-cour-ag-ing word, And the skies are not cloud-y all day.____

*CHORUS*

Home, home on the range,____ Where the deer and the an-te-lope play,____ Where sel-dom is heard a dis-cour-ag-ing word, And the skies are not cloud-y all day.____

**2.** Oh, give me a land where the bright diamond sand
Flows leisurely down the stream;
Where the graceful white swan goes gliding along
Like a maid in a heavenly dream.
CHORUS

**3.** Where the air is so pure, the zephyrs so free,
The breezes so balmy and light,
That I would not exchange my home on the range
For all of the cities so bright.
CHORUS

243

# Git Along, Little Dogies

1.As I was a-walk-ing one morn-ing for pleas-ure, I
spied a cow-punch-er a-rid-ing a-long; His
hat was throwed back and his spurs were a-jin-glin,'
CHORUS
As he ap-proached me a-sing-in' this song: Whoo-pee
ti yi yo, git a-long, lit-tle do-gies, It's
your mis-for-tune and none of my own; Whoo-pee
ti yi yo, git a-long, lit-tle do-gies, For you
know Wy-o-ming will be your new home.

**2.** It's whooping and yelling and driving the dogies,
Oh, how I wish you would go on,
It's whooping and punching and go on, little dogies,
For you know Wyoming will be your new home.

CHORUS

**3.** When the night comes on and we hold them on the bed-ground,
These little dogies that roll on so slow;
Roll up the herd and cut out the strays,
And roll the little dogies that never rolled before.

CHORUS

# Cowboy's Gettin'-Up Holler

Wake up, Ja-cob, day's a-break-in',

Fry-in' pan's on an' hoe cake bak-in'.

Ba-con in the pan, cof-fee in the pot,

Git up now and git it while it's hot.

# Background and Vocabulary

**A Very Important Day**

**Read to find the meanings of these words.**

*e* • Glossary

allegiance

citizens

citizenship

downtown

enrich

oath

# A NEW YORK CITY
## Welcome

*Welcome to New York,* one of the largest cities in the world. More than seven million people live here.

From uptown to **downtown**, New York City is a busy place.

# WELCOME TO NEW YORK CITY!

New York, NY

*The Statue of Liberty welcomes everyone to New York.*

People come from around the world to make New York City their new home. Many become American **citizens**, and swear an **oath** of loyalty — a pledge of **allegiance** — to the United States. **Citizenship** gives them the same rights as people born in the United States. These new citizens **enrich** their new country and their new city.

In *A Very Important Day* you will meet New Yorkers who came from many lands, and find out why this day is so special to them.

*Skating in Central Park*

*A neighborhood celebration*

247

# Meet the Author
## Maggie Rugg Herold

**Where she was born:** New Jersey

**Places she's been:** the states of Ohio and California; the countries of Greece and Jordan

**Places she's worked:** a children's library, a publishing company

**First book:** *A Very Important Day*

**Fun fact:** She and Catherine Stock are close friends.

# Meet the Illustrator
## Catherine Stock

**Where she was born:** Sweden

**Where she lives now:** She splits her time between New York and France.

**Places she's been:** Haiti, Great Britain, South Africa, Hong Kong

**Hobbies:** hiking, reading, doing crossword puzzles

**Other books she's illustrated:** *Justin and the Best Biscuits in the World* by Mildred Pitts Walter, *Kele's Secret* by Tololwa Mollel, *Nellie Bly's Monkey* by Joan Blos

**Fun fact:** *A Very Important Day* is based on a very important day in Stock's life. Read the story to find out what that day was!

To find out more about Maggie Rugg Herold and Catherine Stock, visit Education Place.
**www.eduplace.com/kids**

248

# A Very Important Day

### Maggie Rugg Herold

ILLUSTRATED BY
### Catherine Stock

## Strategy Focus

In this selection, many different families prepare for one very important day. As you read, think of **questions** to ask about how each family reacts to this day.

Nelia Batungbakal was too excited to sleep. She was looking out her window, listening to music, when she thought she saw snow!

Sure enough, before long the station DJ came on. "It's three A.M. here in New York City, and it's snowing. Four to six inches are expected by noon."

Nelia's mind raced. Imagine, snow on such a very important day. This would never happen in the Philippines. Her son and daughter-in-law and the grandchildren were fast asleep. She would need to awaken them early, to allow extra time for the trip downtown.

"Wake up, Miguel. It's snowing," Rosa Huerta [WHERE-tah] called to her brother. "There are at least two inches on the fire escape."

"All *right*!" said Miguel, bounding from his room. He opened the window and scooped up some snow.

"Close that window," their father ordered. "It's cold in here, and — Miguel, is that snow in your hand?"

"Yes, Papa, the first this year."

"Back outside with it before it melts. And on such a very important day. This would not happen in Mexico, at least not in the south."

"Let's move quickly," urged their mother. "It's six-thirty. We can get an early start downtown."

Veena Patel had just set the table when the doorbell rang. "That will be the children," her husband, Mohandas, said.

But it was their neighbors, the Pitambers. They apologized for stopping by so early. "We were afraid of missing you, and we wanted to wish you well on this very important day."

"Join us for breakfast," said Veena. "Our daughter and her family will be here any minute. They think we must allow extra time, that the snow will slow us down. That's one worry we never had in India."

The doorbell rang again, and this time it was the children. Everyone gathered quickly at the table, talking eagerly about the special morning ahead.

Out the door and down the steps came the Leonovs [lay-OH-nufs] — first Eugenia [yev-GAY-nee-ah], then her brother, Lev [LEF], followed by their grandfather, grandmother, mother, and father.

"Snow reminds me of Russia," said their mother.

"I love snow!" exclaimed Eugenia.

Her grandfather stooped, grabbed two handfuls, and threw them at his grandchildren.

The fight was on.

Just then Mr. Dionetti lobbed a snowball from the door of his corner grocery. "Is this the big day?" he called out. "Are you headed downtown?"

"Yes," answered their father. "This snowball fight is headed for the subway."

"Congratulations!" cried Mr. Dionetti. And tossing a big handful of snow straight up in the air, he crossed the street to shake their hands.

Kostas and Nikos Soutsos were clearing the sidewalk in front of the family restaurant when their mother came out the side door from their apartment above. She was carrying their baby sister, Kiki.

"Kiki, this is snow," said Kostas.

"How do you like it?" Nikos asked.

Kiki seemed puzzled by the flakes that hit her nose.

Their mother laughed. "She'll get used to it, living here. Not like Greece, where it snows maybe once in ten years. But where's your father? We should be on our way."

"He went to make a sign for the door. See, there he is."

"Set those shovels inside, and let's be off," their father called. "And read this sign, everyone. What does it say?"

They chorused together, "Closed for a very important day."

"Finally!  There's the bus," said Duong Hao [ZUNG HAH-oh].

He and his older sister, Trinh [CHING], brushed snow off each other and followed their mother on board.  It was crowded at first, but a few stops later they all got seats.

"Here we are," said their mother, "in the middle of a snowstorm on the most important day since we arrived from Vietnam — "

Suddenly the driver braked hard.

They were all thrown forward.

"Car skidded at the light and couldn't stop," the driver yelled. "Everybody okay?"

Fortunately only bundles had landed on the floor.

"That was close," said their mother.

"Yes," said Trinh, "but our driver's good."

Duong nodded.  "Maybe he knows that today of all days we just have to get downtown."

"I love the ferry," said Jorge Báez [HOR-hay BYE-es].

"So do I," agreed his cousin Pedro Jiménez [PAY-droe hee-MEN-es], "especially in snow.  Let's go up on deck."

"Not by yourselves, but I'll go with you," said Pedro's father.

"And I'll keep you company," Jorge's father added.

"Me too," begged Jorge's sister.  "I want to go outside."

"All right," said her father.  "You are old enough."

They went up on deck, leaving the little ones inside with Jorge's mother and aunt.

"I'm so glad this day takes us across the harbor," said Pedro's father. "I never tire of the ride."

"Neither do I," said Jorge's father. "Even in snow, this view is the best in the city. And now we will all remember it as part of the most important day since we came from the Dominican Republic."

258

Through the narrow streets on the unshoveled sidewalks the Zeng [DZENG] family made their way on foot. Suddenly, from above them, a voice called out.

Yujin's [EEOO-JING] friend Bailong [BYE-LONG] was leaning out the window. "I've been watching for you," he said. "Don't open this until later. Catch!"

Down through the snowflakes came a small brightly wrapped package, straight into Yujin's outstretched hands.

"Thanks, Bailong."

"Thanks for remembering."

"This is such an important day."

"The most important since we arrived from China."

Yujin tucked the package safely inside his coat, and with waves and good-byes the Zengs set off again, heading south.

Jihan Idris [ji-HAN i-DREES] and her parents had also left home early to make the trip downtown. Now their subway ride was over, and there was time for breakfast.

"I see a coffee shop ahead," Jihan's mother called out.

"I want to sit at the counter!" Jihan exclaimed.

They entered and sat on three stools, Jihan in the middle.

"I'd like waffles," Jihan told their waitress.

"And I'll have pancakes," said her father. "With coffee and grapefruit juice."

"Scrambled eggs and a toasted bagel, please," said her mother. "With orange juice and tea."

Quickly the waitress was back with their breakfasts. "What brings you out so early on a snowy day like today?" she asked.

"Can you guess?" said Jihan's mother.

"It's the most important day for us since we came from Egypt," said Jihan's father.

"And I'm celebrating with waffles," said Jihan. "I never get them at home."

"There's the courthouse," said Kwame Akuffo [KWA-mee ah-KOO-foo] to his wife, Efua [eh-foo-WAH], as they rounded a corner, walking fast.

She stopped. "Only two blocks to go. I'll race you to the steps."

He stopped, too. "Are you crazy?"

"It's not slippery."

"You're on! Ready?"

She nodded.

"On your mark, get set, go!"

And off they dashed, down the sidewalk.

"Tie," Efua declared at the bottom of the steps.

"I used to run in Ghana," Kwame said, "but never in snow."

"Wait," said Efua, taking a camera from her purse. "Before we go in on this very important day, let's get someone to take our picture."

So they asked a stranger, who gladly obliged, and then hand in hand they climbed the courthouse steps.

As Robert MacTaggart came through the courthouse door, he heard familiar voices calling, "Robert. Over here."

Near the entrance stood his friends Elizabeth and Alan. Each of them gave him a big hug.

"You made it," Robert said. "Thank you so much for coming. I was afraid the snow would stop you."

"Oh, no, not on such an important day," said Elizabeth.

"We were getting worried about *you*, though," said Alan.

Robert chuckled. "A few snowflakes defeat a man from the highlands of Scotland? Come on. Let's find the chamber. It's on this floor."

Leaving relatives and friends to wait in the hall outside, Alvaro Castro, his wife, Romelia, and their children entered the crowded chamber. They were among the last to find seats.

Soon the examiner appeared, and the room became quiet. "When I call your name," he said, "please come forward to receive your certificate."

Many names were called; many people went forward. Then, "Alvaro and Romelia Castro and children Marta, José [hoe-SAY], and Oscar."

The Castros approached the examiner.

"Please sign here," he said to Alvaro. "And here," he said to Romelia. "These are your papers."

"Thank you," said Alvaro. "This is a proud moment."

The Castros returned to their seats. "The long journey from El Salvador has ended," Romelia whispered to her husband, and he squeezed her hand.

When the examiner had finished, he said, "Please open the door to relatives and friends."

People poured in. There were so many they filled the aisles and lined the walls at the back and sides of the chamber.

"Everyone please rise," said the examiner, and as everyone did, a judge entered the chamber.

"Your Honor," said the examiner, "these petitioners have qualified for citizenship in the United States of America."

"Then," said the judge, "will you repeat after me the oath of citizenship. Let us begin. 'I hereby declare, on oath . . .'"

"I hereby declare, on oath . . ."

Echoing the judge phrase by phrase, sentence by sentence, the many voices resounded as one, swearing loyalty to the United States of America.

"Congratulations," said the judge. "Those of you who can be, please be seated."

As the room became quiet again, the judge cleared his throat. "Two hundred nineteen of you from thirty-two countries have become United States citizens here today. You are carrying on a tradition that dates back to the earliest days of our country, for almost all Americans have come here from somewhere else. May citizenship enrich your lives as your lives enrich this country. Welcome. We are glad to have you. This is a very important day."

Everyone then rose and joined the judge in the Pledge of Allegiance.

Family and friends and strangers turned to one another. "Best wishes!" "I'm so happy for you." "You must be so proud." "Isn't it wonderful?" "What a day!" "Let me shake your hand." "Let me give you a kiss." "Let me give you a hug."

Zeng Yujin tore open the package from his friend Bailong. Inside he found small American flags, a dozen or so, enough to share with everyone in his family and with other new citizens surrounding him.

In a wave of excitement, they all made their way out of the
chamber, through the hallway, and back to the courthouse door.

"Look!" they exclaimed, everybody talking at once. "The
snow has stopped." "The sun is shining." "It will be easy to get
home and go on celebrating." "This has become our country on
this very important day!"

## Think About the Selection

**1.** Why do the people in the story react differently to snow?

**2.** Why do you think the author writes about so many different families, instead of concentrating on one family?

**3.** How do you know that becoming American citizens means a lot to these families?

**4.** Why was Bailong's gift to Yujin (page 266) a good choice on this particular day?

**5.** The author waits until the end of the story to show the importance of this day. Why do you think she does this?

**6.** **Connecting/Comparing** Tanya's family reunion is an important day for her. If she and Yujin could discuss their very important days, what do you think they would say?

## Write a Newspaper Article

How would you describe the citizenship ceremony in this story? Write a newspaper article about it. Include interviews with the families. Check the Media Link on pages 272–275 for examples of real news articles.

**Tips**

- Write a beginning that captures the reader's attention.
- Use quotations to make the article come alive.
- Write a short, attention-grabbing headline for the article.

270

## Math
## Take a Poll

Where were students in your class born? Take a poll to find out. Write your birthplace (city, state, and country) on an index card. One person collects everyone's cards. Sort the cards by country, by state, and by city. Tally and discuss the results. How does your class compare to the families in the story?

**Bonus** Make a table of the information you collect and present it to the class.

| Birthplace | Tally | Total |
|---|---|---|
| New York, NY USA | ℍℍ III | 8 |
| San Juan, Puerto Rico | | |
| Sunny Pines, MN USA | | |

:

## Social Studies
## Use a World Map

Write the name of each family from the story on a label. Also make a label for New York City. Then use a large world map or globe to locate where each family came from. Attach the labels to the right places on the map. Discuss which families traveled the farthest to get to New York City.

## Internet
## Send an E-postcard

If you want to tell a friend what you've learned about America in this theme, send an e-postcard. You'll find one at Education Place.

**www.eduplace.com/kids**

271

**Skill: How to Read a Newspaper Article**

❶ **Look** first at the parts of the article: headline, byline, photographs, and captions.

❷ **Scan** the article to get an idea of what it is about.

❸ While you **read**, ask yourself questions when you don't understand and then reread.

❹ If there are several articles on the same topic, **compare** the information.

# KIDS VOTING USA

What if you could vote in a real election? Thousands of kids around the United States are doing just that. Through a program called Kids Voting USA, students "vote" for real candidates in real elections. In class, students discuss the candidates and the issues. Then, on Election Day, they go to the polls with their parents and cast votes at special booths. The students' results are often reported in the local news. Even though their votes are counted separately from the official adult votes, students in Kids Voting USA learn a great lesson about participating in a democracy.

These students make their voices heard at a Kids Voting rally.

# EL PASO TIMES

EL PASO, TEXAS                                    APRIL 25, 1999

# Children cast Kids Voting ballots

By Christina Ramírez
EL PASO TIMES

A small row of posterboard booths decorated with American flags and pinwheels beckoned the next generation of voters at the Kids Voting early voting site Saturday.

"I think it's fun because I get to practice what I'll do when I grow up," said Jeanine Rubio, 9, a Del Norte fourth-grader who also voted last year. "I tell my friends to vote because they should have a voice and a habit of this."

About 200 children 17 and younger filed into the Towne East shopping strip's early voting site Saturday and marked their choices for mayor, City Council and the three major school districts. The idea is to get children interested in voting in hope that they'll stick with it as adults.

Nashelly González, 11, a fifth-grader at Del Norte Heights, said she would have gone to vote even if she weren't receiving extra credit.

"I want to pick the best person," said Nashelly. "I'm not voting for who my friends vote for, but for who I think is best."

While Nashelly feels that all the candidates are good people, she feels positive that the people she picked were better.

"I read the paper and watch the TV ads to find out about the politicians," Nashelly said.

J.R. HERNANDEZ/EL PASO TIMES

**Sloan Bowen, 10, was one of the children who cast ballots Saturday at the Towne East shopping center's Kids Voting early voting site.**

# FT. LAUDERDALE SUN-SENTINEL

FORT LAUDERDALE, FLORIDA                    MARCH 10, 1999

## A real lesson in democracy
### Fort Lauderdale students vote on name for city cleanup boat

By Peter Bernard
STAFF WRITER

As Broward County voters flowed in and out of polling places on Tuesday, students cast votes as well — in the classroom.

In Fort Lauderdale, students actually got to decide a municipal issue. They had the final say on a name for the city's new waterway cleanup boat.

After Fort Lauderdale fifth-graders sent in 170 suggestions for a name, local leaders narrowed the vote to three: *Clean Sweep*, *Pollution Solution*, and *Trash Master*. Students from ages 4 to 18 voted. *Pollution Solution* was ahead in early results with 1,691 votes; 1,372 students voted for *Trash Master*; and *Clean Sweep* garnered 891 votes.

Kids Voting Broward, a nonprofit student voter-education group, distributed a special ballot to Broward County's 245,000 students for most local elections. Participants cast their votes on a range of election topics including the library bond issue and voter education.

Normally the results of the student ballot are used for educational purposes, but the city of Fort Lauderdale gave students the responsibility of voting on a name for the boat.

STAFF PHOTO/LOU TOMAN

**Alicia Jester, 9, and Zack Angelos, 10, mark their ballots at Oakland Park Elementary on Tuesday.**

Other firsts in this year's Kids Voting program included moving the election from polling places to classrooms and allowing mock municipal elections in Broward County cities.

"This gives them a taste of what thousands of people around the world would like to do and cannot," said Patricia Houchens, a Sunrise Middle School teacher who coordinated the election at her school. "That's to have a choice in their government."

# Honolulu Advertiser

HONOLULU, HAWAII                                    NOVEMBER 5, 1998

## Kids Voting results match adults' tally

By Karen Peterson
ADVERTISER EDUCATION WRITER

Oh, the perils of working the polls.

On Tuesday, Tori Brumfield endured 12 hours of checking names off the polling list at Solomon Elementary School. Voters ate her food, thinking it was for them. And sometimes she had to do two jobs because fellow workers didn't show up as promised.

Tori, a Solomon fifth-grader and student council president, spearheaded her school's Kids Voting program.

About 220,000 children in Hawaii's public and private schools were issued voter identification cards in the program and nearly 70,000 cast ballots Tuesday in the governor's race and five other contests.

In Hawaii, Kids Voting results mirrored official results in all six races. Kids Voting organizers will analyze the results this week to determine how closely children in each precinct tracked with adult voters. They also will have school-by-school voting tallies.

Besides the student workers, more than 1,000 Rotary Club members helped children at the state's 213 polling places. Local businesses volunteered their computers to tally votes.

Kids Voting USA began in Arizona in 1988 and has spread to 41 states and the District of Columbia. In some areas of the country, it is credited with improving adult voter turnout by 3 percent to 11 percent.

Lyla Berg, director of Hawaii Kids Voting, will offer copies of this year's voting report to school principals, the state superintendent of education, and maybe even the governor.

Berg would like the Legislature to pass a law supporting the presence of children in polling places. She said she hopes the state's children can lead the way on the legislation.

# Check Your Progress

You have just read four very different selections. Each one presents a unique snapshot of life in America. Now you will read and compare two new selections and sharpen your test-taking skills.

To begin, revisit Valerie Flournoy's letter on pages 152–154. Think about her ideas on what makes a good American Story. In what ways have special people and places, as well as memorable moments, played an important part in the theme so far?

Now you will read two new selections about some high-flying, larger-than-life Americans. Compare their experiences, and think about how these stories compare with the ones you've already read. There are countless American Stories to tell. Here are two more — among millions.

# Read and Compare

Join two incredible friends as they share a special evening together flying across the night skies of Washington, D.C.

**Try these strategies:**
Predict and Infer
Question

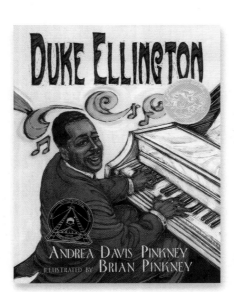

Learn about Duke Ellington, a master American musician, who played and composed a great American form of music — jazz!

**Try these strategies:**
Monitor and Clarify
Evaluate

**Strategies in Action**  *Be sure to use all your reading strategies while you read.*

# AMELIA AND ELEANOR GO FOR A RIDE

### BY PAM MUÑOZ RYAN   PICTURES BY BRIAN SELZNICK

*Amelia and Eleanor are good friends. Whether it's flying in an airplane or driving a fast car, they both love a good adventure. One night, Eleanor invites Amelia to her house for dinner. But Eleanor's house is no ordinary house, and these two are no ordinary friends. Eleanor is Eleanor Roosevelt, the heroic First Lady of the United States. Amelia is Amelia Earhart, the first female pilot to fly alone across the Atlantic Ocean. When two friends like this get together for an evening, something incredible might just happen. . . .*

"Mrs. Roosevelt just received her student pilot's license," said one of the reporters.

Amelia wasn't surprised. She had been the one to encourage Eleanor. She knew her friend could do anything she set her mind to.

"I'll teach you myself," offered Amelia.

"I accept! Tell us, Amelia, what's it like to fly at night in the dark?"

Everyone at the table leaned closer to hear. Very few people in the whole world had ever flown at night, and Amelia was one of them. Amelia's eyes sparkled. "The stars glitter all about and seem close enough to touch."

"At higher elevations, the clouds below shine white with dark islands where the night sea shows through. I've seen the planet Venus setting on the horizon, and I've circled cities of twinkling lights."

"And the capital city at night?" asked Eleanor.

"There's no describing it," said Amelia. "You just have to experience it on a clear night, when you can see forever. Why, we should go tonight! We could fly the loop to Baltimore and back in no time!"

The Secret Service men protested. "This hasn't been approved!"

"Nonsense!" said Eleanor. "If Amelia Earhart can fly solo across the Atlantic Ocean, I can certainly take a short flight to Baltimore and back!"

Before dessert could be served, Amelia had called Eastern Air Transport and arranged a flight.

Within the hour, Amelia and Eleanor boarded the Curtiss Condor twin-motor airplane. For a moment, both women looked up at the mysterious night sky. Then, without changing her gloves, Amelia slipped into the cockpit and took the wheel.

The plane rolled down the runway, faster and faster. Lights from the airstrip flashed in front of them. And they lifted into the dark.

"How amusing it is to see a girl in a white evening dress and high-heeled shoes flying a plane!" Eleanor said.

Amelia laughed as she made a wide sweep over Washington, D.C., and turned off all the lights in the plane.

Out the window, the Potomac River glistened with moonshine. The capitol dome reflected a soft golden halo. And the enormous, light-drenched monuments looked like tiny miniatures.

Soon the peaceful countryside gave way to shadowy woodlands. The Chesapeake Bay became a meandering outline

on the horizon. And even though they knew it wasn't so, it seemed as if the plane crawled slowly through starstruck space.

Eleanor marveled, "It's like sitting on top of the world!"

When it was time to land, Amelia carefully took the plane down. A group of reporters had gathered, anxious to ask questions.

"Mrs. Roosevelt, did you feel safe knowing a girl was flying that ship?"

"Just as safe!" said Eleanor.

"Did you fly the plane, Mrs. Roosevelt?" asked one reporter.

"What part did you like best?" said another.

"I enjoyed it so much, and no, I didn't actually fly the plane. Not yet. But someday I intend to. I was thrilled by the city lights, the brilliance of the blinking pinpoints below."

Amelia smiled. She knew just how Eleanor felt.

As the Secret Service agents drove them slowly back to the White House, Amelia and Eleanor agreed that there was nothing quite as exciting as flying. What could compare? Well, they admitted, maybe the closest thing would be driving in a fast car on a straightaway road with a stiff breeze blowing against your face.

Arms linked, they walked up the steps to the White House. Eleanor whispered something to Amelia, and then they hesitated, letting the rest of the group walk ahead of them.

"Are you coming inside, Mrs. Roosevelt?" someone asked.

But by then, they had wrapped their silk scarves around their necks and were hurrying toward Eleanor's new car.

Without changing her gloves, Eleanor quickly slipped into the driver's seat and took her turn at the wheel. With the wind in their hair and the brisk air stinging their cheeks, they flew down the road.

And after they had taken a ride about the city streets of Washington, D.C., they finally headed back to the White House . . . for dessert! Eleanor Roosevelt's pink clouds on angel food cake.

# DUKE ELLINGTON

BY ANDREA DAVIS PINKNEY
ILLUSTRATED BY BRIAN PINKNEY

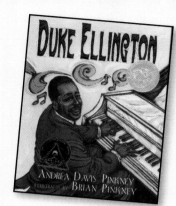

You ever hear of the jazz-playin' man, the man with the cats who could swing with his band? He was born in 1899, in Washington, D.C. Born Edward Kennedy Ellington. But wherever young Edward went, he said, "Hey, call me Duke."

Duke's name fit him rightly. He was a smooth-talkin', slick-steppin', piano-playin' kid. But his piano playing wasn't always as breezy as his stride. When Duke's mother, Daisy, and his father, J. E., enrolled him in piano lessons, Duke didn't want to go. Baseball was Duke's idea of fun. But his parents had other notions for their child.

Duke had to start with the piano basics, his fingers playing the same tired tune — *one-and-two-and-one-and-two*. Daisy and J. E. made Duke practice day after day.

To Duke, *one-and-two* wasn't music. He called it an *umpy-dump* sound that was headed nowhere worth following. He quit his lessons and kissed the piano a fast good-bye.

Years later, on a steamy summer night, Duke heard that *umpy-dump* played in a whole new way. Folks called the music ragtime — piano that turned *umpy-dump* into a soul-rousing romp.

The ragtime music set Duke's fingers to wiggling. Soon he was back at the piano, trying to plunk out his own ragtime rhythm. *One-and-two-and-one-and-two....* At first, this was the only crude tinkling Duke knew.

But with practice, all Duke's fingers rode the piano keys. Duke started to play his own made-up melodies. Whole notes, chords, sharps, and flats. Left-handed hops and right-handed slides.

Believe it, man. Duke taught himself to press on the pearlies like nobody else could. His *one-and-two-umpy-dump* became a thing of the past. Now, playing the piano was Duke's all-time love.

When Duke was nineteen, he was entertaining ladies and gents at parties, pool halls, country clubs, and cabarets. He had fine-as-pie good looks and flashy threads. It wasn't long before Duke formed his own small band, a group of musicians who played all over Washington, D.C. But soon they split the D.C. scene and made tracks for New York City — for Harlem, the place where jazz music ruled.

They called themselves the Washingtonians, and performed in all kinds of New York City honky-tonks. Barron's Exclusive. The Plantation. Ciro's. And the Kentucky Club. Folks got to know the band by name and came to hear them play.

Then, on an autumn day in 1927, Lady Luck smiled pretty on the Washingtonians. They were asked to play at the Cotton Club, Harlem's swankiest hangout, a big-time nightspot.

The Cotton Club became a regular gig for Duke and his band. They grew to twelve musicians and changed their name to Duke Ellington and His Orchestra. Night after night, they played their music, which was broadcast live over the radio.

For all those homebodies out in radio-lovers' land — folks who only dreamed of sitting pretty at the Cotton — the show helped them feel like they were out on the town. Duke's *Creole Love Call* was spicier than a pot of jambalaya. His *Mood Indigo* was a musical stream that swelled over the airwaves.

Sometimes the Orchestra performed their tunes straight-up. But other nights, when the joint started to jump, Duke told his band to play whatever came to mind — to improvise their solos. To make the music fly! And they did.

Each instrument raised its own voice. One by one, each cat took the floor and wiped it clean with his own special way of playing. Sonny Greer pounded out the bang of jump-rope feet on the street with his snare drum. A subway beat on his bass drum. A sassy ride on his cymbal. Sonny's percussion was smooth and steady. Sometimes only his drumsticks made the music, cracking out the rattly beat of wood slapping wood.

Along with Sonny, Joe "Tricky Sam" Nanton went to work on his trombone, sliding smooth melodic gold. He stretched the notes to their full tilt, pushing and pulling their tropical lilt. When Tricky Sam was through, he'd nod to Otto "Toby" Hardwick. "Your turn," he'd say. "Take the floor, Daddy-O!"

**T**oby let loose on his sleek brass sax, curling his notes like a kite tail in the wind. A musical loop-de-loop, with a serious twist.

Last came James "Bubber" Miley, a one-of-a-kind horn player. He could make his trumpet wail like a man whose blues were deeper than the deep blue sea. To stir up the sound of his low-moan horn, Bubber turned out a growl from way down in his throat. His gutbucket tunes put a spell on the room.

Yeah, those solos were kickin'. Hot-buttered bop, with lots of sassy-cool tones. When the band did their thing, the Cotton Club performers danced the Black Bottom, the Fish-Tail, and the Suzy-Q. And while they were cuttin' the rug, Duke slid his honey-colored fingertips across the ivory eighty-eights.

The word on Duke and his band spread, from New York to Macon to Kalamazoo and on to the sunshiny Hollywood Hills. The whole country soon swung to Duke's beat. Once folks got a taste of Duke's soul-sweet music, they hurried to the record stores, asking:

"Yo, you got the Duke?"

"Slide me some King of the Keys, please!"

"Gonna play me that Piano Prince and his band!"

People bought Duke's records — thousands of them.

In 1939, Duke hired Billy Strayhorn, a musician who wrote songs. Billy became Duke's ace, his main man. Duke and Billy worked as a team. Together they composed unforgettable music. Billy's song *Take the "A" Train* was one of the greatest hits of 1941.

With the tunes that he and Billy wrote, Duke painted colors with his band's sound. He could swirl the butterscotch tones of Tricky Sam's horn with the silver notes of the alto saxophones. And, ooh, those clarinets. Duke could blend their red-hot blips with a purple dash of brass from the trumpet section.

In time, folks said Duke Ellington's real instrument wasn't his piano at all — it was his Orchestra. Most people called his music jazz. But Duke called it "the music of my people."

And to celebrate the history of African American people, Duke composed a special suite he called *Black, Brown, and Beige*. A suite that rocked the heart and lifted the soul.

*Black, Brown, and Beige* sang the glories of dark skin, the pride of African heritage, and the triumphs of black people, from the days of slavery to years of civil rights struggle.

Duke introduced *Black, Brown, and Beige* at New York's Carnegie Hall, a symphony hall so grand that even the seats wore velvet. Few African Americans had played at Carnegie Hall before. Duke and his Orchestra performed on January 23, 1943. Outside, the winter wind was cold and slapping. But inside, Carnegie Hall was sizzling with applause. Duke had become a master maestro.

Because of Duke's genius, his Orchestra now had a musical mix like no other.

Now you've heard of the jazz-playin' man. The man with the cats who could swing with his band.

King of the Keys.
Piano Prince.
Edward Kennedy Ellington.
The Duke.

# Think and Compare

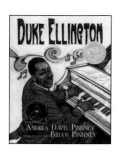

1. What qualities do Duke Ellington and Amelia Earhart have in common? How does each of them show these qualities in what they love to do?

2. Compare the different ways the authors of *Amelia and Eleanor Go for a Ride* and *Duke Ellington* tell their stories.

3. Why do you think *Amelia and Eleanor Go for a Ride* and *Duke Ellington* belong in a theme called "American Stories"?

4. In what ways are Duke Ellington and John Stetson from *Boss of the Plains* alike? What qualities do you think helped each man to reach his goals?

5. Which selection in this theme best describes your idea of what it means to be an American? Give examples.

**Strategies in Action** Explain how you used reading strategies while reading one of the selections.

# Write a Book Jacket

Write a book summary that might appear on the back cover of one of the selections in this theme. Tell about the story without giving away the ending. Remember, your summary should make people want to read the book you choose.

**Tips**

- Make an outline or story map.
- Focus on the most important parts of the story.
- Use exciting, descriptive words.

# Filling in the Blank

**Some test items ask you to complete a sentence. You must choose the best answer from three or more choices. A test about *Amelia and Eleanor Go for a Ride* might have this question.**

---

**Read the sentence. At the bottom of the page, fill in the circle for the answer that best completes the sentence.**

1. Amelia wasn't surprised that Eleanor had received her student pilot's license because _____.

   **A** Eleanor was married to the president

   **B** Amelia helped her study for the test

   **C** they were good friends

   **D** Amelia had encouraged Eleanor to learn to fly

   | ANSWER ROW 1 | Ⓐ Ⓑ Ⓒ ● |
   |---|---|

---

 **Understand the sentence.**

**Find the key words in the sentence. Use them to understand what you need to do.**

> The key words are *wasn't surprised*, *pilot's license,* and *because*. The word *because* tells me I must decide *why* Amelia wasn't surprised.

**Look back at the selection.**

Think about where to find the answer. You may need to look in more than one place. Skim the selection, using the key words.

> I need to look back to where I read about Eleanor's pilot's license. They talked about this during the dinner party. I'll reread that scene.

 **Narrow the choices. Then choose the best answer.**

Read the sentence, trying each answer choice in the blank. Find the choices that are clearly wrong. Have a good reason for choosing an answer. Guess only if you have to.

> **A** and **C** are true, but they don't tell why Amelia wasn't surprised. The story says that Amelia encouraged Eleanor. It doesn't say that she helped Eleanor study. So **D** is the best answer.

PLAYS

# Plays

The curtains open . . . the play begins. A play is a story that actors bring to life on a stage. You can go to a play — or you can read one.

A play may begin with a list of characters, or the **cast**. The lines they speak are called **dialogue**. **Stage directions** tell how the characters move and speak. Events take place in parts, or **scenes**.

**Now turn the page.
The play is about to begin!**

## CONTENTS

# Tales of a Fourth Grade Nothing

**by Judy Blume**
**adapted by Bruce Mason**

**Cast List** *(In order of appearance)*

| | | |
|---|---|---|
| Peter | Dad | Mom |
| Mrs. Yarby | Mr. Yarby | Fudge |

**Setting**

This scene takes place in the Hatcher family apartment in New York City.

**Time**

The present.

*In Scene I Peter Hatcher, a fourth grader, brings home a turtle he has won at a party. His mother is busy cooking because Peter's father, who works in advertising, is bringing an important client to dinner. As Peter and Mom talk, Peter's little brother, Fudge, begins eating the flowers on the table. Peter's mother rushes to the phone to call the doctor.*

## SCENE II — MR. AND MRS. JUICY-O

PETER *(To audience)*: Dr. Cone said Mom shouldn't worry about the flowers. She told her to give Fudge a spoon of that yucky pink stuff I get when I have a stomachache. By the time Dad came home with the Yarbys, Mom was all cleaned up. You'd never have guessed that Fudge ate some flowers, either. Mr. Yarby is the President of the Juicy-O Company, one of Dad's biggest clients. We always had plenty of Juicy-O around the house. Mr. Yarby sent us crates of it at Christmas. I wouldn't want to insult Dad's client, but between you and me, Juicy-O is gross. Anyway, the Yarbys were coming to New York for a visit and Dad invited them to stay with us. Mom wanted to know why they couldn't stay in a hotel like most of the people who come to New York. Dad said they could, but he thought they'd be more comfortable staying here. Mom said that was the silliest thing she had ever heard.

*(Lights up on the living room. DAD enters with the YARBYS. MRS. YARBY immediately goes to FUDGE.)*

DAD: Well, here they are . . . the Yarbys. Howard, I'd like you to meet my wife, Anne. Darling, Mr. and Mrs. Yarby.

MOM: Hello, nice to meet you. Welcome.

MRS. YARBY *(With eyes only for FUDGE)*: Ohhh . . . . Isn't he the cutest little boy? I just love babies.

DAD: And this is our older son, Peter.

PETER: Hi. I'm nine and I'm in fourth grade.

MR. YARBY: How do you do, Peter?

*(MRS. YARBY just gives PETER a nod.)*

MRS. YARBY: I have a surprise for this dear little baby. It's in my suitcase. Should I go get it now?

FUDGE: Yes! Go get it!

PETER *(To audience)*: I kept waiting for someone to tell her that Fudge was no baby. But no one did.

*(MRS. YARBY opens her suitcase and takes out a box tied with a red ribbon. FUDGE claps his hands.)*

FUDGE: Ohhh! Goody!

MRS. YARBY: Why don't you sit up here with me. I'll help you unwrap the pretty box.

*(FUDGE begins untying the ribbon.)*

MOM: Really, Mrs. Yarby, this is very nice of you.

MRS. YARBY: I just love babies. And Fudge is so adorable.

*(FUDGE has the box unwrapped. He pulls out a wind-up train.)*

MRS. YARBY:  See?  You just turn the key a couple of times and then . . .

*(FUDGE does so. The train careens about the floor and makes much noise.  Every time the train bumps into something, it turns around.  FUDGE is delighted with his gift; because of the noise it makes, MRS. YARBY is less delighted.)*

PETER:  That's a nice train.

MRS. YARBY:  Oh, I have something for you, too, uh . . . uh . . .

PETER:  Peter.  My name is Peter.

MRS. YARBY:  Yes.  *(She rummages through her suitcase.)*  Well, it's here somewhere . . .

*(MRS. YARBY looks at MOM.)*

MOM:  Fudge, give Mommy the train.

FUDGE:  No.

MOM:  Fudge, let's see what Peter got.

*(FUDGE reluctantly gives the train to MOM.  She puts it in her lap.)*

PETER *(To audience)*:  I unwrapped my gift carefully in case Mom wanted to save the paper — and to show Mrs. Yarby that I'm more careful with my things than my brother.  She didn't even notice.

*(The present is a picture book dictionary.  PETER holds the book up.  FUDGE watches, then exits.)*

MRS. YARBY:  I don't know much about big boys.  So the lady in the store said a nice book would be a good idea.

PETER *(To audience)*:  A nice book would have been a good idea.  But a picture dictionary!  That's for babies!  I've had my own Webster's Merriam Collegiate dictionary since I was eight.  And besides, I had one of these when I was four.  It's in Fudge's bookcase now.

PETER:  Thank you very much.  It's just what I always wanted.

MRS. YARBY *(Sighing)*:  I'm so glad.

DAD: Well, would you folks like a drink?

MR. YARBY: Good idea . . . good idea.

DAD: What'll it be?

MR. YARBY: What'll it be? What do you think, Hatcher? It'll be Juicy-O! That's all we ever drink. Good for your health!

*(MR. YARBY pounds his chest.)*

DAD: Of course. Juicy-O for everybody. I'll take your bags into your bedroom first.

*(DAD exits and then enters to the kitchen to fix the drinks.)*

MR. YARBY *(To MOM)*: Hatcher tells me that you're taking classes.

MOM: Yes, I am. I'm studying art history.

MRS. YARBY: My! And with two growing boys.

*(FUDGE enters. He is carrying a beat-up copy of the same dictionary that Mrs. Yarby gave Peter.)*

FUDGE:  See?

PETER *(To audience)*:  I wanted to vanish.

FUDGE:  See the book?

PETER:  That's okay.  I can use another one.  I really can.  That old one is falling apart.

FUDGE:  MINE!  *(He holds the book close to his chest.)*  It's MINE!  It's MINE!

MOM:  It's the thought that counts, Mrs. Yarby.  It was so nice of you to think of our boys.  Put the book away now, Fudgie.

MRS. YARBY *(Insulted)*:  It's returnable.  Really, it's silly to keep it if you already have one.  Let me have it back.

PETER:  No.  I'll keep it.  *(To audience)*  Like it was my fault she brought me something I already had.

*(DAD brings the drinks in.)*

DAD:  Isn't it Fudge's bedtime?

MOM:  Oh yes.  I think it is.  Say goodnight, Fudge.

FUDGE:  Goodnight Fudge.

*(MOM exits with FUDGE in tow.  FUDGE waves good-bye.  Lights down on the living room except for on PETER.)*

PETER *(To audience)*:  Fudge was supposed to fall asleep before we sat down to dinner.  But just in case, Mom put a lot of toys in his crib.  I don't know who she thought she was fooling.  We all knew that Fudge could climb out of his crib anytime he wanted.  He stayed away until the middle of the roast beef.

*(Lights up on the dining area.  FUDGE enters carrying Dribble's bowl.)*

FUDGE *(To MRS. YARBY)*:  See Dribble?

MRS. YARBY (*Shrieking*):  Oh!  I can't stand reptiles.  Get that thing away from me.

*(FUDGE looks disappointed.  He shows Dribble to MR. YARBY.)*

MR. YARBY:  HATCHER!  Make him get that thing out of here.

PETER:  Give Dribble to me!  *(He takes the bowl away from Fudge.)*  You know you're not allowed to touch my turtle.

MRS. YARBY:  Please.  Please, remove the reptile.  I can't eat.

DAD:  Go put Dribble back in your room, son, and then come back and finish your dinner.

MOM:  And I'll put Fudge back in his crib.  Excuse me a moment.

*(PETER and MOM exit with FUDGE.)*

MRS. YARBY:  It must be interesting to have children.  We never had any ourselves.

MR. YARBY:  But if we did, we'd teach them some manners.  I'm a firm believer in old-fashioned good manners.

DAD (*Weakly*):  So are we, Howard.  So are we.

*(Lights dim on the dining area. Lights up on PETER in his bedroom. He is still holding the turtle bowl.)*

PETER *(To audience)*: I think Mr. Yarby had a lot of nerve to suggest we had no manners. Didn't I pretend to like their dumb old picture dictionary? If that isn't good manners, I don't know what is . . . Well, anyway, Mom got Fudge back into his crib. Things were fine until dessert . . .

*(Lights back up on the dining area. PETER remains where he is and watches the scene. FUDGE runs in, wearing a realistic gorilla mask. MOM is pouring coffee. FUDGE so startles MRS. YARBY that her screaming startles MOM. MOM pours coffee all over the table and the floor. DAD grabs FUDGE and pulls the gorilla mask off.)*

DAD: That's not funny, Fudge.
FUDGE *(Laughing)*: Funny.
MRS. YARBY: This is more than I can handle.
MR. YARBY: There, there dear.

*(Both MOM and DAD begin cleaning up the mess.)*

MOM: We're so sorry, Mrs. Yarby.
DAD: I just don't know what's got into Fudge this evening. Ah, excuse me a moment.

*(Dad exits with FUDGE.)*

MRS. YARBY: Howard, could I see you in the other room, please?

*(MR. and MRS. YARBY cross to the living room. They confer silently.)*

MOM *(To herself; as the YARBYS cross)*: Oh dear.
PETER *(To audience)*: . . . by that time, I'm sure Dad wished the Yarbys had stayed in a hotel.

*(DAD enters and helps MOM. MRS. YARBY exits to the off-stage bedroom area.)*

MR. YARBY: Hatcher, my wife is a delicate woman, so we've decided . . .

DAD: I understand, Howard.

MR. YARBY: . . . that we should stay in a hotel after all. If you'd call us a cab.

MRS. YARBY *(Off)*: Oh! Howard! *(She enters carrying her suitcase. FUDGE, smiling, toddles in behind her. He is carrying something behind his back.)* Just look at what that little . . . just look at what he did to my suitcase.

*(MRS. YARBY's suitcase is covered in green trading stamps.)*

FUDGE: Pretty . . .

*(FUDGE laughs. No one else does. He licks a final trading stamp and sticks it on the suitcase.)*

FUDGE:  All gone!

MRS. YARBY:  Howard!

MR. YARBY *(To DAD)*:  Yessir!  Old-fashioned MANNERS!

*(Lights out except for on PETER.)*

PETER *(To audience)*:  The next week Dad came home from the office . . .

*(Lights up on the kitchen area.  DAD is collecting every can of Juicy-O he can find and dumping them in the trash.)*

PETER:  . . . and collected all the Juicy-O cans.

MOM:  I'm sorry you lost such an important account.

DAD:  Don't worry.  The stuff's not selling that well.  Nobody seems to like the combination of oranges, grapefruits, pineapples, pears and bananas.

PETER *(In scene)*:  You know, Dad, I just drank the stuff to be polite.  But really . . . I thought it was gross.

DAD:  You know something, Peter . . . I thought it was pretty gross myself.

# Think About the
# PLAY

1. How is a play different from a fictional story, such as the ones you have already read in *Journeys* or *American Stories*? What features do they have in common?

2. In what ways does a play remind you of movies or television shows? What elements of a play do they contain? How are they different?

3. How would the play have been different if a character other than Peter had narrated it? Or if there were no narrator at all?

4. Why are stage directions so important in a play? Give three examples of how stage directions helped you to better understand *Tales of a Fourth Grade Nothing*.

5. If you had the chance to play a character from *Tales of a Fourth Grade Nothing*, who would you choose? Why?

**Internet**

# Go on a Web Field Trip

Ready to learn more about the theater? We're expecting you backstage! You won't even have to get dressed up. Just log on and take our online field trip. **www.eduplace.com/kids**

Creating

# Write Your Own Play

Be a playwright! Make up an original story or choose one that has only a few characters, lots of dialogue, simple action, and one or two settings. Decide what the characters will say out loud, and write their words as lines of dialogue. Write their actions as stage directions. To show what the characters are feeling, add dialogue in which they tell their feelings, or use stage directions.

---

### Tips

- Write a list of characters and a short description of the setting.
- For dialogue, write the character's name in capital letters, a colon, and then the words the character speaks.
- Put stage directions in parentheses.
- Remember, the characters must tell or show the audience everything!

# 3

# That's Amazing!

If sunlight fell like snowflakes,
gleaming yellow and so bright,
we could build a sunman,
we could have a sunball fight . . .

*— Frank Asch*
*from "Sunflakes"*

# That's Amazing!

## with Chris Van Allsburg

Dear Reader,

There are different kinds of "amazing." For instance, if you had a dog who could walk down the block on his hind feet, that would be amazing. But if your dog walked down the block on his hind feet while reading out loud from the newspaper, well, that would be truly AMAZING. The stories in this theme are that second kind of "amazing."

Being amazed means being surprised — learning, hearing, or seeing something that is so different from what we are used to that it makes us feel a little strange, almost like being caught in a dream.

Now and then we all see the regular kind of amazing thing: our little brother eats a chocolate ice cream cone and doesn't get any on his face, our teacher forgets to give us homework two days in a row. Truly AMAZING things, however, practically never happen. We'd all like to meet a friend with a magic wand, as Cendrillon does in one of the stories that follows, but we never will.

If you're the kind of person who would really like to live in a world with magic wands and talking dogs, you're out of luck.

That's not the world we live in, but you can visit places like that very easily. As a matter of fact, it might be better to visit than to actually live there. It could turn out that it's not your friend who has the magic wand, but some really nasty person, and it might be impossible to get the dog to stop talking. After many hours he might still be reading, just getting to the weather page and giving the afternoon temperature in Amsterdam, Athens, Brussels, Cairo. . . .

So, how can you visit these interesting places? Easy. Just go to the library, a truly AMAZING place. If you can't find what you're looking for in between the covers of the books, just take out some paper and a pencil. Put down in words and pictures the AMAZING things that come from your own imagination. Then you'll find out there is such a thing as a magic wand. It's the pencil in your hand.

Sincerely,

# Amazing or AMAZING?

Chris Van Allsburg believes that there are two different kinds of "amazing." What amazing — or AMAZING — experiences have you had? Think about what makes an experience AMAZING for you. Are all impossible events AMAZING simply because they aren't real?

Look at the book covers shown below. What unexpected events do you think you might discover in these selections? While you read each story, think about which events could really happen and which ones would truly be impossible.

Prepare to be AMAZED! Things are about to get a bit *stranger*. . . .

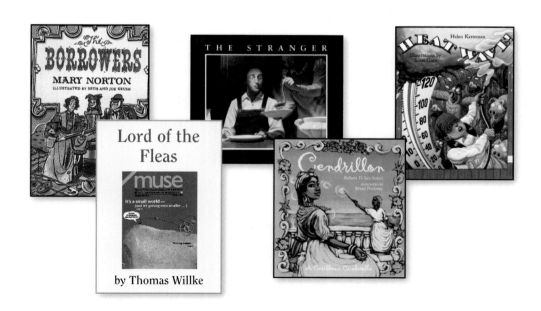

To learn about the authors in this theme, visit Education Place. **www.eduplace.com/kids**

## Background and Vocabulary

THE STRANGER

**The Stranger**

**Read to find the meanings of these words.**

*e* • Glossary

autumn
draft
etched
frost
mercury
thermometers
timid

# When the Leaves Fall

**A**utumn is the season that comes between summer and winter. In much of North America, autumn weather begins in late September and lasts until late November. The days grow shorter and the nights get cooler. You might start to feel a cold **draft** from an open window. The **mercury** in outdoor **thermometers** begins to fall, and in the morning you will sometimes find lines of **frost etched** on leaves and windows. Read *The Stranger* to find out about an autumn that doesn't quite follow the rules.

◀ Animals that are normally **timid** leave their homes to gather food for the winter.

▲
Some birds fly south
to spend the winter
in warmer climates.

◀ Autumn is also called
*fall*, because this is
when the leaves on
many trees turn bright
colors and then fall to
the ground.

▲
Autumn is also
when apples,
pumpkins, and
other crops
are harvested.

299

# MEET THE AUTHOR AND ILLUSTRATOR
## Chris Van Allsburg

If you've read books by Chris Van Allsburg before, you know that he writes mysterious stories that leave a lot for you to figure out. To help you, he provides clues throughout each book. In order to find the clues, you must read the story and look at all the pictures very carefully. What things seem strange to you in *The Stranger*? What explanations can you find in the author's words and illustrations to explain these mysteries?

Van Allsburg says that his stories usually start out as simple pictures or ideas. "It almost seems like a discovery, as if the story was always there," he says. "The few elements I start out with are actually clues. If I figure out what they mean, I can discover the story that's waiting." It takes him about seven months to write and draw a book, from start to finish.

**Other books:** *The Polar Express, Jumanji, The Mysteries of Harris Burdick, Just a Dream*

Find out more about Chris Van Allsburg by visiting Education Place. **www.eduplace.com/kids**

# THE STRANGER

## Strategy Focus

When a mysterious stranger arrives at the Baileys' house, unusual things begin to happen. **Monitor** your reading. If something doesn't make sense, reread to **clarify**.

It was the time of year Farmer Bailey liked best, when summer turned to fall. He whistled as he drove along. A cool breeze blew across his face through the truck's open window. Then it happened. There was a loud "thump." Mr. Bailey jammed on his brakes. "Oh no!" he thought. "I've hit a deer."

But it wasn't a deer the farmer found lying in the road, it was a man. Mr. Bailey knelt down beside the still figure, fearing the worst. Then, suddenly, the man opened his eyes. He looked up with terror and jumped to his feet. He tried to run off, lost his balance, and fell down. He got up again, but this time the farmer took his arm and helped him to the truck.

305

Mr. Bailey drove home. He helped the stranger inside, where Mrs. Bailey made him comfortable on the parlor sofa. Katy, their daughter, peeked into the room. The man on the sofa was dressed in odd rough leather clothing. She heard her father whisper ". . . must be some kind of hermit . . . sort of fellow who lives alone in the woods." The stranger didn't seem to understand the questions Mr. Bailey asked him. "I don't think," whispered Mrs. Bailey, "he knows how to talk."

Mr. Bailey called the doctor, who came and listened to the stranger's heart, felt his bones, looked in his eyes, and took his temperature. He decided the man had lost his memory. There was a bump on the back of his head. "In a few days," the doctor said, "he should remember who he is and where he's from." Mrs. Bailey stopped the doctor as he left the house. He'd forgotten his thermometer. "Oh, you can throw that out," he answered. "It's broken, the mercury is stuck at the bottom."

Mr. Bailey lent the stranger some clean clothes. The fellow seemed confused about buttonholes and buttons. In the evening he joined the Baileys for dinner. The steam that rose from the hot food fascinated him. He watched Katy take a spoonful of soup and blow gently across it. Then he did exactly the same. Mrs. Bailey shivered. "Brrr," she said. "There's a draft in here tonight."

The next morning Katy watched the stranger from her bedroom window. He walked across the yard, toward two rabbits. Instead of running into the woods, the rabbits took a hop in his direction. He picked one of them up and stroked its ears, then set it down. The rabbits hopped away, then stopped and looked back, as if they expected the stranger to follow.

When Katy's father went into the fields that day, the stranger shyly tagged along. Mr. Bailey gave him a pitchfork and, with a little practice, he learned to use it well. They worked hard. Occasionally Mr. Bailey would have to stop and rest. But the stranger never tired. He didn't even sweat.

That evening Katy sat with the stranger, watching the setting sun. High above them a flock of geese, in perfect V formation, flew south on the trip that they made every fall. The stranger could not take his eyes off the birds. He stared at them like a man who'd been hypnotized.

Two weeks passed and the stranger still could not remember who he was. But the Baileys didn't mind. They liked having the stranger around. He had become one of the family. Day by day he'd grown less timid. "He seems so happy to be around us," Mr. Bailey said to his wife. "It's hard to believe he's a hermit."

Another week passed. Farmer Bailey could not help noticing how peculiar the weather had been. Not long ago it seemed that autumn was just around the corner. But now it still felt like summer, as if the seasons couldn't change. The warm days made the pumpkins grow larger than ever. The leaves on the trees were as green as they'd been three weeks before.

One day the stranger climbed the highest hill on the Bailey farm. He looked to the north and saw a puzzling sight. The trees in the distance were bright red and orange. But the trees to the south, like those round the Baileys', were nothing but shades of green. They seemed so drab and ugly to the stranger. It would be much better, he thought, if all trees could be red and orange.

The stranger's feelings grew stronger the next day. He couldn't look at a tree's green leaves without sensing that something was terribly wrong. The more he thought about it, the more upset he became, until finally he could think of nothing else. He ran to a tree and pulled off a leaf. He held it in a trembling hand and, without thinking, blew on it with all his might.

At dinner that evening the stranger appeared dressed in his old leather clothes. By the tears in his eyes the Baileys could tell that their friend had decided to leave. He hugged them all once, then dashed out the door. The Baileys hurried outside to wave good-bye, but the stranger had disappeared. The air had turned cold, and the leaves on the trees were no longer green.

Every autumn since the stranger's visit, the same thing happens at the Bailey farm. The trees that surround it stay green for a week after the trees to the north have turned. Then overnight they change their color to the brightest of any tree around. And etched in frost on the farmhouse windows are words that say simply, "See you next fall."

# Think About the Selection

**1.** What is the Bailey family like? Use details from the story to support your description.

**2.** What are the first few clues that tell you that something is unusual about the stranger?

**3.** The stranger feels that something is "terribly wrong" when he sees green leaves on the trees. What do you think is wrong?

**4.** Who do you think the stranger is? List three clues that help you guess his identity.

**5.** If the stranger stayed for a while in the area where you live, what effect do you think he would have on the climate?

**6.** **Connecting/Comparing** What does Chris Van Allsburg do to make this story mysterious and amazing? Look at both the words and the illustrations.

**Describing**

## Write a Character Sketch

The stranger is an unusual person. Write a character sketch of him so that someone who has not read this story will understand what he is like.

**Tips**

- To get started, look for details in the story and the illustrations.
- Include what the stranger looks like and how he acts.

# Find the Average Temperature

Use a thermometer and some math to find the average temperature for a week where you live. Find each day's average temperature for seven days in a row. Write the temperatures in a notebook. When you have seven readings, find the average temperature for that week.

**Bonus** Use a newspaper to find the average temperature for another city during the same week. Calculate how much hotter or colder that city was than where you live.

# Draw a Picture

Where do you think the stranger goes after he leaves the Baileys' farmhouse? Make a drawing of the stranger in the place where he stays next or lives during the rest of the year. You might want to draw a picture that is somewhat mysterious, like the ones Chris Van Allsburg draws.

# Post a Review

Would you like to share your opinion of *The Stranger* with other students on the Internet? Write a review of the book and post it on Education Place. **www.eduplace.com/kids**

**Skill: How to Read a Poem**

- Read the poem several times. Try reading it aloud.

- Listen for the words that **rhyme**.

- Listen for a **rhythm**, and try to tap out the beats.

- Look at the words to see if they form a **picture** on the page.

- Finally, reread the poem. Try to picture what the poet is describing. Also, think about the meaning of the poem.

# Autumn Poems

## Fall Wind

I scarcely felt a breath of air;
I didn't hear a sound,
But one small leaf came spiraling
In circles to the ground.

And then the wind began to rise.
I felt it on my face.
It blew my jacket out behind
And made the white clouds race.

It seized the branches of the trees
And shook with might and main.
The leaves poured down upon the earth
Like drops of colored rain.

*by Margaret Hillert*

going out of my way
to crunch them as I walk;
first leaves of autumn

*by Lee Gurga*

320

# Falling Leaves

Some glide,
Some slide,
And some bide their time.

Some hurl,
Some twirl,
And some whirl and climb.

Some slip,
Some zip,
And some dip and play.

Falling leaves
Depart their trees
In every sort of way.

*by Lucinda A. Cave*

# Canada Geese

Padded drum
of beating wings
fills the steel gray sky.
See them sketching, stretching skyward.
Hear their lonely cry.  See them in the windswept
autumn.  Hear them call
goodbye.

*by Kristine O'Connell George*

        migrating geese
      one falls farther and farther
behind

*by Charles Dickson*

# Moon of Falling Leaves

Long ago, the trees were told
they must stay awake
seven days and nights,
but only the cedar,
the pine and the spruce
stayed awake until
that seventh night.
The reward they were given
was to always be green,
while all the other trees
must shed their leaves.

So, each autumn, the leaves
of the sleeping trees fall.
They cover the floor
of our woodlands with colors
as bright as the flowers
that come with the spring.
The leaves return the strength
of one more year's growth
to the earth.

This journey
the leaves are taking
is part of that great circle
which holds us all close to the earth.

*by Joseph Bruchac and Jonathan London*
*based on a traditional Cherokee story*
*of the Tenth Moon*

# A Story

Toothpaste

A story tells about a true or fictional experience. It has a main character and a beginning, a middle, and an end. Use this student's writing as a model when you write a story of your own.

| | |
|---|---|
| **Dialogue** helps make **characters** come to life. | # My Wish |

**Dialogue** helps make **characters** come to life.

**Readers** want to know the **setting** of a story right away.

A good story has a **problem** that needs to be solved.

# My Wish

Shirley yelled, "Get ready for bed!"
Javis said, "Yes, ma'am."

Javis climbed into his bunkbed. When he got into his bed, he saw someone who looked like a fairy godmother. She told him that she was his godmother, and that her name was Jamie. She exclaimed, "What would you like as a wish, little boy?"

Now Javis was a short little boy, about three feet tall. He thought a lot, and then he said, "I wish to be ten feet tall." The fairy godmother waved her wand, and Javis fell asleep.

The next morning Javis woke up and he was ten feet tall. He was gigantic, huge, tall, and strong all put together.

When he went in to brush his teeth he didn't see his toothbrush. He looked all over but still didn't see it. It was too small to use! By this time he had messed up the whole bathroom.

Of course all that noise woke up his parents. When they saw him, they were worried and rushed him to the doctor. Javis couldn't fit into the car, so his parents drove and he walked. He stepped on many cars but didn't feel a thing.

When they got to the doctor's office, Javis reached out to shake hands. The doctor saw Javis's belt buckle, and he immediately fell unconscious.

When the doctor woke up, he said Javis had a disease. It was called "tallest." So Javis's parents took him to a specialist.

The specialist decided to put Javis in a shrinking machine. He stayed there for one hour. When he came out, the only thing big was his head, so they put him back in. Then Javis was back to normal. So, if you ever get a free wish, wish for something that won't cause problems.

**Details** should be exact, never vague.

A good story ends with a **resolution** to its problem.

## Meet the Author

Javis B.
**Grade:** four
**State:** Florida
**Hobbies:** drawing, basketball, and singing
**What he'd like to be when he grows up:** a church worker

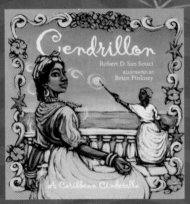

**Cendrillon**

**Read to find the meanings of these words.**

*e* ● Glossary

elegant

godmother

orphan

peasant

proud

# The Island of Martinique

If you visit Martinique, be ready to say *"Bonjour!"* That is the French word for "good day." Located in the Caribbean Sea, Martinique is known for its green forests, colorful flowers, and calm blue waters. Many of the island's traditions come from France and Africa. This mix of traditions is called Creole. Martinique's Creole traditions can be found in all parts of life: in language, in food, in clothing styles — even in fairy tales.

Martinique is 425 square miles, less than half the size of Rhode Island.

North America

Caribbean Sea

South America

**Martinique**

Martinique's warm climate makes flowers like these a year-round sight.

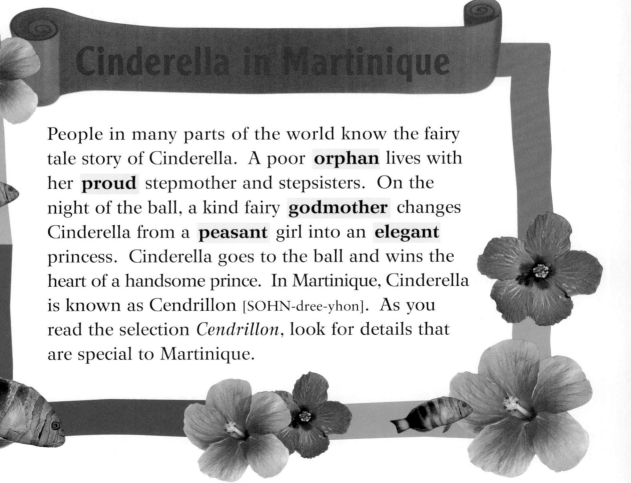

# Cinderella in Martinique

People in many parts of the world know the fairy tale story of Cinderella. A poor **orphan** lives with her **proud** stepmother and stepsisters. On the night of the ball, a kind fairy **godmother** changes Cinderella from a **peasant** girl into an **elegant** princess. Cinderella goes to the ball and wins the heart of a handsome prince. In Martinique, Cinderella is known as Cendrillon [SOHN-dree-yhon]. As you read the selection *Cendrillon*, look for details that are special to Martinique.

# Robert D. San Souci

Robert D. San Souci likes to tell old stories with a new twist. Whenever he retells a folktale, he researches the history of the country to make sure that all his details will be accurate. Even when it's a tale that's hundreds of years old, San Souci gets ideas from the modern world. He likes to ride the bus just to hear how ordinary people talk!

## MEET THE ILLUSTRATOR

# Brian Pinkney

Illustrator Brian Pinkney gets totally involved in his subjects. When he illustrated a book on ballet, he took dance lessons. When he wrote and illustrated a book about a boy who plays drums, he used his own experience playing drums. Pinkney illustrates in a style called scratchboard. He scratches lines into a board coated with a special black paint over white clay. The lines in the white clay show the picture he's drawn.

**Other books by the team of Robert D. San Souci and Brian Pinkney:** *Sukey and the Mermaid, Cut from the Same Cloth*

To learn more about the author and the illustrator, visit Education Place. **www.eduplace.com/kids**

328

Cendrillon

Robert D. San Souci

ILLUSTRATED BY
Brian Pinkney

A Caribbean Cinderella

## Strategy Focus

This version of the Cinderella story takes place
in Martinique. As you read, think of **questions**
to ask about how the setting affects the story.

329

You may *think* you know this story I am going to tell you, but you have not heard it for true. I was there. So I will tell you the truth of it. Now.

330

I live on a green-green island in the so-blue Mer des Antilles [MEHR de-ZON-teeyl], the Caribbean Sea. Long ago, when I was a child, my family was poor. When my mother died, she left me only one thing: a wand of mahogany. "Three taps will change one thing into another," my mother had whispered. "But only for a short time. And the magic must be used to help someone you love."

Of what use was this to an orphan like me, who every day struggled to find shelter and fill her belly? I could not use the wand. I had no one to love and no one who loved me.

When I grew up, I worked as a *blanchisseuse* [blahn-SHEEZ-seuz], a washerwoman, scrubbing other people's sheets and shirts at the riverside. Drying them in the sun.

One woman I worked for was kind. I often nursed her, for she was always sickly, poor creature. In thanks, she made me the *nannin'* [non-NIHN], godmother, of her baby girl, Cendrillon [SOHN-dree-yhon]. When I held that *bébé* [BEEYH-beeyh] in my arms on her christening day, I felt such love! And I saw love returned from her sweet brown eyes.

Alas! Cendrillon's mamma died soon after this. Then her papa, Monsieur [MOHN-sur], married again. Madame Prospèrine [Pros-SPER-in] was a cold woman, and puffed-up proud because her grandfather had come from France.

When a new daughter, Vitaline [VEE-tah-LEEN], was born,
Madame gave a christening party for her rich friends. What a feast
it was!

Madame and the other fine ladies were dressed in satin and
velvet, all the colors of the rainbow. They laughed at my worn
white skirts and peasant's way of speaking.

Pretty Cendrillon came and kissed me. "*Bonjou'* [BOH-zhew],
*Nannin'*." She gave me a cup of punch. Her hands were
blistered and red.

"*Pauv' ti* [pov tee] *Cendrillon*, poor little child!" I cried. "What have you done to yourself?"

She shrugged. "My father's wife works me like a serving-girl."

"And Monsieur allows this?"

Sighing, she said, "He fears Madame. But I am strong. The work hurts my hands but not my heart."

"Someday, I will find a way to help." Even as I spoke them, my words sounded hollow. What could I — a poor washerwoman — do for my dearest?

When she was older, Cendrillon would come to the river each morning to do the family's laundry. Her sweet *"Bonjou'"* was music. Her smile was sunshine even when clouds hid the sun. We knelt beside the other *blanchisseuses* and talked and sang and laughed as we scrubbed the clothes. Cendrillon seemed so happy, I wished that I could always see her so.

Nothing was easy for her at home. Madame and spoiled Vitaline ate dainties. Cendrillon often had only a handful of manioc flour and tail ends of codfish. All day she worked. At night she slept on a hard straw pallet.

Then, one day, she came sad-faced to the river. No singing or joking would make her smile. I asked, "What troubles you so, my child?"

"There is a ball tonight, but I am not to go," she said, looking so miserable, my heart nearly snapped in two. "Vitaline and Mamma will go. But Mamma says I am lazy."

"Does it mean so much to you, this ball?"

"Oh, yes, *Nannin'*!" she cried. "It is a birthday *fet'* [FET] for Paul, Monsieur Thibault's [TEE-bowlz] son. He is so handsome and well spoken, he is like a prince. Yet he is kind."

"Do not cry, dear one," I said, hugging her. "Tonight you will go to the ball."

"For true?"

"Upon my soul, I promise this," I said. Though I was fearful of risking so much when I had no plan.

But her smile lightened my heart. As she gathered up her laundry, I heard her singing.

Long after she left, I sat watching the river. *How am I to keep my promise?* I asked myself. Then, as the day grew late, I began to think what I must do.

It was dark when I reached home, took my mother's wand from the shelf, and hurried to my sweet Cendrillon.

What a hubble-bubble at the house! Cendrillon's papa stood on the porch, holding his gold watch, while the coachman waited beside the family carriage. "We are late," Monsieur said, as if the fault belonged to me. Inside, Madame and Vitaline were shouting, "Cendrillon, find my shoulder-scarf!" "Cendrillon, comb my hair!" I helped arrange Madame's gown, while Cendrillon combed Vitaline's hair.

Finally they were off, away. Good riddance!

Upon the instant, I told Cendrillon, "Now *you* will go to the ball."

"But I have no carriage," she protested. "I have no gown."

"Go into the garden and pick a *fruit à pain* [FREE-ya pan]," I said.

The child looked at me as if she thought, *My poor* nannin' *has gone mad.* But she found a big, round breadfruit.

I tapped this three times — *to, to, to!* — with my wand, and it became a gilded coach.

So far so good!

Cendrillon gasped, but I told her, "Do not waste your breath on questions; we still have much to do."

*To, to, to!* Six *agoutis* [ah-GOO-teez] in a cage became six splendid carriage horses. *To, to, to!* Five brown field lizards became five tall footmen. *To, to, to!* A plump *manicou* [MAN-ee-coo] was changed to a coachman.

Then I tapped Cendrillon. Her poor calico dress was changed to a trailing gown of sky-blue velvet. Upon her head sat a turban just as blue, pinned with a *tremblant* [TRHEM-blahn], pin of gold. She had a silk shoulder-scarf of pale rose, rings in her ears, bracelets, and a necklace of four strands of gold beads, bigger than peas.

Upon her feet were elegant pink slippers, embroidered with roses. It was enough to hurt my eyes to look at my darling.

Finally, I turned my washerwoman's shift into a fine red dress. I would chaperone Cendrillon, as suited a proper young lady.

Away we went, over the bridge, through the town, along the shore to the *granmaison* [grahn-MAY-zohn] of Monsieur Thibault.

Just before we stepped down from our carriage, I warned Cendrillon, "The magic lasts only a short time. We must leave before the midnight bell is rung."

"Yes, *Nannin'*," she promised.

341

What a grand entrance Cendrillon made! All eyes turned toward her and could not turn away. I heard whispers all around: "Who is that pretty girl?" "Look how fine her clothes are!" "Did she come from France?"

Even Cendrillon's stepmother and sister did not recognize the two of us, though they peered crossly at us.

Then Paul, his eyes blazing with love, asked her to dance. And he refused to dance with any other. I know. I watched as I ate. Oh, what fine food I helped myself to, as I watched the handsome couple. Even chocolate sherbet.

Cendrillon was so happy, and I was happy seeing her so, that we forgot to mark the time. Suddenly, I heard distant bells strike the first chime of midnight.

Astonishing all with my rudeness, I grabbed Cendrillon's hand and cried, "It is nearly midnight! We must go!"

For a moment, I feared she would not obey. Then she turned, and we ran toward the door.

Paul cried, "Wait! I do not even know your name!"

He ran after us, but guests and servants, confused by such running and shouting, blocked his way. As it was, we barely escaped to our carriage because Cendrillon stumbled on the stair. She had to leave behind one embroidered slipper.

Off we sped into the night as I counted the chimes. And the moment I heard the twelfth stroke, we found ourselves in the dusty road, beside a smashed breadfruit. Around us, *agoutis* and lizards and a fat *manicou* scurried into the brush.

We walked home like two ragged washerwomen. Our fine clothes were gone — all except Cendrillon's one pink slipper.

She took it off, saying, "I will keep this to remind me of this wonderful night and a happiness I will never know again."

"But," I said, "I will help you visit Paul again."

347

She shook her head. "I see now that it was not Cendrillon he fell in love with," she said. "He was under the spell of your wand. When the magic goes, the love, too, will fade from his eyes."

"Alas!" I said. "My plans have come to nothing. I cannot give you the gift of a love that would change your life for true."

"Dear Godmother," she said, kissing my cheek, "you gave me this night. It is enough."

I did not see Cendrillon at the river the next day. When I called at the house, I found she was in bed. Madame and Vitaline said she was being lazy. But I saw she was sick with a broken heart. I stroked her brow for a good long time — until I heard a great commotion.

When I looked for the cause, I found that Paul had arrived. He was followed by a footman carrying Cendrillon's lost pink slipper on a satin pillow.

To Madame and Vitaline, he explained, "I am searching for the lovely stranger who was at the *fet'* last night. This is her slipper. I am asking all unmarried young women on the island to try it on. I will wed the one whose foot it fits."

From the doorway I heard Madame say, "My pretty daughter is the only unmarried girl in the house."

Then Vitaline and her mamma tried to force the girl's big foot, with toes like sausages, into the slipper. Such grunting and groaning you never heard! So eager were they, I feared they would destroy the slipper.

"If you cut off those big toes," I called out, "it would be a fine fit."

Madame screeched, "Go away, old woman!"

And I did. Straight back to Cendrillon's room I marched.

"Now, child, if you love me," I charged her, "do this one thing for me: Go out into the hall."

She drew a shawl around her cotton shift. Barefoot, she went into the hall, where panting Madame and sobbing Vitaline had given up the battle of the slipper. But just as Paul was turning to go, I tapped Cendrillon — *to, to, to!* — with my wand. To the astonishment of all, she appeared as she had at the ball.

"No, Godmother dear," she said. "No more spells."

With a sigh, I touched her again, and she was as before, in her shift and shawl.

Without hesitation, Paul knelt before her. Gently he placed the slipper on her foot. Then he said, "You are as beautiful this minute as you were last night." And everyone in the room could see the true-love in his eyes.

351

Cendrillon and Paul were married soon after this. Even the king and queen of France never had such a wedding! The guests ate and danced and sang and ate again for three days.

I know because I was there. I danced the *gwo-kā* [gwoh-KAH] and ate nine helpings of chocolate sherbet and came away only to tell you this tale.

353

# Think About the Selection

**1.** How do you think Madame and Vitaline felt when they found out that Cendrillon was the mysterious guest at the ball?

**2.** Which events in the story could happen in real life? Which amazing events could never happen in real life?

**3.** Why does Cendrillon want to wear her own clothes when Paul puts the slipper on her foot?

**4.** How would this story have been different if Cendrillon had left the ball on time?

**5.** Many countries have versions of the Cinderella story. Why do you think this story is so popular all over the world?

**6.** **Connecting/Comparing** Which story do you think is more amazing, *Cendrillon* or *The Stranger*? Give reasons for your answer.

# Write Another Scene

How would *Cendrillon* be different if it were told by another character, such as the stepmother or Paul? Choose one scene from the story. Then pick a different character to narrate the events of that scene. Write the scene from that character's point of view.

**Tips**
- Start your story with "Now let me tell you what happened . . ."
- Tell only what that character would know about events.

# Make a Travel Brochure

If you were going to Cendrillon's island home, what would you see there? Make a travel brochure of Martinique. Look in the selection and in the Get Set to Read on pages 326–327 for details about Martinique to include in your brochure.

# Watch a Movie Version

View one of the many film or television versions of *Cinderella*. Then, in a small group, discuss how the movie compares to the story *Cendrillon*. Which version do you like better? Why?

An animated version of *Cinderella*

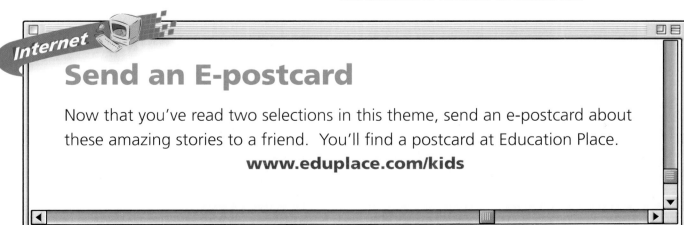

*Internet*

## Send an E-postcard

Now that you've read two selections in this theme, send an e-postcard about these amazing stories to a friend. You'll find a postcard at Education Place.

**www.eduplace.com/kids**

# Dance Link

**Skill: How to Read a Time Line**

- Read the **title** to see what the time line is about.

- Look for **dates** and notice the **time span** each section of the time line shows.

- Scan the time line from left to right. The earlier **events** will be on the left. The later events will be on the right.

# Let's Have a BALL!

Fantastic balls like the one in *Cendrillon* aren't just in fairy tales. In real life, people still go to fancy parties like balls. Guests wear their most formal clothing. And what type of dancing do they do? Ballroom dancing, of course!

## The History of Ballroom Dance

### 1600s

One of the first ballroom dances, the **minuet**, was popular in Europe in the **1600s**. Dancers stood in two lines. They moved along the floor in an *S* or *Z* pattern, joining hands at different parts in the dance.

### 1700s

People first danced the **waltz** in Germany during the **1700s**. With its gliding steps and graceful turns, it quickly became popular all over the world.

*The graceful minuet was a favorite among the lords and ladies of Europe.*

356

Guests loved to waltz at balls like this one, held by the Skidmore Guard in the 1870s.

Dancers had to be quick on their feet for the lively fox trot.

These professional dancers perform an elegant tango.

## 1800s

The waltz stayed popular throughout the **1800s**. Some of the best-loved waltz music was written in that century. You may even have ice-skated to "The Skaters' Waltz."

## 1900s

The **fox trot** was a favorite ballroom dance of the **1900s**. The dance was named after Harry Fox, a famous performer who used to trot across the stage! At that time, Latin American dances such as the **rumba** and the **tango** became popular too.

## 2000s

Today, you can still see guests waltzing at weddings or doing the **tango** on televised dance contests. Hundreds of years after the first dancers twirled across the floor, ballroom dancing is as popular as ever.

**Heat Wave!**

# What Is a HEAT WAVE?

Have you ever heard the saying "It's so hot you could fry an egg on the sidewalk"? Sometimes the **temperature** soars so high, it feels as if the sun could **singe** the hair on top of your head. When the weather is unusually hot and sticky for a long period of time, it is called a heat wave.

Read to find the meanings of these words.

*e* • Glossary

affected
horizon
singe
temperature
thermometer

Sometimes the heat can play tricks on your eyes. Here, a dry road looks wet, and the **horizon** appears blurred and wavy.

Here's how to keep your cool in a city fountain.

Heat waves can last for a few days or for as long as several weeks. They are caused when large masses of hot air get stuck over a particular region — and don't budge. These hot spells can send the **thermometer** to over 100 degrees.

Such hot weather can be dangerous — even deadly. People, animals, and crops can all be seriously **affected**. For example, too much heat can make you sick by forcing your body to work extra hard. In the story you are about to read, one Kansas farm girl tries to save her farm from a heat wave that may just prove too hot to handle.

**TIPS FOR**

# Beating the HEAT

- Take it easy! Avoid working or playing too hard.

- Stay out of the sun or wear sunscreen.

- Wear light colors. They bounce some of the sun's energy away from you.

- Even if you're not thirsty, drink lots of water. Your body needs water to cool down.

- Eat lightly.

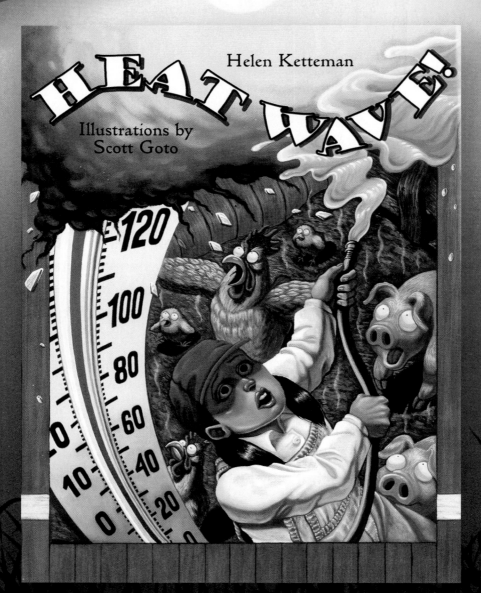

Helen Ketteman

Illustrations by
Scott Goto

HEAT WAVE!

## Strategy Focus

What amazing things happen when a heat
wave strikes a Kansas farm? **Evaluate** how the
author and the illustrator make this story funny
and incredible.

My big brother, Hank, used to tease me that girls couldn't be farmers. But he sure changed his tune the day the Heat Wave hit.

I was feeding the chickens when I heard a loud roar. I looked out across the horizon and saw a big old clump of crinkled, yellow air rolling across the sky. A flock of geese flew in one side and came out the other side plucked, stuffed, and roasted.

361

I hollered for Ma and Pa and Hank, but before they got outside, the Heat Wave hit. The mercury blasted out of the porch thermometer like a rocket. Ma's flowers pulled themselves up by their roots and crawled under the porch looking for shade.

By the time everybody ran outside, the Heat Wave had gotten snagged on the barn's weather vane. It was near harvest time, so we raced to the cornfield to save what we could. But by the time we got there, it was already too late. The corn had started popping. It looked like a blizzard had hit. One of our old hound dogs turned blue and froze when he saw it. I wrapped him in a blanket, and he thawed out okay.

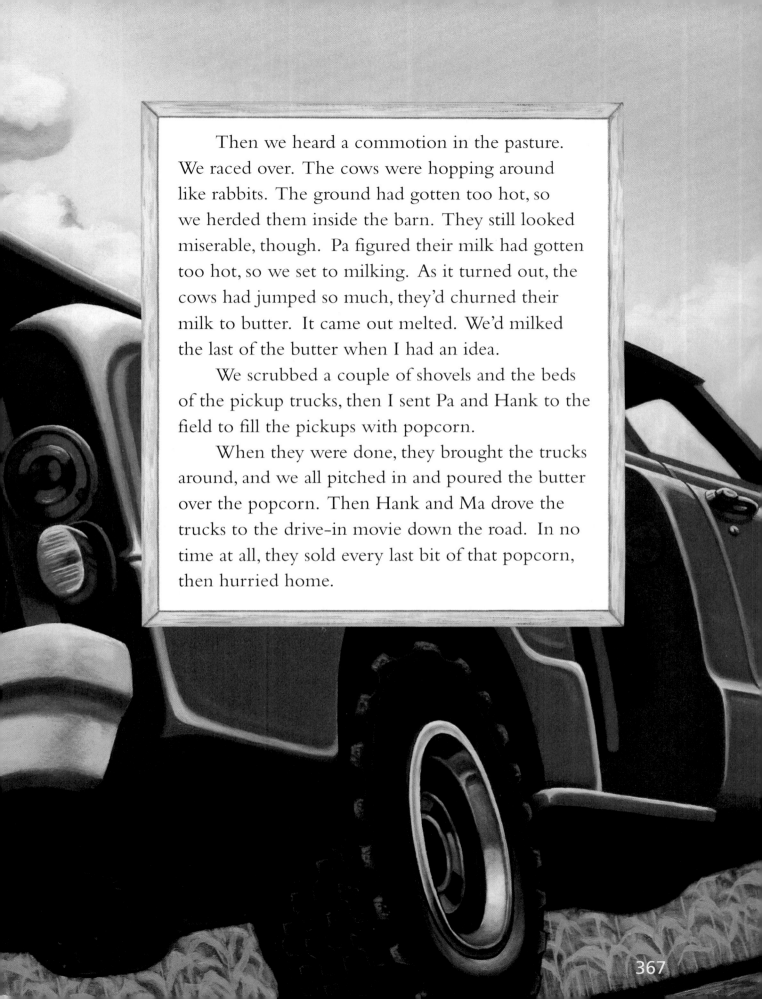

Then we heard a commotion in the pasture. We raced over. The cows were hopping around like rabbits. The ground had gotten too hot, so we herded them inside the barn. They still looked miserable, though. Pa figured their milk had gotten too hot, so we set to milking. As it turned out, the cows had jumped so much, they'd churned their milk to butter. It came out melted. We'd milked the last of the butter when I had an idea.

We scrubbed a couple of shovels and the beds of the pickup trucks, then I sent Pa and Hank to the field to fill the pickups with popcorn.

When they were done, they brought the trucks around, and we all pitched in and poured the butter over the popcorn. Then Hank and Ma drove the trucks to the drive-in movie down the road. In no time at all, they sold every last bit of that popcorn, then hurried home.

We still had plenty of worries. We hurried to the field where we had oats planted. Sure enough, they had dried out. I tried wetting them down, but that didn't turn out to be such a good idea.

Soon I felt something slimy and thick rising up around my ankles. In another minute, it was waist high, and I could barely move. Turned out I'd created a whole field of oatmeal. It was lumpy, just like Ma's, and I about drowned in the stuff.

I dog-paddled to the edge and crawled out. Whoo-ee! That oatmeal was sticky! I told Pa we should bottle it, which we did later. It made fine glue.

It was then that I caught a whiff of something burning. I followed my nose to the barn and hurried inside. The cows were steaming, and their coats were starting to singe. Those poor critters were about to cook! We hosed them down and turned fans on them. It helped, but not enough. Pa always said I was the quickest thinker in the family, and I knew it was up to me to think of something else.

I figured it was time to take on the Heat Wave. I thought blowing air on it would help, but we needed the fans for the cows. Besides, we didn't have near enough fans to cool the Heat Wave down. Then I had another idea. A huge flock of crows, all beating their wings at once, might work. One thing Kansas has is plenty of crows. And I knew how to get them to come.

We dumped several fifty-pound bags of flour and a bunch of yeast in the trough by the barn, then stirred in water with shovels. That dough rose so fast we had to run for our lives. It rolled over several chickens, then picked up the tractor and Sally the mule. Ended up big as the barn.

A few minutes later, the dough started baking in
the heat. Smelled awful good, and that's what I was
counting on. Crows can't resist the smell of baking
bread, and soon every crow in Kansas came flocking
to the farm. Their wings made so much wind, we
had to tie ourselves around a giant tree trunk to
keep from being blown away. It felt cooler already.

374

The trouble was, those crows didn't keep flying. They lit on the bread and started eating. The temperature shot right back up, and I figured we might be licked.

The crows pecked at the bread until they freed Sally and the chickens. None of them were a bit worse for wear. In fact, they were right frisky. I figured all that yeast had caused their spirits to rise.

Seeing Sally gave me one more idea. I told Pa to hitch her to the plow, and she plowed up a section of land in record time. While Pa was plowing, I found what I needed. I gave everyone lettuce seeds, and we started planting. Those seeds sprouted as soon as they hit the dirt.

The bigger the lettuce grew, the cooler the air got. That Heat Wave put up a fight, all right. It rippled and twisted and squirmed like a bucking bronco. But as the lettuce cooled the air more, the Heat Wave started shrinking, until it finally disappeared altogether.

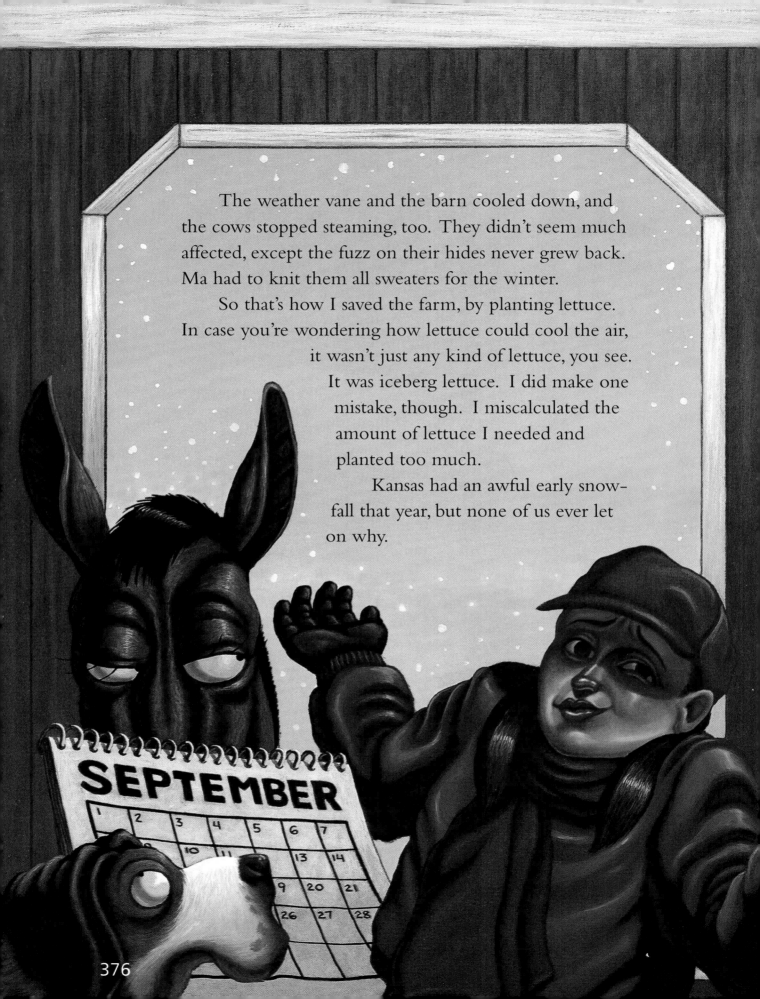

The weather vane and the barn cooled down, and the cows stopped steaming, too. They didn't seem much affected, except the fuzz on their hides never grew back. Ma had to knit them all sweaters for the winter.

So that's how I saved the farm, by planting lettuce. In case you're wondering how lettuce could cool the air, it wasn't just any kind of lettuce, you see. It was iceberg lettuce. I did make one mistake, though. I miscalculated the amount of lettuce I needed and planted too much.

Kansas had an awful early snowfall that year, but none of us ever let on why.

SEPTEMBER

| 1 | 2 | 3 | 4 | 5 | 6 | 7 |
|---|---|---|---|---|---|---|
| | | 10 | 11 | | 13 | 14 |
| | | | 19 | 20 | 21 |
| | | 26 | 27 | 28 |

# Meet the Author
# HELEN KETTEMAN

**W**hat would you do if you didn't have a television in your house? That's just how Helen Ketteman grew up in a small Georgia town. Believe it or not, she says she is glad about that now. Instead of watching TV, she turned to books for entertainment.

She also invented stories for her sisters, and acted out plays for her neighbors. "I know that the reason I'm a writer today is because I read so much as a child," she says.

**Other books:** *Luck with Potatoes, The Year of No More Corn, Bubba the Cowboy Prince*

# Meet the Illustrator
# SCOTT GOTO

**S**cott Goto is certainly no stranger to heat waves. He lives in Hawaii, where hot weather is common. So it is no surprise that he did not have to do any weather research for his work on *Heat Wave!*

When Goto creates art for a children's book, he pretends he is the age of the reader. "This isn't very hard since a big part of me never grew up," says Goto. "I still love playing video games, watching cartoons, and buying toys."

 **Internet**

To find out more about Helen Ketteman and Scott Goto, log on to Education Place.

**www.eduplace.com/kids**

# Think About the Selection

**1.** What qualities make the girl so good at fighting the heat wave?

**2.** How is the heat wave like a character in the story? If the heat wave could speak, what would it say?

**3.** Many scenes in this selection exaggerate an ordinary event until it becomes amazing. Give three examples.

**4.** If the farm had been out of lettuce seeds, how else could the girl have defeated the heat wave?

**5.** Before the heat wave, the girl's brother teased her that girls couldn't be farmers. What do you think he says about her now?

**6. Connecting/Comparing** What do you think would happen if the stranger from Chris Van Allsburg's story were at the farm during the heat wave attack?

# Write a Sequel

Think about what would happen if the cool weather caused by the iceberg lettuce became a cold wave. Write a scene involving the girl doing battle with a cold wave that's just as amazing as the heat wave.

**Tips**

- Continue the tall-tale style of the story by using exaggeration and puns.
- Include dialogue. Remember to use quotation marks.

# Make a Fact File

Without the sun, there couldn't be heat waves. Using an encyclopedia or your science book, create a fact file about the sun. How does it heat the earth? How hot is it? How far away is it? Use illustrations to help support the facts you include.

**Bonus** Make and label a diagram showing how the earth's revolution around the sun affects the seasons.

The Sun

Average Distance from Earth:

Age:

What it is made of:

Temperature:

# Tell a Tall Tale

Sit in a circle with a group and tell a story that will become more and more amazing as you go along. One person starts the story by telling about a realistic event. After one or two sentences, the next person continues the story by adding an exaggerated event. As the plot grows, each storyteller will make the tale stranger and stranger.

**Tips**

- Start with a sentence about something ordinary, such as "One day, on my way home from school, it started to rain."
- Review this theme to help you think of some wacky ideas.

**Internet**

# Take a Web Field Trip

Have you ever wanted to visit the hottest places in America without having to worry about keeping cool? Now's your chance! Log on to Education Place and take our sizzling field trip.

**www.eduplace.com/kids**

# Constructing a STRAW Thermometer

by Muriel Mandell

*Simple Weather Experiments With Everyday Materials*

### How *does* a thermometer work? Make your own and find out.

### You need:
- a medicine bottle or small jar
- a cork to fit
- a few drops of food coloring
- a felt-tipped pen
- a glass straw or medicine dropper tube
- a nail
- water

### What to do:

1. Dig out a hole in the cork with the nail and fit the straw or tube through it.

2. Fill the bottle halfway with water colored with a drop or two of food coloring and cap it securely. Mark the line the water rises to in the tube with a felt-tipped pen.

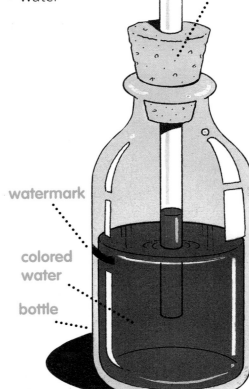

straw

cork

watermark

colored water

bottle

**3.** Note the height of the water in the straw at room temperature, and also at different times and places —

on a sunny windowsill . . .    in the refrigerator . . .    in a pot of hot water.

## What happens:

**The water goes up the tube when the temperature is warm and goes down when it is cold.**

## Why:

We measure temperature by the changes made. Temperature is really a measure of whether one object absorbs heat from or loses heat to another object.

Liquids expand when heated and contract when cooled. The liquid of the thermometer absorbs heat. It expands when it contacts anything warmer than itself, and contracts when contacting something cooler. Mercury and colored alcohol are usually used as the liquid in thermometers because they react so quickly.

Makers of commercial weather thermometers use a sealed glass tube that has a little bulb blown out at one end. They mark the thermometer's scale by placing its bulb in contact with melting ice.

The point at which the liquid contracts is 32° for a Fahrenheit scale and 0° for a centigrade scale. Then the bulb is placed in the steam from boiling water. The point at which it expands is marked 212°F or 100°C.

You can make a scale for your straw thermometer by comparing its levels with a commercial weather thermometer.

Gabriel Fahrenheit, a German physicist, devised the first commonly used scale in 1714. About thirty years later, a Swedish astronomer, Anders Celsius, established the centigrade scale, also known as the Celsius scale.

The first thermometer was invented in 1593 by the Italian physicist Galileo.

# Check Your Progress

You have just visited a fantastic world of wands, weird weather, and wonder — a place where anything can, and does, happen. Now it is time to read and compare two more incredible selections and to practice some important test-taking skills.

Turn back to pages 294–296. Do you agree with Chris Van Allsburg that reading, writing, and imagination are great ways of experiencing the truly AMAZING? Why or why not?

The next two selections, too, will take you to places where the impossible seems possible. As you read, ask yourself what you find amazing in each one. Think about what fantastic qualities they share with the stories you have already read. And now, believe it or not, it's time for more unbelievable tales.

# Read and Compare

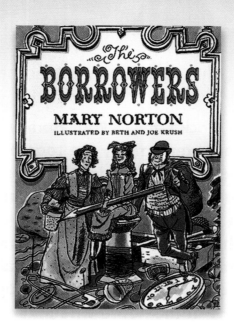

Find out what happens when a family of tiny people meets a regular-sized boy who towers over them like a giant!

**Try these strategies:**
Monitor and Clarify
Evaluate

Meet a man who trains real fleas to juggle, play soccer, and even pull miniature carts.

**Try these strategies:**
Question
Summarize

**Strategies in Action** *Try to use all your reading strategies while you read.*

# The Borrowers

by Mary Norton, illustrated by Bruce MacPherson

Meet the incredible Clock family.  Pod, Homily, and their 13-year-old daughter Arrietty live together in an old English home — that is, under the floor-boards.  They fit quite comfortably there because they are Borrowers, tiny people who live unseen among humans.  They survive by secretly taking, or "borrowing" items they need from their giant neighbors.  The Clocks may be in danger, though.  There is a curious boy in the house who might spot them, making big trouble for them.  Pod and Homily have warned young Arrietty about keeping hidden, but curiosity has gotten the best of her.  She strikes up a friendship with the boy.  When her parents find out, they are upset and confused.  Her mother, Homily, feels frightened that being "seen" will force them to move away.  Then one night, just as the Clocks have drifted off to sleep . . .

And Homily woke up.  She saw the room again and the oil lamp flickering, but something, she knew at once, was different:  there was a strange draught and her mouth felt dry and full of grit.  Then she looked up at the ceiling:  "Pod!" she shrieked, clutching his shoulder.

Pod rolled over and sat up.  They both stared at the ceiling: the whole surface was on a steep slant and one side of it had come right away from the wall —  this was what had caused the draught — and down into the room, to within an inch of the foot of the bed, protruded a curious object:  a huge bar of gray steel with a flattened, shining edge.

"It's a screwdriver," said Pod.

They stared at it, fascinated, unable to move, and for a moment all was still.  Then slowly the huge object swayed upward until the sharp edge lay against their ceiling and Homily heard a scrape on the floor above and a sudden human gasp.  "Oh, my knees," cried Homily, "oh, my feeling —" as, with a splintering wrench, their whole roof flew off and fell down with a clatter, somewhere out of sight.

Homily screamed then.  But this time it was a real scream, loud and shrill and hearty; she seemed almost to settle down in her scream, while her eyes stared up, half interested, into empty lighted space. There was another ceiling, she realized, away up above them — higher, it seemed, than the sky; a ham hung from it and two strings of onions. Arrietty appeared in the doorway, scared and trembling, clutching her nightgown. And Pod slapped Homily's back. "Have done," he said, "that's enough," and Homily, suddenly, was quiet.

A great face appeared then between them and that distant height. It wavered above them, smiling and terrible: there was silence and Homily sat bolt upright, her mouth open. "Is that your mother?" asked a surprised voice after a moment, and Arrietty from the doorway whispered: "Yes."

It was the boy.

Pod got out of bed and stood beside it, shivering in his nightshirt. "Come on," he said to Homily, "you can't stay there!"

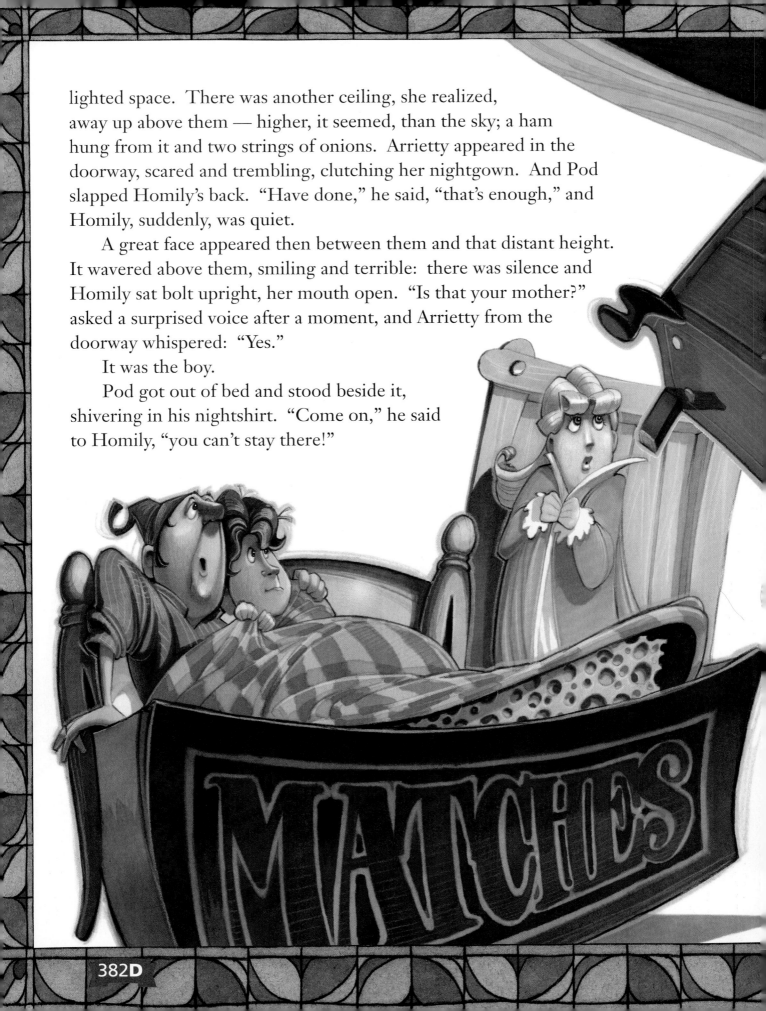

But Homily could. She had her old nightdress on with the patch in the back and nothing was going to move her. A slow anger was rising up in Homily: she had been caught in her hair curlers; Pod had raised his hand to her; and she remembered that, in the general turmoil and for once in her life, she had left the supper washing-up for morning, and there it would be, on the kitchen table, for all the world to see!

She glared at the boy — he was only a child after all. "Put it back!" she said, "put it back at once!" Her eyes flashed and her curlers seemed to quiver.

He knelt down then, but Homily did not flinch as the great face came slowly closer. She saw his under lip, pink and full — like an enormous exaggeration of Arrietty's — and she saw it wobble slightly. "But I've got something for you," he said.

Homily's expression did not change and Arrietty called out from her place in the doorway: "What is it?"

The boy reached behind him and very gingerly, careful to keep it upright, he held a wooden object above their heads. "It's this," he said, and very carefully, his tongue out and breathing heavily, he lowered the object slowly into their hole: it was a doll's dresser, complete with plates. It had two drawers in it and a cupboard below; he adjusted its position at the foot of Homily's bed. Arrietty ran round to see better.

"Oh," she cried ecstatically. "Mother, look!"

Homily threw the dresser a glance — it was dark oak and the plates were hand-painted — and then she looked quickly away again. "Yes," she said coldly, "it's very nice."

There was a short silence which no one knew how to break.

"The cupboard really opens," said the boy at last, and the great hand came down all amongst them, smelling of bath soap. Arrietty flattened herself against the wall and Pod exclaimed, nervous: "Now then!"

"Yes," agreed Homily after a moment, "I see it does."

Pod drew a long breath — a sigh of relief as the hand went back.

"There, Homily," he said placatingly, "you've always wanted something like that!"

"Yes," said Homily — she still sat bolt upright, her hands clasped in her lap. "Thank you very much. And now," she went on coldly, "will you please put back the roof?"

# LORD of the FLEAS

by Thomas Willke
photographs by Volker Steger

Hans Mathes reaches for a hair-fine strand of copper wire and twists it into a braid until only a tiny loop is left at the end. Then he gets one of his artists. They are magnificent athletes. For them it's no problem to kick balls more than 30 times heavier than themselves or to turn a carousel 20,000 times their weight. They are barely two millimeters long, the size of a grain of sand — a fraction of a gram of concentrated strength: they are fleas.

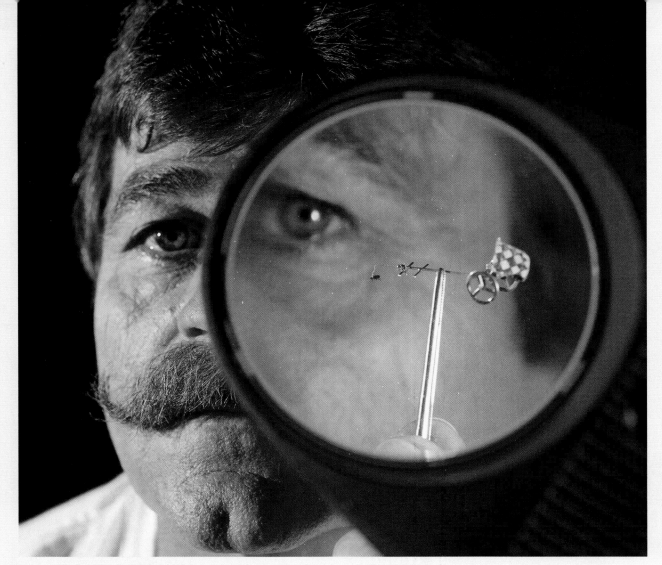

**Hans Mathes with one of his star performers.**

Hans Mathes is their master. He is the last of his kind, the only remaining flea-circus director in Europe. Mathes carefully holds a flea between his thumb and index finger, moving the little loop of wire over its head. Then he takes a fine needle and pokes the flea's first pair of legs through the loop. Now comes the most difficult part: Mathes squeezes the loop just a teeny-tiny bit so the flea can't escape its harness. Too much pressure, and the flea meets his maker. But Mathes has decades of experience, and nine out of ten fleas survive being harnessed.

Flea circuses were very common in medieval Europe, an attraction at just about every county fair. Everybody had fleas, and anybody able to handle them could create his own circus in a box.

Mathes learned the art from his ancestors. The flea circus has been a family business for over 150 years. The Mathes family performed for a Pope and a Russian czar. But times have changed and these days the director of Europe's last flea circus works a day job as a janitor in a semiconductor factory in Nuremberg, Germany. The flea circus leaves its little box only two weeks a year to perform at *Oktoberfest*, a traditional festival held each October in Munich, Germany.

Here's what the fleas can do: play soccer, pull carriages, turn carousels, juggle, and dance!

How does Mathes get them to perform their stunts? He uses the natural instincts of the fleas and their astounding athletic talents. Fleas normally hop around like popcorn popping in a hot pan because a good jump just might land them on their next victim. But for some tricks Mathes needs the fleas to walk. So first he sorts his performers. "You have to observe them very carefully," Mathes explains. "They all like to jump but some of them like to jump more than others. That's how you have to sort them!"

**"Floh-circus" is just German for flea circus (as if you couldn't guess).**

The natural jumpers become soccer players, since that's where their talents lie. Fleas can jump higher than twenty centimeters and farther than thirty-five centimeters, incredible distances compared to their size. Fleas are very strong. If they were the size of people, they would be able to jump right over a building. What's more, they are fast.

A flea can catapult itself out of danger in less than a thousandth of a second. It can take off so quickly because its leg muscles have help. Fleas grow two tiny spheres made of a rubbery protein just above their hind legs. When a flea jumps, it squeezes these little "rubber balls" with the muscles on its hind legs, then locks its legs with a hook-shaped part of its exoskeleton under its belly. Now the flea is like a cross-bow ready to fire: the hook is released and the insect shoots off with an acceleration of as much as 140 *g*s — more than twenty times the acceleration of the space shuttle on liftoff!

**Soccer, flea-style. The flea sits on a tiny styrofoam ball.**
**When it tries to jump, it ends up kicking the ball into the goal.**

In the circus, the soccer fleas are held by their wire harnesses to a little styrofoam ball and placed in a brightly lit miniature soccer stadium. "I'm using the flight instinct of the animals," says Mathes. "They want to get away from the light." The fleas feel the ball under their feet, think it is the ground and try to jump — kicking the ball into a miniature soccer goal. "As a treat, I put them into the dark after they score," explains the circus's director.

It takes a lot more training to teach fleas not to jump and to turn them into the dedicated workhorses Mathes needs for his delicate carriages and carousels, most of which he inherited from his grandfather. In these tricks, fleas show off their muscles: a single flea moves a gold carriage weighing several grams or turns the thirty-five gram carousel. The equivalent feat for a person would be to pull 600 cars or ten blue whales at once. If an animal jumped while pulling the carriage, the act would be ruined, so Mathes only trains fleas that don't like to jump very much for these tricks. "I have a set of boxes for them. First I put them into relatively tall boxes so they can jump around

**Mathes' assistant uses a magnifying glass to show the fleas performing. Kids always get the front seats.**

a little, then the boxes gradually become flatter and flatter. In the end, they completely give up jumping!"

All the fleas in the flea circus are females, because males would be too small and too weak for the stunts. Mathes prefers real human fleas, because the kind that live on dogs and cats are too small. But where does he get them? Human fleas are practically extinct in western Europe, but Mathes insists he knows where to find them. He once caught one of the little pests in a subway in Paris, although most are collected by friends elsewhere. "I won't name the countries," he says, "since I don't want to get in trouble with the people in charge of tourism there!"

Some of Mathes' flea carriages are more than 150 years old. In the foreground (top) are dancing fleas: dressed in tiny aluminum costumes, they look like twirling ballerinas when they move.

# Think and Compare

1. What qualities make *The Borrowers* and "Lord of the Fleas" so amazing? Compare and contrast the two stories.

2. Which stories in this theme are fantasies? For each story, list two qualities that support your answer.

3. Compare the Borrowers' home with yours. Name four tiny items the Clocks might borrow from you. What would they do with them?

4. "Lord of the Fleas" shows that real life can be amazing. List two things you think are amazing in real life. Explain.

5. What selection in this theme do you find most amazing? Explain.

**Strategies in Action** When did you use reading strategies in this theme? Tell how you used them.

## Write an Advertisement

Create a poster advertising a "Borrower Circus" planned by Hans Mathes, starring the Clocks. Give important information, such as where and when the show will be held. Tell just enough about the show to make people curious. Include exciting illustrations.

**Tips**

- Review similar ads in newspapers for reference.
- List the information you need to include.
- Use short sentences and exclamations.

# Writing a Personal Response

Some test items ask you to write a personal response to a topic, based on your reading and your own ideas and experience. Look at the sample below.

---

**Write at least one paragraph about the topic below.**

In the theme *That's Amazing!*, you have met many interesting characters. Which character reminds you most of someone you know? Explain.

---

**①** ## Understand the question.

Find the key words. Use them to understand what you need to do. Decide what to write about.

**②** ## Get ready to write.

Look back at the selection. List details that help answer the question. Think about yourself. List thoughts or experiences that help answer the question.

Here are some examples of good lists.

| Selection Details from *Heat Wave!* | Personal Thoughts or Experiences |
|---|---|
| The girl's brother thinks she can't be a farmer because she is a girl. | My friend Hannah's brother thinks girls are not good at baseball. |
| The girl fights bravely against the hot weather. | Hannah likes to face challenges. |
| The girl finds clever solutions. | Hannah is good at solving problems. |

## 3 Write your answer.

Use details from both of your lists. Write a clear and complete answer.

Here is an example of a good answer.

The main character in <u>Heat Wave!</u> reminds me of my best friend Hannah. In the story, the girl's brother thinks a girl can't be a good farmer. Hannah's brother feels the same way about girls and baseball. But last season Hannah got more hits than he did! Both the girl and Hannah are always trying new things. Hannah just signed up for singing lessons. But most of all, the girl is a very good problem solver, and so is Hannah. Last week Hannah figured out a way to get her cat Shadow to stop scratching her mother's curtains.

# Problem Solvers

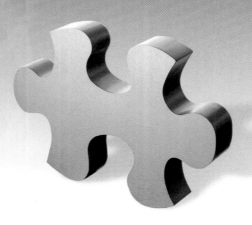

A problem is just
a solution waiting
to be discovered.

— *Anonymous*

# Problem Solvers

## with Alma Flor Ada

Dear Reader,

Have you ever had a problem? Did it feel as if there was nothing you could do to solve it? Sometimes we get into trouble without meaning to and then don't know how to get out of it. This happens to the main character in my book *My Name Is María Isabel*. She is frustrated at school and searches for ways to explain her feelings.

Telling the truth to ourselves and to others helps solve most problems. Hiding from the truth and pretending nothing is wrong makes the problems grow larger.

In writing this letter to you, I found myself with a problem. I tried different approaches, but I was never really satisfied. First, I tried remembering being in fourth grade. Then I thought about books with fourth grade characters. Finally, I decided to ask my granddaughter Camille (pictured above) to help me list problems fourth graders may have.

"Some subjects may be hard," she began. "And someone may have forgotten to do their homework. Or maybe they did not understand and did it wrong. Sometimes, even when you want to listen to the teacher, a friend keeps talking."

I asked Camille if she could think of other problems. "Having to go to a new school," she replied. "Nobody recognizes you. Everyone is looking at you. It's very stressful!"

Since Camille changed schools last year, I asked her how she faced it. "You just have to stay with it and be ready to make new friends," said Camille. "It helps if you can still talk to your old friends after school. It's harder if the family has to move far away — that can really be hard on kids."

My conversation with Camille helped me to see a new point of view. We identified two types of problems: ones we can try to solve ourselves, and ones where we must involve others. An example of this second kind of problem would be if parents decided not to live together anymore. We might not be able to change the situation, but we can always make things better by being kind and loving.

Thinking about my own problem, I see that I was able to follow these steps:

## Tips for Solving Problems

**Recognize the problem.** I was not satisfied with my writing.

**Identify the type of problem.** This problem involved just me.

**Look for solutions.** I used my memories and books I have read.

**Ask for help.** Camille's advice was helpful, because she was willing to listen. Also, she is an expert, since she is a child.

**Make decisions.** I decided how to apply what I learned from my conversation with Camille.

**Get to work.** It is not enough to have ideas. They must be put into action!

It feels great once a problem is solved. So, next time you have a problem, look at it honestly, telling yourself the truth. If the problem involves your relationships with others, share your feelings with them. I hope sharing my process will help you the next time you think about solving problems. May you always find good solutions!

Much love from your author friend,

# Problem Solved!

Alma Flor Ada writes that telling the truth is an important part of solving a problem. Think of a problem you once had. How did being honest help clear the way toward solving your problem?

Think about what problems the characters in the selections shown below might have. As you read, ask yourself which of Alma Flor Ada's steps the main characters use as they struggle to overcome their own problems.

Can't wait to read some more? No problem! It's time for *Problem Solvers*!

To learn about the authors in this theme, visit Education Place. **www.eduplace.com/kids**

# Background and Vocabulary

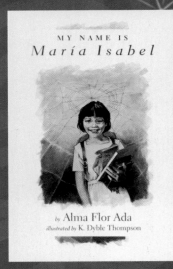

**My Name Is María Isabel**

MY NAME IS
María Isabel

*by* Alma Flor Ada
*illustrated by* K. Dyble Thompson

**Read to find the meanings of these words.**

*e* • Glossary

disappointed
misunderstandings
nervously
troublesome

# New *in the* Neighborhood

No one knows your name or anything else about you. You don't know where things are or how to get from one place to another, and your friends all live far away. What's happened? You've just moved from your old home to a new one.

Nowadays, it's common for families to move from one neighborhood, town, or state to another. For a student, entering a new school can be the most **troublesome** part of a move. Although you might be **disappointed** at first by your new school, soon you'll find exciting things there that you hadn't expected. When you first arrive, you might feel like a stranger as you **nervously** try to make friends. There might be **misunderstandings** because people do things differently in the new school from what you're used to. But soon you will meet people and get to know your way around. Read *My Name Is María Isabel* to find out how one girl deals with the challenge of being the newest one in school.

391

## Meet the Author
# Alma Flor Ada

Alma Flor Ada was born in Camagüey, Cuba. She lived in Spain and Peru before coming to the United States. She writes her books in Spanish. Later, other people translate them into English. One of those translators is her daughter, Rosalma Zubizarreta. Ada has written many books for children, including collections of stories, poetry, and riddles.

Alma Flor Ada began writing when she was a child: "I made a firm commitment while in fourth grade to devote my life to producing schoolbooks that would be fun — and since then I am having a lot of fun doing just that!"

**Other books:** *The Malachite Palace, The Gold Coin, The Lizard and the Sun, Dear Peter Rabbit*

## Meet the Illustrator
# Melodye Benson Rosales

Melodye Benson Rosales grew up in Los Angeles. From the time she was a little girl, she loved all kinds of art, from drawing pictures to singing and acting. There were no televisions or computer games in her home, so she would get her friends together to put on plays. Afterward, she would imagine additional scenes for those plays and then draw pictures of what she imagined. When she grew up, she decided to become an illustrator. Now she does the work she likes the best — illustrating children's books.

If you want to find out more about Alma Flor Ada and Melodye Benson Rosales, visit Education Place.
**www.eduplace.com/kids**

MY NAME IS
*María Isabel*

*by* Alma Flor Ada

*illustrated by* K. Dyble Thompson

## Strategy Focus

María Isabel has a difficult problem to solve.
As you read, stop several times and **predict** what
you think she will do next. Then predict what the
results will be.

María Isabel's family has just moved from one part of the city to another. She has had to switch schools two months after the start of the school year. To make matters worse, there are two other girls named María in her new class, so the teacher has decided to call her Mary López instead of María Isabel López Salazar. This upsets her, for she is proud of her name, which is made up of the names of relatives she loves in Puerto Rico. Because she doesn't realize she is being called on when the teacher says "Mary López," María Isabel has missed the chance to perform in the Winter Pageant.

## The Winter Pageant

Everything at school now revolved around plans for the Winter Pageant. The class was making wreaths and lanterns. The teacher explained to the class that Christmas is celebrated differently in different countries, and that many people don't celebrate Christmas at all. They talked about Santa Claus, and how he is called Saint Nicholas in some countries and Father Christmas in others. The class also talked about the Jewish feast of Hanukkah that celebrates the rededication of the Temple of Jerusalem, and about the special meaning of the nine candles of the Hanukkah menorah.

The teacher had asked everyone to bring in pictures or other things having to do with the holidays. A lot of kids brought in photographs of their families by their Christmas trees. Mayra brought in pictures of New Year's Day in Santo Domingo. Michelle brought in a picture of herself sitting on Santa's lap when she was little. Gabriel brought in photos of the Three Kings' Day parade in Miami, Florida. He had been there last year, when he went to visit his Cuban grandmother. Marcos brought in a piñata shaped like a green parrot that his uncle had brought back from Mexico. Emmanuel showed everyone a photo album of his family's trip to Israel, and Esther brought in cards her grandfather had sent her from Jerusalem.

One day, Suni Paz came to the school. She sang Christmas songs from different countries and taught the class to sing a Hanukkah song, "The Candles of Hanukkah."

María Isabel went home humming softly "Hanukkah . . . Hanukkah . . . Let us celebrate." The bus trip seemed a lot shorter as the song ran through her head. It almost felt as if she had traveled to all those different countries and had celebrated all those different holidays.

María Isabel was still singing while she made dinner and set the table:

> "With our menorah,
>
> Fine potato latkes,
>
> Our clay trumpets,
>
> Let us celebrate."

Her voice filled the empty kitchen. María Isabel was so pleased she promised herself that she'd make a snowman the next time it snowed. And she'd get it finished before the garbage men picked up the trash and dirtied up the snow.

But after Suni Paz's visit to the school, the days seemed to drag by more and more slowly. María Isabel didn't have anything to do during rehearsals, since she didn't have a part in *Amahl*.

The teacher decided that after the play the actors would sing some holiday songs, including María Isabel's favorite about the Hanukkah candles. Since she didn't have a part, María Isabel wouldn't be asked to sing either.

It didn't seem to matter much to Tony and Jonathan, the other two kids who weren't in the play. They spent rehearsal time reading comics or whispering to each other. Neither boy spoke to María Isabel, and she was too shy to say anything to them.

The only fun she had was reading her library book. Somehow her problems seemed so small compared to Wilbur the pig's. He was in danger of becoming the holiday dinner. María Isabel felt the only difference was that the characters in books always seemed to find answers to their problems, while she couldn't figure out what to do about her own.

As she cut out bells and stars for decorations, María Isabel daydreamed about being a famous singer. Someday she would sing in front of a large audience, and her teacher would feel guilty that she had not let María Isabel sing in the Winter Pageant.

But later María Isabel thought, My teacher isn't so bad. It's all a big misunderstanding. . . . If only there was some way I could let her know. Even if I'm not a great singer someday, it doesn't matter. All I really want is to be myself and not make the teacher angry all the time. I just want to be in the play and to be called María Isabel Salazar López.

## Trapped in a Spider's Web

"I've asked my boss if I can leave work early the day of the school pageant," María Isabel's mother said one evening as she served the soup. "Papá is also going to leave work early. That way we'll be able to bring the rice and beans."

"And best of all, we can hear María Isabel sing," her father added.

María Isabel looked down at her soup. She had not told her parents anything. She knew they were going to be very disappointed when they saw the other kids in her class taking part in the play. She could just hear her mother asking, "Why didn't you sing? Doesn't the teacher know what a lovely voice you have?"

María Isabel ate her soup in silence. What could she say?

"Don't you have anything to say, Chabelita?" asked her father. "Aren't you glad we're coming?"

"Sure, Papá, sure I am," said María Isabel, and she got up to take her empty bowl to the sink.

400

After helping her mother with the dishes, María Isabel went straight to her room. She put on her pajamas and got into bed. But she couldn't sleep, so she turned the light on and continued reading *Charlotte's Web*. María Isabel felt that she was caught in a sticky, troublesome spider's web of her own, and the more she tried to break loose, the more trapped she became.

When the librarian had told her that she would like the book, María Isabel had felt that they were sharing a secret. Now as she turned the pages, she thought that maybe the secret was that *everyone* has problems. She felt close to poor little Wilbur, being fattened up for Christmas dinner without even knowing it. He was a little like her parents, who were so eager to go to the pageant, not knowing what was waiting for them.

"It just isn't fair that this can't be a happy time for all of us!" María Isabel said out loud. She sighed. Then she turned off the light, snuggled under her blanket, and fell asleep trying to figure out a way to save Wilbur from becoming Christmas dinner.

## My Greatest Wish

Two days were left until the pageant. The morning was cloudy and gray. On the way to school, María Isabel wondered if it was going to snow. Maybe she would be able to make that snowman. But shortly after she got to school, it started to drizzle.

Since they couldn't go outside, the students spent their time rehearsing. No one made a mistake. Melchior didn't forget what he had to say to Amahl's mother. Amahl dropped his crutch only once. Best of all, though, the shepherds remembered when they were supposed to enter, without bumping into the Three Kings.

Even Tony and Jonathan seemed interested in the play. They volunteered to help carry the manger and the shepherds' baskets on- and offstage.

Satisfied with the final rehearsal, the teacher decided there was time for one last class exercise before vacation. "It's been a couple of days since we've done some writing," she said when the students returned to class. "The new year is a time for wishes. Sometimes wishes come true; sometimes they don't. But it's important to have wishes and, most of all, to know what you really want. I'd like you all to take out some paper and write an essay titled 'My Greatest Wish.'"

María Isabel sighed and put away *Charlotte's Web*. Charlotte had just died, and María Isabel wondered what was going to happen to the sack of eggs that Wilbur had saved, and when Charlotte's babies would be born. But María Isabel would have to wait to find out. She bit down on her pencil and wrote: "My greatest wish . . ."

This shouldn't be so hard, María Isabel thought. If I finish writing early, I can probably finish my book. She started to write: "My greatest wish is to make a snowman. . . ."

María Isabel read over what she had just written, and realized that it wasn't what she really wanted. She put the paper aside, took out a new sheet, and wrote down the title again. "My greatest wish is to have a part in *Amahl.* . . ."

María Isabel stopped writing again. She thought, Would Charlotte have said that her greatest wish was to save Wilbur? Or would she have wished for something impossible, like living until the next spring and getting to know her children? The teacher just said that wishes don't always come true. If I'm going to wish for something, it should be something really worth wishing for.

María Isabel took out a third sheet of paper and wrote down the title again. This time, she didn't stop writing until she got to the bottom of the page.

## My Greatest Wish

When I started to write I thought my greatest wish was to make a snowman.  Then I thought my greatest wish was to have a part in the Winter Pageant.  But I think my greatest wish is to be called María Isabel Salazar López.  When that was my name, I felt proud of being named María like my papá's mother, and Isabel, like my grandmother Chabela.  She is saving money so that I can study and not have to spend my whole life in a kitchen like her.  I was Salazar like my papá and my grandpa Antonio, and López, like my grandfather Manuel.  I never knew him but he could really tell stories. I know because my mother told me.

If I was called María Isabel Salazar López, I could listen better in class because it's easier to hear than Mary López.  Then I could have said that I wanted a part in the play.  And when the rest of the kids sing, my mother and father wouldn't have to ask me why I didn't sing, even though I like the song about the Hanukkah candles so much.

The rest of the class had already handed in their essays and were cleaning out their desks to go home when María Isabel got up. She quietly went to the front of the room and put her essay on the teacher's desk. María Isabel didn't look up at the teacher, so she didn't see the woman smiling at her. She hurried back to her desk to get her things and leave.

## One Little Candle, Two Little Candles

Holiday spirit was everywhere at school the next day. The paper wreaths and lanterns the class had made were hung up all over the room. The teacher had put the "greatest wish" essays up on the bulletin board, next to the cutouts of Santa Claus, the Three Kings, and a menorah.

All the students were restless. Marta Pérez smiled when María Isabel sat down next to her. "Look at the pretty Christmas card I got from my cousin in Santo Domingo," she said excitedly. María Isabel looked at the tropical Christmas scene, all trimmed in flowers. But she couldn't answer Marta because the teacher had started to speak.

"We're going to do one last rehearsal because there's a small change in the program."

The rest of the kids listened attentively, but María Isabel just kept looking down at her desk. After all, she had nothing to do with the pageant.

Then she heard the teacher say, "María Isabel, María Isabel Salazar López . . ." María Isabel looked up in amazement.

"Wouldn't you like to lead the song about the Hanukkah candles?" the teacher said with a wide grin. "Why don't you start by yourself, and then everyone else can join in. Go ahead and start when you're ready."

María Isabel walked nervously up to the front of the room and stood next to the teacher, who was strumming her guitar. Then she took a deep breath and began to sing her favorite holiday song.

While her mother was getting the rice and beans ready that night, Mr. Salazar called María Isabel over to him. "Since you can't wear makeup yet, Chabelita, I've brought you something else that I think you'll like." In the palm of his hand were two barrettes for her hair. They were shaped like butterflies and gleamed with tiny stones.

405

"Oh, Papi. They're so pretty! Thank you!" María Isabel exclaimed. She hugged her father and ran to her room to put them on.

At school the next day, María Isabel stood in the center of the stage. She was wearing her special yellow dress, a pair of new shoes, and the shining butterflies. She spoke clearly to the audience. "My name is María Isabel Salazar López. I'm going to sing a song about the Jewish feast of Hanukkah, that celebrates the rededication of the Temple in Jerusalem." The music started, and María Isabel began to sing:

## The Candles of Hanukkah

One little candle,
Two little candles,
Three little candles,
Let us celebrate.
Four little candles,
Five little candles,
Six little candles,
Let us celebrate.
Hanukkah, Hanukkah,
Let us celebrate.
Seven little candles,
Eight little candles,
Nine little candles,
Let us celebrate.
Hanukkah, Hanukkah,
Let us celebrate.
With our menorah,
Fine potato latkes,
Our clay trumpets,
Let us celebrate.
With our family,
With our friends,
With our presents,
Let us celebrate.

And the butterflies in María Isabel's hair sparkled under the stage lights so much that it seemed that they might just take off and fly.

# Responding

## Think About the Selection

**1.** Why is the book *Charlotte's Web* so important to María Isabel?

**2.** Why do you think María Isabel feels that she is "caught in a sticky, troublesome spider's web of her own"?

**3.** María Isabel doesn't tell her parents that she is upset. Why do you think she keeps her feelings to herself?

**4.** How does writing the essay help María Isabel solve her problem?

**5.** If you had a difficult problem to solve, would you solve it the way María Isabel did, or would you choose a different way? Explain.

**6. Connecting/Comparing** What does this selection teach you about solving problems?

## Write a Review

At the end of this selection, María Isabel participates with her classmates in the Winter Pageant. Write a review of the pageant for a school newspaper. Use information from the story and what you think the pageant would be like.

**Tips**

- **Start by telling where and when the pageant happened.**
- **Describe several performances, including María Isabel's.**
- **Use reviews in magazines or newspapers as models.**

408

## Social Studies

### Learn About Names

María Isabel was named after relatives in Puerto Rico. Interview classmates about the stories behind their first and last names. Then tell the class what you learned about the names of one of your classmates.

## Listening and Speaking

### Role-Play Meeting a New Student

If a new student joined your class, what would you want to ask him or her? What advice or information would you give? Get together with a classmate and take turns playing the role of the new student.

**Internet**

## Complete a Web Word Search

Try finding names of characters from *My Name Is María Isabel* in a word search puzzle. Print the puzzle from Education Place.

**www.eduplace.com/kids**

**Skill: How to Skim and Scan**

*To skim . . .*

❶ **Read** the title and the headings.

❷ **Look at** the illustrations, photographs, and captions.

❸ **Look at** boxed lists, tables, and charts.

❹ **Read** the first and last paragraphs.

*To scan . . .*

❶ **Read quickly** to find key words.

❷ **Read more carefully** when you find important information.

# The Name GAME

### BY IRA WOLFMAN

What makes us laugh if we meet a Judy Tailor who works as a tailor, or a Billy Baker who specializes in cakes?  What makes us do a double-take when we see a sign that reads "Law Offices of Ellen M. Law"?

There is one simple reason:  We don't expect names to *mean* anything.  But they do.  Names are filled with meaning, symbolism, and history.  First and middle names frequently have family tradition behind them.  Family names may reveal where ancestors lived, what they looked like, how they acted or spoke, how they earned a living, or who their parents were.

The most common family name in the world is Li.  More than 87 million Chinese carry that moniker.  But the name that is most common in Western countries is — are you surprised? — Smith.

Is this carpenter's name Carpenter?

# The Mighty SMITH

The name Smith comes from the Old English word *smite*, which means "to strike." Smiths worked with metals, using hammers or other tools to smite the metal and make something useful like horseshoes, plows, tools, or swords. These implements were important to the people in the village, which must have made Smith a prominent figure in town.

That must be part of the reason why in every nation there are people whose names translate as "Smith." For example:

A blacksmith in Spain

| | | | |
|---|---|---|---|
| Arabic: | Haddad | Hungarian: | Kovacs |
| Armenian: | Darbinian | Irish Gaelic: | Gough, Goff |
| Bulgarian: | Kovac | Italian: | Feffaro, Ferraro |
| Catalan: | Feffer | Norwegian: | Smid |
| Czech: | Kovar | Persian: | Ahangar |
| Dutch: | Smid, Smidt, Smit, Smed | Polish: | Kowal |
| | | Portuguese: | Ferreiro |
| Estonian: | Raudsepp, Kalevi | Romanian: | Covaciu |
| Finnish: | Rautio, Seppanen | Russian: | Kuznetsov, Koval |
| French: | Lefevre, Lefebvre, Ferrier, Ferron, Faure | | |
| | | Spanish: | Herrera |
| German: | Schmidt, Schmitt, Schmid, Schmitz | Swedish: | Smed |
| | | Turkish: | Temirzi |
| Greek: | Skmiton | Welsh: | Goff, Gowan |
| Gypsy: | Petulengro | | |

An Australian blacksmith working at an anvil

# A Persuasive Essay

The purpose of a persuasive essay is to convince someone to think or act in a particular way. Use this student's writing as a model when you write a persuasive essay of your own.

# The Pledge

The **introduction** usually states the **goal** of a persuasive essay.

I strongly believe that the Pledge of Allegiance should be said in the morning by all staff and students. I have three reasons why the Pledge of Allegiance should be said.

A good persuasive essay states strong **reasons** supported by **facts** and **examples**.

First of all, when I say the Pledge of Allegiance, I get such a great patriotic feeling that my voice vibrates with happiness. I think my classmates get that good feeling too.

Usually facts and examples have separate paragraphs.

Second, saying the Pledge of Allegiance every day in school helps you remember the words. If you repeat something a lot, you can learn it without too much trouble.

Last but not least, the more you say the Pledge of Allegiance the more you understand what it means. You appreciate living in the United States and being free.

So please say the Pledge of Allegiance every day, because it is a good way to start the school day. I have given you three good reasons.

The **conclusion** restates the goal and encourages the reader to take action.

## Meet the Author

Alexander M.

**Grade:** four

**State:** Michigan

**Hobbies:** fishing and hockey

**What he wants to be when he grows up:** a NASA scientist or an astronaut

**Marven of the Great North Woods**

**Read to find the meanings of these words.**

*e* • Glossary

bunkhouse

cords (of wood)

immense

lumberjack

snowshoes

timber

woodsman

# Life in a Logging Camp

*Camp cooks and fiddlers pose before a meal prepared for hungry lumberjacks.*

In the early 1900s, northern logging camps were like small communities located deep in the woods. Cutting **timber** was dangerous work, and for a **lumberjack**, days were long and hard. Turning an **immense** tree into neat **cords** of wood was no simple task. Each lumberjack had his own special job to do, but they all worked as a team.

On an average day a lumberjack awoke before the crack of dawn. Leaving the warm, cozy **bunkhouse** could be unpleasant, especially on a freezing, snowy day. But the thought of a tasty pancake breakfast served by the camp cook probably helped! Lumberjacks would then trudge off into a vast landscape of trees. Some days, a **woodsman** even needed to wear **snowshoes** to avoid falling waist-deep into thick snow.

Logging camp deep in
the woods of Minnesota

CANADA

Minnesota

UNITED STATES

MEXICO

In *Marven of the Great North Woods*, you will
read about a city boy who leaves his familiar home
for a strange world of snow, towering trees — and
towering lumberjacks.

Minnesota lumberjacks haul timber, 1900.

# Selection 2

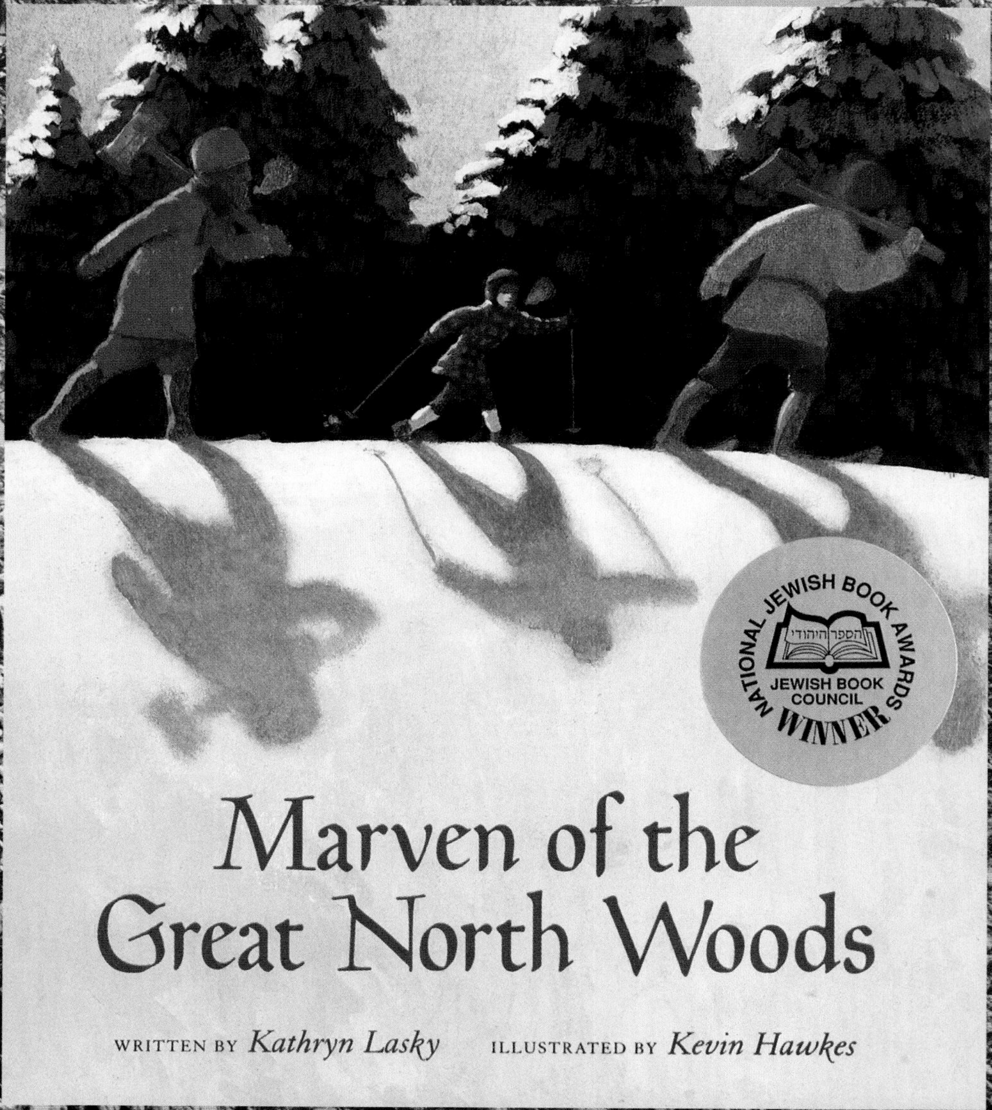
NATIONAL JEWISH BOOK AWARDS
JEWISH BOOK COUNCIL
WINNER
Marven of the Great North Woods
WRITTEN BY Kathryn Lasky
ILLUSTRATED BY Kevin Hawkes

## Strategy Focus

In this selection, a boy faces many challenges in an unfamiliar place. **Evaluate** how well the author helps you to see this new world through the boy's eyes.

After his great-aunt Sadie died of the influenza, Marven's mother and father decided to send him away from the city to keep him safe. Marven heard them talk it over with Uncle Moishe and Aunt Ghisa one night as he sat hidden on the stairs.

"How will he get along in a logging camp? A boy of ten, all by himself?" asked Aunt Ghisa.

"I want him to live to be a man," said Mama quietly. "He must go."

"But Marven's very small for his age," said Uncle Moishe. "He won't even be able to lift a saw." Marven glowered and huddled closer to the wall.

"He's got a head for numbers. He'll keep the books," said Papa. Marven knew that he was good at math in school. But a logging camp? "I've already talked to my friend Mr. Murray at the camp up north," Papa continued. "Marven should go right away."

The next day Marven's mother cut down an old overcoat of Papa's and lined it with scraps of beaver fur. From the scraps of the scraps, she lined Marven's cap and made earflaps.

Marven turned to his mother. "Mama, I don't know how to speak French. You said most of the men who work there are French Canadian, except for Mr. Murray."

"You just say *bonjour.*"

"*Bonjour,*" Marven repeated.

"It means hello," Mama said. "You'll learn the rest. Like your father and I did when we came from Russia."

"Your mother's right," said Papa. "Look, we are living proof. When we came here, not a word of English. Just Russian and Yiddish. Now look at us. We talk English to all our children. I talk English to my boss. We sing in English. We make jokes in English."

Marven hoped his father wouldn't tell the chicken joke. It was a dumb joke.

Two days later, the morning Marven was to leave, Mama made latkes and knishes. While they were piping hot, she wrapped them in newspaper and put two in each of his coat pockets and one inside his cap to keep him warm.

"Don't eat them until they're almost cold," she told him. "Then they'll warm you twice."

At the train station, Papa handed Marven the skis he had made for his son's sixth birthday.

"Papa, I've never skied in the country before," Marven said anxiously.

"You've skied in the city. Up and down every hill in Duluth, and there are many."

"How far do I have to ski?"

"Five miles, remember? It's all flat. You'll go like a shot."

The train pulled out of the station, and the glass grew foggy with Marven's breath as he said soft good-byes through the window. Would his family be all right until he came home in the spring? He wished he could take his sisters to the logging camp to keep them safe from the influenza, too. He saw them all there on the platform — Mama, Papa, his two big sisters, his two little sisters — bundled in their coats, waving. As the train moved away, the little sisters blurred into the big ones; the big sisters blended into Papa and Mama. They were all one bundle waving good-bye to him — Marven, alone on the train, going far, far away to the great north woods.

Marven ate his first latke when the train stopped in Floodwood.  It was almost cold.  An hour passed, and Marven ate another latke, then another. Outside, the land stretched white until it reached the trees.  The dark band of the forest rested on the horizon as the train sped through the white world of the north.

Almost five hours later, in Bemidji, Minnesota, Marven stood alone on the platform as the train rolled away.  Beyond the depot a road ran straight and flat to where the white landscape met the forest.  Marven felt small, very small, and the road looked like it went on forever.  He thought of the big waving bundle on the train platform back in Duluth.  What were they doing now — his sisters, his mother, his father?

It was too cold to stand still.  So Marven ate the knish in his cap, slapped his cap back on his head, strapped on his skis, and started for the shadowy thread on the horizon.  His father had told him that five miles down the road, Mr. Murray, a very big man with a handsome waxed mustache, would be waiting for him.

The way was flat and the snow was well packed. Marven thought that if he kept up a good pace, he would reach the camp just after sunset. The thin thread of the forest thickened to a dark ribbon.

Soon he could smell the sharp green fragrance of freshly cut timber, and soon after that he spotted a speck in the distance. The speck grew into a smudge; before long the smudge wore a muffler and a fur hat. Between the top of the muffler and the bottom of the hat, a huge mustache bristled with frost.

"Come along, boy." Mr. Murray turned his snowshoes toward the camp at the edge of the forest. "I'm like to freeze my *derrière* off. That's French for 'bottom.'"

*So,* Marven thought, *now I know two words in French. I can say, "Hello, bottom."*

As they entered the camp, the longest shadows Marven had ever seen stretched across the snow, and he realized with a start that the shadows were the lumberjacks walking in the moonlight. He could smell hay and manure and saw the silhouettes of horses stomping in a snowy corral. From a nearby log building he heard the lively squeaks of a fiddle. It seemed for a moment as if the horses were keeping time to the music. Mr. Murray must have thought the same. "You want to watch the horses dance, or the jacks?" He laughed. "Come along, we'll take a look."

When they entered the building, the long shadows from the yard suddenly sprung to life. Marven stared. Immense men with long beards and wild hair were jumping around to the fiddler's tunes like a pack of frantic grizzly bears. They were the biggest and wildest men Marven had ever seen.

Marven could have watched the dancing all night, but Mr. Murray said, "Come on, Marven. We start early in the morning. I'll show you where you'll be living."

Mr. Murray took Marven to the small office where he would work and sleep. In Duluth, Marven had to share a bedroom with his two younger sisters and all of their dolls and toys, but this room was his — all his — and he liked it. A bed with a bearskin on it sat across from a woodstove; nearby, wood was stacked neatly. The big desk had cubbyholes for papers, envelopes, glue pots, and blotter strips. And on the desk there were blocks of paper and a big black ledger. There were pencils in a blue glass jar, as well as an inkwell. Marven hoped that somewhere there was a very good pen — a fountain pen.

"In addition to keeping the payroll," Mr. Murray said, "you have another job. The first bell in the morning is at four o'clock; second bell at four-fifteen. Third bell is at four-twenty. By four-twenty-five, if any jack is still in the sack, he's *en retard,* 'late.' So you, son, are the fourth bell. Starting tomorrow, you go into the bunkhouse and wake *les en retards.*"

"How?"

"You tap them on the shoulder, give 'em a shake, scream in their ear if you have to."

Then Mr. Murray said good night, and Marven was alone again.

It seemed to Marven he had just crawled under the bearskin when he heard the first bell. The fire was out and the room was cold and dark. He lit the kerosene lamp and pulled on his double-thick long underwear, two pairs of socks, two pairs of knickers, and two sweaters. Then he put on his cut-down overcoat.

After the second bell, Marven heard the jacks heading toward the eating hall. It was nearly time for his first job.

He ran through the cold morning darkness to the bunkhouse, peeked in, and counted five huge lumps in the shadows. Five jacks in the sacks. Marven waited just inside the door.

At the third bell, Marven was relieved to see two jacks climb out of bed. He thought there must be a *broche,* a Hebrew blessing, for something like this. His father knew all sorts of *broches* — blessings for seeing the sunrise, blessings for the first blossom of spring. Was there a *broche* for a rising lumberjack? If he said a *broche,* maybe the other three would get up on their own.

One lump stirred, then another. They grunted, rolled, and climbed out from under the covers. Their huge shadows slid across the ceiling.

One jack was still in the sack. Marven took a deep breath, walked bravely over to the bed, reached out, and tapped the jack's shoulder. It was like poking a granite boulder. The jack's beard ran right into his long, shaggy hair; Marven couldn't even find an ear to shout into. He cupped his hands around his mouth and leaned forward.

"Up!"

The jack grunted and muttered something in French.

"Get up," Marven pleaded.

Another jack pulled on his boots, boomed, "*Lève-toi!* Jean Louis [JHUH loo-EE]. *Lève-toi,*" and shuffled out the door.

427

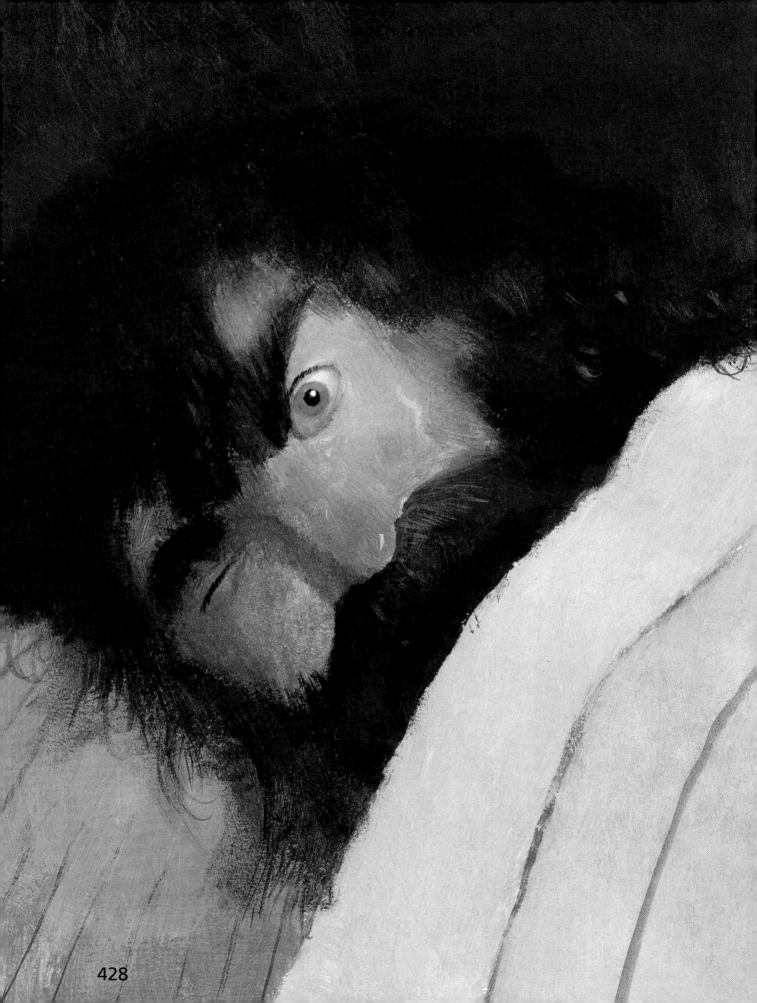

"*Lève-toi!* Jean Louis. *Lève-toi,*" Marven repeated.

Jean Louis opened one eye. It glittered like a blue star beneath his thick black eyebrow. He squinted, as if trying to make out the shape in front of him, then blinked and sat up.

"*Bonjour,*" Marven whispered.

"*Qui es tu? Quel est ton nom?*"

"I don't speak French — just *bonjour, derrière,* and *lève-toi.*"

"That's all? No more?" The man opened his eyes wide now. "So what is your name?"

"Marven."

"Ah . . . Marven," Jean Louis repeated, as if tasting the sound of his name.

"Will you get up?" Marven asked anxiously.

Jean Louis growled and fixed him in the hard blue squint of one eye.

"Please." Marven stood straight and tried not to tremble.

Jean Louis grunted and swung his feet from beneath the covers. They were as big as skillets, and one of his huge toenails was bruised black and blue. Marven tried not to stare.

Marven and Jean Louis were the last to arrive at the breakfast table. The only sounds were those of chewing and the clink of forks and knives against the plates. At each place were three stacks of flapjacks, one big steak, eight strips of bacon, and a bowl of oatmeal. In the middle of the table were bowls of potatoes and beans with molasses, platters with pies and cakes, and blue jugs filled with tea, coffee, and milk.

Marven stared at the food in dismay. *It's not kosher,* he thought. In Marven's house it was against ancient Jewish law to eat dairy products and meat together. And never, ever, did a Jew eat bacon. Marven came to a quick decision. One day he would eat the flapjacks and oatmeal with milk. The next day he would eat the steak and the oatmeal without milk. And never the bacon.

After breakfast, as they did every morning, the jacks went to the toolhouse to get their saws and axes. Then, wearing snowshoes and pulling huge sleds piled with equipment, they made their way into the great woods, where they would work all day.

Marven went directly to his office after breakfast. Mr. Murray was already there, setting out Marven's work. A fresh pot of ink was thawing in a bowl of hot water on the woodstove. There were two boxes on the desk filled with scraps of paper.

"Cord chits," Mr. Murray said. "The jacks are paid according to the number of cords they cut in a pay period — two weeks. You figure it out. I'm no good as a bookkeeper and have enough other things to do around here. Each chit should have the jack's name — or, if he can't write, his symbol."

"His symbol?" Marven asked weakly.

"Yes. Jean Louis's is a thumbprint. Here's one!" He held up a small piece of paper with a thumbprint on it the size of a baby's fist. Marven blinked.

It was all very confusing. Sometimes two names were on one chit. These were called doublees; there were even some triplees. This meant more calculations. And sometimes chits were in the wrong pay-period box.

Marven sat staring at the scraps. "There is no system!" he muttered. Where to begin? His mother always made a list when she had many things to do. So first Marven listed the jacks' names alphabetically and noted the proper symbol for those who could not write. Then he listed the dates of a single pay period, coded each chit with the dates, and, with a ruler, made a chart. By the end of the morning, Marven had a system and knew the name or symbol for each man. There were many chits with the huge thumbprint of Jean Louis.

Every day Marven worked until midday, when he went into the cookhouse and ate baked beans and two kinds of pie with Mr. Murray and the cook. After lunch he returned to his office and worked until the jacks returned from the forest for supper.

By Friday of the second week, Marven had learned his job so well that he finished early. He had not been on his skis since he had arrived at camp. Every day the routine was simply meals and work, and Marven kept to his office and away from the lumberjacks as much as he could. But today he wanted to explore, so he put on his skis and followed the sled paths into the woods.

He glided forward, his skis making soft whisking sounds in the snow. This certainly was different from city skiing in Duluth, where he would dodge the ragman's cart or the milkman's wagon, where the sky was notched with chimney pots belching smoke, where the snow turned sooty as soon as it fell.

Here in the great north woods all was still and white. Beads of ice glistened on bare branches like jewels. The frosted needles of pine and spruce pricked the eggshell sky, and a ghostly moon began to climb over the treetops.

Marven came upon a frozen lake covered with snow, which lay in a circle of tall trees like a bowl of sugar. He skimmed out across it on his skis, his cheeks stinging in the cold air, and stopped in the middle to listen to the quietness.

And then Marven heard a deep, low growl. At the edge of the lake a shower of snow fell from a pine. A grizzly bear? Marven gripped his ski poles. A grizzly awake in the winter! What would he do if a bear came after him? Where could he hide? Could he out-ski a grizzly?

Marven began to tremble, but he knew that he must remain still, very still. Maybe, Marven thought desperately, the grizzly would think he was a small tree growing in the middle of the lake. He tried very hard to look like a tree. But concentrating on being a tree was difficult because Marven kept thinking of the bundle on the train platform — his mother, his father, his two big sisters, his two little sisters. He belonged in Duluth with them, not in the middle of the great north woods with a grizzly. The hot tears streaming down his cheeks turned cold, then froze.

When another tree showered snow, Marven, startled, shot out across the lake. As he reached the shore, a huge shadow slid from behind the trees. The breath froze in Marven's throat.

In the thick purple shadows, he saw a blue twinkle.

"Aaah! Marven!" Jean Louis held a glistening ax in one hand. He looked taller than ever. "I mark the tree for cutting next season." He stepped closer to the trunk and swung the ax hard. Snow showered at Marven's feet.

434

"Ah, *mon petit,* you cry!" Jean Louis took off his glove and rubbed his huge thumb down Marven's cheek. "You miss your mama? Your papa?" Marven nodded silently.

"Jean Louis," he whispered. The huge lumberjack bent closer. "I thought you were a grizzly bear!"

"You what!" Jean Louis gasped. "You think I was a grizzly!" And Jean Louis began to laugh, and as he roared, more snow fell from the tree, for his laugh was as powerful as his ax.

As they made their way back to the sled paths, Marven heard a French song drifting through the woods. The other jacks came down the path, their saws and axes slung across their shoulders, and Marven and Jean Louis joined them. Evening shadows fell through the trees, and as Marven skied alongside the huge men, he hummed the tune they were singing.

One day followed the next. Every morning, in that time when the night had worn thin but the day had not yet dawned, Marven shouted, "Up! *Lève toi! Lève-toi!*" to Jean Louis. Together they would go to the dining hall, where one day Marven would eat steak and oatmeal without milk; the next day he would eat oatmeal with milk and flapjacks but no steak. Jean Louis always ate the bacon and anything else Marven left.

And every afternoon after that, Marven would finish his work well before sunset and ski into the woods. Although the worry that his family might catch the terrible sickness nagged at him constantly, when he was in the woods his fears grew dim in the silence and shadows of the winter forest. And every day he would fall in beside Jean Louis as the jacks returned to camp, and he would hum the French songs that Jean Louis told him were about a beautiful woman in the far, far north, or a lonely bear in its den, or a lovely maiden named Go With Clouds.

437

At night, after supper was done, Marven learned the lumberjacks' songs and how to play their games — the ones he could manage, like ax throwing. A jack would heave an ax from thirty paces at the tail end of a log; for Marven they moved the mark up to ten feet. The jacks challenged each other to barrel lifting and bucksaw contests, but Marven was too small for those.

He was not, however, too small to dance. Sometimes he danced on the floor, and sometimes Jean Louis lifted him and Marven did a little two-step right there in his stocking feet on the shoulders of the big lumberjack.

In April, four months after Marven had arrived at the camp, the snow began to melt. Mr. Murray said to Marven, "I promised your parents I'd send you back while there was still enough snow for you to ski on. Every day it grows warmer. You better go before you have to swim out of here. I'll send your parents a letter to say you're coming home. But I don't know what I'll do for a bookkeeper."

So it was planned that Marven would leave on the last day of the month. When the day came, he went to the bunkhouse to find Jean Louis.

"Ah, Marven." Jean Louis tasted Marven's name as he had the first time he had ever said it, as if it were the most delicious French pastry in the world. "I have something for you, *mon petit.*" He got up and opened the chest at the end of his bed.

"You are a woodsman now," he said, and handed Marven a brand-new ax. The head was sharp and glinting; the handle glistened like dark honey.

"*Merci,* Jean Louis. *Merci beaucoup,*" Marven whispered.

Jean Louis went with Marven all the way to the train station. When the snow ran out on the banks of a muddy creek near the depot, he turned to Marven, grinned widely, and said, "Up, up. *Lève-toi,* Marven." The giant of a man swung the small boy onto his shoulders, skis and all, and carried him across to the opposite bank.

As the train pulled away, Marven waved at Jean Louis through the window, which had become foggy with his breath. "*Au revoir,*" he murmured. "*Au revoir,* Jean Louis."

Marven sat alone on the train and thought of his family. Who would be waiting for him at the station? He felt the edges of his new ax. It was so sharp, so bright. But it was good only for cutting wood. What could it do against the terrible flu that had sent him away?

With each mile the land slid out from under its snowy cover. When the train finally pulled into the station in Duluth, Marven pressed his face against the window, the glass fogging as he searched the crowd on the platform.

When Marven stepped down from the train he was still searching. Everyone looked pale and winter worn, and not a single face was familiar. Then suddenly he was being smothered with kisses and hugs. His little sisters were grabbing him around his waist, his big sisters were kissing his ears, and then all of them tumbled into Mama's and Papa's arms, and they were one big hugging bundle.

"You're not dead!" Marven said. His sisters, Mama, Papa, Aunt Ghisa, and Uncle Moishe crowded around him in a tight circle. He turned slowly to look at each face.

"Nobody's dead," Marven repeated softly.

"The sickness is over," said Mama. "And you are finally home!"

441

# A NOTE FROM THE AUTHOR

Marven Lasky was born in 1907 in Duluth, Minnesota. He was the first child born in America to Ida and Joseph Lasky, who had emigrated from Tsarist Russia to escape the persecution of Jews. The story of their escape in 1900 was told in my novel *The Night Journey*.

In 1918 an influenza epidemic swept through the United States. The disease was the worst in the cities, among large populations. Old people and young children were the most vulnerable. Ida and Joseph believed that they might save at least one of their children if they could arrange for that child to

go far from the city. Marven was not chosen because he was loved most; Joseph and Ida loved all of their children. Girls in that era, however, were never permitted to travel far from home by themselves — and the last place a girl would ever be sent was to a logging camp. Marven, therefore, was sent by himself on a train to a logging camp in the great north woods of Minnesota.

Marven Lasky, my father, is now more than ninety years old. The last time he skied was at age eighty-three in Aspen, Colorado. He still has a good head for figures.

Marven of the
Great North Woods

written by *Kathryn Lasky*   illustrated by *Kevin Hawkes*

# Responding

## Think About the Selection

1. What does Marven think of Jean Louis at first? How and why does his opinion change?

2. Why is Marven so good at adjusting to life in the logging camp? Give examples of how he solves some problems there.

3. How do you think Marven's experience in the great north woods might have changed him?

4. What do you think Marven will miss about the logging camp when he returns home?

5. If you had to spend the winter at a logging camp, what would you be worried about? What would you look forward to?

6. **Connecting/Comparing** Both María Isabel and Marven have problems getting used to a new place. Compare their experiences.

**Expressing**

## Write a Letter

Think about what happens when Marven returns home from the great north woods. Write a letter from Marven to his new friend Jean Louis. Marven could tell how he feels about his time in the logging camp or explain the good news he received when he got home.

- Before you write, list details from the story that you could include in the letter.
- Use commas after your greeting and closing.

## Social Studies

# Estimate Latitude and Longitude

Using a map of Minnesota, locate the places at the beginning and end of Marven's train trip. Then find the longitude and latitude of each city. On tracing paper, draw the outline of Minnesota and trace the route Marven might have taken. Label the longitude and latitude for the beginning and ending points of his journey.

**Bonus** Use the scale of miles on the map to estimate the distance Marven travels.

## Listening and Speaking

# Have a Discussion

Marven makes the best of a tough situation by adjusting to life at the logging camp. In a small group, discuss some of the problems Marven faces there and how he overcomes them. Talk about what makes him such a good problem solver and other ways he might have solved his problems. Would you have done the same things in his situation?

*Internet*

# Complete a Web Crossword Puzzle

What is a nine-letter word for the place where a logger sleeps? Test what you've learned from *Marven of the Great North Woods* by cracking the crossword puzzle on Education Place.

**www.eduplace.com/kids**

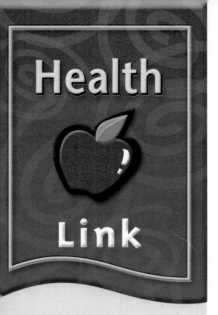

**Skill: How to Take Notes**

❶ To begin, write the **title** of the article at the top of a piece of paper.

❷ As you read, look for **main ideas** and supporting details.

❸ Write a **heading** for each main idea.

❹ List important **details** below each heading.

# Snow Runners

*Text by William G. Scheller • Photographs by Scott S. Warren*

Make tracks to snowshoeing, hot sport for cold weather.

**Kicking up powder** with their snowshoes, Metzi Anderson, 13, on the left, and her sister, Robyn, 11, make tracks across a snowy meadow near their home in Stowe, Vermont.
▼

When winter blows into Stowe, Vermont, snowdrifts can bury the world outside the front door. That's when Metzi Anderson, 13, and her sister Robyn, 11, head outside and buckle up their snowshoes.

They get around just fine instead of sinking deep into the white stuff. The snowshoes spread their weight over a wide area so they "float" on top of the drifts.

Snowshoeing has been around a while. As early as 6,000 years ago, people in Asia strapped big, basket-like "shoes" onto their feet to make travel over snow possible. Native Americans wore snowshoes while hunting and trapping. Early European explorers and settlers in North America also used snowshoes. They would never have been able to travel far from home during winter if they hadn't learned about snowshoeing from the Native Americans.

Today snowshoeing is making a big comeback — as a sport. Some snowshoers prefer the latest designs made with lightweight aluminum frames and synthetic lacings (bottom right). Others prefer traditional snow-shoes made with wood and leather strips (top right). Either way, the sport's biggest advantage may be that it's so easy. As Robyn discovered on her first attempt, "to snow-shoe, all you have to know is how to walk."

447

If you'd like to scoot across the snow, this is the sport for you!

Look! My snowshoes keep me on top of the snow.

Metzi and Robyn snowshoe through some of the prettiest countryside in Vermont. They've learned to put safety first, always. "I went snowshoeing with a friend in another part of town," Metzi explains. "We were in the woods when it started snowing and getting dark. We were lost for quite a while." Her advice? "Always snow-shoe with a partner." And tell an adult where you're going. Don't overdress, Robyn adds. "Snowshoeing is great exercise," she says, "and it really warms you up!" What else would you expect from the hottest sport around?

# The Race Is On

On your mark, get set . . . snow! After you get used to walking on snowshoes, the next step is to run. The town of Stowe, Vermont, holds a Winter Carnival every January. A two-kilometer snowshoe race is part of the fun. Last year Metzi Anderson, on the right, wearing a yellow parka, came in third overall — and first among the girls. To avoid tripping when running, she says, don't bury the front of your shoes in the snow. And try not to step on the snowshoe of the runner in front of you.

"Hare Jordan."

The widespread toes of a snowshoe hare's large hind feet work like a snowshoe. They distribute weight and keep the animal from sinking into the snow — even when the hare lands after leaping 12 feet.

# Background and Vocabulary

**The Last Dragon**

The
Last Dragon
By Susan Miho Nunes
Illustrated by Chris K. Soentpiet

**Read to find the meanings of these words.**

*e* • Glossary

characters

crest

fierce

homage

scales

teeming

# A Visit to Chinatown

In many big cities across the United States, neighborhoods called Chinatown keep the customs of China alive. People who live in Chinatown celebrate many traditional holidays. One of the most important holidays is the Chinese New Year.

The New Year's celebration lasts for two weeks. People go to family reunions and eat traditional foods. On the last day of the celebration, the Lantern Festival, the whole neighborhood gathers for a parade.

The star of the New Year's parade is the dragon. It's not a real dragon, but a costume carried by people. The dragon costume can be just a few feet long or hundreds of feet long. The entire neighborhood gives **homage** to the dragon. Through the

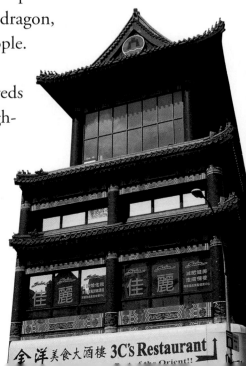

This New York City building is designed to look like buildings in China.

Signs in Chinatown are in Chinese **characters** as well as in English.

**teeming** streets, dancers make the dragon come alive. The **crest** on its head rises above the crowd, and the **scales** on its back shine brightly. The dragon looks **fierce** enough to breathe fire! But as you'll read in *The Last Dragon*, this dragon has many friends.

This dragon dances through Los Angeles streets.

## MEET THE AUTHOR
# Susan Miho Nunes

Susan Miho Nunes got the idea for *The Last Dragon* from real life. Nunes was walking one day when she saw an enormous dragon's head in a bank's window. A sign said it was the largest dragon in the world! "In time," says Nunes, "'Largest Dragon' became 'Last Dragon.'"

Nunes was born in Hawaii and has traveled to Hong Kong, Russia, and China. When she's not writing, she likes reading, jogging, and cooking for her friends.

## MEET THE ILLUSTRATOR
# Chris K. Soentpiet

Chris Soentpiet is used to living in different places. He was born in Korea but moved to Hawaii when he and his sister were adopted by an American family. He has also lived in Oregon and Alaska. Today, Soentpiet lives in Brooklyn, New York, where he's currently working on a picture book about his adoption.

Soentpiet enjoys bike riding, weightlifting, and sightseeing in New York — especially in Chinatown!

To find out more about Susan Miho Nunes and Chris Soentpiet, visit Education Place.

**www.eduplace.com/kids**

452

# The Last Dragon

By Susan Miho Nunes

Illustrated by Chris K. Soentpiet

## Strategy Focus

Peter finds a new challenge when he discovers a dusty dragon costume. As you read, stop and **summarize** the steps he uses to solve his problem.

454

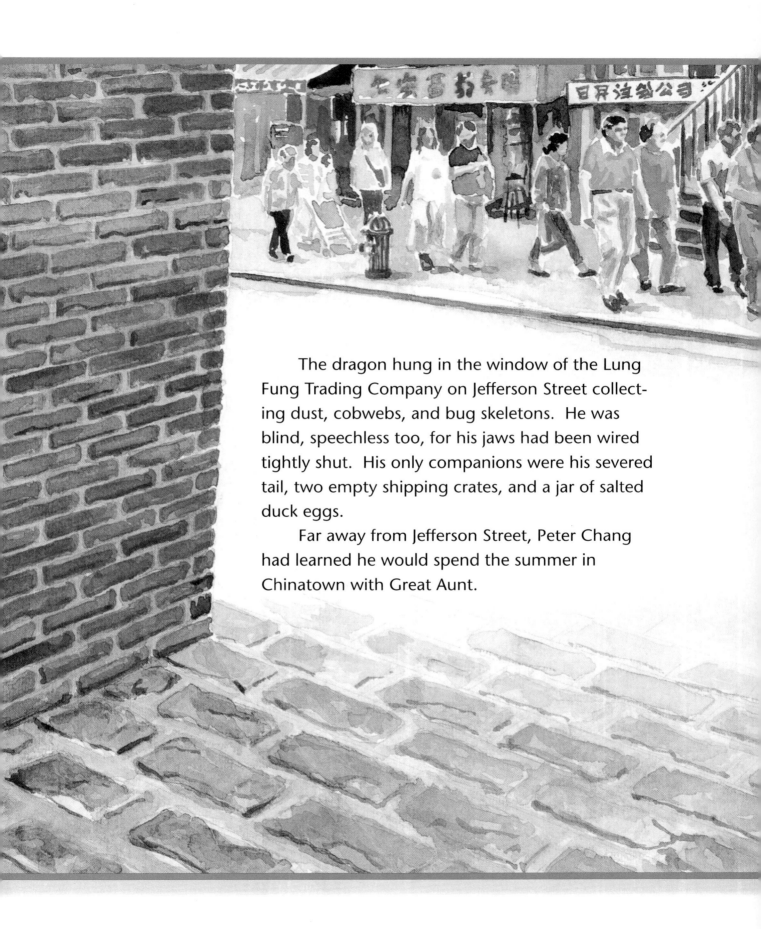

The dragon hung in the window of the Lung Fung Trading Company on Jefferson Street collecting dust, cobwebs, and bug skeletons. He was blind, speechless too, for his jaws had been wired tightly shut. His only companions were his severed tail, two empty shipping crates, and a jar of salted duck eggs.

Far away from Jefferson Street, Peter Chang had learned he would spend the summer in Chinatown with Great Aunt.

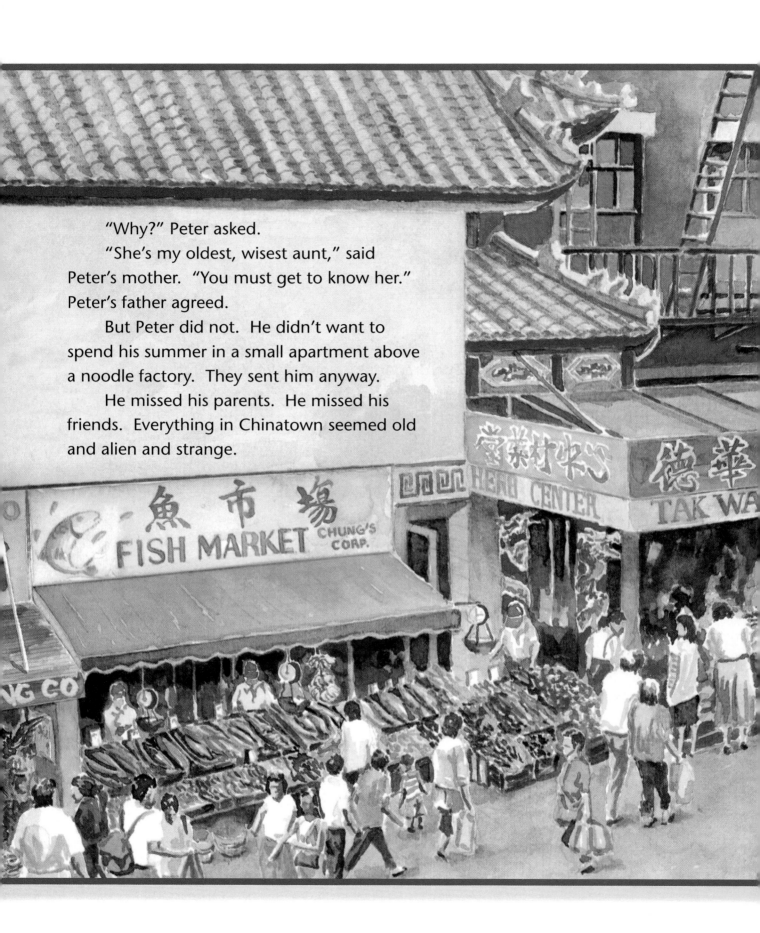

"Why?" Peter asked.

"She's my oldest, wisest aunt," said Peter's mother.  "You must get to know her." Peter's father agreed.

But Peter did not.  He didn't want to spend his summer in a small apartment above a noodle factory.  They sent him anyway.

He missed his parents.  He missed his friends.  Everything in Chinatown seemed old and alien and strange.

457

Until he saw the dragon.

Something about it made Peter forget his sack of squirming black crabs. Before Great Aunt could protest, he walked through the doorway.

"Yes?" said an old man behind a desk.

"Is that dragon for sale?" Peter demanded.

"You forgot your manners," Great Aunt scolded. She spoke to the old man in Chinese.

The man lifted the dragon's head off its hook. He shook it, raising great clouds of dust and raining bug skeletons all over the floor.

"Hoo!" said Great Aunt.

"Our last dragon," said the man.

"The Last Dragon?" asked Peter.

The man nodded. "The others we sold long ago."

"Bad luck to keep a dragon that way," said Great Aunt, brushing dust from her sleeve.

"He's very old," said the man. "You sure you want him?"

Peter stroked the dragon's tangled whiskers. "Yes," he said.

"A very sad dragon, if you ask me," sniffed Great Aunt.

"Please, Most Favored Aunt," said Peter. "I'll clean him myself."

Great Aunt looked doubtful but finally agreed.

Peter carried the dragon's head down Jefferson Street. Great Aunt followed with the rest of him, and the groceries, too. She grumbled about how the dragons of her childhood were royal in appearance and received the homage of every living thing. This was no such creature.

Back in Great Aunt's kitchen, Peter put the dragon's head on the hat rack. The Last Dragon had a faded face, a scraggly crest, and no eyes. No eyes at all.

Great Aunt laid the tail on the floor and unfolded the body. "A ten-man dragon," she said. "Full of holes. Tail in bad shape."

Peter found something shiny on the dragon's forehead. "Looks like a pearl," he said.

"All dragons have pearls, don't you know?" said Great Aunt. "People say the pearl gives the dragon power, but I don't know how, exactly."

Peter untwisted the wires that held the jaws together. The dragon's mouth fell open with a loud *whump*.

"Hoo!" said Great Aunt.

"No teeth," said Peter.

Great Aunt swept up the bug skeletons and complained, "A very sorry dragon, if you ask me."

They ate their crab dinner with the dragon gaping crookedly at them from the hat rack.

The next morning, the dragon's mouth did not gape crookedly. His whiskers were combed and the pearl polished until it shone.

Great Aunt shrugged. "Humph. Couldn't have his mouth hanging open like a fool."

"What about his body?" Peter wondered.

"Today I play mahjongg with my friends," said Great Aunt. "Perhaps you should visit the tailor, Mr. Pang." She explained where to find him. "And don't forget your manners," she said as Peter ran out the door.

461

Mr. Pang peered over his newspaper. "What did you bring?" he asked suspiciously.

Peter unfolded the dragon's body. It stretched from the worktable to the front door.

"My goodness!" said Mr. Pang. "Where's the head?"

"In Great Aunt's kitchen," said Peter.

Mr. Pang ran his hand over the dragon's body. "Look at these holes! A big job."

Peter explained about the Lung Fung Trading Company, the bug skeletons, the broken jaw, and the pearl.

"Enough! Enough!" said Mr. Pang. He rubbed the dragon's body between his fingers. "Hmmm. Good silk. Feels warm."

"There's something about him," Peter said.

Mr. Pang laid the dragon's body over his worktable and handed Peter a package. "Deliver this to the computer store on River Street," he said, "and every morning you check with me. Agreed?"

Then he disappeared behind his newspaper.

Every morning Peter checked with Mr. Pang. Sometimes Mr. Pang had a small errand, sometimes not. When Peter asked about the dragon's body, Mr. Pang said, "Don't be impatient. This is a big job."

One mahjongg day Peter found Great Aunt and her friends huddled over the kitchen table. But they were not playing mahjongg.

"This sorry creature has robbed us of our afternoon," said Great Aunt.

Peter pulled a strip of silver paper out of Great Aunt's hair. "What's this?" he asked.

"Surprise!" said Mrs. Li, who lived downstairs. She held up the dragon's new crest. Everyone admired the fine horns.

Then Miss Tam, who made the best dumplings in the neighborhood, pointed a chubby finger at the dragon's tail. "What about *that*?"

Great Aunt bit into a dumpling. "A big problem," she agreed.

464

"Perhaps not too big," said Mrs. Lo, who taught English at the community center. "Once, when I was a girl, I saw a kite just like that. If someone could make such a kite, then someone could fix a dragon's tail."

Peter carried the dragon's tail through the busy streets of Chinatown. People stared and shook their heads. Two doors past the Imperial Travel Company, he found the Big Wind Kite Shop, just as Mrs. Lo described.

"Did you run into a tree?" exclaimed the owner, Miss Rose Chiao.

"It's a dragon's tail," Peter said with a smile.

Miss Rose Chiao set her pliers aside and examined the tail. "Needs a new frame," she said.

"Can you fix it?" Peter asked.

Miss Rose Chiao kept studying the tail. "Maybe," she said.

Peter explained about the Lung Fung Trading Company, the bug skeletons, the mended jaw, the body at Mr. Pang's, the dragon's new crest, and Mrs. Lo's memory of kites in China.

"There's something about this dragon, don't you think?" he asked.

"Indeed," said Miss Rose Chiao.

"I can't pay you," said Peter.

"No problem," said Miss Rose Chiao, "but I could use a hand once or twice a week."

Every day Peter did something new. He learned the streets of Great Aunt's neighborhood. He knew where to find a bookstore, a bargain bakery, a stall with the best salted plums. Some days he joined Mr. Pang for morning tea. He swept the kite shop, oiled the tools. He learned to fly a fighting kite, which entertained Great Aunt's mahjongg friends.

All the while, Miss Rose Chiao repaired the frame, covered it with silk. One day she began to sew on shining scales.

"Got any ideas for the eyes?" Peter asked.

Miss Rose Chiao thought for a moment. "Check out the medicine shop on the corner," she said.

Peter found the sign that said TAK WAH TONG HERB CENTER, DR. WAI SING FONG. Inside, Dr. Fong weighed herbal tea on a set of ancient scales. "What can I do for you, young gentleman?" he asked.

"Do you sell dragon eyes?" asked Peter.

"*Dragon* eyes?" asked Dr. Fong.

Peter explained about the Lung Fung Trading Company, the bug skeletons, the mended jaw, the body and new crest, about Miss Rose Chiao and the dragon's tail.

"He's the Last Dragon," Peter concluded, "and he's blind."

Dr. Fong sucked thoughtfully on his moustache and said, "The Last Dragon. How very sad. I have many hundreds of herbs. Herbs to sleep, herbs to wake up, herbs to settle stomachs or burn out fevers. I have snake scales, lizard skin, and dried sea horses. But, unfortunately, no dragon eyes."

Dr. Fong folded the package of tea and tied it with string. He said, "Dragon eyes are very special. Any old eyes will not do. They must be blessed by a priest, or the dragon will never see."

Peter walked back to Great Aunt's apartment. Around him swirled the sights, sounds, and smells of Chinatown. A man stood on the sidewalk and painted a new sign on a restaurant window. Peter stopped to watch. The red characters looked strong and fierce. They reminded him that the Last Dragon still looked pale and unhealthy. Dragons should be strong and fierce, too. "I need an artist," thought Peter. While the sign painter was cleaning his brush, Peter told him what he wanted.

After painting for several afternoons, Mr. Sung was finally satisfied. The dragon now had bold eyebrows, red cheeks, and lots of sharp teeth.

"Want them sharper?" Mr. Sung asked.

"They are sharp enough now," grumbled Great Aunt. "Why, he looks fierce enough to cause a typhoon."

"What about his eyes?" asked Peter. He had almost forgotten them in the excitement of watching the artist.

Mr. Sung shook his head.

Great Aunt sighed. "Dragon eyes cannot be painted by a mere artist."

"What shall we do?" asked Peter. The summer was almost over.

"Wait and see," said Great Aunt.

The day came when Miss Rose Chiao stitched on the last scale and knotted the thread. The tail glistened in the light of the shop.

"Thank you, Miss Rose Chiao," said Peter. He had waited for this day. Now he felt a little sad.

"I'll miss you," said Miss Rose Chiao. "Will you be back next summer?"

"Indeed," said Peter.

469

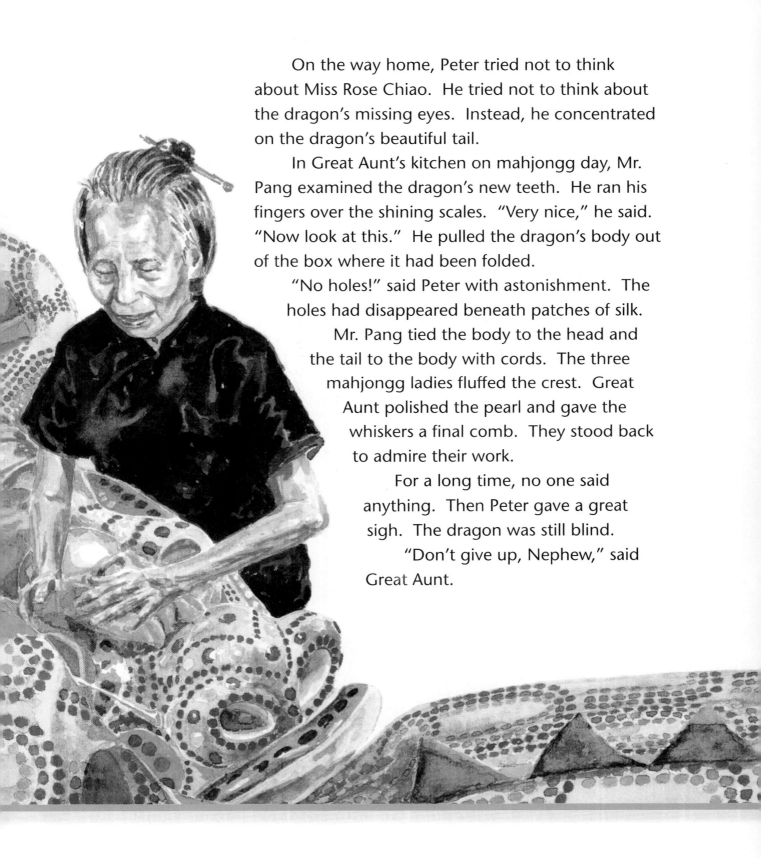

On the way home, Peter tried not to think about Miss Rose Chiao. He tried not to think about the dragon's missing eyes. Instead, he concentrated on the dragon's beautiful tail.

In Great Aunt's kitchen on mahjongg day, Mr. Pang examined the dragon's new teeth. He ran his fingers over the shining scales. "Very nice," he said. "Now look at this." He pulled the dragon's body out of the box where it had been folded.

"No holes!" said Peter with astonishment. The holes had disappeared beneath patches of silk.

Mr. Pang tied the body to the head and the tail to the body with cords. The three mahjongg ladies fluffed the crest. Great Aunt polished the pearl and gave the whiskers a final comb. They stood back to admire their work.

For a long time, no one said anything. Then Peter gave a great sigh. The dragon was still blind.

"Don't give up, Nephew," said Great Aunt.

The words were barely out of her mouth when someone knocked at the door.  It was Dr. Fong.

He handed Peter a small wooden box and said, "Something for the young gentleman."

Peter lifted the lid and parted the tissue paper.  Inside were two milky white balls.  Dragon eyes!

"Can he see with these?" he asked.

"Very soon," said Great Aunt, "very soon."

On Peter's last night in Chinatown, Great Aunt hosted a farewell celebration at the Golden Palace Restaurant and invited Peter's new friends.

474

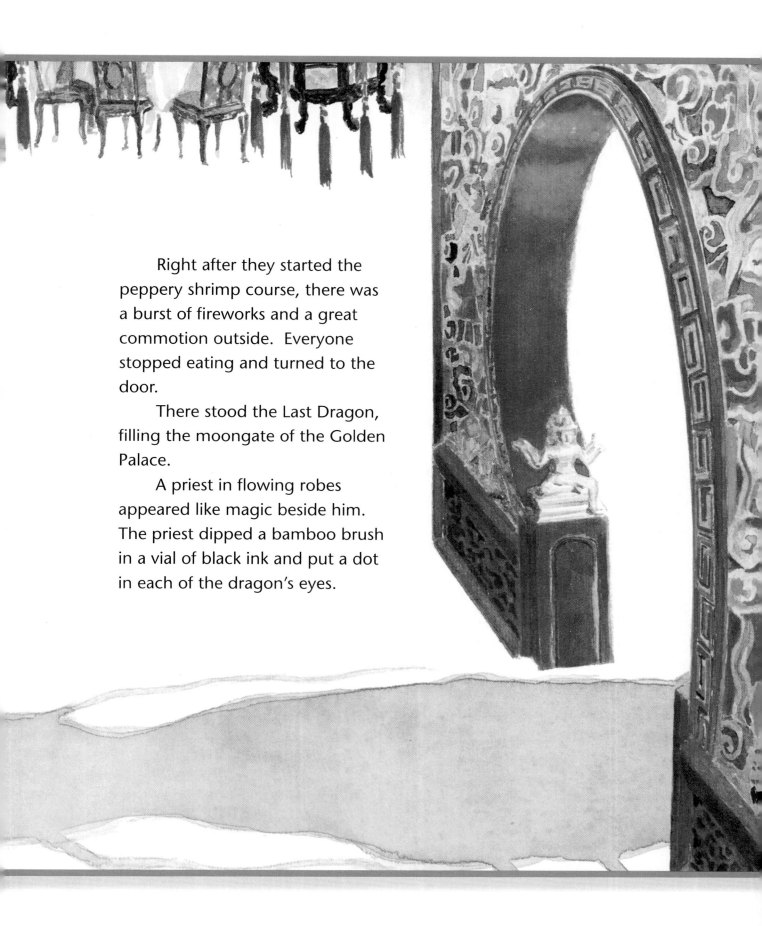

Right after they started the peppery shrimp course, there was a burst of fireworks and a great commotion outside. Everyone stopped eating and turned to the door.

There stood the Last Dragon, filling the moongate of the Golden Palace.

A priest in flowing robes appeared like magic beside him. The priest dipped a bamboo brush in a vial of black ink and put a dot in each of the dragon's eyes.

Everyone stared at the dragon.  The Last Dragon stared back.

"He can see!" cried Peter.

The Last Dragon's eyes raked the room from side to side.  A drum began to beat.

"That's his heart," said Great Aunt.

With a toss of his head and a snap of his jaws, the Last Dragon came through the moongate borne on ten pairs of silken black legs. His crest glistened.  His face glowed with health.  His body rippled from proud head to glittering tail.

First slowly, then with ever-quickening steps, he snaked among the tables and around the room.  His bell-like voice filled the air.

Everyone cheered.

The Last Dragon stopped at Great Aunt's table.  He looked at each person.  When he came to Peter, he bent his head in a deep bow.

"Don't forget your manners," said Great Aunt.

Peter stood up and bowed to the dragon.  Everyone clapped, Peter loudest of all.

Then, to the beat of his great heart, the Last Dragon danced out through the moongate of the Golden Palace.  Diners crowded the door and spilled into the street to watch him depart.

"He is like the dragons of my childhood," said Great Aunt to Peter. But Peter had disappeared.

And so the Last Dragon paraded through the teeming streets of Chinatown.  Indeed, like the dragons of old, he was royal in appearance and received the homage he so richly deserved.

"There's something about that dragon," said Great Aunt to her friends.

Everyone agreed there certainly was.

*The* Last Dragon
By Susan Miho Nunes
Illustrated by Chris K. Soentpiet

## *Think About the Selection*

**1.** What does Peter mean when he says, "There's something about this dragon"?

**2.** Give examples from the story of how Great Aunt helps Peter with his dragon.

**3.** Why are Great Aunt's neighbors willing to help Peter?

**4.** How does Peter change because of his experience fixing the dragon?

**5.** Would this story be different if one person had repaired Peter's entire dragon? Explain.

**6.** **Connecting/Comparing** Compare Peter's experiences away from home with the experiences of another character in this theme.

Persuading

## *Write a Flier*

A flier announces an event. Write a flier announcing a special performance by Peter's dragon. Give the date, time, and place of the performance. Include information about how everyone in the neighborhood helped to fix the dragon.

**Tips**

- Use artwork and a bold headline to get the reader's attention.

- Use phrases like "Don't miss out!" or "Fun for all!"

## Math

### Estimate Length

Peter's dragon is a "ten-man dragon," meaning that it takes ten people to carry it. Estimate the length of the dragon. Suppose one person carries the head, which is five feet long. One person carries the tail, which is four feet long. If each remaining person carries three feet of the dragon's body, figure out the length of the entire dragon.

**Bonus** Using the same measurements, figure out how long a fifteen-man dragon would be.

## Viewing

### Look at Great Aunt's Neighborhood

Great Aunt's neighborhood is full of busy stores and markets. Work with a partner. Go back to the story and choose your favorite illustration of a store in Great Aunt's neighborhood. Then discuss what is interesting about that place.

### Solve a Web Word Scramble

Use what you've learned about the New Year's dragon to solve a word scramble. You'll find one at Education Place.

**www.eduplace.com/kids**

## Skill: How to Follow Directions

1. **Read** through all of the directions carefully.

2. **Study** pictures or diagrams to help you understand what to do.

3. **Gather** the materials you will need.

4. **Follow** the steps in order. If you don't understand a step, go back and **reread**.

5. As you work, keep the directions where you can see them easily.

# Happy New Year!

by Meryl Doney

**Chinese New Year** is celebrated wherever in the world there is a Chinese community. New Year's Day occurs on the second new moon after the midpoint of the winter months, called the winter solstice. The festivities can last for many days. People clean their homes and often re-decorate rooms in preparation. Food has to be cooked beforehand because some Chinese people believe that you should never use a knife on New Year's Day. You might cut your luck in two!

On New Year's Day, everyone is on their best behavior; they believe that any bad manners will continue throughout the year. Gifts are wrapped in red paper, with the words "new happiness for the New Year" written in gold.

The last day of the New Year celebrations is called the Lantern Festival. Lights like the one at right, made from red paper, are hung everywhere. The highlight is the parade when a dragon, symbol of goodness and strength, weaves its way among the crowds. It is made from cane and paper, and may be so long that more than 50 people can dance underneath. Many children follow the dragon, carrying lanterns to light the way. They often hold small dragon toys like the one on page 485.

# Make a Chinese Dragon Toy

## You will need

- three pieces of red construction paper, $13 \times 4\frac{1}{2}$ inches, $6\frac{1}{2} \times 6$ inches, $8\frac{1}{2} \times 3$ inches
- pencil
- scissors
- black felt-tip pen
- gold paint
- strips of red and green construction paper, $1\frac{1}{2}$ inch and $\frac{1}{2}$ inch wide
- sticky tape
- glue
- two corks
- two garden sticks
- tracing paper

**1.** Draw the dragon's head on one side of the 13- × $4\frac{1}{2}$-inch red construction paper. Trace the head a second time onto the other side.

Draw the tail shape onto the $6\frac{1}{2}$- × 6-inch paper.

Draw the inside mouth on the $8\frac{1}{2}$- × 3-inch paper.

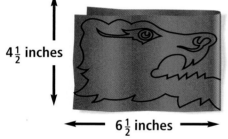

$4\frac{1}{2}$ inches

$6\frac{1}{2}$ inches

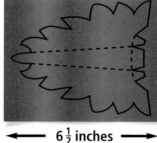

6 inches

$6\frac{1}{2}$ inches

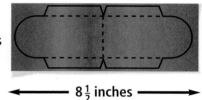

3 inches

$8\frac{1}{2}$ inches

**2.** Cut out and decorate head and tail with black felt-tip pen and gold paint.

**3.** To make body, cut one strip of $1\frac{1}{2}$-inch red construction paper and one of $1\frac{1}{2}$-inch green paper. Tape strips together at one end at right angles.

Fold green strip over red strip, red over green, and so on to form an accordion.

Join more red and green strips with tape, to form long body.

484

**4.** Fold tail along dotted lines. Tuck flaps inside end of body and glue.

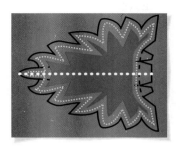 

**5.** Fold inside of mouth in half and fold flaps out. Tape to inside of head. Stick body to the head on the underside of mouth.

**6.** Make tongue from strips of $\frac{1}{2}$-inch construction paper in same way as body. Cut ends to a point and glue inside mouth.

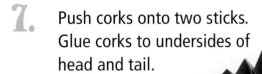

**7.** Push corks onto two sticks. Glue corks to undersides of head and tail.

**Sing to the Stars**

Sing to the Stars

Mary Brigid Barrett
Illustrated by Sandra Speidel

**Read to find the meanings of these words.**

*e* ● Glossary

blaring

classical

debut

jazz

rhythm

stride

# Musicians at WORK

Have you ever heard the old saying "Practice makes perfect"? Well, it's true for musicians! Whether they play **classical** music or **jazz**, musicians must practice every day to sharpen their musical skills.

Long before they make their **debut** in front of an audience, musicians rehearse by themselves or with other musicians. They learn written notes and practice keeping a steady **rhythm**. They also practice how to ignore the many distractions onstage, such as bright lights and sounds from the audience.

After years of hard work, musicians can **stride** onstage and perform with confidence. Good musicians can make the listener feel happy or sad. They can perform through the sound of a car horn **blaring** or a baby crying. Good musicians can perform even if they are nervous or if they have a cold! As you'll see in *Sing to the Stars*, a little practice can even prepare you to perform at unexpected times.

## MEET THE AUTHOR
## Mary Brigid Barrett

Mary Brigid Barrett gets story ideas from the world around her. She keeps lots of notebooks handy — even near her bed and in her car — so that she is always ready to write down new ideas! Barrett advises young writers to "read as much as you can and everything you can — cereal boxes, books, magazines, anything!" When she's not writing, Barrett likes spending time with her family, reading, biking, and going to the movies.

## MEET THE ILLUSTRATOR
## Sandra Speidel

Sandra Speidel has always loved to draw pictures. She started drawing as a young girl, filling the pages of sketch books with her illustrations. Speidel has illustrated more than ten children's books. Her favorite activities include acting and spending time with friends. She lives in California with her daughter.

To learn more about Mary Brigid Barrett and Sandra Speidel, visit Education Place. **www.eduplace.com/kids**

Selection 4

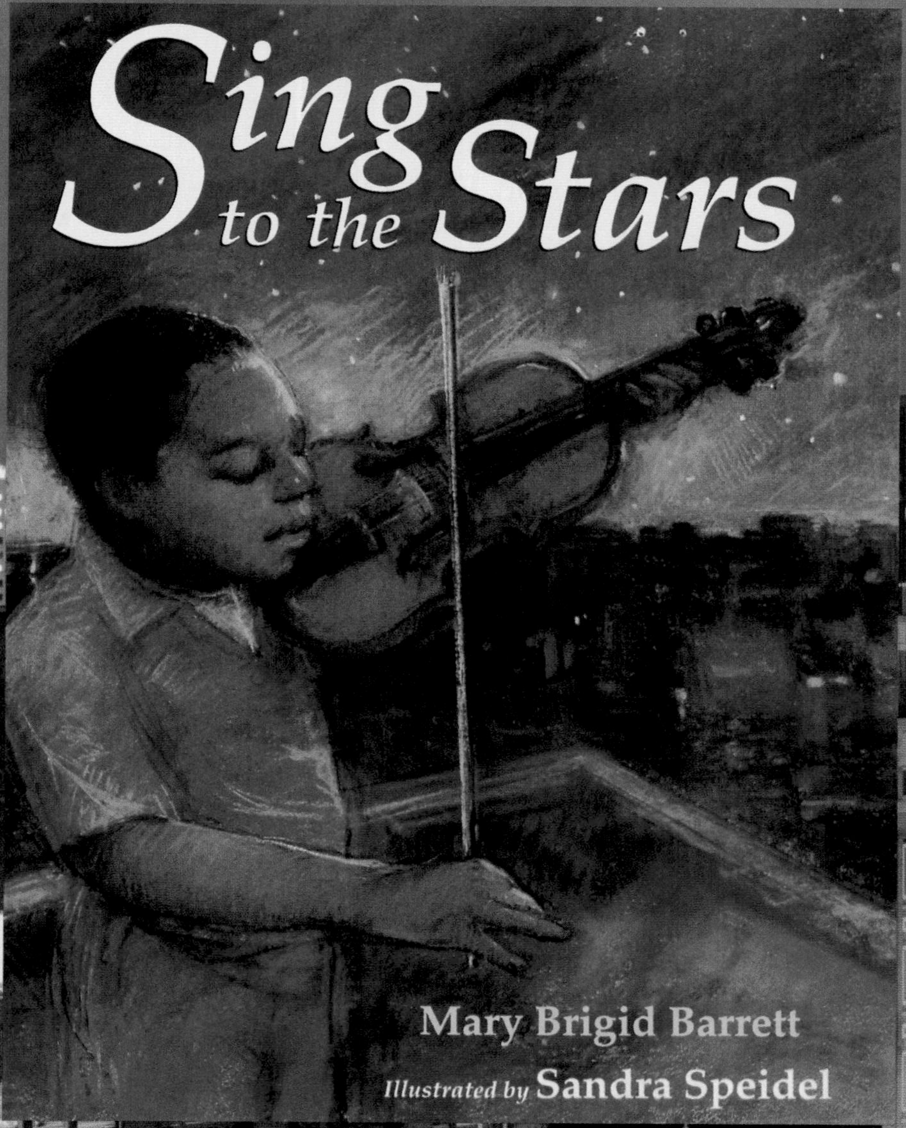
Sing to the Stars
Mary Brigid Barrett
Illustrated by Sandra Speidel

## Strategy Focus

In this selection, a boy uses his love of music to change someone's life. As you read, think of **questions** to ask about the importance of the music they share.

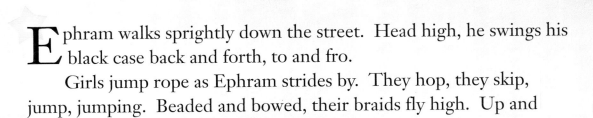

Ephram walks sprightly down the street. Head high, he swings his black case back and forth, to and fro.

Girls jump rope as Ephram strides by. They hop, they skip, jump, jumping. Beaded and bowed, their braids fly high. Up and down, up and down. The rope slaps the sidewalk, *plat, plat, plat*.

It's late afternoon. Mr. Washington steps out of his Laundromat, his dog's harness in one hand, his toolbox in the other. He eases himself into a folding chair. Bending forward, he touches his dog, nose to wet nose. Shiloh licks his chin and cheeks. Chuckling, Mr. Washington wipes his face with a big plaid handkerchief. His hand pat, pat, pats his dog and his foot tap, tap, taps the cracked cement.

"How are you today, Ephram?"

Ephram stops. "Evening to you, Mr. Washington," he says, thumping his case against his leg. "Hello there, Shiloh." He pauses. "Mr. Washington, sir, how do you always know it's me walking by?"

491

"Well, son, every walk's got a rhythm. My ears tell me light step, brush, light step, brush, must be Ephram walking home from his violin lesson, stepping glad and swinging his violin case."

"You can tell I'm happy by the sound of my walk?" asks Ephram.

"Boy, I can tell when your violin teacher has been razzing you and you're full up pitiful with yourself!"

"Really?"

"Oh yes, your shoes clap the cement slow and dull. Your case thuds low against your leg. But that's rare, Ephram. Most times you walk with the song of life in your step. You must make sweet music on that violin. Your grandma says you've got a gift."

"Don't know about that, Mr. Washington," says Ephram. "But I do like to play this violin. It speaks when I haven't got any words. I like to practice after supper, up on the roof."

Mr. Washington smiles broadly. He reaches for Ephram's hand. "Here I thought it was old Mr. Bach, sliding down his 'Jesu, Joy of Man's Desiring' from his heavenly station. And all the time it was you, Ephram, up on that roof."

Ephram pulls his hand away from Mr. Washington. "You heard me on the roof? I thought nobody could hear me out there."

"I keep my apartment windows open in this heat," says Mr. Washington, pointing up toward the windows above the Laundromat. "I heard you playing last night. A breeze swept your music down from the roof, and boy, you play to take my breath away.

"There's a neighborhood concert in the park tomorrow night, a fundraiser for a new playground. It's an open mike. Anyone can play. How 'bout it, Ephram?"

493

Ephram steps back from Mr. Washington. "A stage and all those people, I — I just don't know," he stammers, clutching his violin case tight against his chest. "I've got to go now, Mr. Washington. Grandma will be keeping supper."

"Good-bye, Ephram." Grabbing Shiloh's harness, Mr. Washington stands. "Remember, Ephram," he calls, "music speaks best when some-one listens."

Ephram walks on. Past the rap group on the corner. Past the boom box blaring. Past the glaring neon signs flashing on-off, on-off.

"Hey, man, get yourself an electric guitar!" yells one of the group.

Ephram swings around and fingers his violin case as if he were playing a guitar. Then he slaps the case, spins it, and raises it up onto his shoulder, playing it with an imaginary bow. The rapper flashes him a thumbs-up signal. Smiling, Ephram nods back.

Ephram ducks into his building. Pots and pans clank and clatter through thin walls. Televisions blare. A baby squalls. The air is hot and still in the hallways.

"Grandma, I'm home," says Ephram.

"Hello, Sugar," she says. She wipes the sweat from Ephram's brow and kisses him on top of his head. "Supper's ready. Did you have a fine lesson?"

"Yes. I stopped and talked to Mr. Washington on the way home. I think he knows music, Grandma."

"You bet he knows music, Sugar. Mr. Washington was a professional."

496

"He was?" says Ephram, sitting down to eat.

"Yes, indeed.  Mr. Washington trained as a classical pianist. He was your grandfather's and my neighbor when we were young and living in Harlem.  One sweltering summer night we were all invited upstairs to a rent party in our building.  Mr. James P. Johnson was there, his hands pounding on the piano keys, one hand playing the rhythms of New Orleans, the other making the keys sing the song of New York. Our music pulsated through the air on that sultry night.  From then on Flash Fingers Washington played hot, joyful jazz and cool, soulful blues.  You should have heard him play, Ephram," says Grandma.  "His fingers flew across the keys.  Any piece of music, classical, jazz, old spirituals, he gave it style."

"Grandma, he never told me he could play an instrument.  Does he play anymore?"

"Not since he and his little girl were in a car accident.  That's when Mr. Washington lost his sight."

"His little girl, Grandma, what happened to his little girl?"

Grandma wraps her arms tight around him.  "His little girl died in the accident.  I suppose he just lost all his joy.  He hasn't played since."

Ephram pushes his plate away.  His chair scrapes across the floor as he leaves the table.

"Where are you going?" asks Grandma.  "You haven't finished your supper."

Ephram picks up his violin.  "I need to practice, Grandma."

Up on the roof, the hubbub bustle of cars and people fades to a murmur. In the twilight, Ephram plays his violin, and its sweet song floats out into the wide night.

500

The next morning Ephram dresses quickly and runs to the park, his feet beating the sidewalk fast time. The stage is set for the concert. Microphones and amplifiers are tested one, two, three, four. On the stage floor, Ephram sees a piano.

He pauses, then walks on, steady, determined, straight to Mr. Washington's Laundromat.

"You're up early this morning, Ephram."

"I don't have my violin case today, Mr. Washington. How d'you —"

"How did I know it was you? Well, son," says Mr. Washington, unlocking the coin box on the dryer. "I told you before, you've got the song of life in your step. This morning it sounds like you're as bold as Mr. Louis Armstrong's horn laying down the 'Tiger Rag.'"

"Mr. Washington," says Ephram, "I've been thinking about playing at the benefit concert tonight. It'd be an honor to play with Flash Fingers Washington."

"Your grandma told you?"

"Yes, sir."

"Ephram, it's been years since I've played." Placing his hands on a laundry table, Mr. Washington spreads his fingers wide, lifting each one individually, clasping and unclasping his hands. "I don't even know if these hands can make a piano sing anymore, Ephram. And I'm not sure I want to find out."

Ephram slips his hands into Mr. Washington's. "Just come, Mr. Washington. The concert begins at eight o'clock."

At the benefit concert, neighbors greet each other. Parents tap their feet and children clap hands to the music. Ephram sits next to his grandmother, his violin case on his lap. "Do you think Mr. Washington will come, Grandma?" asks Ephram.

"Yes . . . yes, I do believe he'll come," says Grandma. "Save this seat for him, here at the end, so Shiloh can sit right by him."

Ephram looks at his watch, trying to read its face in a beam from the streetlight. "It's too late, Grandma. I told him eight o'clock and it's already past eight-thirty! He would have been here by now."

The group from the corner is rapping onstage. Their drums fill the air with a pulsating beat. Suddenly, the lights go out. There's a loud thump and a clang from onstage. "Power outage," someone yells. Metal chairs clink as people rise then sink back into their seats, some chattering, some shouting, all wondering what to do.

"It's this heat," says Grandma. "Too many air conditioners blowing in this town. A brownout, I think they call it."

Ephram takes out his violin. "It's time for me to play now, Grandma."

"Ephram," says Grandma, "how can you play in the dark?"

A wet nose tickles Ephram's elbow, a hand firmly grasps his shoulder. "It's always dark . . . up on the roof, isn't it, Ephram?"

Mr. Washington smiles. "Evening, Rachel," he says. "Shiloh and I couldn't miss your grandson's neighborhood debut. Hope we're not too late."

"It's never too late, Balthazar Washington," says Grandma.

"Mr. Washington, people are beginning to leave. I'm going onstage to play some of the old songs Grandma sings in church. There's a piano onstage. Will you play with me, sir?"

Mr. Washington tightens his grip on Shiloh's harness and sits down on the empty chair. He pulls out his handkerchief and wipes the sweat from his face and neck.

"Mr. Washington," says Ephram, "music speaks best when someone listens."

Mr. Washington turns toward Ephram's voice. "Shiloh, you stay here with my friend Rachel. Ephram and ole Flash Fingers Washington, we gonna make some sweet sounds tonight."

Ephram grins widely. "Do you know 'Amazing Grace,' Mr. Washington?"

"Ephram, I was playing 'Amazing Grace' when you were a thought in the good Lord's mind!" Mr. Washington places his hand on Ephram's forearm. "Ready, son?"

"Be careful getting up on that stage, you two," cautions Grandma.

"Don't worry, Grandma," says Ephram. "Mr. Washington sees in the dark."

Up on the stage, Ephram seats Mr. Washington at the piano. The crowd buzzes. Ephram shoulders his violin. He raises his bow and begins "Amazing Grace." Mr. Washington joins in. The hum of the crowd fades, and in the darkness the music sings to the stars.

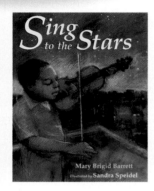

Sing to the Stars

Mary Brigid Barrett
Illustrated by Sandra Speidel

## Think About the Selection

**1.** Why do you think Ephram likes to practice on the roof?

**2.** What does Mr. Washington mean when he tells Ephram, "Music speaks best when someone listens"?

**3.** Why does Ephram want Mr. Washington to perform with him at the concert?

**4.** Why do you think Mr. Washington finally decides to play the piano with Ephram?

**5.** Ephram says that music speaks for him when he can't talk about his feelings. How do *you* feel when you listen to music?

**6.** **Connecting/Comparing** Explain how music helps Ephram and María Isabel solve their problems.

## Write a Sound Poem

Mr. Washington recognizes Ephram by the sound of his walk: *light step, brush, light step, brush*. Write a poem about sounds you hear around you. Create rhythms by repeating words, such as *tap tap tap* or *tap-tap, tap-tap*.

**Tips**

- Read your poem out loud for rhythm.
- Use words that sound like real sounds, such as *click* and *buzz*.

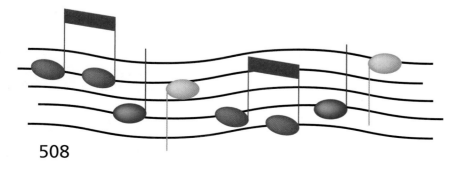

## Science

## Make Musical Pitches

Sounds such as musical pitches are caused by vibrations in the air. To make musical pitches, wrap a rubber band around a plastic cup. Pluck the rubber band with your fingers. Try a thinner rubber band or a thicker one. Then try using more than one rubber band. Discuss the different sounds you hear.

## Vocabulary

## Create a Music Glossary

The author uses many musical terms in this story, such as *classical* and *jazz*. Create a music glossary. Go back to the story and write down words that are about music. Write the definition next to each word. Look up words you don't know in a dictionary.

## Follow Web Instructions

Would you like to make a simple musical instrument? You'll find instructions at Education Place. **www.eduplace.com/kids**

# THE ART of Music

by Richard Mühlberger

At the beginning of the twentieth century, an archaeologist was exploring one of the many small islands of Greece. He knew that people had lived there four thousand years ago. When he came upon one of their graves, he carefully dug it up. *The Lyre Player* was buried in it. Carved from a small block of marble, the statue has the smooth, round lines of a modern sculpture. It shows a person playing a lyre, the ancestor of the harp.

The people who created, and then buried, the statue believed that it would make music forever. Missing hands still pluck the five invisible strings of the instrument.

***The Lyre Player***
artist unknown

*The Boy with a Flute*
by Judith Leyster

*The Boy with a Flute* was painted by Judith Leyster. She lived in Holland more than three hundred years ago.

Judith Leyster made every detail exact. Even the light entering the room seems soft. The one detail beyond her talent, however, was the sound of the flute — impossible for anyone to paint.

This musical fantasy, called *The Green Violinist,* was painted in 1923 and 1924 by a famous Russian artist, Marc Chagall.

Because the fiddler has a green face, we know it is not a real face. The fiddler's purple coat is alive with triangles, shaped like the gables of the houses at his feet. Propelled by the colors of his clothes and the tapping of his heels, the fiddler seems to dance into the sky.

*The Green Violinist*
by Marc Chagall

# Check Your Progress

In this theme, you have read four selections about creative problem solvers. Soon, you will read and compare two more selections about solving problems and review some test-taking strategies as well.

First, take a moment to review Alma Flor Ada's letter on pages 386–388. Which of her strategies do characters in the theme use? How do you think her suggestions might be useful in your own life?

Now it's time to read about more characters with hurdles to overcome. As you read, compare the different problems and solutions in each selection. Ask yourself what qualities the problem solvers throughout the theme have in common. Which problem-solving strategies seem to work best for the characters overall?

# Read and Compare

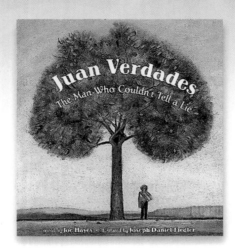

Meet Juan Verdades, a man who must think quickly in order to defend his legendary reputation for honesty.

**Try these strategies:**
Predict and Infer
Monitor and Clarify

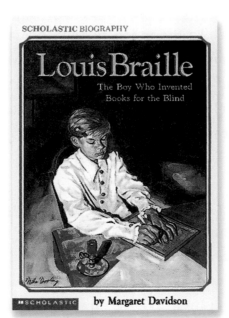

Learn about Louis Braille, a young man whose solution to an important problem nearly two hundred years ago continues to help blind people today.

**Try these strategies:**
Question
Summarize

**Strategies in Action** *Find ways to use all your reading strategies while you read.*

# Juan Verdades
## The Man Who Couldn't Tell a Lie

by **Joe Hayes** • illustrated by **Joseph Daniel Fiedler**

Long ago in the Southwest, a wealthy *ranchero* named don Ignacio owned a wonderful apple tree called *el manzano real* — his most prized possession. His ranch-hand, Juan Verdades, famous for his honesty, guards the tree.  One day, another *ranchero* named don Arturo bets don Ignacio his entire ranch that he can force honest Juan to lie.  To do this, don Arturo sends his beautiful daughter Araceli to the ranch, hoping she can convince Juan to give her the fruit of *el manzano real*.  Juan soon falls in love with Araceli, who treats him so kindly.  But how will he answer Araceli's request for the one thing he cannot give her?  Can the honesty of the man who could not tell a lie pass such a difficult test?

The next morning Juan and Araceli met again.  As they sipped their coffee together, Juan said, "I truly would like to repay you for the kindness you've shown me.  There must be something on this ranch you would like.  Tell me what it is.  I'll see that it's given to you."

But again Araceli replied, "There's only one thing on this ranch I want:  the apples from *el manzano real*."

Each day they repeated the conversation. Araceli asked for the same thing, and Juan said he couldn't give it to her. But each day Juan was falling more hopelessly in love with Araceli. Finally, just the day before the two weeks of the bet would have ended, the foreman gave in. He said he would go pick the apples right then and bring them to the girl.

Juan hitched up a wagon and drove to the apple tree. He picked every single apple and delivered the wagonload of fruit to Araceli. She thanked him very warmly, and his spirits rose for a moment. But as he mounted his horse to leave, they sank once again. Juan rode away alone, lost in his thoughts, and Araceli hurried off to tell her father the news and then to wait for a chance to talk to don Ignacio too.

Juan rode until he came to a place where there were several dead trees. He dismounted and walked up to one of them. Then he took off his hat and jacket and put them on the dead tree and pretended it was don Ignacio. He started talking to it to see if he could tell it a lie.

"Good evening, *mi capataz*," he pretended he heard the tree say.

"Good evening, *mi patrón*."

"How goes it with my cattle and land?"

"Your cattle are healthy, your pastures are green."

"And the fruit of *el manzano real*?"

"The . . . the crows have carried the fruit away. . . ."

But the words were hardly out of his mouth when he heard himself say, "No, that's not true, *mi patrón*. I picked the fruit. . . ." And then he stopped himself.

He took a deep breath and started over again with, "Good evening, *mi capataz*."

And when he reached the end, he sputtered, "The . . . wind shook the apples to the ground, and the cows came and ate them. . . . No, they didn't, *mi patrón*. I . . ."

He tried over and over, until he realized there was no way he could tell a lie. But he knew he could never come right out and say what he had done either. He had to think of another way to tell don Ignacio. He took his hat and coat from the stump and sadly set out for the ranch.

All day long Juan worried about what he would say to don Ignacio. And all day long don Ignacio wondered what he would hear from his foreman, because as soon as Araceli had shown the apples to her father he had run gleefully to tell don Ignacio what had happened.

"Now you'll see, *compadre*," don Arturo gloated. "You're about to hear a lie from Juan Verdades."

Don Ignacio was heartsick to think that all his apples had been picked, but he had agreed that don Arturo could try whatever he wanted. He sighed and said, "Very well, *compadre*, we'll see what happens this evening."

Don Arturo rode off to gather the other ranchers who were witnesses to the bet, leaving don Ignacio to pace nervously up and down in his house. And then, after don Ignacio received a visit from Araceli and she made a request that he couldn't deny, he paced even more nervously.

All the while, Juan went about his work, thinking of what he would say to his don Ignacio. That evening the foreman went as usual to make his report to his employer, but he walked slowly and his head hung down. The other ranchers were behind the bushes listening, and Araceli and her mother were watching anxiously from a window of the house.

The conversation began as it always did:

"Good evening, *mi capataz*."

"Good evening, *mi patrón*."

"How goes it with my cattle and land?"

"Your cattle are healthy, your pastures are green."

"And the fruit of *el manzano real?*"

Juan took a deep breath and replied:

"Oh, *patrón*, something terrible happened today.

Some fool picked your apples and gave them away."

Don Ignacio pretended to be shocked and confused. "Some fool picked them?" he said. "Who would do such a thing?"

Juan turned his face aside. He couldn't look at don Ignacio. The rancher asked again, "Who would do such a thing? Do I know this person?"

Finally the foreman answered:

"The father of the fool is my father's father's son.

The fool has no sister and no brother.

His child would call my father 'grandfather.'

He's ashamed that he did what was done."

Don Ignacio paused for a moment to think about Juan's answer. And then, to Juan's surprise, don Ignacio grabbed his hand and started shaking it excitedly.

The other ranchers ran laughing from their hiding places. "Don Arturo," they all said, "you lose the bet. You must sign your ranch over to don Ignacio."

"No," said don Ignacio, still vigorously shaking Juan's hand. He glanced toward the window where Araceli was watching and went on: "Sign it over to don Juan Verdades. He has proved that he truly deserves that name, and he deserves to be the owner of his own ranch as well."

Everyone cheered and began to congratulate Juan. Don Arturo's face turned white, but he gritted his teeth and forced a smile. He shook Juan's hand and then turned to walk away from the group, his shoulders drooping and his head bowed down.

But Araceli came running from the house and put her arm through her father's. "*Papá*," she said, "what if Juan Verdades were to marry a relative of yours? Then the ranch would stay in the family, wouldn't it?"

Everyone heard her and turned to look at the girl and her father. And then Juan spoke up confidently. "*Señorita* Araceli, I am the owner of a ranch and many cattle. Will you marry me?"

Of course she said she would, and don Arturo heaved a great sigh. "Don Juan Verdades," he said, "I'll be proud to have such an honest man for a son-in-law." He beckoned his wife to come from the house, and they both hugged Juan and Araceli.

The other ranchers hurried off to fetch their families, and a big celebration began. It lasted all through the night, with music and dancing and many toasts to Juan and Araceli. And in the morning everyone went home with a big basket of delicious apples from *el manzano real*.

# Louis Braille
## The Boy Who Invented Books for the Blind

by Margaret Davidson, illustrated by Steve Noble

Today, blind people all over the world owe their thanks to Louis Braille. At the age of three, he lost his vision in a tragic accident. In the 1800s, when Louis was growing up in France, blind people did not have the same opportunities as others. Being unable to read or write posed huge problems. At a special school for the blind, Louis, now in his early teens, longs to read and write — to live a more normal life. A man named Captain Barbier has created a reading system for the blind called "nightwriting," but it is too complicated. Louis decides to change the situation. He creates his own reading system for sightless people by using a made-up alphabet of raised dots that blind people can "read" by touch. Find out how young Louis overcomes the odds and achieves what everyone else thinks is impossible.

Louis tried not to waste a single minute. Even when he was home on vacation, he worked on his dots. Often his mother would pack him a lunch of bread and cheese and fruit, and he would wander out to sit on some sunny hillside. Other times, he sat by the side of the road, bent over his paper and board. "There is Louis, making his pinpricks," the neighbors said with a smile as they passed. What was he doing? Was it some kind of game the blind boy was playing to keep himself busy? Louis didn't try to explain. He just went on punching patterns of dots.

At home in Coupvray Louis had plenty of free time to work on his experiments. At school it was not nearly so easy.

There were so many other things to do. Louis had to go to class. He had to spend an hour or two in one of the workshops every day. He had to practice his music and do his homework. He had to eat meals with the rest of the boys — or someone would come looking for him.

But Louis still found time to work on his ideas. He worked in bits and pieces. He worked before breakfast. And between classes. He worked after dinner. And late at night.

That was the best time of all. The boys were all asleep, and everything was quiet. Hour after hour Louis bent over his board, experimenting with different patterns of dots.

Sometimes he got so tired he fell asleep sitting up. Sometimes he became so excited he forgot what time it was and worked until he heard the milk wagons rattling by under his window. Louis would raise his head with surprise then. For he knew it was early morning. He had worked the whole night through again! Then Louis would crawl into bed to nap for an hour or two — before he had to get up yawning for breakfast and his first class.

Louis's friends became more and more worried about him.

"You never sleep!"

"Half the time you forget to eat!"

"And for what?" a third boy snapped. "A wild goose chase! That's what!"

"Maybe you're right," Louis always answered softly. And he kept on working.

Three years went by — three years of hard work and trying and not quite succeeding.

Sometimes Louis got so tired he could hardly lift his hand. And sometimes he became very, very discouraged.

Again and again, Louis had simplified Captain Barbier's patterns of dots. But still they were not simple enough. No, reading with dots was still hard to do. Were the boys right? Was this a wild goose chase? Men had been working on this problem for hundreds of years — smart men, important men, older men. And one after another they had failed. Who did he think he was? What right did he have to think he could do better than they?

Then Louis had a new and very different idea. It seemed so simple — after he'd had it. Captain Barbier's nightwriting had been based on sounds. But there were so many sounds in the French language. Sometimes it took almost a hundred dots to write out a simple word. This was far, far too many to feel easily with the fingertips. But what if he used dots in a different way? What if the patterns of dots didn't stand for sounds at all? What if they stood for the letters of the alphabet instead? There were only twenty-six of them, after all!

Louis was filled with excitement. He was sure he was right! Now he worked even harder. And everything began to fall into place.

First Louis took a pencil and marked six dots on a heavy piece of paper. He called this six-dot pattern a *cell*. It looked like this:

```
o   o
o   o
o   o
```

He numbered each dot in the cell:

```
1o   o4
2o   o5
3o   o6
```

Then he took his stylus and raised dot number one — that would stand for A:

```
●   o
o   o
o   o
```

He raised dots number one and two — and that would stand for B:

Raised dots number one and four would be C:

Louis made letter after letter. And when he was finished Louis Braille's alphabet of dots looked like this:

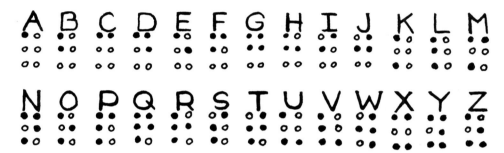

Louis ran his fingers over his alphabet. It was so simple! So simple! Fifteen-year-old Louis Braille felt like shouting or crying or laughing out loud. All the letters of the alphabet had been made out of the same six dots — used over and over again in different patterns! He knew it wouldn't look like much of anything to people who could see. But it wasn't supposed to! It was meant to be felt! Quickly. Easily. And it worked!

Louis was home in Coupvray when he finished his alphabet. He could hardly wait to get back to school and show it to the other boys. What would they say? Would they like it? They just had to!

Louis wasn't disappointed. The boys loved his alphabet from first touch.

"It's so simple!"

"So easy to feel."

"And so small — so much fits right under my fingertips."

"We can write! We can write letters to each other!"

"And keep diaries!"

"We can take notes in class. . . ."

"And read them back later!"

"And books," Louis said quietly. "Don't forget about books. Soon we will have all sorts — just for us to read."

News of the alphabet spread quickly through the school. Soon the director of the Institute sent for Louis.

"Tell me," Dr. Pignier said. "What is this . . . this alphabet of dots I've been hearing so much about?"

"Please, sir," answered Louis eagerly. "If you will read something aloud, I'll show you."

So Dr. Pignier picked up a book and began to read — slowly.

"You can go faster, sir," said Louis. Soon Louis's hand was flying across the paper — punching words into dots. When the director stopped reading, Louis turned the paper over. He brushed his fingers lightly over the lines of raised dots. Then quickly, easily — without a single mistake — he read back every word.

"Amazing," Dr. Pignier kept murmuring. "Amazing. . . . How old are you, my boy?"

"Fifteen," Louis answered.

"Fifteen! To think that men have been searching for just such an alphabet for hundreds of years — and one of my boys has found it instead. Fifteen. Amazing!"

Louis glowed with pride. Now was the time to ask the most important question of all. "Sir, when can we start making books?"

# Think and Compare

1. Compare the problems facing Louis Braille and Juan Verdades. What is the biggest difference between them?

2. List two traits shown by each problem-solver in this theme. What qualities do they all share?

3. If Louis Braille could be friends with any character in the theme, whom might he choose? Why?

4. Identify a problem shared by both Louis Braille and Marven from *Marven of the Great North Woods*. How do their solutions to this problem differ?

5. If you had a problem, which character in this theme would you be most likely to ask for advice? Explain, using details from the story.

**Strategies in Action** Tell about two or three places in *Louis Braille* where you used reading strategies.

# Write an Explanation

Write two paragraphs explaining what braille is, how it works, and how to use it. Include a few sentences explaining why braille is such an important invention.

**Tips**

- Review the selection and take notes.
- Write an outline to organize your thoughts.
- Present your information in the right order.

# Vocabulary Items

Some test questions ask you to identify a synonym, or a word that means almost the same as another word. Try this kind of test item. Use the steps to help you.

---

Read the sentence. Choose the answer that means about the same as the underlined word. Fill in the circle for the correct answer.

1. "All day long don Ignacio wondered what he would hear from his foreman, because as soon as Araceli had shown the apples to her father he had run <u>gleefully</u> to tell don Ignacio what had happened." What does *gleefully* mean?

   **A** amazing

   **B** angrily

   **C** as slowly as possible

   **D** joyfully

   ANSWER ROW 1   Ⓐ Ⓑ Ⓒ ●

---

 **Understand the question.**

Find the word that the question asks about. Is it shown in context? Decide what you need to do.

> The question asks about *gleefully*. I need to choose the answer that means the same as *gleefully*.

## 2 Think about what the word means.

Think about the word's parts. Look for the base word and a prefix or suffix. How is the word used in the context?

*Glee* is the base word. Together, the suffixes *-ful* and *-ly* mean "in a way that is full of." So I know that *gleefully* describes *how* Araceli's father runs — in a way that is full of glee.

## 3 Narrow the choices. Then choose the best answer.

Try each choice in the context. Which choices are clearly wrong? Have a reason for choosing the best answer. Only guess if you have to.

**A** and **C** don't make sense. Both **B** and **D** have suffixes that match *gleefully*. I think *joy* means the same as *glee*, and I know Araceli's father was happy, not angry, that Juan took the apples. **D** must be correct.

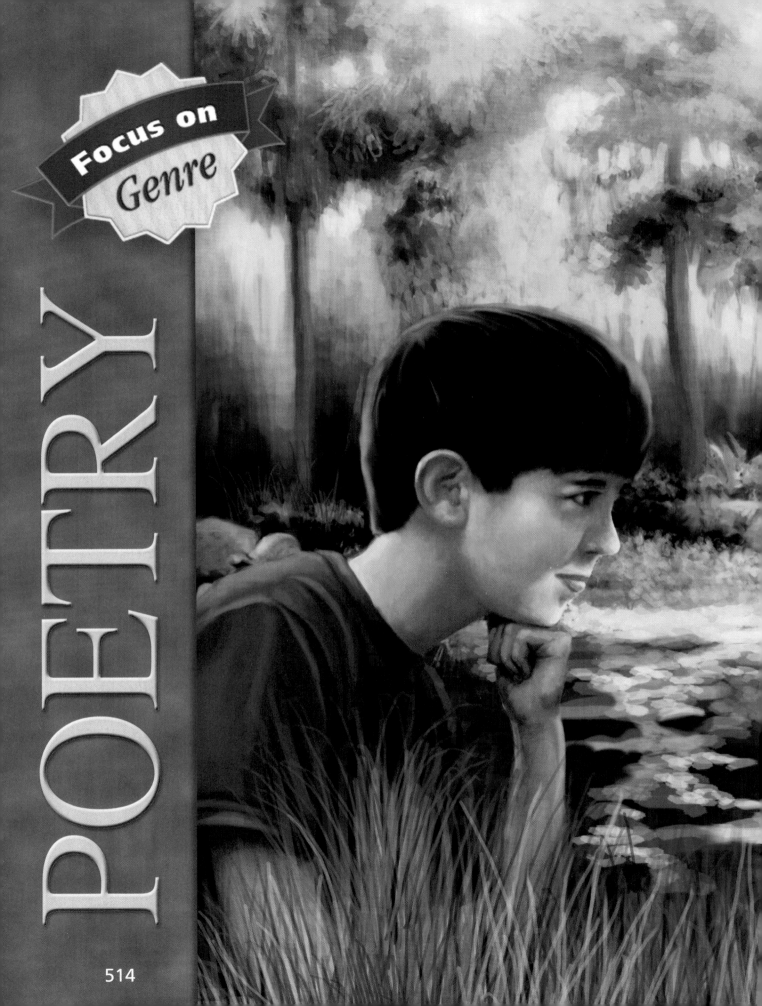

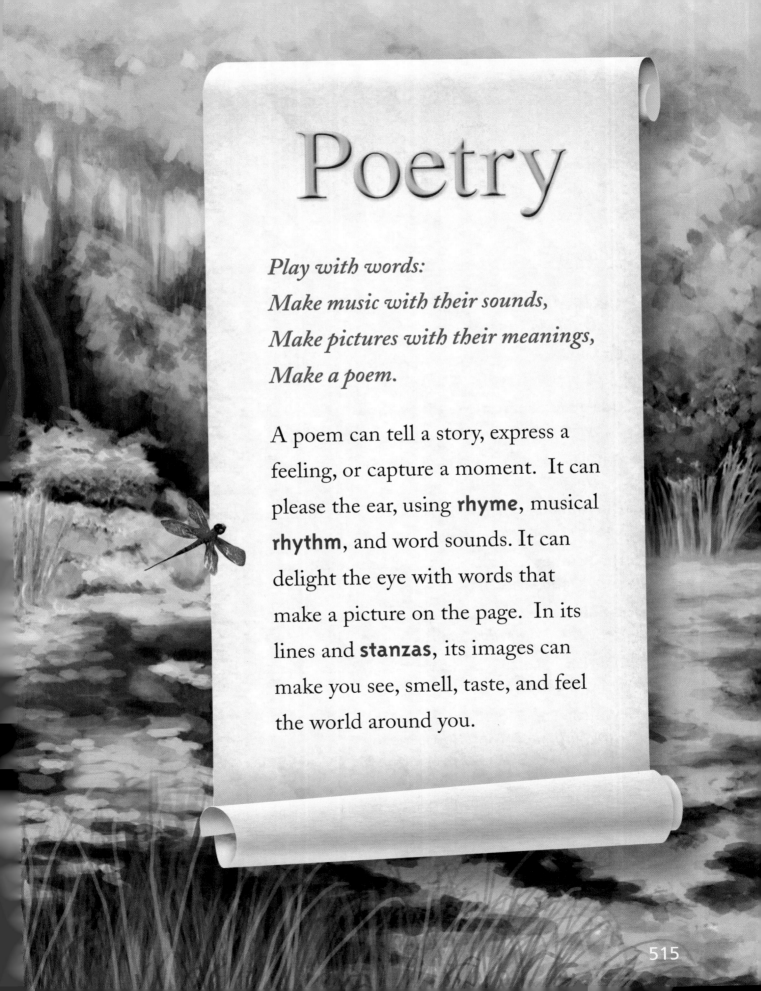

# Poetry

*Play with words:*
*Make music with their sounds,*
*Make pictures with their meanings,*
*Make a poem.*

A poem can tell a story, express a feeling, or capture a moment. It can please the ear, using **rhyme**, musical **rhythm**, and word sounds. It can delight the eye with words that make a picture on the page. In its lines and **stanzas**, its images can make you see, smell, taste, and feel the world around you.

## Contents

# The Seed

How does it know,
this little seed,
if it is to grow
to a flower or weed,
if it is to be
a vine or shoot,
or grow to a tree
with a long deep root?
A seed is so small,
where do you suppose
it stores up all
of the things it knows?

*by Aileen Fisher*

# By Myself

When I'm by myself
And I close my eyes
I'm a twin
I'm a dimple in a chin
I'm a room full of toys
I'm a squeaky noise
I'm a gospel song
I'm a gong
I'm a leaf turning red
I'm a loaf of brown bread
I'm a whatever I want to be
An anything I care to be
And when I open my eyes
What I care to be
Is me

*by Eloise Greenfield*

517

# Oda a mis zapatos

mis zapatos
descansan
toda la noche
bajo mi cama

cansados
se estiran
se aflojan
las cintas

muy anchos
se duermen
y sueñan
con andar

recorren
los lugares
adonde fueron
en el día

y amanecen
contentos
relajados
suavecitos

# Ode to My Shoes

my shoes
rest
all night
under my bed

tired
they stretch
and loosen
their laces

wide open
they fall asleep
and dream
of walking

they revisit
the places
they went to
during the day

and wake up
cheerful
relaxed
so soft

*by Francisco X. Alarcón*

# Pencils

The rooms in a pencil
are narrow
but elephants      castles and
watermelons
fit in

In a pencil
noisy words yell for attention
and quiet words wait their turn

How did they slip
into such a tight place?
Who
gives them their
lunch?

From a broken pencil
an unbroken poem will come!
There is a long story living
in the shortest pencil

Every word in your
pencil
is fearless     ready to walk
the blue tightrope lines
Ready
to teeter and smile
down        Ready to come right out
and show you
thinking!

*by Barbara Esbensen*

# The Anteater

The
    anteater's
        long
           and
               tacky
                  tongue
                     is
                        snaking
                           from
                              its
                                snout.

A thousand termites riding in,
But no one riding out.

*by Douglas Florian*

# THE PANTHER

The panther is like a leopard,
Except it hasn't been peppered.
Should you behold a panther crouch,
Prepare to say Ouch.
Better yet, if called by a panther,
Don't anther.

*by Ogden Nash*

520

# Rabbit

A rabbit
bit
A little bit
An itty-bitty
Little bit of beet.
Then bit
By bit
He bit
Because he liked the taste of it.
But when he bit
A wee bit more,
It was more bitter than before.
"This beet is bitter!"
Rabbit cried.
"I feel a bit unwell inside!"
But when he bit
Another bite, that bit of beet
Seemed quite all right.
Besides
When all is said and done,
Better bitter beet
Than none.

*by Mary Ann Hoberman*

# Sky-Fish

Yesterday
we thought of fishing
when the lake was purpled-out.
But we didn't
take our fish poles
or our hooks . . . we went without.

Uncle Stephen
rowed the rowboat
where the moon made silver bands,
and our fingers
fished for moonfish,
but they slithered from our hands.

Then we tried
to catch the starfish
bobbing bright, with shiny scales,
but they dribbled
through our fingers
as they flicked their starfish tails.

Yesterday
we went out fishing
where the sky-fish glittered bright,
and I'm glad
we didn't catch them
so they'll still be there tonight.

*by Aileen Fisher*

# I Watched an Eagle Soar

Grandmother,
I watched an eagle soar
high in the sky
until a cloud covered him up.
Grandmother,
I still saw the eagle
behind my eyes.

*by Virginia Driving Hawk Sneve*

# Think About the POETRY

1. Choose three poems you especially enjoyed. What do these poems have in common? What are some key differences among them?

2. Which of the poems is your favorite? Why? Which elements of poetry are featured in the poem you chose?

3. Identify two poems about animals or nature and compare and contrast them. What are the different ways each poet chooses to describe his or her subject?

4. If you were going to write a poem, would you choose to use rhyme? Why or why not? What are some good points of each approach?

5. What are the most important differences between poetry and fiction? Between poetry and nonfiction?

## Internet

## E-mail a Friend

Now it's *your* turn to be a poet. Write a short poem using what you have just learned about different kinds of poetry. When you are done, e-mail it to a friend and ask them what they think of it.

**Creating**

# Write Your Own Poem

You can be a poet, too. There are many kinds of poems, so choose the kind that suits you best. Think of several things you want to write about. Then brainstorm words, rhymes, or even shapes that you might use in your poem. Try out a few lines, a few rhymes, a few images. Rearrange them. Try to hear or create a rhythm.

## Tips

- **Use word webs, draw pictures, or do freewriting to collect ideas and words.**
- **Try different ways of writing the lines to create different effects.**
- **As you revise, read each draft of your poem aloud.**

# HEROES

### A Song of Greatness

When I hear the old men
Telling of heroes,
Telling of great deeds
Of ancient days,
When I hear that telling
Then I think within me
I too, am one of these.

— *Traditional Chippewa,*
*as translated by Mary Austin*

527

# HEROES

## with David Adler

Dear Reader,

In this theme, you will read about people who have shown great courage, including one of my heroes — baseball player Lou Gehrig. Here are a few more heroes of mine.

Lou Gehrig
(1903–1941)

### Harriet Tubman
#### (1821–1913)

Harriet Tubman was born a slave. In 1849 she escaped. She ran from one safe house to the next on the Underground Railroad. When she reached Pennsylvania, a free state, she later said, "I felt I was in heaven."

After all she went through, it took great courage to go back, but she did. She made nineteen trips south and helped more than 200 other slaves escape.

Harriet Tubman was at war with slavery. For the many slaves she saved, she won that war.

### Helen Keller
#### (1880–1968)

As an infant, Helen Keller lost her sight and hearing. Still, she went to college and became a writer and a public speaker. She learned how to swim and even ride a bicycle.

Helen Keller worked all her life to help others, especially blind people. Her visits meant a lot to injured soldiers during World War II. Her good spirit and achievements brought hope to people with handicaps.

Helen Keller taught me and millions of others that no matter what our problems might be, we still have to do our best.

## Benjamin Franklin
### (1706–1790)

Ben Franklin was a printer, writer, inventor, scientist, and statesman. He helped prove that lightning is electricity and invented the lightning rod, the Franklin stove, and bifocal eyeglasses.

His work in France for our new nation helped win the Revolution. He signed both the Declaration of Independence and the Constitution.

Benjamin Franklin is a hero of mine for all he did, and for his good sense and good humor.

## Edward M. Adler
### (1948–1979)

My brother Eddie worked in a hospital. He headed the blood bank. He was careful and made sure his workers were careful, too. Their work, done well, saved lives.

One afternoon, in the parking lot of the hospital, Eddie saw the beginning of an attack on a nurse. Eddie saved her life, but he was severely injured. Five weeks later, he died.

After his death, Eddie was given many awards for his heroism, including The Carnegie Medal.

Eddie had such courage! I am so very proud of Eddie, but I miss him terribly.

You have met some of my personal heroes. Now, as you read the selections in this theme, ask yourself, who are *your* heroes?

Sincerely,

*David A. Adler*

# What Is a Hero?

David Adler has just shared some of his heroes with you. Think about the qualities you feel are important in a hero. How do they compare with the qualities of David Adler's heroes?

Now you're ready to read the selections shown below and meet some more extraordinary people. Find out why many people consider them worthy of the title *hero*. Could they be your heroes, too?

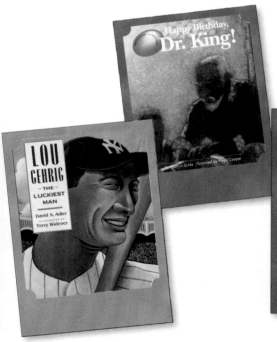

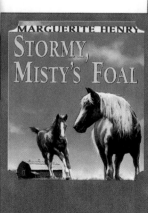

Internet

To learn about the authors in this theme, visit Education Place. **www.eduplace.com/kids**

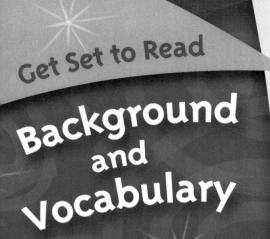

**Happy Birthday, Dr. King!**

**Read to find the meanings of these words.**

*e* ● Glossary

boycott

civil rights

fare

protest

stupendous

# A FAMOUS BUS RIDE

One day in 1955, in Montgomery, Alabama, Rosa Parks paid her bus **fare** and sat down at the front of the bus. This part of the bus was reserved for white people. When the bus driver told Mrs. Parks, an African American, that she had to move to the back of the bus, she refused. The police arrested her.

Many people wanted to **protest** how African Americans were treated on the buses. Dr. Martin Luther King, Jr., helped to organize a **boycott** of all the city buses in Montgomery.

Rosa Parks, riding at the front of a Montgomery city bus in 1956, just after the bus boycott ended

The response was **stupendous**. So many African Americans refused to ride the buses that a year later, the law was changed. African Americans in Montgomery could now sit anywhere they wanted on city buses.

In 1955, African Americans didn't have all the rights that white people did. But many people — both African American and white — were organizing to change this situation. Dr. King became one of the most important leaders of this peaceful battle called the **civil rights** movement.

Read *Happy Birthday, Dr. King!* to learn more about Dr. King and Mrs. Parks, and how they inspired a young boy many years later.

Dr. Martin Luther King, Jr., leading a peaceful march for civil rights in 1965

## Meet the Author
# Kathryn Jones

**Her birthday:** November 4
**Where she lives:** Dorchester, Massachusetts
**Another place she's lived:** Guyana (a country in South America)
**Other jobs she's done:** Worked at the Children's Museum in Boston, taught elementary school
**Advice for students who want to become authors:** Pay attention in English class, read a lot, and use your imagination when you write.
**Other books:** *Carnival*

## Meet the Illustrator
# Floyd Cooper

**His first job as an artist:** Working at a greeting card company
**Why he became a children's book illustrator:** He wanted to be creative and make the art he loved. He also wanted to create art for children that made them feel good.
**Other work he does:** He also writes some of the children's books he illustrates, such as *Mandela*.
**Other books:** *Grandpa's Face* by Eloise Greenfield, *Meet Danitra Brown* by Nikki Grimes, *I Have Heard of a Land* by Joyce Carol Thomas

Internet

If you want to find out more about Kathryn Jones and Floyd Cooper, visit Education Place.
**www.eduplace.com/kids**

# Happy Birthday, Dr. King!

MULTICULTURAL CELEBRATIONS II

by Kathryn Jones   Illustrated by Floyd Cooper

## ⭐ Strategy Focus

In this story, a boy learns a valuable lesson when his grandfather tells him about an important time in history.  As you read, **predict** what will happen next.

"Class, don't forget your assignment for tonight. Think about the Martin Luther King, Jr., assembly. His birthday is almost here," Mrs. Gordon said to her fourth grade class.

"Jamal, Arthur, you two wait. You have another assignment. Please take these notes from the principal home for your parents."

"A pink slip! I'm really in trouble now!" Jamal thought to himself walking home through the January slush. "Maybe Mom won't ask me about school."

Jamal decided to go in the front door and quietly upstairs to his room. Usually, he liked that his mother was home from her job at the hospital before he got home from school. Today was different.

"Jamal, is that you? Is Alisha with you?" Mrs. Wilson called from the kitchen.

"It's just me, Mom," Jamal answered.

"How did your day go?" she asked.

"Well, we're planning Dr. King's birthday celebration and I have some math and . . ." Jamal pulled the crumpled pink slip out of his pocket.

"A pink slip? Did you get into trouble?" she asked looking him straight in the eye. Grandpa Joe came into the kitchen.

"What's this I hear about trouble — and Dr. King?" he asked. "What's the pink paper?"

"It's just a note from the principal. It's no big deal," Jamal said. "Yesterday I got into a fight with another kid on my bus. We both wanted to sit in the back seat."

Grandpa Joe's smile disappeared.

"FIGHTING to sit at the BACK of the bus! I can't believe what I'm hearing!" Grandpa Joe said in that voice — that voice that tells the family to sit up and listen.

"Why would you want to fight over something like that?" he said, walking toward the basement door. "I just can't believe it."

"Why is Grandpa Joe so angry?" Jamal asked his mother. "It's no big deal."

"It is a very big deal — especially to your grandfather. Why don't you go and talk to him about it?"

"Grandpa Joe, I'm sorry that I got into trouble for fighting.  I won't do it again."

"Jamal, you are ten years old and old enough to understand.  It's almost Martin Luther King, Jr.'s birthday.  What are you doing for the celebration this year?"

"What does Dr. King's assembly have to do with a little fight?"

Grandpa Joe took a deep breath and began . . .

"A long time ago I was raising my family in Montgomery, Alabama.  This is what used to happen when African Americans wanted to ride the city buses.

"First, we'd get on at the front of the bus, pay our fare, and get off.  Then we'd get back on again at the rear of the bus.  We didn't like it, but that's how things were.  It was the law.  Then one day, in 1955, a lady named Rosa Parks . . ."

"Rosa Parks," Jamal interrupted, "we read about her.  She sat in the front of the bus and wouldn't give her seat to a white man, and she got arrested."

"But, Jamal, there is more to the story. When African Americans heard about her arrest, many of us stopped riding the buses. We wanted to protest her arrest and get the same rights that white people had. That was the Montgomery Bus Boycott. And the boycott worked. We finally won — without fighting.

"Now, you go think about that bus boycott. Maybe you can figure out why I'm so unhappy about your pink slip."

"Jamal. Your sister's home. Come and set the table," Mrs. Wilson called. Jamal hurried up the stairs. He had some hard thinking to do.

"Heard you got into trouble," Alisha said to her brother.

"Oh, be quiet."

"Okay you two," said Jamal's dad coming in. "Jamal knows he did something wrong. How is your homework going?"

"Well . . . we have to think of something to do for the Martin Luther King, Jr., assembly."

"Everyone in my class is learning parts of his 'I Have a Dream' speech," Alisha chimed in.

"I'll think of something. Grandpa Joe and I were talking about the bus boycotts."

"That should give you some ideas," his dad said. "Did you know that Grandpa Joe took me to hear Dr. King speak when I was your age?"

"You heard Martin Luther King, Jr., yourself?" Jamal asked.

"I sure did. It was during the boycott, too. Grandpa Joe took me to a meeting at a church one night. This man went up to the front and suddenly everyone stood and clapped. Then, he started talking. I couldn't believe the power of his speech.

"That man was Dr. King. He told us why to boycott the buses, and how we needed to help each other. Dr. King became a great leader of the civil rights movement."

"I know about that part," Jamal said. "That's why we celebrate his birthday. But *how* to celebrate is the problem."

"Then remember, Dr. King always spoke out about peaceful ways to make things happen. Does that help?"

"Peaceful . . ." Jamal said slowly, thinking. "You mean like not fighting?  And those peaceful ideas worked back then?"

"Jamal, peaceful ideas work today, too," his dad answered.

"Peaceful," Jamal said again and his face brightened.  "That's it!  Our class could do something to show that fighting is not the way to get things done.  Maybe we could do a skit.  Everyone could have a part and we could have costumes and I could be the star and . . ."

"Whoa," his dad said.  "First you'd better eat your dinner.  Then you can write down your ideas for Mrs. Gordon."

"Grandpa Joe," Jamal asked as his grandfather joined them.  "When you were a kid, did you ever do something *really* stupid that turned out to be *stupendous* instead?"

Grandpa Joe's smile returned and he nodded his head.

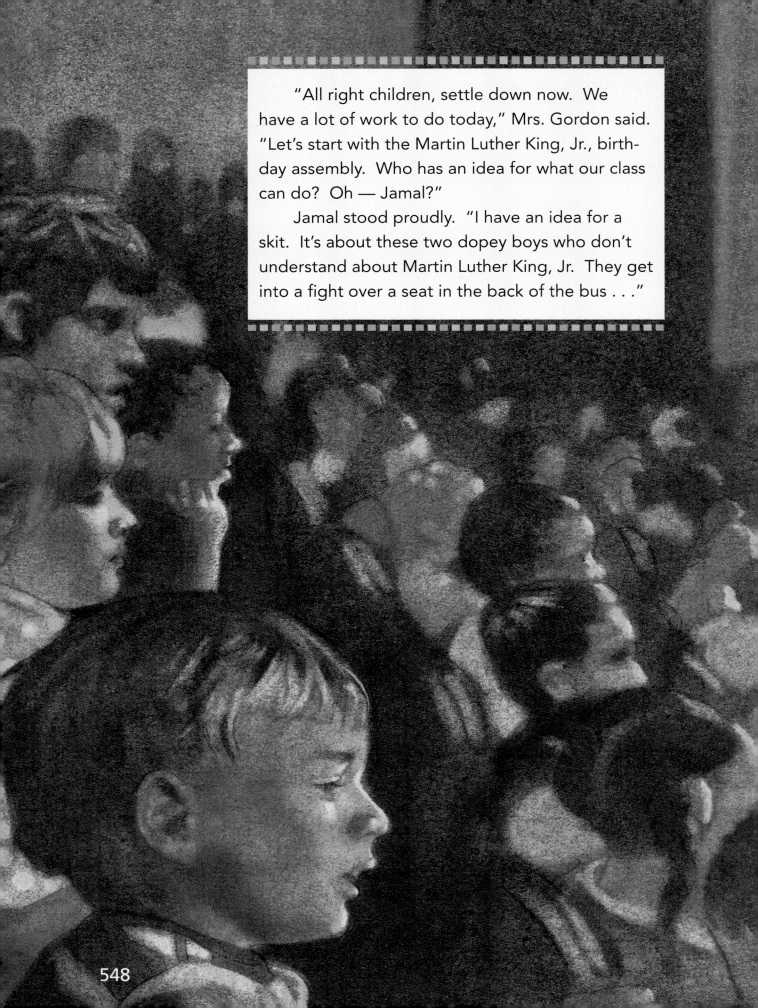

"All right children, settle down now. We have a lot of work to do today," Mrs. Gordon said. "Let's start with the Martin Luther King, Jr., birthday assembly. Who has an idea for what our class can do? Oh — Jamal?"

Jamal stood proudly. "I have an idea for a skit. It's about these two dopey boys who don't understand about Martin Luther King, Jr. They get into a fight over a seat in the back of the bus . . ."

549

## Think About the Selection

**1.** Why is Jamal's grandfather so unhappy that Jamal fought to sit at the back of the bus?

**2.** What does Jamal learn from talking with his grandfather? How is he different after the talk?

**3.** How does Jamal use what he learns from his grandfather in his skit?

**4.** Jamal says that he did something "really stupid that turned out to be stupendous instead." What do you think he means?

**5.** What would you like to do for a school celebration of Dr. King's birthday?

 **6.** **Connecting/Comparing** Who do you think are the heroes in this story? What makes them heroic?

## Write a Scene

Jamal has an idea for a skit to honor Dr. King. Write the opening scene for the skit. Use the style for writing a play described in Focus on Plays (pages 278–291). Give your scene to other students so they can act it out.

**Tips**

- Review the story to decide what to include.
- Write lines that sound like real people talking.
- Before you revise, test your ideas by acting out your scene with a partner.

550

## Make Posters of Peaceful Ideas

Write MARTIN, LUTHER, and KING, JR., in capital letters down the left side of a big sheet of paper. With a group, choose words or phrases that begin with each letter and that are about solving problems peacefully. Write the words beside each letter. Look at your poster and discuss your ideas for peace.

## Listen to a Speech

Listen to a recording of Dr. King's "I Have a Dream" speech. Discuss your reactions to the speech with two or three other students. Talk about the ideas and how Dr. King expressed them. Also discuss how he used his voice to make the speech effective.

M-Make friends
A - Always listen
R -

## Do a Web Crossword Puzzle

Identify the names of places and people mentioned in *Happy Birthday, Dr. King!* You'll find a crossword puzzle to solve at Education Place.

**www.eduplace.com/kids**

# Dear Mrs. Parks

## Rosa Parks Answers Letters from Young People

by Rosa Parks

### Skill: How to Take Notes

1. To begin, write the **title** at the top of a piece of paper.

2. As you read, look for important **ideas**, **facts**, and **opinions**.

3. Write a **heading** for each main idea.

4. List important **details** and **key words** below each heading.

## Dear Mrs. Parks,

**How old are you? (If you can't tell me, I'll understand.)**

I'm glad to answer that. I am thankful for each day that I'm alive. This year (1996) I turned 83. I was born February 4, 1913.

*Dear Mrs. Parks,*

The sixth graders are doing a history project. We chose you. The theme is "Taking a stand in history." We have some questions. Can you answer them? How did you feel when you were on the bus?

Jennifer and Jamie
La Puente, California

Your theme is a good one. A person should not take a stand to make history. Taking a stand for what is right is most important.

When I sat down on the bus on the day I was arrested, I decided I must do what was right to do. People have said over the years that the reason I did not give up my seat was because I was tired. I did not think of being physically tired.

My feet were not hurting. I was tired in a different way. I was tired of seeing so many men treated as boys and not called by their proper names or titles. I was tired of seeing children and women mistreated and disrespected because of the color of their skin.

I thought of the pain and the years of oppression and mistreatment that my people had suffered. I felt that way every day. December 1, 1955, was no different. Fear was the last thing I thought of that day. I put my trust in the Lord for guidance and help to endure whatever I had to face. I knew I was sitting in the right seat.

### Dear Mrs. Parks,

In school and when I am around certain people, I want to ask questions, but I am having trouble doing this. What would you do, Mrs. Parks?

Jimmy
Cleveland, Ohio

You can never learn very much if you do not ask questions. Many times questions are more important than answers. A person should never be afraid to admit he or she does not know an answer. Once you do this, then you are on the path of learning.

I am 83 years of age, and I am still learning. I am fascinated by the computer age, and I am still learning how to use some of the new technology. I just started taking water aerobics and swimming lessons last year. I ask a lot of questions during my swimming lessons. Take a deep breath! You can drown yourself with problems if you do not ask questions.

### Dear Mrs. Parks,

It seems that my grandparents are always right, and they always want to help someone. Why do older people seem to be smarter than young people?

James
Highland Park, Michigan

It is true that with age comes wisdom. Yet we never stop learning. From the moment we are born, we begin to learn. The longer you live, the more you understand this basic truth: All people want self-respect and the chance to use their gifts and talents. You should treat people as you would want them to treat you. We should show each other respect and help others to keep their dignity.

Your grandparents understand that adults are needed to reach out and help the younger generation. You and many young people are waiting to benefit from our wisdom and experience. There is still work to do.

*Dear Mrs. Parks,*

**My teacher told us that you just celebrated your 83rd birthday. My great-grandmother is 85 years old. She talks about the old days all the time. Sometimes I wonder what the old days have to do with me.**

**Adrienne**
**Vienna, Virginia**

When your great-grandmother talks to you about those days, you must listen, listen, listen. When she talks to you that way, she is trying to keep history alive. She seeks to inspire you by sharing stories of the past, of good times and bad times. There is no better way for us to learn from the mistakes of the past than through stories handed down from people who have lived through those times.

Listen to your great-grandmother and her stories from the past. She is preparing you to take your place in the world of tomorrow. Treasure her stories, and remember them so that you can share them with future generations.

# A Personal Essay

A personal essay explains the writer's opinion and gives reasons to support the opinion. Use this student's writing as a model when you write a personal essay of your own.

## H*E*R*O

My dad is a hero to me, and I want to tell everyone about him. My dad has brown hair with golden blond streaks. He usually wears shorts and a golf shirt, or a suit. He is about 5'8" tall, and when he is angry his face is like a cherry red rose that just opened up, and his voice is like a lion that is right on your trail.

My dad also has a sweet side, like when we make cut-and-bake cookies, or when he makes his famous s'mores pie with hot pudding and melted marshmallows.

> A good **opening** draws the reader into the essay.

> A good essay stays with the main point, or **focus**.

> **Examples** clarify ideas in an essay.

By the end of the day he kisses me with his fatherly goodnight kiss and turns out the light.  So when I see my dad, I don't see Superman, Batman, or any other superhero, but I do see my very special hero.

The **closing** sums up the essay.

## Meet the Author

Amanda B.
**Grade:** four
**State:** Florida

**Gloria Estefan**

**Read to find the meanings of these words.**

*e* ● Glossary

career
contract
demonstrated
eventually
specializes
tireless
worldwide

# Success in the Music Business

Have you ever wondered how your favorite music star achieved **worldwide** fame? Chances are the answer involves talent — and **tireless**, hard work. Many young musicians dream of a successful music **career**, but few actually reach that goal.

For many musicians, fame is earned slowly, one step at a time. Playing in a band might begin as only a hobby. **Eventually**, after much practice, the band might perform in front of audiences, slowly winning fans.

**Singers rehearsing**

**A band performing in a concert**

If a band has **demonstrated** enough determination and talent, it might earn a **contract** from a major recording company and make a CD. If enough people like a song from the recording, the song is a hit! The result could even be a gold record — and musical fame.

Now meet Gloria Estefan, a successful Cuban-American singer who **specializes** in blending different kinds of popular music into a style all her own.

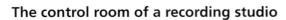

**Singer Patty Larkin recording a song**

**The control room of a recording studio**

REAL-LIFE READER BIOGRAPHY

# GLORIA ESTEFAN

Grammy Award–Winning Recording Artist

## ⭐ Strategy Focus

As you read about Gloria Estefan's rise to musical fame, **monitor** your reading to make sure you follow the order of events. **Clarify** anything you don't understand.

# CHAPTER 1
# Escaping with Music

Gloria Estefan was born Gloria Maria Fajardo [fa-HAR-doe] on September 1, 1957. She was the first child born to Gloria and José [hoe-SAY] Manuel Fajardo. She has a younger sister, Rebecca (Becky). For about the first year and a half of her life, Gloria lived with her family in Havana, Cuba. Her mother taught kindergarten there. Her father was an officer in the Cuban army.

In 1959, however, a war began in Cuba, and many Cubans fled to the United States for safety. These people were called refugees. The Fajardos were among the refugees. By the time Gloria was two years old, José Fajardo had settled the family in Miami, Florida. He then went back to Cuba to fight against Fidel Castro, who had taken control of the government.

A street scene (left) and a festival (above)
in a Cuban American neighborhood in Miami

Other Cuban men in Florida had also gone back to Cuba to
fight. Many, including José, were captured and kept in a Cuban
prison for nearly two years. Gloria and her mother were alone in the
United States. The U.S. government tried to help get the prisoners
back to the United States. Finally, just a few days before Christmas
in 1962, José Fajardo was freed. He returned to Miami.

Life in the United States wasn't easy for the family. The
Fajardos spoke only Spanish. Many Americans didn't want Cuban
refugees in the United States. They treated the refugees badly.

But Gloria was determined to succeed. At school she quickly
learned English and caught up with the other children. She was
always at the head of her class, even when her home life became very
difficult.

When Gloria's father came back from Cuba, he joined the U.S.
Army. In 1966, when war began between the United States and
Vietnam, José Fajardo volunteered for duty. He served in Vietnam
for two years.

Gloria was ten when her father came home. The girls and their mother knew something was wrong with him. Even though he had not been hurt in the fighting, Gloria says, "He'd fall for no reason."

Her father was told he had multiple sclerosis. This disease can cause many kinds of problems because it attacks the nerves. In just a few months, her father could not walk. Mrs. Fajardo went back to work to support the family. She also went back to college and got an American teaching degree. Then she taught public school in Miami.

Gloria helped out at home as much as she could. She became a little mother to her family. From the age of 11 until she was 16, Gloria took care of her sister, Becky, and her father.

José Fajardo needed constant care. "It was around the clock," says Gloria. "It wasn't easy. His mind went before his body. There were times when he wasn't aware of who I was, or who any of us were. It was very hard."

During those years, music became very important to Gloria. She remembers, "When my father was ill, music was my escape. I'd lock myself up in my room with my guitar."

In her room, Gloria would listen to music for hours and hours. She loved to sing along with the ballads and pop songs. She learned to play the guitar. Soon she could play along with her favorite songs.

**Gloria and her mother in a recent photograph**

## CHAPTER 2

# Making Music with Emilio

**M**usic became more and more important to Gloria as she went through her teen years. During her senior year in high school, she and some friends put together a band to play for a party.

The father of another band member knew Emilio Estefan, a popular band leader in Miami. The father invited Emilio to one of the girls' rehearsals, to give the girls a few tips.

Gloria met Emilio again three months after the first meeting. She says, "My mother dragged me to this wedding that I really didn't want to go to, and Emilio's band was playing. Emilio remembered me and asked me to sing a song with the band." A few weeks after that, Emilio asked Gloria to join the band permanently.

At first, Gloria said no. She had just begun classes at the University of Miami. Because her high school grades were so good — she made honor roll every semester — Gloria had received a scholarship.

She had never thought about joining a band or following a full-time musical career. Of course, she loved music and liked to sing, but mostly for fun. She worried that if she joined Emilio's band, she would not have enough time for her studies. Gloria's mother worried, too.

But Emilio promised Gloria that she would perform only on weekends and vacations. Her mother agreed that Gloria could sing, but only if Gloria agreed to finish college. Gloria promised, then accepted Emilio's offer. "I loved music so much that I couldn't let a great opportunity like this pass me by," she says.

With Gloria as lead singer, the band had a better, different, very special sound. Soon, Emilio changed the band's name from the Miami Latin Boys to Miami Sound Machine. "All of a sudden," Gloria says, "I was going to parties every weekend, singing with the whole band behind me." She loved to perform and came to realize that music was her calling.

**Gloria performing with the band**

Through their music, Gloria and Emilio got to know each other. Like the Fajardos, Emilio and his family had come from Cuba. Like many Cuban refugees, they had settled in Miami. They were very poor when they arrived in the United States, so Emilio worked at many jobs to help support the family. By the time he met Gloria, Emilio was the director of marketing at a Miami company.

But Emilio's real passion was music, and his part-time band was one of the most popular dance bands in Miami. By the time Gloria joined the band, Emilio had long been thinking about quitting his job and working with his band full time.

Gloria sang with the band for a year and a half before Emilio asked her out. They fell in love, dating steadily during Gloria's last two years at the university. In May 1978, Gloria graduated from college. Three months later, on September 1, 1978, she married Emilio.

**Gloria and Emilio Estefan**

# CHAPTER 3
# Changes

After their marriage, Gloria and Emilio began a long, hard job — getting the band known all over the world. The Miami Sound Machine's first album, *Renacer* (1978), was a collection of disco, pop, and original ballads sung in Spanish. During the next two years, the band released two more albums. All the albums sold well in Miami, but they didn't get much attention anywhere else.

In 1980, two changes took place in Gloria's family. Her father died after twelve years of crippling illness. He had been in a Veteran's Administration Hospital since 1975. His long illness had brought the family much grief. Gloria says, "It just gets to the point where you pray that the suffering will end, because you can't imagine why anyone has to go through something like that."

That same year, though, Gloria and Emilio's first child was born, bringing much joy and happiness to the family. The couple named the boy Nayib. They decided at once that their son was the most important thing in their lives.

Not long after Nayib was born, Emilio quit his full-time job. He wanted to give all of his attention to making a success of Gloria and the Miami Sound Machine.

Soon the group signed a contract with Discos CBS International, the Miami-based Hispanic division of CBS Records. Discos CBS International specializes in Latin music. Company officials decided that the Miami Sound Machine should release albums only in Spanish. The band's recordings would be sold in the Latin American countries, where the people speak mostly Spanish.

Gloria explains, "CBS thought we would sell better in Latin America if we sang in Spanish. But we kept the right to record in English, because eventually we wanted to try for the States."

During the next several years, Miami Sound Machine recorded four Spanish-language albums. From those albums came a dozen songs that became worldwide hits. By 1984, Miami Sound Machine was one of the most popular recording groups in Latin America. And — even better — Gloria Estefan and the Miami Sound Machine were becoming popular all over the world.

**The Miami Sound Machine in concert**

# CHAPTER 4
## World Fame and Tragedy

**T**hroughout the rest of the 1980s, Gloria and the Miami Sound Machine recorded song after song. Each was a bigger success than the one before. During those years, too, the group began to record English-language songs.

The string of hits began with "Dr. Beat" (1984), a Latin-style dance song that the group recorded in English. "Dr. Beat" was on the record's B side, the side that usually gets no air time on the radio. But it wasn't long before "Dr. Beat" could be heard on many Miami radio stations, both Spanish- and English-language. When CBS released it nationally as a dance single, it zoomed to number ten on the dance charts.

In 1984 the group also recorded the album *Eyes of Innocence; Primitive Love* came out the next year. These two albums made Gloria and the Miami Sound Machine a success all over English-speaking America. In fact, "Conga," a single from *Primitive Love*, went to number two on the American pop charts. The song also made *Billboard*'s dance, Latin, and Black charts — the first song in American music history to appear on four charts at the same time.

*Let It Loose* (1987) stayed on the pop charts for more than two years. The album sold three million copies in the United States alone, and it produced four top ten hits. The group performed at the closing of the 1987 Pan American games — even though the Cuban government protested because it wanted a Latin-American band to play. And, in 1989, *Cuts Both Ways* demonstrated Gloria's talent as a songwriter. The album contained ten of the many songs she had written during a 20-month tour.

**Gloria receiving flowers from a fan**

**The Estefan family meeting with President George Bush at the White House**

The early months of 1990 carried on the streak of success. Gloria and the band performed at the American Music Awards and the Grammy Awards ceremonies. From CBS, they received the Crystal Globe award, a prize that goes to performers who sell more than 5 million records outside their own country. Gloria met President George Bush at the White House, where he honored her for her drug prevention work with teenagers. Life shined brightly for Gloria, her family, and the band.

But on March 20 — the day after she visited the White House — tragedy struck.

Headed for their next concert in Syracuse, New York, Gloria, Emilio, and Nayib were traveling through a snowstorm. Near the Pennsylvania-New York state line, a tractor trailer had jackknifed across the road and was blocking traffic. As Gloria's tour bus came to a stop, it was hit from behind. The tour bus was pushed into a truck that was stopped ahead of it on the road. The front of the bus caved in, and all three family members were thrown to the bus floor.

Emilio was not seriously hurt. He found Nayib lying under a mountain of purses, books, and bags with a broken collarbone.

Gloria was relieved that her husband and son were alive. But she was in terrible pain. She had been thrown from the couch on which she had been lying, and she could not move. For more than an hour, Gloria sat waiting for a police helicopter. She didn't want Nayib to know how much pain she was in. "I was forced to really keep a lot of control," Gloria remembers, "because I didn't want him to feel that we had lost that grip for him, so he helped me hang on."

**On the road
to recovery**

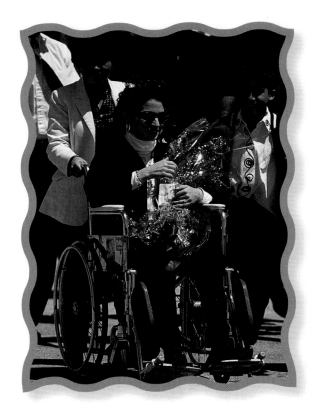

**Gloria's first performance after the bus accident**

When Gloria finally arrived at the hospital in Scranton, the doctors told her what she had suspected: her back was broken. Gloria thought her career as a performer was over.

Flown to the Hospital for Joint Diseases in New York City, she underwent a new and very risky kind of surgery on March 23. If the operation failed, she would be paralyzed forever.

The operation was a complete success. However, complete recovery was another matter. It took many months of rest and therapy.

Thousands of cards and letters from fans all over the country brought good wishes and support to Gloria. That support helped her through the long months of recovery. By January 1991, Gloria was performing again.

# CHAPTER 5
## "Here for Each Other"

**S**ince the accident, Gloria has had many more successes. She and the Miami Sound Machine keep turning out hit albums. They perform for world leaders and at important events. And Gloria keeps piling up honors and awards. She is most proud of her Ellis Island Congressional Medal of Honor. The medal makes her a representative for all Americans when she travels. She also represents the millions of Hispanics who, like her family, make their homes in the United States.

In 1994, there was more good news for Gloria and Emilio. They became parents again when Emily Marie Estefan Fajardo was born on December 5. Emily was a dream come true for the Estefans. Before the bus accident, they had talked about another baby. But,

**Damage caused by Hurricane Andrew (above). Gloria viewing the damage with the National Guard (right).**

after the accident, no one was sure that Gloria would be able to have another child.

Gloria is also a passionate, tireless worker for those with troubles. People throughout Miami call her "a star with a heart." When Hurricane Andrew roared through Miami, she wrote and recorded the song "Always Tomorrow." The song brought nearly $3 million to Gloria and Emilio — all of which they gave to the people who lost their homes and loved ones to Hurricane Andrew.

For many years, Gloria has also worked hard to help battered and abused children in Miami. "I've seen things that have ruined the lives of children," she says.

"The children in our care are fortunate that Gloria and Emilio have both given so much of themselves," says Dr. Mary Louise Cole of the Children's Home Society of Florida. Laurie Kay, the Society's Director of Development, gives Gloria credit for the very existence of Children's Home Society. "Gloria and her husband have done wonders for us," she says. "I wish there were more Gloria Estefans."

To be with her own children, Gloria has turned down several offers for movie roles. "Right now, I just want to concentrate on my children and watch them grow up into happy, healthy adults," she states. She tries to see to it that their home on one of Miami Beach's islands is always filled with fun and friends.

Gloria is ever thankful she was able to recover from her accident and return to the performing she loves. "I was always a thankful person," she says, "because I did go through some difficult things, but you tend to forget and get caught up in petty stuff. The bottom line is that we're here for each other."

**A benefit concert for the American Cancer Society (right)**

**The Estefan family "here for each other" (left)**

## MEET THE AUTHOR

# Sue Boulais

Sue Boulais says that it is her curiosity that has kept her writing for twenty-five years. "I want to know why and what kind and how much and who," she says. "Writing gives me an opportunity and a direction in which to explore a subject. . . . Writing also lets me share what I learn with others."

Boulais's first writing job was for the *Weekly Reader* school newspaper. Since then, she has published many books, articles, puzzles, and games. She says she was very pleased to have a chance to write about Gloria Estefan.

"The more I read and learned about her, the more I respected her," says Boulais. "She uses her talent well; she works very hard to be a great singer. I especially respected her determination to get well after her accident. She didn't cry or feel sorry for herself or make a lot of excuses — she used all her energy to do what she had to do to get her body well."

**Other books:** *Famous Astronauts* and *Hispanic American Achievers*

To learn more about Sue Boulais, log on to Education Place. **www.eduplace.com/kids**

## Think About the Selection

**1.** Why do you think Gloria Estefan enjoyed music so much while she was growing up?

**2.** Do you think Gloria and Emilio Estefan make a good musical team? Explain.

**3.** Why was it such a great achievement for Gloria Estefan's song "Conga" to appear on four different music charts at the same time?

**4.** What do you learn about Gloria Estefan's personality from the way she recovered from her accident?

**5.** Would you enjoy having the kind of fame that Gloria Estefan has achieved? Why or why not?

**6. Connecting/Comparing** What qualities and accomplishments make Gloria Estefan a hero?

**Summarizing**

## Write a Book Jacket Summary

Many book jackets present highlights of the story to tempt people to buy and read the book. Write a summary of Sue Boulais's book *Gloria Estefan* that could be printed on its jacket. Tell the most important events.

**Tips**

- Look at book jackets for models of story summaries.
- To get started, list the main events. Then circle the most important and interesting ones.
- Follow the sequence of events in the book.

## Social Studies

# Create a Time Line

Make a time line showing the most important events in Gloria Estefan's life. Draw a straight line across a sheet of paper. Mark off every ten years: 1950, 1960, and so on. Put the events and their dates on the appropriate places on the time line.

**Bonus** Using the same time line, add at least three historical events that occurred during this time period.

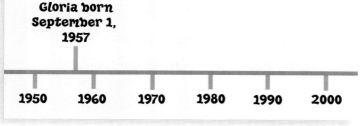

Gloria born September 1, 1957

1950   1960   1970   1980   1990   2000

## Listening and Speaking

# Present a Song

Listen to recordings of some popular songs. Then meet with a group to brainstorm a creative way to present one song to the class. A volunteer from your group might introduce the song the way a radio disc jockey would. Other ideas include dancing or lip-synching to the recording.

# Take an Online Poll

What is *your* favorite kind of music? Tell the world and learn what other students think about music by taking the Education Place online poll.

**www.eduplace.com/kids**

**Skill: How to
Follow a Recipe**

❶ **Read** the entire
recipe carefully.

❷ **Ask** an adult to help
if you have to use
knives or the stove
or oven.

❸ **Gather together** all
the ingredients and
kitchen tools.

❹ When you are
preparing the food,
**reread** each step of
the recipe before
you follow it.

❺ **Follow** the steps in
the correct order.

# ¡Sabroso!

## A Recipe from
## Gloria Estefan's Restaurant

If you like the Cuban flavor of Gloria
Estefan's music, you should try the food at one
of her restaurants. It's *sabroso* — delicious!

Gloria Estefan owns Larios on the Beach in
Miami Beach, Florida, with her husband and the
Larios family. Larios on the Beach serves typical
Cuban food. One of their popular dishes is a
beef stew called *ropa vieja* [ROH-pah BYEH-hah],
which means "old clothes." Another is *ensalada
de fruta tropical,* a tropical fruit salad that com-
bines many fruits from the Caribbean, where
Cuba is located.

Gloria Estefan and her
mother stir it up in her
restaurant kitchen.

# Ensalada de fruta tropical

This salad can be served with a meal or by itself. It serves about four people — depending on how much people eat!

## Ingredients

$\frac{3}{4}$ cup pineapple

$\frac{1}{2}$ cup cantaloupe

$\frac{1}{2}$ cup honeydew melon

$\frac{1}{2}$ cup watermelon

$\frac{1}{2}$ cup papaya

$\frac{1}{2}$ cup mango

$\frac{1}{2}$ cup grapes

$\frac{1}{2}$ kiwi

$\frac{1}{3}$ cup shredded coconut

lettuce leaves

fresh mint leaves

## Steps

1. Ask an adult to help you peel and cut the fruit (except for the grapes) into one-inch cubes. Combine the fruit in a large bowl.

2. Clean and dry the lettuce leaves and put them in four plates or bowls.

3. Put about one cup of the fruit mixture on the lettuce in each plate or bowl.

4. Sprinkle shredded coconut and a few mint leaves on top.

5. Serve and enjoy.

## Background and Vocabulary

*Lou Gehrig:
The Luckiest Man*

**Read to find the meanings of these words.**

*e* ○ **Glossary**

fielding

first baseman

honor

modest

shortstop

sportsmanship

# Good SPORTSMANSHIP

Lou Gehrig was good at hitting as well as **fielding**.

**G**reat baseball players love to win games. But they also know that good **sportsmanship** counts just as much: working hard, being **modest** when their team wins, and not complaining when their team loses. Players with these qualities are called good sports.

When you read *Lou Gehrig: The Luckiest Man*, you'll meet one of the greatest baseball players in history. Lou Gehrig played for the New York Yankees in the 1920s and 1930s. You'll see why people still **honor** Gehrig both for his achievements and for his good sportsmanship.

center fielder

left fielder

right fielder

shortstop

second baseman

third baseman

pitcher

first baseman

catcher

During his career Lou Gehrig was both a **shortstop** and a **first baseman**.

For professional athletes, good sportsmanship includes meeting fans and signing autographs.

LOU
GEHRIG
~THE~
LUCKIEST
MAN

David A. Adler

ILLUSTRATED BY
Terry Widener

## Strategy Focus

Lou Gehrig was a hero both on and off the base-ball field. As you read about his life, **evaluate** how well the author shows Gehrig's heroism.

**1903** was a year of great beginnings. Henry Ford sold his first automobile and the Wright Brothers made the first successful flight in an airplane. In baseball, the first World Series was played. The team later known as the Yankees moved from Baltimore to New York. And on June 19, 1903, Henry Louis Gehrig was born. He would become one of the greatest players in baseball history.

Lou Gehrig was born in the Yorkville section of New York City. It was an area populated with poor immigrants like his parents, Heinrich and Christina Gehrig, who had come to the United States from Germany.

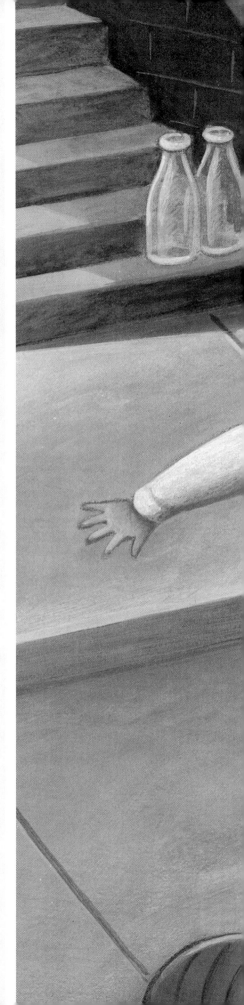

Christina Gehrig had great hopes for her son Lou. She dreamed that he would attend college and become an accountant or an engineer. She insisted that he study hard. Through eight years of grade school, Lou didn't miss a single day.

Lou's mother thought games and sports were a waste of time. But Lou loved sports. He got up early to play the games he loved — baseball, soccer, and football. He played until it was time to go to school. In high school Lou was a star on his school's baseball team.

After high school Lou Gehrig went to Columbia University. He was on the baseball team there, too, and on April 26, 1923, a scout for the New York Yankees watched him play. Lou hit two long home runs in that game. Soon after that he was signed to play for the Yankees.

The Yankees offered Lou a $1,500 bonus to sign plus a good salary. His family needed the money. Lou quit college and joined the Yankees. Lou's mother was furious. She was convinced that he was ruining his life.

On June 1, 1925, the Yankee manager sent Lou to bat for the shortstop. The next day Lou played in place of first baseman Wally Pipp. Those were the first two games in what would become an amazing record: For the next fourteen years Lou Gehrig played in 2,130 consecutive Yankee games. The boy who never missed a day of grade school became a man who never missed a game.

Lou Gehrig played despite stomachaches, fevers, a sore arm, back pains, and broken fingers. Lou's constant play earned him the nickname Iron Horse. All he would say about his amazing record was, "That's the way I am."

Lou was shy and modest, but people who watched him knew just how good he was. In 1927 Lou's teammate Babe Ruth hit sixty home runs, the most hit up to that time in one season. But it was Lou Gehrig who was selected that year by the baseball writers as the American League's Most Valuable Player. He was selected again as the league's MVP in 1936.

Then, during the 1938 baseball season — and for no apparent reason — Lou Gehrig stopped hitting. One newspaper reported that Lou was swinging as hard as he could, but when he hit the ball it didn't go anywhere.

Lou exercised. He took extra batting practice. He even tried changing the way he stood and held his bat. He worked hard during the winter of 1938 and watched his diet.

But the following spring Lou's playing was worse. Time after time he swung at the ball and missed. He had trouble fielding. And he even had problems off the field. In the clubhouse he fell down while he was getting dressed.

Some people said Yankee manager Joe McCarthy should take Lou out of the lineup. But McCarthy refused. He had great respect for Lou and said, "Gehrig plays as long as he wants to play." But Lou wasn't selfish. On May 2, 1939, he told Joe McCarthy, "I'm benching myself . . . for the good of the team."

When reporters asked why he took himself out, Lou didn't say he felt weak or how hard it was for him to run. Lou made no excuses. He just said that he couldn't hit and he couldn't field.

On June 13, 1939, Lou went to the Mayo Clinic in Rochester, Minnesota, to be examined by specialists. On June 19, his thirty-sixth birthday, they told Lou's wife, Eleanor, what was wrong. He was suffering

from amyotrophic lateral sclerosis, a deadly disease that affects the central nervous system.

Lou stayed with the team, but he didn't play. He was losing weight. His hair was turning gray. He didn't have to be told he was dying. He knew it. "I don't have long to go," he told a teammate.

Lou loved going to the games, being in the clubhouse, and sitting with his teammates. Before each game Lou brought the Yankee lineup card to the umpire at home plate. A teammate or coach walked with him, to make sure he didn't fall. Whenever Lou came onto the field the fans stood up and cheered for brave Lou Gehrig.

But Yankee fans and the team wanted to do more. They wanted Lou to know how deeply they felt about him. So they made July 4, 1939, Lou Gehrig Appreciation Day at Yankee Stadium.

Many of the players from the 1927 Yankees — perhaps the best baseball team ever — came to honor their former teammate. There was a marching band and gifts. Many people spoke, too. Fiorello La Guardia, the mayor of

New York City, told Lou, "You are the greatest prototype of good sportsmanship and citizenship."

When the time came for Lou to thank everyone, he was too moved to speak. But the fans wanted to hear him and chanted, "We want Gehrig! We want Gehrig!"

Dressed in his Yankee uniform, Lou Gehrig walked slowly to the array of microphones. He wiped his eyes, and with his baseball cap in his hands, his head down, he slowly spoke.

"Fans," he said, "for the past two weeks you have been reading about a bad break I got. Yet today I consider myself the luckiest man on the face of the earth."

It was a courageous speech. Lou didn't complain about his terrible illness. Instead he spoke of his many blessings and of the future. "Sure, I'm lucky," he said when he spoke of his years in baseball. "Sure, I'm lucky," he said again when he spoke of his fans and family.

Lou spoke about how good people had been to him. He praised his teammates. He thanked his parents and his wife, whom he called a tower of strength.

The more than sixty thousand fans in Yankee Stadium stood to honor Lou Gehrig.  His last words to them — and to the many thousands more sitting by their radios and listening — were, "So I close in saying that I might have had a bad break, but I have an awful lot to live for.  Thank you."

Lou stepped back from the microphones and wiped his eyes.  The stadium crowd let out a tremendous roar, and Babe Ruth did what many people must have wanted to do that day.  He threw his arms around Lou Gehrig and gave him a great warm hug.

The band played the song "I Love You Truly," and the fans chanted, "We love you, Lou."

When Lou Gehrig left the stadium later that afternoon, he told a teammate, "I'm going to remember this day for a long time."

In December 1939 Lou Gehrig was voted into the Baseball Hall of Fame. And the Yankees retired his uniform. No one else on the team would ever wear the number four. It was the first time a major-league baseball team did that to honor one of its players.

Mayor Fiorello La Guardia thought Lou's courage might inspire some of the city's troubled youths to be courageous, too. He offered Lou a job working with former prisoners as a member of the New York City Parole Commission. Lou had many opportunities to earn more money, but he believed this job would enable him to do something for the city that had given him so much.

Within little more than a year, Lou had to leave his job. He was too weak to keep working. He stayed at home, unable to do the simplest task.

Lou had many visitors. He didn't speak to them of his illness
or of dying. When he saw one friend visibly upset by the way he
looked, Lou told him not to worry. "I'll gradually get better," he said.
In cards to his friends Lou wrote, "We have much to be thankful for."

By the middle of May 1941, Lou hardly left his bed.  Then on Monday, June 2, 1941, just after ten o'clock at night, Lou Gehrig died.  He was thirty-seven years old.

On June 4 the Yankee game was canceled because of rain. Some people thought it was fitting that the Yankees did not play; this was the day of Lou Gehrig's funeral.

At the funeral the minister announced that there would be no speeches. "We need none," he said, "because you all knew him." That seemed fitting, too, for modest Lou Gehrig.

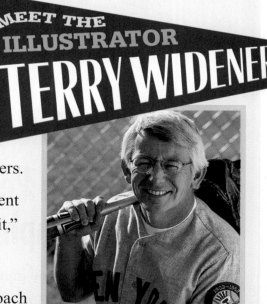

**D**avid Adler has always been a dreamer. He grew up in New York "in a large house filled with brothers, sisters, and books." He dreamed that a baseball scout would see him playing ball in his back yard and immediately sign him to the Yankees. Adler also wanted to be an actor, an artist, a lawyer, and a writer. Becoming an author, Adler says, "is one of the dreams I had that came true."

Adler loves his work because he can still follow his many interests. He has published more than one hundred books on topics such as math, science, and history. He's also written puzzle books, biographies, mysteries, and adventures.

**Other books:** the *Cam Jansen* mystery series, *A Picture Book of Helen Keller*, *Fraction Fun*

## MEET THE ILLUSTRATOR TERRY WIDENER

**W**henever Terry Widener illustrates a book, he tries to make the author's words come alive through his pictures. He hopes that his illustrations are exciting and entertaining, especially to young readers.

Widener's advice to young artists is to be patient to achieve their dreams. "It's very hard to wait," he says, "but I have found that if you work towards your goal, things seem to happen." When he's not illustrating, Widener likes to coach

Internet

To find out more about David Adler and Terry Widener, visit Education Place.
**www.eduplace.com/kids**

# Think About the Selection

**1.** What made Lou Gehrig a great ballplayer? Give facts about both his achievements and his character.

**2.** How did Gehrig's childhood habits help him when he joined the Yankees?

**3.** What does Gehrig's life teach you about good sportsmanship?

**4.** How do you think the fans felt when they heard Gehrig's speech at Yankee Stadium? Would you have felt the same?

**5.** Why did Lou Gehrig call himself "the luckiest man on the face of the earth"? Do you agree?

**6.** **Connecting/Comparing** Lou Gehrig and Gloria Estefan are not only stars but also good citizens. Explain.

*Persuading*

# Write a Persuasive Paragraph

There are many great baseball players, but Lou Gehrig's story has a special meaning in baseball history. Write a paragraph to persuade a reader that Lou Gehrig was one of the country's greatest baseball heroes. Go back to the story for details.

**Tips**

- To help you get started, write out the goal of your paragraph.
- Be sure to support your statements with facts and examples.

## Math

# Find the Difference

Lou Gehrig's record for consecutive games was broken in 1995 by Cal Ripken, Jr., of the Baltimore Orioles. The new record is 2,632 consecutive games. Figure out how many more consecutive games Cal Ripken played than Lou Gehrig. Go back to the story for clues.

**Bonus** Lou Gehrig played an average of 152 games a year for 14 years. Estimate how many more years Lou Gehrig would have had to play to reach the current record of 2,632 games.

## Viewing

# Compare Baseball Then and Now

Work with a partner. Go back to the story and look at the illustrations of baseball uniforms, baseball stadiums, and the fans. Then compare those with modern pictures from magazines or television. How are the styles different? How are they similar?

# Go on a Web Field Trip

Connect to Education Place to explore Yankee Stadium, the National Baseball Hall of Fame, and other fun sports sites.

**www.eduplace.com/kids**

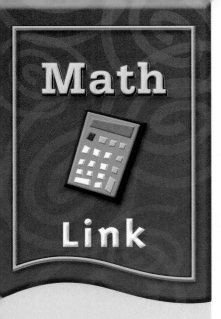

# Math Link

## Skill: How to Read a Chart

❶ Read the **title** of the chart. It tells what information the chart shows.

❷ Read the **headings** of the **rows** (which go across) and the **columns** (which go up and down) to see how the chart is organized.

❸ Move your finger across the rows and columns to find the information you want.

❹ Look for a **key** to help you understand symbols or abbreviations.

# FIGURING IT OUT

### by Marty Appel

**Y**ou can follow your favorite player or team by checking the newspapers each day, which are loaded with information on the major leagues.

You can see the standings of the clubs, the box scores of games, and the league leaders in many categories. You can often see a chart showing how everyone on the home team is hitting or pitching.

It is good to know how all of these baseball averages are figured. You can do it yourself with the help of a calculator.

## Lou Gehrig's Statistics

| Year | Team | HR | RBI | BA |
|------|----------|----|-----|------|
| 1925 | New York | 20 | 68 | .295 |
| 1926 | New York | 16 | 107 | .313 |
| 1927 | New York | 47 | 175 | .373 |
| 1928 | New York | 27 | 142 | .374 |
| 1929 | New York | 35 | 126 | .300 |

**Key:** **HR**–home runs; **RBI**–runs batted in; **BA**–batting average

**Batting Averages.** A batting average measures how many hits a player would get if he were to bat 1,000 times. Anything over .300 (say "three hundred") is considered excellent.

Use the division sign for the word *for*. If a batter has 71 hits *for* 253 at bats, you would calculate $71 \div 253 = .2806324$. Since batting averages are only shown in three numbers, you would round off the third number and this average would be .281. If the fourth number is five or more, add a number in the third column.

Try another one. Look at the league leaders and see if the math is correct!

**Earned Run Average.** This is a very important statistic for pitchers. The number tells you how many earned runs they allow for every nine innings they pitch. An earned run is a run that scores without help from errors, even a pitcher's own error. It is a run that has scored simply by hits, walks, and hit batters.

Clear the calculator. Punch in the earned runs (say, 60) and multiply it by 9. $60 \times 9 = 540$. Leave the 540 showing. Don't clear the calculator. Hit the $\div$ sign, and then punch in the innings pitched, say 210. That gives you an ERA of 2.5714285, which rounds off to 2.57. This is a good pitcher, one who allows fewer than three runs for every nine innings.

# Check Your Progress

You have just met three heroes, each of whom rises to heroism in unique ways. Now you will read and compare two more selections about heroism and polish your test-taking skills.

Before reading on, return to David Adler's letter on pages 528–530. Think about the qualities displayed by the people in this theme. Which of those character traits do you think David Adler would find most heroic? Why?

Now you will read about some unexpected heroes. As you read, think about what qualities the main characters both share. Do they remind you of yourself or someone you know? How do their quiet acts of heroism compare with the positive deeds of the other heroes you have met in this theme?

# Read and Compare

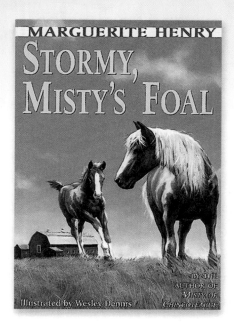

A fierce hurricane bears down on Paul's island home. Will this ordinary boy meet this extra-ordinary challenge? Read and find out!

**Try these strategies:**
Question
Summarize

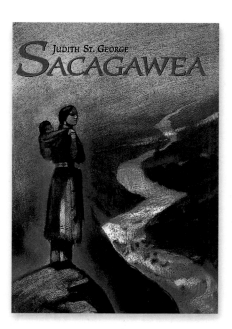

Learn how Sacagawea, a young Native American woman, changes history by saving an important scientific journey from near disaster.

**Try these strategies:**
Predict and Infer
Monitor and Clarify

**Strategies in Action**  *Look for ways to use all your reading strategies as you read the selections.*

# Stormy, Misty's Foal

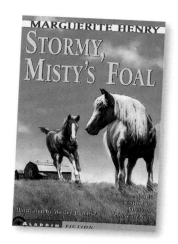

**by Marguerite Henry**
**illustrated by Keith Neely**

*A powerful hurricane rages over the island of Chincoteague, off the coast of Virginia.
As the wind dies down, Paul Beebe and his grandpa set out on horseback to see what
damage the hurricane has done. As they ride along the storm-tossed shore, they are
stopped by the driver of a Coast Guard DUKW, a large, half-boat, half-truck emergency
vehicle. The driver needs Paul and Grandpa's help in town. As Paul boards the DUKW,
he worries about his prized pony, Misty, who is about to have a foal. For now, though,
he must try and concentrate on others who need him....*

As they turned onto Main Street, which runs along the very shore
of the bay, Paul was stunned. Yesterday the wide street with its white
houses and stores and oyster-shucking sheds had been neat and prim,
like a Grandma Moses picture. Today boats were on the loose, bashing
into houses. A forty-footer had rammed right through one house, its
bow sticking out the back door, its stern out the front.

Nothing was sacred to the sea. It swept into the cemetery, lifted up
coffins, cast them into people's front yards.

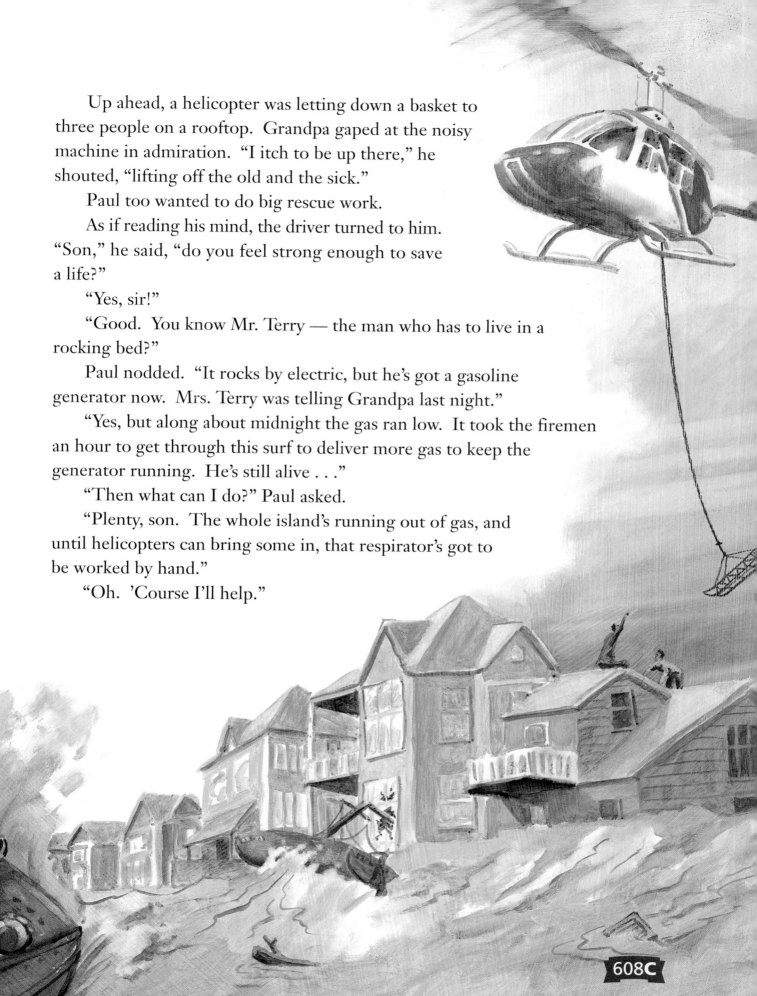

Up ahead, a helicopter was letting down a basket to three people on a rooftop. Grandpa gaped at the noisy machine in admiration. "I itch to be up there," he shouted, "lifting off the old and the sick."

Paul too wanted to do big rescue work.

As if reading his mind, the driver turned to him. "Son," he said, "do you feel strong enough to save a life?"

"Yes, sir!"

"Good. You know Mr. Terry — the man who has to live in a rocking bed?"

Paul nodded. "It rocks by electric, but he's got a gasoline generator now. Mrs. Terry was telling Grandpa last night."

"Yes, but along about midnight the gas ran low. It took the firemen an hour to get through this surf to deliver more gas to keep the generator running. He's still alive . . ."

"Then what can I do?" Paul asked.

"Plenty, son. The whole island's running out of gas, and until helicopters can bring some in, that respirator's got to be worked by hand."

"Oh. 'Course I'll help."

608C

The driver now turned to Grandpa. "These folks," he said, indicating his passengers, "are flooded out. We'll take them to the second story of the Fire House for shelter. Then we got to chug up to Bear Scratch section and rescue a family with six children. Whoa! Here we are at the Terrys'."

The DUKW skewered to a stop in front of a two-story white house.

"Good luck, Paul. When the gas arrives, grab any DUKW going by, and we'll meet you back at Barrett's Store along about noon."

Paul got out and plowed up to the house. The door opened as he stumbled up the flooded steps, and Mrs. Terry greeted him. Her face was pale, and there were deep circles under her eyes, but she smiled. "You've come to man the generator?"

"Yes, sir — I mean, yes, ma'am," Paul stammered. "I'm Paul Beebe."

"Oh," she smiled again. "So you're the Beebe boy. You're the one who rescued Misty when she was a baby and nearly drowned."

"Yes, ma'am."

"And to think that now she's going to have a baby of her own."

"Yes, ma'am. Any minute."

All the while she watched Paul pulling off his boots and jacket Mrs. Terry talked to him, but her head was cocked, ears alert, listening to the steady hum of the generator in the next room.

"We've got so little gas left," she said. "The doctor says I'm to save it in case relief-men get worn out." She led the way down the hall to Mr. Terry's bedroom.

Paul blanched. Hospitals and sick rooms gave him a cold clutch of fear. But the moment he saw Mr. Terry smiling there in his rocking bed he was all eagerness to help. Maybe he could do a better job than an old machine. Maybe he could pump stronger and faster, so Mr. Terry'd get a lot more air in his lungs and his face wouldn't look so white.

Mrs. Terry showed Paul how to work the controls. "He's used to just twenty-eight rocks a minute," she explained. "No faster."

"Hi, son." The voice from the bed was weak but cheerful. "It's good of you to help."

Paul bent to his work, pushing up and down in steady rhythm, twenty-eight strokes to the minute. Maybe, he thought as the minutes went by, now I can qualify for a volunteer fireman. He was glad he was used to pumping water for the ponies. And that set him thinking of Misty, and the bittersweet worry rushed over him again so that he barely heard Mrs. Terry.

"How wonderful people are, Paul," she was saying. "With their property wrecked and their own lives endangered, they are so concerned about us. And we aren't even Chincoteaguers. We just came here to retire."

Paul heard the words far off. He was thinking: Sometimes newborn colts don't breathe right away and horse doctors have to pump air into their lungs with their hand — like this, like this, like this. Down, up, down, up, down, up. Would it be twenty-eight times a minute for a little foal? Or more? Or less? How would he know? Why hadn't he asked Dr. Finney, the veterinarian from Pocomoke?

Runnels and rivulets of sweat were trickling down his back; his face and hair were dripping as if he were still out in the rain.

"Paul!" Mrs. Terry was saying, "Look! A whole beautiful tank of gas has come. And the DUKW man is waiting to give you a ride back. High time, too. You're all tuckered out, poor lamb!"

Mr. Terry smiled and shook hands with Paul. "In my book, you are a hero," he said.

# SACAGAWEA

by Judith St. George
illustrated by Pablo Torrecilla

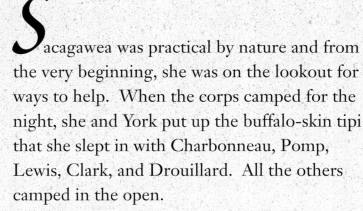

*It is 1804. The United States has just doubled in size with the purchase of the Louisiana Territory — thousands of square miles of vast, western lands. The newly formed Corps of Discovery, led by Captains Meriwether Lewis and William Clark, has set out to explore and map this unknown territory. At Fort Mandan, their winter camp, a young Shoshone woman named Sacagawea joins the explorers along with her husband, Charbonneau, and their infant son, Pomp. As they set out along the mighty Missouri River, the group soon recognizes her as a key member of this historic Journey of Discovery.*

Sacagawea was practical by nature and from the very beginning, she was on the lookout for ways to help. When the corps camped for the night, she and York put up the buffalo-skin tipi that she slept in with Charbonneau, Pomp, Lewis, Clark, and Drouillard. All the others camped in the open.

On the third day out, Sacagawea noticed a mound of loose dirt near some driftwood. She knew right away what it was. Poking in the dirt with a sharp stick, she found a large stock-pile of white roots that a gopher had stored away. The roots were the size of a man's finger, and quite delicious. The men told her that they tasted just like Jerusalem artichokes.

Every time the corps stopped, Sacagawea searched for flavorful berries and roots. And she knew what she was doing. She was a Shoshone and for most of the year, Shoshones lived on wild plants, roots, and fish. With Pomp in his cradle bundle, Sacagawea picked baskets of redberries, serviceberries, gooseberries, chokecherries, and purple currants. She dug up prairie turnips, small white onions, and wild licorice.

Because game was plentiful, almost every meal was boiled, fried, or roasted meat. Although the men especially liked buffalo tongues and beaver tails, their favorite was a buffalo sausage that Charbonneau cooked, which he called *boudin blanc*. His finishing touch was to fry the sausage in bear oil.

An all-meat diet caused a disease called scurvy. Sacagawea had no way of knowing that fruits and vegetables prevented scurvy. Nevertheless, the berries and roots that she constantly gathered went a long way in keeping the men healthy.

Young as she was, Sacagawea also proved herself to be cool in a crisis. A few weeks into their journey up the Missouri River, she and Pomp were sitting under an awning in the white pirogue. Charbonneau, Cruzatte, and four other men were also aboard, as were the captains' journals, instruments, papers, medicine kit, and trade goods, which they planned to give to the Indians along the way.

Lewis called Charbonneau "the most timid waterman in the world." Only a short time before, he had been steersman when a strong gust of wind had almost overturned the pirogue. He had instantly panicked. Nevertheless, for some unknown reason, he was once again at the helm.

All of a sudden, a squall hit. The wind ripped the sail away from the man holding it and the pirogue tipped at a dangerous angle. Charbonneau again panicked. Instead of putting the boat into the wind, he luffed it broadside and it heeled over. Only the *awning* over Sacagawea and Pomp saved the pirogue from capsizing.

*Pages from Lewis and Clark's journal*

*A Sacagawea gold dollar coin*

Sure that he was about to die, Charbonneau started screaming for mercy. Granted, he couldn't swim, but then neither could two other men on board. Although Sacagawea was a strong swimmer, Pomp was strapped in his cradle bundle on her back, and she was as helpless as anyone else.

As the pirogue filled with water, Cruzatte yelled at Charbonneau to turn the boat into the wind. Charbonneau returned to his senses and grabbed the rudder. Cruzatte then ordered two of the men to take down the sail and the other two to start bailing.

If anyone had reason to panic, it was Sacagawea, who carried her darling Pomp in his cradle bundle. But she didn't. Barely able to balance herself in the stern of the boat that was already filled with water, Sacagawea first made sure that Pomp was safe. She then reached out and grabbed everything that was floating past her into the river. She had no idea what she was rescuing. All she knew was that the captains set great store by all these papers and equipment they had packed in watertight bags.

By the time Cruzatte and the other men were able to row to shore, the pirogue was barely above water. Although Cruzatte's quick thinking may have saved them from drowning, Sacagawea's quick thinking had saved what Lewis later said was worth his life. Until now Lewis hadn't paid much attention to Sacagawea one way or the other, but he praised her courage and cool-headedness. Sacagawea thought nothing of it. She had seen what needed to be done and did it. That was all.

Sacagawea couldn't speak English to the soldiers, or even French to her husband. But their journey had hardly gotten underway when she proved herself to be as valuable to Lewis and Clark as any man in the company.

*After the episode on the river, the Corps of Discovery journeyed on for two more years through boiling river rapids, and over high, snowy mountain passes. Sacagawea's quiet, daily heroism would help ensure the success of their long and dangerous journey west. Serving as interpreter, navigator, and advisor all-in-one, Sacagawea's knowledge of the lands and peoples of the West would help her to become a valuable member of the exploration party — and to claim her rightful place in American history.*

# Think and Compare

1. Compare and contrast the heroic acts performed by both Paul and Sacagawea. How are the two main characters most alike?

2. How is the heroism described in *Stormy, Misty's Foal* and *Sacagawea* different from that of the other selections in the theme?

3. Which character from the theme do you feel is the most heroic? Why? Give details from the selection.

4. How might each character in this theme feel about being called a hero? Which character would be most surprised? Why?

5. Name someone you think is a hero. Give reasons for your answer.

**Strategies in Action** Explain how some of the reading strategies you used in this theme helped you to better understand your reading.

## Write a Journal Entry

Write a journal entry that Sacagawea might have written about the day she saved the materials from being washed away. Explain how Sacagawea might have felt that day and about being on the voyage with Lewis and Clark.

 **Tips**

- Review the selection.
- Tell what happened from Sacagawea's point of view.
- Think about her feelings and use descriptive words.

# Writing an Answer to a Question

Some test items ask you to write an answer to a question about something you have read. Usually you can answer these questions in a few sentences. Here is an example of this type of question for *Stormy, Misty's Foal.*

---

**Write your answer to this question.**

**1.** Paul's day is filled with unusual events. How and why do his feelings change with each new experience? Give four examples.

---

 **Understand the question.**

Find the key words in the question. Use them to understand what you need to do.

**Get ready to write.**

Skim the selection, using the key words. List the details that will help you answer the question.

Here is an example of a good list.

| What Happens | How Paul Feels |
|---|---|
| sees a helicopter rescue | eager to help; excited |
| goes to help Mr. Terry | like he's in a hospital; scared, nervous |
| Mr. Terry smiles. | relieved |
| pumps the bed and thinks of Misty | worried |

 **Write your answer.**

Use details from your list. Write a clear and complete answer.

Here is an example of a complete answer.

> At first, Paul is excited. He sees the helicopter rescue and is eager to help. Then Paul goes to help Mr. Terry. He is nervous because Mr. Terry's bedroom reminds him of a hospital. Then Mr. Terry smiles, and Paul feels relieved. But as he pumps the bed, Paul thinks of Misty and her foal, and he worries about them in the storm.

POURQUOI TALES

# Pourquoi Tales

Why do stars twinkle? How did the elephant get its trunk? **Pourquoi** (poor-KWA) **tales** are folktales that explain how something in **nature** came to be. It could be a feature of an animal or a force like the sun or the wind. A character might be a talking elephant or the ocean. See for yourself how pourquoi tales invent the world!

## CONTENTS

611

**Focus on Genre**

# WHY THE SUN AND THE MOON LIVE IN THE SKY

### by Julius Lester

IN THE TIME OF THE BEGINNING of beginnings, everything and everyone lived on earth. If you had been living in those times, you could've sat on your porch in the evening and watched the Sun, the Moon and the Stars taking a stroll and chatting with all the neighbors.

The Sun had many friends, but his best friend in all the universe was Water. Every day Sun visited Water and they talked about this and that and enjoyed each other's company, which is what friends do.

There was one thing wrong with their friendship, however. Water never came to visit Sun at his house. That hurt Sun's feelings.

He could've held onto his hurt feelings and gotten angry. But that's not the way to treat your feelings when they're hurt. You feel better if you talk to the one who hurt them. Maybe Water didn't know that he had hurt Sun's feelings.

"Why don't you ever visit me?" Sun asked Water.

"I would love to visit you," Water replied, "but your house might not be big enough for me and all of my relatives. I wouldn't want to force you out of your house. If you want me to visit, you must build a very, very, very, very, very large house. I need a lot of room."

Sun went home and told his wife, the Moon, that they had to build a very, very, very, very, very large house. His friend, Water, was coming to visit.

They set to work immediately. He sawed. She nailed. He hammered. She measured, and they built a very, very, very, very, very large house indeed.

The house was so large that it took a whole day to walk from the front door to the back door. The house was so wide that when you stood on one side, you couldn't see the other side.

Sun went and told Water that he could come visit now.

The next morning Water flowed up the road. "Is it safe to come in?" he asked when he got to the house.

"Please enter," said Sun and Moon, opening the door to the house they had built.

Water began flowing in. With him came the fish and all the other water creatures.

Soon the water was knee-deep. "Is it still safe for me to come in?"

"Of course," Sun and Moon said.

More water flowed in. Soon it was halfway to the ceiling. "Do you want more of me to come in?"

"Of course," said Sun and Moon, rising to the ceiling so they wouldn't get wet and have their lights put out.

More water and more water and more water flowed in. Sun and Moon had to go sit on the roof.

"Do you want more of me to come in?" asked Water.

Sun and Moon said yes, not knowing what they were saying.

More and more Water poured in. With him came more and more fish and whales and sharks and seaweed and crabs and lobsters. Water covered the roof of the house and got higher and higher.

The higher Water rose, the higher in the sky Sun and Moon had to go to stay dry.

Finally Sun and Moon were so high in the sky they weren't sure how to get down. But they liked being so high up and looking down on the world.

And that's where they've been ever since.

Focus on Genre

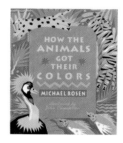

# Tiger

## by Michael Rosen

A meeting is taking place on Great Mountain.

Tiger says Tiger's the best, the strongest, the fastest on earth. Thunder says Thunder's the best, the loudest, the fiercest on earth. Echo says Echo's the best, the toughest, the cleverest on earth. Dragon says Dragon's the best, the mightiest, the hottest on earth.

"Yes, yes, yes," says Tiger. "I know all about you. But the thing that makes me the best is I'm not afraid of anything."

Tiger, Thunder, Echo, and Dragon cannot decide who is the greatest.

"Let us have a contest," says Tiger. "In this contest we will see which of us is the most terrifying. Whoever can make the other three cry, 'Stop, no more!' is the winner."

They all agree, and Tiger laughs.

"Now I'll show them."

Tiger paws the ground, opens his jaws, shows every tooth in his head, and roars.  Thunder vanishes into thin air and sits among the clouds.  Echo rolls down Great Mountain, across Blue River, up Little Mountain and is gone.  Dragon coils and twists her long body and tail and squirms her way up into the sky, out of reach of Tiger's claws.

No one cries, "Stop, no more!"  Tiger is left pawing the ground and roaring to himself until no roar is left.  Thunder, Echo, and Dragon come back.

"Tiger loses," they say.

"I know, I know, I know," says Tiger.

Now Thunder comes forward, looks around at the clouds, and flies off to the deepest, darkest one in sight.  From that cloud come the most horrendous drumming and deafening rolls.

Tiger can't bear it and shouts, "Stop, no more!"

But Echo listens to Thunder's rolls, waits for them at the top of Little Mountain, and rolls them back at Thunder.  And Dragon just coils and twists her long body and tail and squirms her way up into the sky, up above Thunder's clouds where it is all quiet.

Thunder, Echo, and Dragon come back.

"Thunder loses," they say.

"I'm better than Tiger," says Thunder.

"I know, I know, I know," says Tiger.

Now Echo comes forward and waits.

"Well, aren't you going to start?" says Tiger.

"Going to start?" says Echo.

"Well, don't hang about," says Tiger.

"Don't hang about," says Echo.

"It's not me that's hanging about, you fool," says Tiger.

"You fool," says Echo.

"Who are you calling a fool?" asks Tiger angrily.

"Who are you calling a fool?" asks Echo angrily.

"You," says Tiger.

"You," says Echo.

"Just get on with it," roars Tiger.

"Get on with it," roars Echo.

"It's not my turn," says Tiger.

"It's not my turn," says Echo.

"It is," shouts Tiger.

"It is," shouts Echo.

"You're driving me mad," says Tiger.

"You're driving me mad," says Echo.

"Stop, stop, no more!" cries Tiger.

"Stop, stop, no more!" cries Echo.

"I agree," says Thunder.

"I agree," says Echo.

"Stop, no more!" says Thunder.

Echo looks around for Dragon, but Dragon has coiled and twisted up her long body and tail and squirmed away up into the sky, where not even an echo can reach. Sometime later, Dragon comes back.

"Echo loses," they say.

"Echo was better than Thunder," says Dragon.

"Better than Thunder," says Echo.

"That's true," says Thunder.

"Echo was better than Tiger," says Dragon.

"Better than Tiger," says Echo.

"I know, I know, I know," says Tiger.

Now it's Dragon's turn. Dragon coils and twists her long body and tail and pours fire out of her mouth. Thunder flees to a cloud, but Dragon follows and breathes fire on the cloud and dries it up until there is nowhere for Thunder to sit.

"Stop, no more!" shouts Thunder.

Dragon chases Echo down Great Mountain, across Blue River, and up Little Mountain until they meet going down the other side.

"Do you want to give up?" asks Dragon.

"Give up," says Echo.

"Stop, no more?" asks Dragon.

618

"Stop, no more," says Echo.

"And now for Tiger," says Dragon. But Tiger is hiding in the forest on the side of the Great Mountain. So Dragon coils and twists up her long body and tail and lets fly a huge jet of flame, setting that forest on fire. But Tiger is ready, and he runs from the fire that races through the trees. And Tiger could have escaped, but for the wind in the treetops that flies even faster. Just as Tiger is leaving the forest, the fire crackles overhead. Flaming branches of a tree fall on Tiger, just as he thinks he is free.

"Stop, no more!" shouts Tiger.

"I've won," says Dragon.

"That's true," say Thunder and Echo.

"Never mind that," says Tiger, "look at my coat, the branches have burned my fur."

"Yes," says Dragon. "You're all *stripy*."

"I know, I know, I know," says Tiger.

Focus on Genre

NATIVE AMERICAN STORIES by Joseph Bruchac

# How Turtle Flew South for the Winter

## by Joseph Bruchac

*IT WAS THE TIME OF YEAR* when the leaves start to fall from the aspens.

Turtle was walking around when he saw many birds gathering together in the trees. They were making a lot of noise and Turtle was curious. "Hey," Turtle said. "What is happening?"

"Don't you know?" the birds said. "We're getting ready to fly to the south for the winter."

"Why are you going to do that?" Turtle asked.

"Don't you know anything?" the birds said. "Soon it's going to be very cold here and the snow will fall. There

620

won't be much food to eat. Down south it will be warm. Summer lives there all of the time and there's plenty of food."

As soon as they mentioned the food, Turtle became even more interested. "Can I come with you?" he said.

"You have to fly to go south," said the birds. "You are a turtle and you can't fly."

But Turtle would not give up. "Isn't there some way you could take me along?" He begged and pleaded. Finally the birds agreed just to get him to stop asking.

"Look here," the birds said, "can you hold onto a stick hard with your mouth?"

"That's no problem at all," Turtle said. "Once I grab onto something no one can make me let go until I am ready."

"Good," said the birds. "Then you hold on hard to this stick. These two birds here will each grab one end of it in their claws. That way they can carry you along. But remember, you have to keep your mouth shut!"

"That's easy," said Turtle. "Now let's go south where Summer keeps all that food." Turtle grabbed onto the middle of the stick and

two big birds came and grabbed each end. They flapped their wings hard and lifted Turtle off the ground. Soon they were high in the sky and headed toward the south.

Turtle had never been so high off the ground before, but he liked it. He could look down and see how small everything looked. But before they had gone too far, he began to wonder where they were. He wondered what the lake was down below him and what those hills were. He wondered how far they had come and how far they would have to go to get to the south where Summer lived. He wanted to ask the two birds who were carrying him, but he couldn't talk with his mouth closed.

Turtle rolled his eyes. But the two birds just kept on flying. Then Turtle tried waving his legs at them, but they acted as if they didn't even notice. Now Turtle was getting upset. If they were going to take him south, then the least they could do was tell him where they were now! "Mmmph," Turtle said, trying to get their attention. It didn't work. Finally Turtle lost his temper.

"Why don't you listen to . . ." but that was all he said, for as soon as he opened his mouth to speak, he had to let go of the stick and he started to fall. Down and down he fell, a long, long way. He was so frightened that he pulled his legs and his head in to protect himself! When he hit the ground he hit so hard that his shell cracked. He was lucky that he hadn't been killed, but he ached all over. He ached so much that he crawled into a nearby pond, swam down to the bottom and dug into the mud to get as far away from the sky as he possibly could. Then he fell asleep and he slept all through the winter and didn't wake up until the spring.

So it is that today only the birds fly south to the land where Summer lives while turtles, who all have cracked shells now, sleep through the winter.

# Think About the
# POURQUOI TALES

1. What do the three pourquoi tales you have just read have in common? What are some differences among them?

2. Which character has the most in common with Turtle? What qualities do they share?

3. How is a pourquoi tale different from a traditional folktale? What do the two types of story have in common?

4. Which of these tales do you think does the best job of explaining its subject? Give examples from the story to support your choice.

5. Many cultures all over the world have their own pourquoi tales. Why do you think they are so popular?

**Internet**

## Post a Review

Which pourquoi tale did you like the best? What did you enjoy about it? Post an online review and tell other readers across the nation!

**www.eduplace.com/kids**

**Creating**

# Write Your Own Pourquoi Tale

Become a storyteller. Think of something in nature that would be fun to explain in a creative way. It could be an animal, a geographical feature, or a force of nature. Decide how your "character" came to be the way it is. Write your story so that it sounds as if you were telling it aloud.

## Tips

- **Give your "character" an interesting personality.**
- **Use dialogue as well as action to show the personalities of all the characters.**
- **You might include a lesson in your tale: the character gets what it deserves in the end.**
- **Read your tale aloud to see if it has the effect you want.**

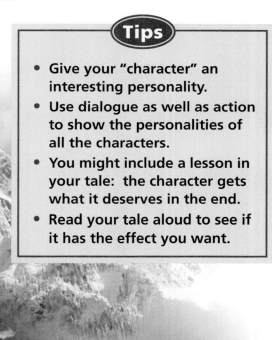

# Nature
## *Friend and Foe*

Nature is a gentle rain
and winds that howl and blow,
a thunderstorm, a hurricane,
a silent field of snow.

— *Jack Prelutsky*
*from "Nature Is"*

# Nature
## *Friend and Foe*
### with Seymour Simon

Dear Reader,

I was born in the Bronx, a part of New York City. It may seem odd to you that an author of books about natural things such as wildfires, icebergs, volcanoes, big cats, wolves, gorillas, the planets, and outer space grew up in a large city. But even though I lived in an apartment house surrounded by other apartment houses, I found nature all around me.

On my street, there was a vacant lot. Wild grasses, weeds, and small trees grew in the lot. Insects buzzed, spiders made webs, and earthworms wriggled in the soil. Birds flew in to look for bugs or seeds to eat. Feral cats (we called them "alley cats") roamed and raised litters of kittens in the city "jungle" of the lot. Wildflowers appeared in the summer and snowdrifts piled up in the winter. The vacant lot was my own little corner of the natural world.

I've been a nature explorer all my life. At first I explored what I found near my home. Not far from me were an ocean beach and the wonderful Bronx Zoo, where I saw lions, tigers, elephants, and gorillas.

When I grew up I traveled to many places and continued to explore the natural world. I've been scared and shaken by earthquakes in California and Mexico, watched erupting volcanoes in Hawaii, icebergs and glaciers in Alaska, and wildfires in the forests of the western states. I've walked in rain forests and deserts, along ocean shores and mountain trails, and listened to the sounds of wolves and the thunder of a lightning storm.

Nature has many moods and is always changing. Nature can be as calm as the sky on a sunny day or as dangerous as the winds of a hurricane or the snows of a blizzard. Nature is not just good or bad, nor only friend or foe. Nature is all of these things. Nature is always with us and around us and in us. We are truly part of Nature.

Sincerely,

Seymour Simon

# The Faces of Nature

As a child, Seymour Simon explored nature in a vacant lot near his home. What are some discoveries you have made about nature in your own neighborhood? Simon also writes that nature has "many moods." What moods have you observed in nature?

Look at the covers shown below. What do you think you will learn about nature from each selection? As you read each one, think about whether it describes nature as a friend, a foe, both, or maybe even neither. From the wilds of Alaska to the shores of Maine — get ready to experience the many faces of nature.

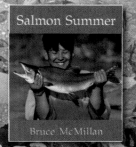

**Internet**

To learn about the authors in this theme, visit Education Place. **www.eduplace.com/kids**

# Background and Vocabulary

Salmon Summer

Bruce McMillan

**Salmon Summer**

**Read to find the meanings of these words.**

*e* ● Glossary

abundance

ancestors

lures

scavengers

spawn

# The Land and People of Kodiak Island

A sculpture of a traditional Alaskan canoe

Kodiak Island is part of Alaska. You might expect the weather to be cold there, but Kodiak Island's climate is mild enough for farming. An **abundance** of fish provides food for the human and animal populations. One of the busiest seasons on Kodiak Island

▲
The town of Old Harbor on Kodiak Island

A grizzly bear (small photo) and ▶
a Kodiak bear hunting for
salmon on Kodiak Island

is summer, when the salmon return to the island's streams to **spawn**, or lay their eggs.

Salmon are important to life on Kodiak Island. The native people, called Aleuts [AL-ee-oots] or Alutiiq [ah-LOO-TIK], have lived on Kodiak Island for hundreds of years. Aleuts today fish for salmon as their **ancestors** did before them, using nets and **lures**. Animals such as the Kodiak bear and the fox also eat the salmon. Even **scavengers** such as seagulls take part in the feast. Learn more about life on Kodiak Island as you read about an Aleut boy's activities in *Salmon Summer*.

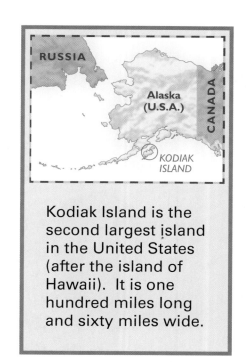

Kodiak Island is the second largest island in the United States (after the island of Hawaii). It is one hundred miles long and sixty miles wide.

# Meet the Author and Photographer

# Bruce McMillan

Can you remember a present you got when you were five years old? Bruce McMillan can. His father gave him a camera for his fifth birthday — and he's been taking pictures ever since! In high school, McMillan was the photographer for his school newspaper. Today, he travels all over the world taking pictures and writing stories.

McMillan takes photographs first and then writes a story to go along with them. Once, he rescued a tricycle from the town dump. He took pictures of the tricycle and wrote a story about it. Although he's been a photographer for most of his life, McMillan is still excited about looking for new things to photograph. "Even now," he says, "every time I shoot I seem to learn more."

**Other books:** *Penguins at Home, Nights of the Pufflings, Summer Ice*

Internet

To find out more about Bruce McMillan, visit Education Place. **www.eduplace.com/kids**

# Salmon Summer

## Bruce McMillan

**Strategy Focus**

In this selection, you'll find out how one Alaskan boy spends his summer. As you read, stop to **summarize** his many activities.

Summer, Matfay Fish Camp, Moser Bay, Kodiak Island, Alaska

Alex loves to snack on tamuuq [tah-MOHK], chewy dry fish. This tamuuq comes from halibut, his favorite fish to catch. But now that the salmon are running, Alex is going fishing for salmon.

He's been waiting for them to return. As young fry they left the nearby stream to live at sea. To complete their life cycle, they're coming back to the same stream to spawn.

This summer nine-year-old Alex is finally old enough to help his father set the gill net. Like their Aleut [AL-ee-oot] ancestors, they catch fish to feed their family.

By next morning the net is full of flapping fish. They are trapped in the almost-invisible mesh of the net as they try to swim past Alex's beach. Alex and his father pull their net. It's time to "pick" fish.

Alex wears gloves to protect his hands not only from the fine mesh of the nets but also from the stings of jellyfish. It's not as much fun as fishing with a line, but there will be time for that later. Now they must finish landing today's catch.

Back on the beach Alex's father asks him if he can tell what kind of salmon they caught. First Alex picks out a humpy, the pink salmon that are running in the greatest numbers. Below that he lays a red salmon, the best kind for eating. Then he lays down a silver salmon and finally, at the bottom, a big dog salmon.

Alex cleans salmon alongside his father as seagulls watch from afar. He uses the same knife his grandmother's uncle used to skin bears. He cuts filets from one of the fish for dinner. With the others, he cuts off the head, pulls out the guts, and leaves the skin and tails on. They're for the smokehouse. But as the cleaned fish hang outside, uninvited visitors fly in to steal a meal.

Magpies sneak in for a bite when nobody's watching. They're not the only hungry birds. Alex leaves salmon scraps to wash away with the tide and be eaten by scavengers. The gulls swoop down for a fish feast. As always, they eat their favorite part of the salmon first — the eyes. At dusk another animal arrives to take home more of Alex's scraps.

A fox slinks by to pick up a meal.  She takes it back to her pups in their den near Alex's cabin.

Farther up the bay, at Dog Salmon Creek, a Kodiak bear grabs a king salmon to feed her two cubs.  Later, when Alex goes by, the bears are gone.  But he knows they were here.  He follows claw tracks in the sand and discovers the remains of their meal.

There's an abundance of salmon for all. There's salmon for the eagles to catch. There's more salmon for Alex to catch and give to the people in town who are too old to fish.

There's also salmon for the family's smokehouse. The fish Alex and his father cleaned are smoked. Alex hangs the smoked red salmon outside in the sun to cure. The fish drip dry, which removes the excess oil.

Soon the smoked salmon is ready to eat. Alex's little brother, Larry, tears off a bite as he watches Alex clean more fish.

When Alex discards some salmon eggs, it reminds him that there are ripe salmonberries behind camp, and he's hungry. Alex picks berries for jam but eats most of what he picks. Then he and his father head out to the family's crab traps. He brings along a few small salmon for bait.

Alex hauls in the family's shallow-water trap for Dungeness crabs but finds nothing. He slices open some salmon and baits the trap again.

In deeper water he helps his father haul their trap for Alaskan king crabs. He finds one inside, but the prickly crab is too small to keep. Overboard it goes. After Alex rebaits the trap, he helps push it over the side and watches until it sinks out of sight. Then he heads up the bay to Dog Salmon Creek. It's time to play.

It's time to fish for fun. The creek is full of salmon. The fish are heading upstream to mate — to lay and fertilize their eggs on the gravelly bottom. Alex ties a silver lure with three hooks on it to his line. There are so many fish that he often hooks one in its body.

Alex catches fish after fish. But he doesn't keep them. Every time he catches one, he releases it. He knows the biggest fish is yet to come — and it won't be a salmon.

The last salmon Alex catches is a male humpy. He can tell this one's a male because it is changing. Its jaws are becoming hooked. Its back is growing a hump. Its life cycle is almost complete.

All the salmon will soon die upstream after expending their last energy to mate and cover their eggs with gravel. The floating bodies will become easy meals for the wildlife. But not this salmon. This one will be Alex's bait for the biggest fish of all — a halibut.

It's time to head out in the boat and go hooking. It's time to get fish for tamuuq.

Alex baits a hook with his salmon, attaches a heavy sinker, and hangs the line overboard. It drops to the bottom. He waits and feels with his fingers for a tug on the line. He feels a nibble. He pulls. Nothing. He feels another nibble and tugs hard. He's got it. The hook is set. Alex holds on and starts pulling it in.

With help from his father, Alex pulls the halibut aboard.  It's almost as big as Alex, and it's not even a very big one.

Back at camp, Alex's grandmother slices the halibut flesh into strips and hangs them up to dry.  Alex can hardly wait.  It takes about ten days.  Finally, the dry fish, his favorite snack, is ready.  It's the same kind of snack his ancestors ate — tamuuq.

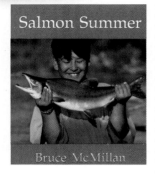

Salmon Summer

Bruce McMillan

# Think About the Selection

**1.** How are salmon important to life on Kodiak Island?

**2.** Why do you think the author begins the selection by telling about tamuuq?

**3.** Give examples of how Alex keeps the traditions of his ancestors.

**4.** Why do you think Alex likes fishing with a line more than fishing with a net?

**5.** If you could spend the summer on Kodiak Island, which activities would you like best? Which ones would you like least?

**6. Connecting/Comparing** How do Alex and his family show respect for nature? Give examples.

**Comparing/Contrasting**

# Write a Comparison

Alex loves to fish, but how about you? Write a paragraph comparing what Alex does for fun with what you like to do. Explain how your favorite activity is similar to and different from Alex's.

### Tips

- Brainstorm a list of your interests and then choose one.
- Use comparison words such as *but*, *similar to*, and *on the other hand*.

## Science

# Make a Food Web

All the inhabitants of Kodiak Island — from humans to animals — eat salmon. Make a food web showing all the creatures that eat salmon. Go back to the story for clues.

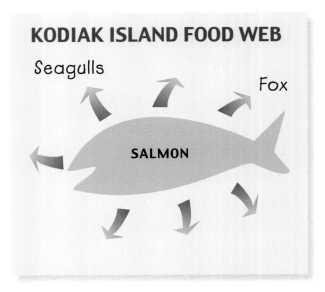

**KODIAK ISLAND FOOD WEB**

Seagulls

Fox

SALMON

## Vocabulary

# Make a Fishing Catalog

What items does Alex use when he goes fishing? Make a fishing catalog. Go back to the selection and list all the fishing equipment. Draw or cut out a picture of each item. Then label each picture.

## Label a Diagram

How many parts of a salmon can you name? Connect to Education Place and label a salmon diagram. **www/eduplace.com/kids**

## Social Studies Link

# SEAL ISLAND KIDS

**Skill: How to Use SQRRR**

*The letters SQRRR stand for five steps:*

❶ **Survey** the article. Look at the title, headings, pictures, and captions. Read the first paragraph.

❷ Turn each heading into a **question**.

❸ **Read** the text under the heading to answer your question.

❹ **Recite** the answer to your question in your own words.

❺ **Review** what you've learned.

**Story and Photos by Yva Momatiuk and John Eastcott**

Seals were a big part of the lives of Aleut people in the far, far North. Today, many Aleut kids say they'd rather drive ATVs and play computer games than deal with seals. But then some of them found out that the seals needed their help. . . .

**Every summer, nearly one million seals return to these small islands to raise their young.**

"Seals are our brothers." That's what many Aleut people say. Some Aleuts live on St. Paul Island (see map). It's one of the Pribilof Islands, near the mainland of Alaska. These people have always depended on northern fur seals for tasty meat and warm clothing.

In the past, Aleut children grew up learning about seals from their parents. During long winter nights, they listened to the elders telling stories about trips in sea kayaks made from animal skins and bones. The children learned how important seals were in the lives of their people.

In recent years, many Aleut grownups began to work in offices. Their kids went to school and played computer games at home. Fewer and fewer kids got to know much about their misty island. They seldom

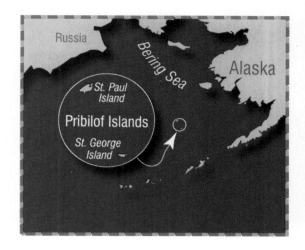

watched the thousands of seals or the millions of birds that return to the Pribilof Islands every summer. Some kids drove all-terrain vehicles (ATVs) in ways that damaged the land. Other kids bothered seals or littered the beach.

**Samantha and Candace are just two of the Aleutian Island kids who want to help seals that come to their island each summer.**

Samantha carefully keeps some fur seals from escaping to the sea.
She and others then will check for seals that are tangled up in trash.

## Seals in Trouble

One day, an Aleut mother named Aquilina Bourdukofsky took a group of these kids to the edge of the sea. She showed them seals that had scraps of fish net and plastic trash caught around their necks. The scraps and trash hurt and sometimes even killed the seals. The kids were upset to see the harm that people had caused. They asked Aquilina how they could save these animals.

To save the seals, Aquilina thought, the kids would have to learn what scientists were doing to help the animals. But the kids would also have to relearn what their parents and grandparents and great-grandparents knew — how to treat nature with respect. So she started a group for the kids called the Pribilof Islands Stewards.

To save this seal's life, the kids hold the animal with a special clamp and clip off the trash that's choking it.

## All About Seals

Aquilina began by asking scientists such as Bruce Robson to teach the kids about seals. She didn't have to ask twice. Bruce took the kids to a beach where male seals were hanging out. There, they found more seals that were tangled up in nets and trash.

"Young seals are curious," Bruce explained. "They love to play with floating things. Sometimes a seal slips its head through a scrap of fish net or a ring of plastic. As the seal grows, the net or plastic gets tighter and slowly strangles the animal."

## Past Helps the Future

Aquilina knew that just saving entangled seals wasn't enough. The kids needed to learn about how the people on St. Paul Island depended on seals and cared about them. So she went to the St. Paul elders, seal hunters, and storytellers and asked for their help.

The hunters took the kids along on the seal harvest, so

Denise and Megan listen to storyteller Larry Merculieff. By listening to these stories, the kids learn about their place in nature.

the kids could learn how their ancestors depended on the seals. The elders cooked delicious Aleut dishes of seal meat. They taught the kids to make beautiful dolls from seal skins and bones. A storyteller told them scary tales about animals and spirits.

The kids also camped by the sea. Being there gave them new ideas. "We could build a house on the beach out of driftwood," one boy said. "We could live inside and take care of any seals that get tangled in trash."

Their small island in the middle of the Bering Sea had become the most important place in the world to them. Now they knew that their island was wonderful and worth protecting.

# A Research Report

A research report presents facts about a topic and uses details to support the facts. Use this student's writing as a model when you write a research report of your own.

# The Rain Forest

**Topic sentences** present the **main idea** of a report.

A rain forest is a tropical forest that contains all kinds of trees, animals, and insects. Many people live there too. Rain forests are important to the whole world for many reasons. For example, the plants and animals found in the rain forest provide food, raw materials, and even medicine. In fact, many medicines used to fight leukemia, high blood pressure, and malaria all came from rain forest plants.

Rain forest plants are also important because they absorb carbon dioxide, a poisonous gas, which all mammals breathe out. Absorbing carbon dioxide is an important function of rain forest plants, since too much carbon dioxide increases the temperature of Earth and could cause global warming.

Half of the rain forests of the world are in Brazil, Indonesia, and the Democratic Republic of Congo. The rain forest is made up of layers. The thick leafy area at the top is called the canopy, which is the warmest and wettest part. More creatures live in the canopy than in any other part of the rain forest. The different plants and insects on top provide food for all of the inhabitants. Hummingbirds sip nectar from the flowers, and monkeys eat fruit and insects.

Many birds, insects, and animals live in the rain forest. Among the birds are toucans and parrots. Some insects are the swallowtail butterfly, the forest millipede, and ants of all kinds. Spider monkeys, tree porcupines, and flying squirrels live there, as well as boa constrictors and poison dart frogs. A unique animal is the sloth, which has a strict leaf-eating diet. Two-toed sloths and three-toed sloths spend almost all of their time in the treetops. Bats are also common in the rain forest. Bats are not birds, but are the world's only flying mammal. Many bats eat insects, but some are fruit eaters. They are useful because they help to spread seeds in the rain forest.

A good report uses **details** to support the facts.

(2)

Town Free Library

Because people are destroying some of the rain forests, thousands of species of animals and plants become extinct each year.   Most tropical rain forests are in countries that are poor and overpopulated. People sometimes cut the trees in order to build or to sell the wood.  In some places, they even burn the forests to leave space for farming, industry, and homes.  Farming doesn't work too well in the rain forest because the soil is poor and cannot support long-term farming of crops.

Many people are aware that we must protect the rain forests that still exist.  The rain forest is the home of many people, animals, insects, and plants, and it is also important for the health of the world and its people.

A good **conclusion** sums up the report.

The rain forest is important to the whole world.

(3)

656

*A rain forest is a tropical forest with many trees, animals, and insects.*

## List of Sources

Clarke, Penny. *Worldwide: Rain Forest.* Franklin Watts: A division of Grolier Publishing, 1996.

Lasky, Kathryn. *The Most Beautiful Roof in the World: Exploring the Rain Forest Canopy.* Gulliver Green/ Harcourt Brace and Company, 1997.

Mutel, Cornelia F. and Mary M. Rodgers. *Our Endangered Planet: Tropical Rain Forest.* Lerner Publications Company, 1991.

A **bibliography** tells where the facts came from.

## Meet the Author

# Brian K.
**Grade:** four
**State:** Florida
**Hobbies:** football, drawing, and reading
**What he'd like to be when he grows up:** a professional football player

WILDFIRES

S E Y M O U R   S I M O N

*Wildfires*

**Read to find the meanings of these words.**

*e* ● Glossary

ablaze
aggressively
charred
consumed
cycles
flammable
renew

# Wildfires and the Cycles of Nature

Fire can cause great damage, but it can also renew the life of forests and grasslands. After a fire, young plants begin to grow and some kinds of trees release their seeds. Read *Wildfires* to find out more about the effects and cycles of fires in the wild.

Yellowstone National Park

Kings Canyon

Everglades National Park

**A wildfire blazes (above). Later, new trees sprout where the fire has burned (left).**

In this selection you will first learn what fire is. You will find out what happens when **flammable** material, like wood, is **consumed** by flames.

Then you will read about several different wildfires, including the 1988 fire in Yellowstone National Park. During that fire, a big part of the park was **ablaze**. You will find out how the fire began, how it spread, how firefighters **aggressively** fought it, and how it was finally put out.

Then you will see how plants and animals return to a burned area after a wildfire and bring new life to a **charred** landscape.

**Fire beetles lay their eggs on scorched trees.**

# Seymour Simon

**When he was born:** August 9

**Where he was born:** New York City

**Where he lives now:** Great Neck, New York

**How many books he has written:** more than one hundred

**Other work he has done:** He was a teacher for more than twenty years.

**Some of his hobbies:** reading, playing chess and tennis, listening to music, traveling, using computers

**Why he writes science books:** When children ask him questions about the world, or he thinks of his own questions, he wants to find out the answers. Then he writes books to explain what he has learned and to ask more questions.

**Other books:** *The Paper Airplane Book, The Smallest Dinosaurs, Killer Whales, Discovering What Earthworms Do, Volcanoes, Icebergs and Glaciers, Soap Bubble Magic*

To find out more about Seymour Simon, log on to Education Place. **www.eduplace.com/kids**

# WILDFIRES

## SEYMOUR SIMON

### Strategy Focus

Some of the effects of wildfires may surprise you.
**Monitor** your reading as you learn about these
fires. If necessary, reread to **clarify**.

661

A raging wildfire is a frightening thing. Living trees burn as fast as cardboard boxes in a bonfire. Flames race through the treetops, sometimes faster than a person can run, burning at a temperature hot enough to melt steel. A wildfire can be a major disaster, capable of destroying hundreds of homes and costing human lives.

But not all fires are bad. Fires in nature can help as well as harm. A burned forest allows young plants to begin growing. And fire is necessary for some trees, such as sequoias, to release their seeds. Instead of being an ending, fire is often a new chapter in the continuing story of the natural world.

A fire is a chemical reaction, and it needs three things to burn: fuel, oxygen, and heat. During a fire, energy is released as heat and light, which is why fires are so hot and so bright. When a fire is done, there is nothing left but ash. Ash is the form the fuel takes after the chemical reaction of fire is over.

Fires not only release heat, they are also caused by heat. A fire can be caused by a burning match, a flash of lightning, or a glowing ember in a dying camp fire. Once a fire starts, the heat from the fire can cause other fires to start in nearby materials. A burning leaf can set fire to a nearby leaf without touching it, just from the intense heat. The flaming leaves can then set fire to a branch, which can set fire to the whole tree. In a short while, a fire can leap to another tree, and then another and another. A whole forest can be set ablaze from a tiny fire no bigger than the flame from a match.

Fires also need oxygen to burn.  Oxygen is an invisible gas in the air we breathe.  One of the reasons wet wood rarely burns is that the water prevents air from getting to the fire.  That's why water is used to fight fires in homes and in forests.

For many years, Smokey the Bear warned that "only you" could prevent forest fires, making people think that all fires were enemies. But wildfires are a fact of life in the wilderness, and plants and animals have adjusted to them.  Many trees are so dependent on fires that they need cycles of fire in order to grow.  Other kinds of trees and shrubs quickly grow back after a fire, often healthier than before. Animals are rarely killed in forest fires.  Most are able to flee from a spreading fire.  And plants that grow quickly after a fire provide food for animals that might otherwise starve.

In fact, aggressively fighting fires has probably decreased the number of wildfires that help a forest renew itself while increasing the number of more dangerous fires.  Scientists say that by stamping out all fires as soon as they start, people have allowed leaves, dead wood, twigs, and bark to accumulate on the forest floor.  This provides much more fuel to feed big wildfires than would be the case if small fires were allowed to burn naturally.  A director of the United States Forest Service has said that it is not a question of "whether these areas will burn, but only a question of when."

665

The summer of 1988 was hot and dry in Yellowstone National Park. Almost no rain fell, less than in any year for the previous hundred years. On June 23, a flash of lightning started a fire near Shoshone Lake in the southwest part of the park. In a few weeks, a total of eight major fires were burning. Six of these fires were caused by lightning and were allowed to burn. The other two fires were caused by human carelessness and were fought from the beginning.

Since 1972, Yellowstone Park officials had allowed fires started by lightning to burn themselves out unless they threatened structures built by people. In the next sixteen years, there had been over two hundred such natural fires. But as the fires and smoke drove tourists from the park in the summer of 1988, officials changed their minds. In mid-July, they ordered firefighters to attack the Shoshone fire, which was coming close to the park buildings at Grant Village. Finally the officials abandoned their policy of letting lightning fires burn naturally, and they launched what was to become the greatest fire-fighting effort in the history of the United States.

Hundreds of firefighters were sent to battle the eight major blazes. But by then, more than fifty smaller ones had started, most from new lightning strikes. The old fires continued to spread, while the small fires raced toward one another and merged into even bigger fires. Giant lodgepole pines and spruce firs burst into flames like matchsticks. Boulders and rocks exploded in the heat of the flames.

There was more bad news. On August 19, gale-force winds gusted to sixty miles per hour, blowing hot embers a mile downwind and starting new fires. The winds also whipped the flames forward and fed them oxygen. Some of the fires moved through the trees at speeds of up to five miles per hour, much faster than most forest fires and as fast as a person can run. On August 20, known as Black Saturday, 165,000 acres of forest, an area more than twice the size of the entire city of Chicago, were burning. But the worst was still ahead.

By early September, most of the fires in the park were completely out of control. Thick clouds of bitter black smoke covered the Yellowstone valley. One of the major fires, the North Fork, was racing toward Old Faithful, the famous geyser. The geyser couldn't burn, but the nearby Old Faithful Inn — the world's largest log cabin, and as flammable as a huge tinderbox — was directly in the fire's path.

Weary firefighters tried to wet down the roof and walls of the inn, but it seemed hopeless. The fire was just too strong. Sparks and glowing embers shot over the cabin and set fire to the trees at the other end of the parking lot. It seemed as if the inn would soon be consumed by flames.

Suddenly, at the last moment, the winds shifted and the fires turned away from Old Faithful. On Saturday, September 10, heavy rains began to drench the area around the inn. The next morning, it snowed. While some fires in the park would continue to burn until November, the worst was over. More than twenty-five thousand firefighters had been called in to help. They had used more than one hundred fire engines and an equal number of planes and helicopters to drop millions of gallons of water and chemicals to slow the advancing flames. But it was the weather, not human beings, that finally ended that summer of fire.

By the time the fires had all died out, about 800,000 acres inside the park had burned, along with another 600,000 acres in the national forests and other lands nearby. About sixty-five buildings had been destroyed, and two people died in the fires. To many people watching on television, it seemed as if the park had been scorched by the flames and would never recover. But that was not so. Nearly two-thirds of the park had not been touched by fire, and even the one-third that had burned was starting to recover.

The wind-driven fires of 1988 left a mosaic of green and black patches in the forests of Yellowstone. Depending upon the extent of the fires, some places looked like green islands in a sea of black trees, while others looked like black tar on a green carpet.

After a fire, burned areas quickly burst into life. In fact, when the ground is still warm from the fires, ants, wood beetles, millipedes, and centipedes are busy. Fire beetles actually seek out fire to breed and lay their eggs in charred logs. The first plants that appear are those whose roots and seeds were there before the fire. But soon new seeds are carried in by the wind and on the fur of animals or in their droppings.

The green-and-black mosaic favors newly arrived plants and animals. Hawks and owls hunt for food in the opened spaces. Tree-drilling woodpeckers hunt for insects beneath the bark of fallen trees. The dead trees also make good nesting sites; bluebirds and tree swallows move in. The fields of new grasses and wildflowers attract grazing animals, and birds come from all over to catch insects in the meadows.

If you watch the movie *Bambi,* you might think that deer and other animals panic and flee in all directions from rapidly approaching flames. But that is not what really happens. Fires often move slowly through forests and grasslands. Larger animals, such as bears, elk, bison, moose, and deer, simply walk away from the fire. Bison and elk graze as usual, sometimes on the flaming edges of the fire. Elk even step over fiery logs to get at patches of unburned grass. The animals that are affected die mostly from smoke inhalation rather than from the flames.

Fires rarely start during the wet spring breeding season, so nests of fledglings are not usually threatened, and at other times of the year mature birds can fly off in advance of a fire. Rodents and other small animals dash away across fields or seek shelter in underground burrows or in rocky places. Bears, coyotes, foxes, hawks, falcons, and ravens feast on animals driven from their burrows or on the bodies of animals killed by the smoke. For these scavengers, fire offers many sources of food. Nature quickly adjusts to changes and finds new life even in death.

The forests of Yellowstone are mostly lodgepole pine trees. Many of the lodgepoles were several hundred years old at the time of the 1988 fire. As a lodgepole ages, it doesn't produce enough resin, or sap, to stop insects from boring into its bark, which eventually kills the tree. In very old lodgepole forests, many of the standing trees are dead. Fires remove these dead trees, making room for new ones.

Fire also helps the lodgepole reproduce. This tree has two kinds of cones. One opens normally, over time, and its winged seeds whirl to the forest floor. That is how lodgepoles usually sprout. The other kind of seed is sealed in a rock-hard pine resin that opens only when the heat of a fire melts and burns away the resin.

Following the Yellowstone fires, seed counts in burned lodgepole stands were very high, ranging from fifty thousand to one million seeds per acre. All had come from sealed pinecones that were opened by the fire. Most of these seeds would be eaten by chipmunks, squirrels, birds, and other small animals, but some seeds would sprout, starting a new cycle of life in the forest.

Just two years after the 1988 fires, burned areas had sprouted new plants of all kinds. The pink flowers of fireweed soon appeared. Asters, lupine, and dozens of other kinds of plants grew among the burned trees. Insects returned in great numbers and began to feast on the plants. In turn, the insects became food for birds and other insect eaters. Elk and bison grazed on the plants. Chipmunks gathered seeds, and small rodents built new nests in the grasses.

The young lodgepole pines are now waist high, and many different kinds of plants surround them. Before the fire, the towering older trees blocked sunlight from the forest floor, allowing only a few other species of plants to flourish there. Without periodic fires, low-growing plants that have survived in the park for thousands of years would die off completely.

In fifty to one hundred years, the lodgepole pines will again be tall enough to deprive other plant species of the light they need to grow. The forest will become mostly pines. Then the fires are likely to return, and the cycle of burning and rebirth will continue.

These firefighters are not trying to put out a fire. Instead they started this fire and are letting it burn. Using a device called a drip torch, firefighters set small blazes on purpose to prevent large-scale forest fires by burning away undergrowth and dead wood in Kings Canyon, California.

Many forests and grasslands in North America are dependent on fire to thin out old, dying trees and other plants. For many years, the main focus of fire prevention has been to put out natural fires as soon as possible, but the longer the fuel builds up in a forest, the worse the fire is going to be — and the more likely it will be to burn out of control. So fire is now actually being put to use. Florida, for example, burns more than a million acres of grasslands a year. In that state, the new slogan is "Using fires wisely prevents forest fires."

Everglades National Park is part of a vast sea of saw grass that covers four thousand square miles in southern Florida. The "glades" are home for many wading birds, as well as for turtles and alligators. During the summer's rainy season, saw-grass fires often start because of lightning. The fires burn the parts of the plant above the water, and the ashes provide minerals for new growth. Without periodic fires, the saw grass would age, die, and decay, filling up the swamps. The Everglades need fires in order to survive. Lightning fires in the glades are permitted to burn except during droughts. Fire crews also burn saw grass along the park boundaries, thus preventing larger fires in dry years.

679

Eight years after the fires of 1988, Yellowstone is still renewing itself. Burned trees are losing their blackened bark and turning a silvery gray. Meadows are growing around them. The burned areas are slowly fading away.

Meanwhile scientists still have a lot to learn about what happens to a forest after a huge fire. One question they ask: How often does an area burn naturally?

The time between natural fires varies, depending upon climate and tree life. In Yellowstone's lodgepole pine forests, the interval between large natural fires is three hundred to four hundred years. In Florida's slash pines, the interval is only seven years, and it is as short as two to five years in the open ponderosa forests of northern Arizona. In the cedar-spruce forests of western Washington State, two thousand years can pass between fires!

Wildfires are neither good nor bad. In forests and grasslands, they are part of the endless cycle of change.

681

## Think About the Selection

**1.** What makes a wildfire "a frightening thing"?

**2.** How do some plants, trees, and animals depend on wildfires?

**3.** Why do some people think it is a good idea to let certain wildfires burn?

**4.** What do you think "using fires wisely" means?

**5.** What is Seymour Simon's opinion of wildfires?

**6. Connecting/Comparing** In *Salmon Summer*, nature was a source of food, work, and enjoyment for people. How would you describe nature in *Wildfires*?

## Write a Magazine Article

Reread the part of *Wildfires* that describes the Yellowstone fire. Write a brief magazine article about that fire. Include as many details as you can. Look at "Flame Busters" on pages 684–685 for an example of an exciting magazine article.

 **Tips**

- Include an interesting title, as well as illustrations with captions.
- Begin your article with an exciting sentence that will get your reader interested.

## Make a Cause-and-Effect Diagram

Make a diagram that shows the cause of a wildfire and the chain of events that results. On the left side of a piece of paper, write one possible cause of a fire. Then write at least four more events that might follow that first cause. Each event should cause the next one. End your diagram with an example of how nature renews itself after a wildfire.

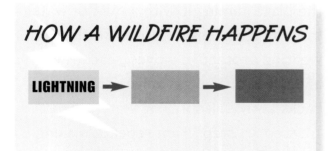

HOW A WILDFIRE HAPPENS

LIGHTNING →　　　→　　　

## Hold a Debate About Wildfires

Form two teams. One team will argue that wildfires are destructive. The other team will support the position that wildfires are helpful. After your team has prepared its argument, present it to the other team. Then listen to their argument. Afterwards, discuss whether there is anything the whole class agrees on.

### Tips

- Before you debate, look for examples in the selection that support your argument.
- Listen carefully to what the other team says before responding to them.

### Internet

# Do a Web Crossword Puzzle

Test what you know about wildfires by solving a crossword puzzle. You will find one at Education Place. **www.eduplace.com/kids**

**Skill: Adjust Your Rate of Reading**

❶ When you read an article that contains a lot of information, **preview** to find the most important or complicated information.

❷ Start to read the article at your **normal rate** of reading.

❸ Read important or complicated information **more slowly** and **carefully**.

# Flame Busters

Teens train to battle heat, fire, and fear.

by R. G. Schmidt

With a huge roar, a gas flame shoots 50 feet high. Another flame leaps out 30 feet to the side. At about 900°F the burning gas is hot enough to melt lead. A team of teens moves in, determined to put it out.

"Step . . . step . . . step," commands Kim Balko, 17, the team leader. With each step the group moves closer to the blaze, taming it with a mist of water from a high-pressure hose. Finally Kim, wearing protective gloves, reaches in and shuts off the gas valve. The team backs away, still spraying water. "Step . . . step . . . step," Kim repeats, making sure everyone moves in unison. "In a fire everyone has a job to do," she says. "Teamwork is important."

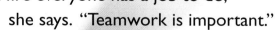

◀ **Super Spray**
Will Connor, 17, aims a hose that sprays 125 gallons of water each minute.

The teens, all from Jacksonville, Florida, participate in Exploring, a program run by Learning for Life for kids 14 to 21 years old. The future firefighters gain knowledge and skills at the Jacksonville Fire and Rescue Training Academy. John Peavy, Explorer Post advisor and training officer, says the teens learn more than just how to spray water. "They learn the mechanics and the hazards of firefighting," he says. "Training includes math, chemistry, CPR, and first aid."

Explorers start their training by performing chores around a firehouse, where they also study procedures and firefighting terms. After several months they take a test; their scores and performance in the training exercises determine when each Explorer qualifies to go on a "ride-along" to a real fire. Although not allowed inside the "hot zone," where the fire is burning, Explorers have important jobs to do at the scene of a fire. "They help take equipment off the apparatus, or fire truck, and connect the hoses," says Peavy.

▲
## Hot Hands

Suiting up to fight a fire, George Green, 17, of Jacksonville, Florida, slides on gloves to protect his hands from the fire's intense heat.

◄ **Treating Heat**

At the academy, Explorers spray water on a fire from a simulated gas tank. Training officers stand along the path to supervise.

## Background and Vocabulary

The sequel to the Newbery Medal winner *Sarah, Plain and Tall*

Patricia MacLachlan

*Skylark*

**Skylark**

**Read to find the meanings of these words.**

*e* ● Glossary

corral
coyote
drought
phonograph
prairie

# Life on the Prairie

Have you ever been to a place so wide open that it looked as though both land and sky could go on forever? A **prairie** is such a place — a vast, flat grassland. Often, you can go miles without seeing a single tree. But you might get a peek at a prairie dog or hear a **coyote** howl in the distance.

A prairie dog

A howling coyote

A prairie is

Life on a prairie farm in the early 1900s was very different from life today. Many items we use every day had not even been invented yet, or else were very costly. Since there were no TVs or radios for entertainment, prairie families listened to records on the **phonograph**, that is, if they were lucky enough to own one.

Water was not available from the faucet and had to be carried from nearby wells or streams. If there was a **drought**, or dry-spell, crops died. Wells could dry up, leaving nothing for people to drink. In *Skylark*, you will read about the painful choice one prairie family must make when their worst fears come true and the wells threaten to run dry.

A family poses before their prairie home. The well in the foreground provided water. The horse was either kept in a barn or fenced into a **corral**.

a vast, flat grassland.

# Meet the Author *Patricia MacLachlan*

Patricia MacLachlan certainly has come a long way since her first childhood story, which read: "My cats have names and seem happy. Often they play. The end." Since then, she has written more than twelve books. Several have won awards and been made into TV movies.

MacLachlan was born in the wide-open, "big-sky" country of Wyoming and was raised in Minnesota. "The Western landscape has always been a powerful force in my life, fueling my mind and imagination and giving me a sense of belonging to a particular place," she says.

**Other books:** *Sarah, Plain and Tall*; *Through Grandpa's Eyes*; *Arthur, for the Very First Time*

# Meet the Illustrator *David Soman*

Because David Soman enjoys painting people, landscapes, and especially horses, *Skylark* was the perfect project for him. To get inspired for his work on *Skylark*, Soman thought back to when he had visited the prairie. The models he worked with even watched the movie *Skylark* when they learned that he would be drawing them for this story.

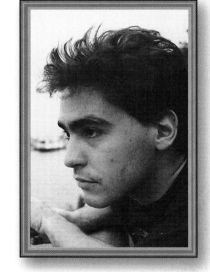

To learn more about Patricia MacLachlan and David Soman, log on to Education Place. **www.eduplace.com/kids**

688

The sequel to the Newbery Medal winner *Sarah, Plain and Tall*

Patricia MacLachlan

# Skylark

## Strategy Focus

As you read about life on a prairie farm, **predict** what challenges the family will face, as well as how the different family members will react.

*Sarah has journeyed all the way from her home by the sea in Maine to marry Jacob and to live with her new family on their prairie farm. There, she has grown to love Anna and Caleb, though she is sometimes homesick because the prairie — a sea of grass — is so different from Maine. After months of happiness together, the family is about to be tested by the forces of nature. The land they have worked so hard to farm is drying up fast. An empty glass placed on the fence by Caleb waits for rain that does not come. All the family can do is watch the skies — and hope.*

Sarah and I sat in the kitchen. The air was thick with the heat, and there was no breeze. There hadn't been any wind for days. Sarah was writing a letter to the aunts in Maine. I wrote in my journal.

"Remember the wildflowers?" I asked Sarah. "And the roses that grew on the fence? Remember singing?"

Sarah looked up.

"Yes," she said. She reached out and touched my hair. "I remember."

"Papa! Papa! Coyote!" shouted Caleb from outside.

Sarah and I ran outside. By the paddock fence a thin coyote was drinking water out of the water pail.

"He'll kill Moonbeam!" shouted Caleb.

Papa came from the field, took a step toward the coyote, then turned and ran to the house. He came out with his rifle.

"Jacob! What are you going to do?" cried Sarah.

"Go inside, Sarah," he said.

Papa raised his rifle to shoot the coyote, but Sarah grabbed the barrel of the rifle.

"No! Don't do it, Jacob. Don't!"

"Sarah! Stop!" yelled Papa.

Papa tried to push her away, and the coyote looked up at the sound of their voices. Slowly he ran away over the fields, stopping once to look back. Then he was gone.

Sarah began to cry.

"He only wanted water. Water, Jacob!"

Caleb climbed over the paddock fence and stood next to me. Papa took Sarah's arm and turned to Caleb.

"Put the animals in the barn, Caleb," he said.

Caleb turned and walked to the barn.

Tears streamed down Sarah's face.

"Water!" she said. "He only wanted water. Just like us. . . ."

She slumped to the ground and put her hands over her face as she cried.

"Get Sarah something to drink, Anna," said Papa.

He took off his hat and sat down on the ground next to her.

"Anna," he said sharply. "Now!"

I turned and went to the water barrel and scooped out a cup of water. Papa put his arms around Sarah.

His voice was soft.

"Sarah. Sarah," he said softly. "It will be all right. It will be all right."

But Sarah cried and cried. And when Papa turned and looked at me, I knew that nothing was all right.

The look in his eyes was fear.

And that night, when I came in from the barn to go to bed, there was something else missing from the fence. Missing like Sarah's roses. Caleb's glass was gone.

———◆——

"They're coming!" said Caleb, looking out the upstairs window.

He wore a clean shirt, and his hair was brushed smooth. I wore the dress I had worn when Papa and Sarah were married. Outside, wagons came into the yard.

"Will this make Sarah happy?" Caleb asked me, worried.

I watched more wagons drive in. I saw Maggie dressed in a rose dress and a straw hat.

"Yes," I said. "This will make Sarah happy."

"Anna? Caleb? What is this?" said Sarah in the bedroom doorway.

We whirled around, silent. Sarah walked to the window to look out, too, but I took her hand and pulled her out into the hallway.

694

Papa looked up the stairs at her. He wore a vest and his hair was slicked back. He smiled at her.

"Happy birthday, Sarah," he said.

"There are guests. And presents, Sarah!" said Caleb.

"But I'm not dressed," said Sarah.

"Then get dressed," said Papa softly.

Outside there was a table in the shade of the house, set with food and lemonade. Maggie and Matthew were there, and Rose and Violet and the baby. All the neighbors were there, too. Papa carried something covered with a cloth out to the table.

"What is it?" asked Maggie.

"You'll see," said Papa.

"Here she is!" someone said.

We all turned, and Sarah came out on the porch in her white dress.

"Happy birthday, Sarah," said Papa.

"Happy birthday," everyone called.

Sarah smiled at the sight of them, everyone washed and clean as if the prairie winds had stopped covering us all with dust.

"A present from the aunts," said Papa.

He took the cloth away, and there was a phonograph. I handed him a record and he put the needle on it. Suddenly, music filled the yard. Sarah stared. Papa walked up to her and held out his hand. She smiled and came down the steps and they began to dance. Maggie and Matthew began to dance, too, the baby between them. Everyone danced, then, in the dirt yard, the light around them all yellow like an old photograph. Sarah buried her face in Papa's shoulder, and Caleb smiled at me. And for a little while, as the sun began to set, as they danced, everyone forgot about the drought. For a while, everyone was happy again. Even Sarah. Even Papa.

———◆———

The last of the wagons left in the moonlight. Sarah and Papa waved good-bye. Caleb was asleep under the table and Papa took him off to bed. Then Papa helped Sarah carry the phonograph inside.

"I have a present for you, Sarah," I said. I handed her a small book.

"Anna, what is this?" said Sarah.

"It's a book I started. About you. About our family," I said.

Papa went out onto the porch. Sarah sat down and opened the book. She began to read.

"'When my mother . . .'"

She stopped and looked at me. Then she began to read again. Papa stood outside the screen door, listening.

"'When my mother, Sarah, came, she came by train. I didn't know I'd love her, but Caleb did. Papa didn't know, either, but he does love her. I have seen them kiss.'" Sarah smiled at me. "'And I have seen the way he looks at her and the way he touches her hair. My mother, Sarah, doesn't love the prairie. She tries, but she can't help remembering what she knew first.'"

Sarah stopped and closed the book, holding it close to her.

"You like it," I said.

"I like it," said Sarah softly.

She put her arms around me, and I saw Papa watching us.

Sarah got up, then, and went to the door.

"It was a fine party, Jacob."

She put her hand up and he did, too, so that they touched through the screen.

"I'd almost forgotten music," whispered Sarah.

Then she looked past Papa at the fence post.

"Where's Caleb's glass, Jacob?"

Papa didn't speak.

"Put it back, please, Jacob," said Sarah. "It should be there when it rains."

Papa stared at Sarah. And when I went to bed later that night, I looked out and saw it there, shining and clean, on the fence post.

The next day, after the party, after the music and dancing, Matthew and Maggie's well went dry. They drove their wagon to our house to say good-bye, and I could hardly look at Sarah's face.

The wagon was packed with furniture and clothes; Rose and Violet sat in the back, the baby on Maggie's lap.

"I'm sorry to be leaving you, Jacob," said Matthew.

"It's all right, Matthew. I know," said Papa.

"I'll miss you," Sarah said to Maggie. Her face was tight, to keep all her feelings from coming out. She reached out to touch the baby's hand.

"We'll be back," said Maggie.

Tears came down her face.

"We'll be back," she repeated.

The baby began to cry as the wagon drove out of the yard. When Sarah turned to look at Papa, tears sat at the corners of her eyes.

"They'll be back," said Papa.

He watched the cloud of dust that followed Matthew's wagon down the road, his eyes narrowed against the sunlight.

<hr>

That night I dreamed about roses, and green fields, and water. A glass of water on the fence post, and ponds of water to swim in; Caleb spitting streams of water in the air like a whale. Sarah laughing and splashing us with water.

A sharp clap of thunder woke me. Lottie and Nick barked as lightning lit up the sky. I turned over in bed, but then Papa's voice from downstairs made me sit up.

"Sarah! Sarah! It's fire!"

I got up and rushed to the window, and there was fire in the field close to the barn. Flames creeping up the fence, flames near the corral.

I ran downstairs and out to the porch, Caleb behind me. Sarah was running carrying wet sacks, her hair down her back. Sarah and Papa beat the flames around the corral. Then Papa stopped to let the frightened horses out.

"Get the cows," he shouted to Sarah.

Sarah ran to the barn and pulled the cows outside.

"Shoo! Shoo!" she cried.

Caleb ran down to get Moonbeam.

"Get on the porch and stay there," Sarah shouted at him as he led Moonbeam away.

I put my arm around Caleb. I could feel him trembling.

Sarah screamed as some hay caught fire and the side of the barn burst into flame.

"Buckets!" shouted Papa. "Get buckets of water! Buckets!"

Sarah ran to the barrel and filled a bucket, running back to him as the fire grew. Papa grabbed it and then Sarah stopped him. I couldn't hear what she said, but I knew what it was. It was the last barrel. Papa stopped, then, and stared at the barn as flames caught the dry wood and then the roof. Sparks flew everywhere. And then part of the roof fell and Sarah and Papa moved back. Sarah put her arm around Papa as the barn burned. They stood there watching for a long time. Papa turned once to look away from the fire and I could see his eyes, shining red from the fire.

I had never seen Papa's face so sad.

701

The sun came up in the morning the way it always did. But everything had changed. The barn was gone, only a few blackened timbers standing. The cows walked in the yard, the sheep in the cornfield, looking for green grass. I stood at my window and watched Sarah and Papa talking by the clothesline. I saw her shake her head, no. I saw Papa take her hand. She shook her head again. Then Papa put his arms around her.

I knew we would have to go away.

They told us at dinnertime.

"Maine?" said Caleb. "Are you coming, too, Papa?"

Papa shook his head and looked at Sarah.

"I have to stay here," he said softly. "I can't go away from the land."

"Can Seal and the dogs come?" Caleb asked.

Papa shook his head.

"They'll be happier here," he said. "I'll take care of them."

"What will you do while we're gone, Papa?" asked Caleb.

"I'll miss you," Papa said softly, reaching out to take Caleb's hand. He looked at me, then, and as if he knew I would cry if I spoke, he took my hand, too.

"What will happen to us?" I asked after a moment.

Papa looked at Sarah, and his words were for her.

"We will write letters," he said, his voice soft. "We've written letters before, you know."

*After the terrible fire, Anna, Caleb, and Sarah leave Papa behind to rebuild the farm. They travel to Maine to stay with Sarah's aunts. To learn more about their adventures in Maine and to find out if they ever return home to rejoin Papa, read the rest of Patricia MacLachlan's* Skylark.

## Think About the Selection

**1.** Why is Sarah so upset about the coyote at the beginning of the selection?

**2.** Who do you think removes the glass from the fence post and why? Why does Sarah want it put back?

**3.** How does Anna feel about Sarah? How does she show her feelings?

**4.** The day after the barn burns down, the narrator says that "everything had changed." What does she mean by that?

**5.** Why is it so hard for the family to decide whether to stay or to leave the farm? Why does Papa stay behind?

**6.** **Connecting/Comparing** How is nature portrayed differently in *Skylark* than in the other two selections in this theme?

## Write a Personal Narrative

The weather affects everyone. Write about a time you experienced some interesting weather. Perhaps you got caught in a thunderstorm or you had to walk home in the snow. Describe what the weather was like. What did you do to overcome it? How did you feel about your experience?

**Tips**

- Make a list of adjectives to describe the weather you are writing about.
- Make sure your narrative has a beginning, a middle, and an ending.

## Social Studies

## Make a Comparison Chart

How would it be different growing up during the time *Skylark* takes place? Make a chart comparing everyday life now with daily life then. Your chart can include topics such as what people did for fun, how they traveled, and how they kept in touch with one another.

|  | Now | Then |
|---|---|---|
| Travel | car, airplane | |
| Clothing | | |
| Communication | | |

## Viewing

## Compare the Movie with the Book

As a class, watch the movie *Skylark*. Afterwards, break into small groups and compare the movie with the book. Were the characters in the movie the way you pictured them? Did the prairie look the way you thought it would? Which version did you like better? Why?

**Bonus** Write a movie review of *Skylark*. Remember not to give away the ending!

A scene from the movie *Skylark*

---

*Internet*

## Take a Web Field Trip

Log on to Education Place to learn more about the American prairie, its long history, and its dramatic weather. **www.eduplace.com/kids**

**Skill: How to Skim and Scan**

*To skim . . .*

❶ **Read** the title and the headings.

❷ **Preview** the introduction.

❸ **Look at** the illustrations.

*To scan . . .*

❶ **Identify** key words.

❷ **Read quickly** to find the key words.

❸ **Decide** which sections seem most important and then **read more carefully.**

# Rain Sayings

FACES

When somebody says *"It's raining cats and dogs,"* you do not really expect to look out the window and see animals coming down from the sky, but sayings usually have a reason behind them. Dr. Franklyn Branley, who used to head the Hayden Planetarium at the American Museum of Natural History, has looked into this and many other questions about rain and written a little book, *It's Raining Cats and Dogs,* on the subject. Here are some rain sayings with Dr. Branley's explanations.

**"Rain before seven,
Clear by eleven."**

Probably true: rain may be caused by a rain belt which often takes four hours or so to pass by.

**"It's raining cats and dogs."**

The saying may go back to Odin, an ancient god of northern Europe. Often in pictures of Odin, wind is shown blowing from the heads of the dogs and wolves with him.

The behavior of cats is often thought to be caused by the weather. They may seem nervous before a storm. British sailors say, "The cat has a gale of wind in its tail."

**"Sea gull, sea gull,**
**Sit on the sand.**
**It's sign of a rain**
**When you are at hand."**

Before a rainstorm, there is often a drop in the density of air and the air is less able to support a bird. Since it's harder for them to fly, the gulls are more apt to stay on land.

And here are a few others, not in that book, which have been popular at various times and places.

**"When it rains,**
**it rains on all alike,"**
a Hindu saying, means that the forces of nature, unlike human societies, treat all people as equals.

**"When it rains, it pours"**
describes what often happens. It also suggests that in nature and in life good or bad things can happen in bunches.

707

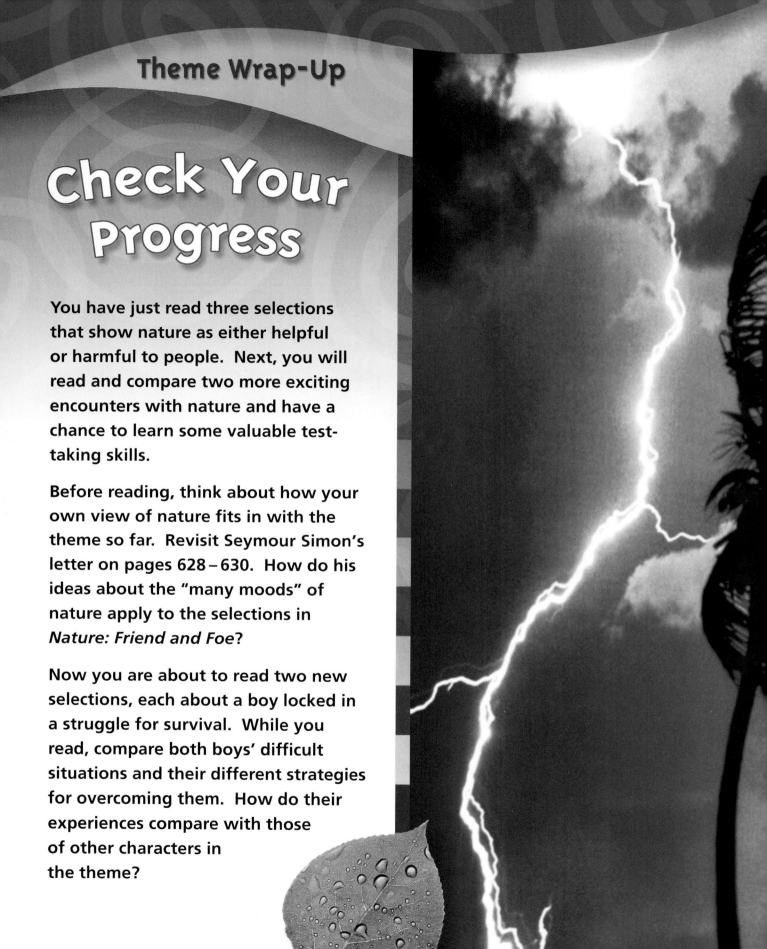

# Check Your Progress

You have just read three selections that show nature as either helpful or harmful to people. Next, you will read and compare two more exciting encounters with nature and have a chance to learn some valuable test-taking skills.

Before reading, think about how your own view of nature fits in with the theme so far. Revisit Seymour Simon's letter on pages 628–630. How do his ideas about the "many moods" of nature apply to the selections in *Nature: Friend and Foe*?

Now you are about to read two new selections, each about a boy locked in a struggle for survival. While you read, compare both boys' difficult situations and their different strategies for overcoming them. How do their experiences compare with those of other characters in the theme?

# Read and Compare

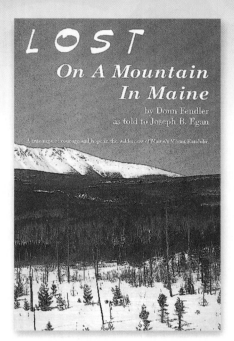

Read the true story of a boy who climbs Maine's highest mountain, only to get lost along its dangerous slopes and within the deep woods below.

**Try these strategies:**
Question
Summarize

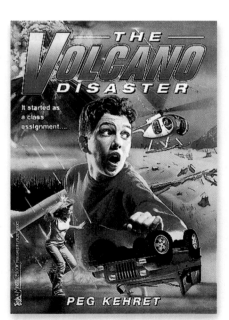

Eruption! It's a race against time for Warren as he dodges fiery mudballs and tries to outrun choking clouds of ash.

**Try these strategies:**
Monitor and Clarify
Evaluate

**Strategies in Action** *Look for ways to use all your reading strategies as you read the selections.*

# *LOST*
## ON A MOUNTAIN IN MAINE

**by Donn Fendler, as told to Joseph B. Egan**
**illustrated by Patrick Whelan**

Twelve-year-old Donn Fendler, along with his friend Henry, has climbed to the top of Mount Katahdin, a rugged peak in northern Maine. While Henry waits, Donn starts down from the rocky summit to meet his father and brothers, who are still climbing. Soon, as a fast-moving fog sweeps over the trail, Donn cannot see Henry, his family, or the blazes that mark the path. Alone in the wilderness, with night approaching, Donn struggles to find his way, looking for trail markers and trying to stay warm.

## Sharp Rocks and Sleet
### FIRST DAY

I knew I couldn't sit where I was very long. The wind was sharp, and it blew so hard that the rain and sleet stung like needles. I was getting wet all over. My fleece-lined jacket kept my chest dry, but my blue jeans were cold and stiff as boards. Jeans are all right for dry hikes, but they're terrible when they get cold and wet.

People want to know why I didn't stay where I was. Someone was sure to find me, they say. Well, I'd like to see anyone stay up there in that wind and sleet with the night coming on. You'd freeze stiff before morning.* I was already getting stiff. I had to keep moving, just to warm up. I shouted once more, as loud as I could — then I stood and listened — nothing but that strange noise.

I turned slowly about so as to be sure of my direction, and started back the way I thought I had come. Pretty soon I ran right into a trail marker. It said "Saddle Trail." Now I was in a fix. I had heard about that trail. I had heard that it went far off into the woods and was dangerous, full of landslides and loose rocks. However, it was a trail and it was marked, often with blue daubs of paint. It would lead me somewhere — perhaps to some lonely spot miles and miles from camp. No, I mustn't take it.* The thing to do is to work off at right angles to it and cut across the main trail. I started on. Right away, I ran into more pucker bush. I climbed over it and fell through and crawled under it. Guides have said no one could crawl under it, but I did — for a long way.

Pretty soon, I was back among big rocks again. Right here, I had a funny experience. The cloud opened for just an instant and far, far below me I saw a lake — I thought was Moosehead — shining in the sun. The cloud closed and the lake was gone and everything was dull gray again. The sight cheered me some, and I hurried faster than ever.

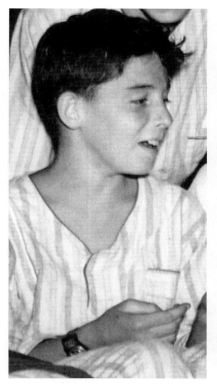

**Donn Fendler tells of his frightening ordeal in the Maine woods.**

* There was a terrific hail and sleet storm on top of the mountain that night, through which it is doubtful if an unprotected person could have lived. Above the timberline, a 40-mile wind was blowing and the temperature dropped to below 40 degrees before morning.
* Although the Saddle Trail is extremely dangerous, had Donn been able to follow it, it would have led him down to a camp at Chimney Pond, which was inhabited that very night.

I started to run and found I couldn't, because of the boulders; that made me frantic and I climbed over them like a cat and yelled and shouted and cried all the time. I yelled for my Dad. I climbed up as high as I could on a big rock and screamed for him — then I waited. No answering shout — nothing — just the noise of that wind and the purring sound of fine sleet driving against my clothes.

I just had to get out of there and back to the trail. I started to run again, as fast as I could. I don't know how long I kept that up, but a long time — over rocks and sharp edges and things I stumbled over and into patches of pucker bush — sometimes falling and then getting up again, and often crawling under brush on my hands and knees. Boy, it was awful! And then, just when the cloud lifted again and I thought sunlight might break through, I ran into another trail sign. It said "Saddle Trail" and looked like the sign I had seen before. I was pretty scared by this time, and I wasn't sure about that sign, so I examined it closely. There was a mark on it that I recalled seeing before. I had come back to the same sign.

For a second I was stunned. I just stood there and looked at it. I knew now, for sure, that I was lost. I was running in a circle. I didn't know what to do, so I stumbled along hunting for other marks, on that same trail. I guess I went a long way over rocks and over pucker bush and some- times under it, too, searching and hunting for another trail marker. I didn't find any, but I kept going down. I remember that. After a while, I came to a place where there was a lot of gravel, and boy, was it slippery! That place was dangerous, for a slip might mean a bad fall — maybe a hundred feet or more. I slowed down. I could imagine myself lying there, in the cold and dark, with a sprained ankle. Meanwhile, the rocks were getting bigger and bigger.

At last I came to a weather-beaten tree. The branches were all pulled out to one side, as though the tree were trying to get away from something. That tree looked scared. Beyond was another and another. I had reached the timberline, and I had to find a trail, because the shrubs grew as thick as doormats and, without a trail, the going down to camp would be pretty bad.

The sight of that tree calmed me down a bit, for I began to think more clearly. It's an awful thing to get lost in the clouds. You see things that aren't there at all. Rocks look like people and shaggy animals, and often you come to an edge and think you are looking down into space, and you draw back and get scared.

The mountain suddenly seemed awfully big under me. I listened. Only the whining noise of the wind in the stunted trees — no, there was another noise — rocks falling, far off to the right — a slow, heavy, crunching sound — then silence, deeper than before.

The rocks in this place had very sharp edges and some of them were loose, too, and slid from under me. I had heard of landslides and had seen the remains of a few on the way up. I kept thinking of how a landslide starts — the slipping stones — just a few at first — then more and more and faster and faster, until the whole mountain seems to move. Then trees tip over like matches, and there are crashings and grindings and dust. Boy! I just stood still, now and then, and shivered. What chance would a fellow have in a mess like that?

However, it was not quite so cold down there in the scrub, and that made me think that farther down, it would be still warmer. Maybe I'd better change my course a little to the right and keep going down. I hunted for an opening through the scrub growth. There wasn't any; so I just had to scramble along as best I could. That's where I cut my sneakers to pieces.* I noticed now that I had to scramble through more and more of those scrubby bushes. My face was badly scratched and I was awfully tired. It was getting dark, too.

I knew I hadn't covered more than three or four miles. That meant that Dad and Henry couldn't be a long way off. The camp must be right down below me in the trees. I felt a little better. What if it were hard going down to it? A fellow could make it, as long as he didn't break a leg or something. I'd just go a little more slowly — that's the way a fellow figures things out. I was all wrong, of course. There wasn't any camp below me — not for miles and miles, and there weren't any trails where I was going.

It's a good thing I didn't know any more than I did. Sometimes, not knowing the worst helps a fellow along, if he just keeps going and doesn't lose his head.

*  "The stones are so sharp on parts of Mt. Katahdin," says veteran guide Earl W. York, Jr., "that a pair of new, heavy sneakers will not last over six trips, even when the regular trail is followed."

Read the entire story of Donn's frightening, nine-day fight for survival and his rescue in the book *Lost on a Mountain in Maine*.

# The Volcano Disaster

by Peg Kehret, illustrated by James Bernardin

*One afternoon, Warren Spalding is tinkering with the Instant Commuter, a time machine his grandfather invented. When his friend Betsy stops by to discuss their project about Mount Saint Helens, Warren tries to hide the time machine from her. In the confusion, a picture of the volcano accidentally touches the time machine. Suddenly, Warren finds himself sent back in time — back to May 18, 1980, the day that Mount Saint Helens erupts! Racing against time, Warren dashes down the lower slopes of the volcano, hoping to stay one step ahead of history.*

Warren raced on.

Partway down the second ridge, he looked at his watch again. Eight thirty-one. Maybe he had remembered the time wrong. Maybe the mountain didn't erupt at eight-thirty.

He stopped running and took a deep breath. He stuck his right foot out in front of him, straightened the leg and hung his head toward his knee, stretching out his tired leg muscles. He held the pose for a few seconds and then did the same thing with his left leg. While he stretched, he watched the mountain warily.

Just as he straightened up, the ground dropped from beneath his feet, and he fell backward onto the gravel road. A low rumbling noise, like a faraway freight train coming through the forest, filled the air. Warren scrambled to his feet and looked back.

Sections of the top of the mountain were shifting downward. It was as if a huge knife had sliced through one side of the volcano, cutting three big pieces loose from the top. The pieces slid quickly, one after another.

Too awestruck to run, Warren stared as the gigantic slabs moved down the side of the volcano. As they fell, a plume of

steam rose from the top of the volcano. Almost immediately the steam turned dark.

"It must be volcanic ash," Warren thought, "or some sort of gas." It ballooned upward like an enormous black cauliflower, filling the sky. More ash came from the face of the landslide.

At the same time an even bigger cloud of ash and debris shot sideways out of the mountain, from the opening created when the pieces slid down. The volcano was erupting sideways, just as Betsy's article had said.

The clouds quickly merged into one huge mass as volcanic debris blasted from inside the volcano.

The ash plume was enormous, and when it mixed with the landslide debris, it became a thick, dark wind.

"It's as if someone set off tons of dynamite inside the mountain," Warren thought. Instead of just one single blast, like a bomb would be, this was a sustained explosion that kept coming and coming. He wished he had brought his camera, but even without pictures Warren knew he would never forget this sight.

He also knew he could not stand and watch any longer. He had already wasted precious seconds because he had been too shocked to react.

He turned and continued to race down the far side of the ridge. It was much hotter now than it had been before. He felt the heat on his back first, and then all around him. The ground seemed to burn through the bottom of Warren's shoes.

Splat! A mud ball landed beside him, splashing his jeans. Another mud ball landed on his shoulder. Warren cried out, and tried to shake the hot mud off his shirt without touching it. Splat! Splat! It was like being in a mammoth snowball fight, except these balls were scorching hot. There was no way to dodge them. Some landed in front of him, some behind, and some on either side.

One hit him right on top of the head. Warren bent over, shaking the mud out of his hair. His scalp felt burned; he touched his hair with his fingers, fearing he might have a bald spot where the mud ball had landed. His hair felt brittle, but it was still where it belonged.

He heard what he thought was someone else running. Looking over his shoulder, he saw a panicked deer bounding from the forest.

The sky grew dark, the way it did before a heavy rain, and then darker still. Ash dropped, quickly covering the road with a layer of gray. It was like running through newly fallen snow.

The old nursery song echoed crazily in Warren's mind: "Ring around the rosie, a pocket full of posies. Ashes, ashes, all fall down."

In less than five seconds the sky had gone from bright sunshine to total darkness. Flaming cinders rained down, sparking several fires.

Fear made him run faster, his muscle aches forgotten.

Warren choked and coughed with every breath. "What does volcanic ash do to human lungs?" he wondered. Was inhaling it like smoking a thousand cigarettes? He bent his arm and buried his nose and mouth in his elbow, trying to breathe in as little ash as possible.

The air was black as a bowling ball; Warren could no longer see the road. The only light came from the burning cinders and the bolts of lightning which now zapped the air above him, one after another. Some of the lightning was orange; some was green, but Warren was too concerned about getting to safety to wonder about the colors.

The gravel beneath his feet felt as if it had just come
out of a hot oven, like the warming stone that his mother put
in the bottom of the bread basket, to keep dinner rolls warm.
Warren coughed harder.
Once, on a Boy Scout camping trip, Warren had stirred
the campfire with a stick, to be sure it was out before he left.
Smoke and ash had risen and filled his nostrils. This air smelled
like the charred remains of that campfire, only this was worse.
Here, he couldn't turn his head away and gulp in fresh air.

# Think and Compare

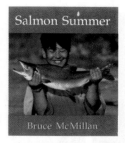

1. In what ways are the problems facing Donn and Warren alike and different?

2. What is the main idea of *Wildfires*? What does this suggest will happen to the natural areas around Mt. Saint Helens after its eruption?

3. If Donn and Warren could meet, what might each boy say he learned about nature during his adventures?

4. Do Donn's decisions show good judgment? Explain and give examples.

5. Describe a time you may have encountered nature as a friend and another as a foe. How did each experience affect the way you view nature overall?

**Strategies in Action** Which reading strategies did you find most useful during this theme? Why?

# Write a Travel Poster

Create a poster advertising a natural place you love, or would like to experience. Describe your location in a way that will make people want to see it. Include your own illustrations, or use pictures from different sources to help bring your poster to life.

**Tips**

- Review travel ads in newspapers for reference.
- List the things that make this place so special.
- Use vivid, descriptive words.

# Writing an Opinion Essay

Some tests may prompt you to write your opinion about a topic. A test about the theme *Nature: Friend and Foe* might include this prompt.

> Write an essay telling whether you think nature is a friend or a foe. Include three reasons explaining your opinion. Support each reason with details.

## 1 Read the prompt.

Find the key words that tell the topic and the kind of writing. Restate in your own words what you need to do. Decide what to write about.

## 2 Explore and plan.

Brainstorm reasons and details to support your opinion. Organize your reasons and details in a chart.

Look at this example of a good planning chart.

**Opinion: Nature is our friend.**

| Reason and Details | Reason and Details | Reason and Details |
|---|---|---|
| Sun and rain are needed for life (light, warmth, water). | Plants and animals feed and help us (crops, livestock, pets). | Nature provides beauty (gardens, art, wilderness). |

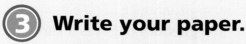

## 3 Write your paper.

Draft your opinion essay. Follow the chart you made. Revise your paper. Look for places to add exact words and details. Proofread your essay to correct errors.

Here is the beginning of a sample essay. It shows the opinion and the first reason and details.

Is nature our friend? Of course! It gives us life and makes life worth living every day.

Sun and rain are both part of nature, and they are necessary for life. The sun helps plants grow and gives us light and warmth. Rain gives people, plants, and animals water to drink. Without the sun and the rain, nothing on our planet could live.

This glossary contains meanings and pronunciations for some of the words in this book. The Full Pronunciation Key shows how to pronounce each consonant and vowel in a special spelling. At the bottom of the glossary pages is a shortened form of the full key.

## Full Pronunciation Key

### Consonant Sounds

| | | | | | | |
|---|---|---|---|---|---|---|
| b | **bib**, ca**bb**age | kw | **ch**oir, **qu**ick | t | **t**igh**t**, stopp**ed** |
| ch | **ch**ur**ch**, sti**tch** | l | **l**id, need**le**, ta**ll** | th | ba**th**, **th**in |
| d | **d**ee**d**, mail**ed**, pu**dd**le | m | a**m**, **m**an, du**mb** | *th* | ba**th**e, **th**is |
| f | **f**ast, **f**i**fe**, o**ff**, **ph**rase, rou**gh** | n | **n**o, sudd**en** | v | ca**v**e, val**v**e, **v**ine |
| | | ng | thi**ng**, i**nk** | w | **w**ith, **w**olf |
| g | **g**a**g**, **g**et, fin**g**er | p | **p**o**p**, ha**pp**y | y | **y**es, **y**olk, on**i**on |
| h | **h**at, **wh**o | r | **r**oar, **rh**yme | z | ro**s**e, si**z**e, **x**ylophone, **z**ebra |
| hw | **wh**ich, **wh**ere | s | mi**ss**, **s**au**c**e, **sc**ene, **s**ee | zh | gara**g**e, plea**s**ure, vi**s**ion |
| j | **j**u**dg**e, **g**em | sh | di**sh**, **sh**ip, **s**ugar, ti**ss**ue | | |
| k | **c**at, **k**i**ck**, s**ch**ool | | | | |

### Vowel Sounds

| | | | | | | |
|---|---|---|---|---|---|---|
| ă | p**a**t, l**au**gh | ŏ | h**o**rrible, p**o**t | ŭ | c**u**t, fl**oo**d, r**ou**gh, s**o**me |
| ā | **a**pe, **ai**d, p**ay** | ō | g**o**, r**ow**, t**oe**, th**ough** | û | c**i**rcle, f**u**r, h**ear**d, t**er**m, t**ur**n, **ur**ge, w**or**d |
| â | **ai**r, c**a**re, w**ea**r | ô | **a**ll, c**augh**t, f**o**r, p**aw** | | |
| ä | f**a**ther, k**o**ala, y**a**rd | oi | b**oy**, n**oi**se, **oi**l | | |
| ĕ | p**e**t, pl**ea**sure, **a**ny | ou | c**ow**, **ou**t | yōō | c**u**re |
| ē | b**e**, b**ee**, **ea**sy, p**ia**no | ōō | f**u**ll, b**oo**k, w**o**lf | yōō | ab**u**se, **u**se |
| ĭ | **i**f, p**i**t, b**u**sy | ōō | b**oo**t, r**u**de, fr**ui**t, fl**ew** | ə | **a**go, sil**e**nt, penc**i**l, lem**o**n, circ**u**s |
| ī | r**i**de, b**y**, p**ie**, h**igh** | | | | |
| î | d**ear**, d**ee**r, f**ie**rce, m**e**re | | | | |

### Stress Marks

Primary Stress ´: bi•ol•o•gy [bī **ŏl´** ə jē]
Secondary Stress ´: bi•o•log•i•cal [bī´ ə **lŏj´** ĭ kəl]

# A

**a·blaze** (ə **blāz´**) *adj.* On fire: *One match set the fire **ablaze**.*

**a·bun·dance** (ə **bŭn´** dəns) *n.* A large amount: *The hikers saw an **abundance** of wildlife in the forest.*

**ad·ven·tur·er** (əd **vĕn´** chər ər) *n.* A person who takes part in bold, dangerous, or risky activities: *The **adventurers** were the first to reach the mountaintop.*

**af·fect** (ə **fĕkt´**) *v.* To cause a change in; have an effect on: *Hot, dry weather **affected** the crops.*

**ag·gres·sive·ly** (ə **grĕs´** ĭv lē) *adv.* Very actively and forcefully: *She worked **aggressively** to get elected.*

**al·le·giance** (ə **lē´** jəns) *n.* Loyalty to one's country, a person, or a cause: *The player showed her **allegiance** to the team by playing her best.*

**am·pli·fi·er** (**ăm´** plə fī· ər) *n.* An electronic device that makes sound stronger or louder: *The **amplifiers** allowed everyone in the large room to hear the speech.*

**an·ces·tor** (**ăn´** sĕs´ tər) *n.* A person in one's family who lived many years ago.

**ar·range·ment** (ə **rānj´** mənt) *n.* Planning done beforehand; preparation: *The family made **arrangements** for their vacation.*

**at·ten·tive·ly** (ə **tĕn´** tĭv lē) *adv.* With attention or alertness: *We listen **attentively** to our teacher.*

**au·tumn** (**ô´** təm) *n.* The season of the year between summer and winter.

# B

**be·wil·der** (bĭ **wĭl´** dər) *v.* To puzzle greatly: *The city's busy streets **bewildered** the young boy.*

**blare** (blâr) *v.* To make a loud harsh noise, as of a horn: *The car horn was **blaring** in the street.*

**bliz·zard** (**blĭz´** ərd) *n.* A very long, heavy snowstorm with strong winds.

**bor·row** (**bŏr´** ō) *v.* To take something with the understanding that it will be returned: *Matt let his friend **borrow** his book.*

**boy·cott** (**boi´** kŏt´) *n.* A refusal to use, buy from, or deal with a store, company, person, or nation: *Many people joined the **boycott** against the store's unfair policy.*

**bunk·house** (**bŭngk´** hous´) *n.* A building in a ranch or camp where a group of people sleeps: *The **bunkhouse** had twenty beds.*

# C

**ca·reer** (kə **rîr´**) *n.* A profession or occupation that a person follows as a life's work: *Raul chose a **career** as a teacher.*

**cham·ber** (**chām´** bər) *n.* A hall or room used by a group of lawmakers or judges: *The mayor spoke in the crowded **chamber**.*

**blizzard**

**chamber**
*Chamber* comes from the Latin word for "room." Now it can refer to a room, like a bedroom, or to a small space, like the chamber of a heart.

ō͞o b**oo**t / ou **ou**t / ŭ c**u**t / û f**u**r / hw **wh**ich / th **th**in / th **th**is / zh vi**si**on / ə **a**go, sil**e**nt, penc**i**l, lem**o**n, circ**u**s

711

**char·ac·ter** (kăr´ ĭk tər) *n.* A symbol, such as a letter or number, used in printing or writing: *Joe painted red characters on a sign for the Chinese New Year.*

**charred** (chärd) *adj.* Burned or scorched by fire: *Only a few charred walls were left after the house fire.*

**check out** (chĕk out) *v.* To sign out and take: *You can check out books from the library.*

**check·point** (chĕk´ point´) *n.* A place along a route where a check or count is made: *The runners were counted at each checkpoint.*

**cit·i·zen** (sĭt´ ĭ zən) *n.* A person who is an official member of a country: *American citizens vote for a president every four years.*

**cit·i·zen·ship** (sĭt´ ĭ zən shĭp´) *n.* The legal position of a citizen of a country, with the duties, rights, and privileges of this position: *The judge granted citizenship to all the people at the ceremony.*

**civ·il rights** (sĭv´ əl rītz) *adj.* Relating to the legal privileges of a citizen, as in the civil rights movement: *The civil rights movement supported fairness for all.*

**clas·si·cal** (klăs´ ĭ kəl) *adj.* Of or relating to a musical style developed in Europe in the 1700s: *The orchestra played classical music.*

**con·duc·tor** (kən dŭk´ tər) *n.* The person in charge of a railroad train or subway: *The conductor collected our tickets on the train.*

**con·sec·u·tive** (kən sĕk´ yə tĭv) *adj.* Following one right after the other: *Chad hit a home run in three consecutive games.*

**con·sume** (kən soom´) *v.* To destroy by burning: *The house was consumed by the fire.*

**con·tract** (kŏn´ trăkt´) *n.* A written agreement that the law can enforce: *The band signed a contract to record two CDs.*

**cord** (kôrd) *n.* A measure for a stack of cut wood. A cord is eight feet long, four feet wide, and four feet high: *The men cut and stacked two cords of wood.*

**cor·ral** (kə răl´) *n.* A fenced-in area for cattle or horses.

**cou·ra·geous** (kə rā´ jəs) *adj.* Having or showing courage; brave: *The courageous policeman saved the child from drowning.*

**coy·o·te** (kī ō´ tē) *or* (kī´ ōt´) *n.* An animal similar to a wolf that lives in western North America.

**crest** (krĕst) *n.* Something that grows out of an animal's head, such as a cluster of feathers: *There was a crest of bright blue feathers on the bird's head.*

**cross·ly** (krôs´ lē) *adv.* In a grumpy or grouchy way: *Evie looked crossly at Gabe when he sat in her favorite chair.*

**cy·cle** (sī´ kəl) *n.* A series of events that is regularly repeated in the same order: *The cycles of seasons are the same each year.*

---

**corral**

*Corral* is a Spanish word that means "an enclosed area for cattle." It comes from an old Latin word for "circle" or "ring."

**conductor**

---

ă r**a**t / ā p**ay** / â c**are** / ä f**a**ther / ĕ p**e**t / ē b**e** / ĭ p**i**t / ī p**ie** / î f**ie**rce / ŏ p**o**t / ō g**o** / ô p**aw**, f**o**r / oi **oi**l / o͞o b**oo**k

# D

**de·but** (dā´ byōō´) *or* (dā **byōō**´) *n.* A first performance in public: *Rosa made her musical debut at the school concert.*

**dem·on·strate** (dĕm´ ən strāt´) *v.* To show clearly; reveal: *This race demonstrated his speed.*

**de·pot** (dē´ pō) *or* (dĕp´ ō) *n.* A railroad or bus station.

**de·ter·mined** (dĭ tûr´ mĭnd) *adj.* Having or showing firmness in sticking to a goal: *Dave was determined to become a doctor.*

**dis·ap·point·ed** (dĭs´ ə **point**´ əd) *adj.* Made unhappy because hopes or wishes were not satisfied: *Chris was disappointed that she wasn't picked for the soccer team.*

**draft** (drăft) *n.* A flow of air: *A cold draft made the boy shiver.*

**drought** (drout) *n.* A period of little or no rain: *The drought dried up the farmer's crops.*

# E

**ea·ger** (ē´ gər) *adj.* Full of strong desire; excited: *Ramón was eager to learn to swim.*

**el·e·gant** (ĕl´ ĭ gənt) *adj.* Marked by good taste; stylish and graceful: *The people at the fancy party looked very elegant.*

**em·ber** (ĕm´ bər) *n.* A piece of glowing coal or wood in the ashes of a fire: *The log burned until only an ember remained.*

**en·rich** (ĕn **rich**´) *v.* To improve the quality of by adding certain parts, qualities, or ingredients: *Music can enrich your life.*

**etch** (ĕch) *v.* To make a drawing or design by cutting lines: *Lynn etched her name in the soft clay.*

**e·ven·tu·al·ly** (ĭ vĕn´ chōō əl lē) *adv.* At the end; finally: *After a long delay, the train eventually arrived at the station.*

**ex·pe·ri·enced** (ĭk spîr´ ē ənst) *adj.* Possessing skill or knowledge from having done a particular thing in the past: *The experienced workers solved the problem quickly.*

# F

**fare** (fâr) *n.* The money a person must pay to travel, as on a plane, train, or bus: *The bus driver collected my fare.*

**field** (fēld) *v.* In baseball, to catch or pick up a ball and throw it to the correct player: *The outfielder had difficulty fielding the ball.*

**fierce** (fîrs) *adj.* Wild and mean; dangerous: *The lion sounded fierce when it roared.*

**first base·man** (fûrst **bās**´ mən) *n.* The baseball player who fields from a position near first base.

**flam·ma·ble** (flăm´ ə bəl) *adj.* Easy to set fire to and able to burn rapidly: *Old wooden buildings are very flammable.*

**fare**

---

ōō b**oo**t / ou **ou**t / ŭ **cut** / û f**u**r / hw **wh**ich / th **th**in / *th* **th**is / zh vi**s**ion / ə **a**go, sil**e**nt, penc**i**l, lem**o**n, circ**u**s

**frost**

**fron·tier** (frŭn **tîr**´) *n.* A remote or distant area beyond which few or no people live: *The family went west and settled on the frontier.* ◆ *adj.* Relating to the frontier: *Frontier life was difficult.*

**frost** (frôst) *n.* A very thin covering of ice: *The cold weather coated the windows with frost.*

# G

**gath·er·ing** (**găth**´ ər ĭng) *n.* A coming together of people: *The party was a family gathering.*

**gear** (gîr) *n.* Equipment, such as tools or clothing, used for a particular activity: *We bought camping gear for our hike.*

**glare** (glâr) *v.* To stare angrily: *After the argument, Mark was glaring at his brother.*

**god·moth·er** (**gŏd**´ mŭth´ ər) *n.* A woman or girl who acts as parent or guardian of a child, in the event that the child's parents are unable to: *Leah was asked to be the baby's godmother.*

# H

**hom·age** (**hŏm**´ ĭj) *n.* Special public honor or respect: *The crowd paid homage to the famous artist at the awards ceremony.*

**home·land** (**hōm**´ lănd´) *n.* The country in which one was born or has lived for a long time: *Seema returned to her homeland after many years in a foreign country.*

**home·stead** (**hōm**´ stĕd´) *n.* A house with the land and buildings belonging to it: *The homestead has belonged to his family for generations.* ◆ In the 1800s, land given by the government to a person who settled on and farmed it: *Finally, the covered wagon reached the family's homestead.*

**hon·or** (**ŏn**´ ər) *v.* To show special respect for: *People came to honor the heroes at the parade.*

**ho·ri·zon** (hə **rī**´ zən) *n.* The line along which the earth and the sky appear to meet: *I watched the sun rise over the horizon.*

# I

**im·mense** (ĭ **mĕns**´) *adj.* Of great size, scale, or degree: *The immense building seemed to touch the clouds.*

# J

**jazz** (jăz) *n.* A type of music with a strong rhythm which developed in the United States from work songs, hymns, and spirituals: *When the pianist plays jazz, she sometimes invents the song as she goes along.*

**jolt** (jōlt) *v.* To move, ride, or cause to move in a jerky way: *The bus was jolting along the bumpy road.*

ă rat / ā pay / â care / ä father / ĕ pet / ē be / ĭ pit / ī pie / î fierce / ŏ pot / ō go / ô paw, for / oi oil / ŏŏ book

# L

**land·scape** (lănd´ skāp´) *n.* A stretch of land: *Emily admired the **landscape** of rolling hills.*

**lap** (lăp) *v.* To take up with the tip of the tongue: *Have you ever watched a cat **lap** up water?* ♦ *n.* The front part of a sitting person's body from the waist to the knees: *The cat slept on Yoshi's **lap**.*

**long** (lông) *v.* To wish or want very much: *My mother **longed** to see her childhood home again.*

**lum·ber·jack** (lŭm´ bər jăk´) *n.* A person who chops down trees and hauls the logs to a sawmill.

**lurch·ing** (lûrch´ ĭng) *adj.* Sudden, heavy, unsteady movements to one side or forward: *The **lurching** boat made Roslyn sway back and forth.*

**lure** (lŏŏr) *n.* Fake bait used to attract and catch fish: *The fisherman tied a silver **lure** to his line.*

# M

**mar·vel** (mär´ vəl) *v.* To be filled with surprise, amazement, or wonder: *Don **marveled** at the beautiful waterfall.*

**mer·cu·ry** (mûr´ kyə rē) *n.* A silvery-white metal that is a liquid at room temperature; used in thermometers.

**mis·cal·cu·late** (mĭs kăl´ kyə lāt´) *v.* To plan or figure incorrectly; make a mistake: *Amy **miscalculated** how much money she needed.*

**mis·un·der·stand·ing** (mĭs´ ŭn dər stăn´ dĭng) *n.* A failure to understand: *Carl's feelings were hurt because of a **misunderstanding** over whose turn it was.*

**mod·est** (mŏd´ ĭst) *adj.* Having a quiet, humble view of one's own talents, abilities, or accomplishments; not boastful: *The piano player was **modest** even though he was very talented.*

**mur·mur** (mûr´ mər) *n.* A low, constant sound: *We often hear the **murmur** of running water from the nearby stream.*

**mush·er** (mŭsh´ ər) *n.* The driver of a dog sled team.

# N

**ner·vous·ly** (nûr´ vəs lē) *adv.* With concern, worry, or fear: *He **nervously** walked onto the stage to deliver his speech.*

# O

**oath** (ōth) *n.* A pledge or promise to act in a certain way: *The new citizens pledged an **oath** to obey the laws of the United States.*

**op·por·tu·ni·ty** (ŏp´ ər tōō´ nĭ tē) *or* (ŏp´ ər tyōō´ nĭ tē) *n.* A good chance to advance oneself: *Joining the school band was an **opportunity** to make new friends.*

**or·phan** (ôr´ fən) *n.* A child whose parents are dead.

**landscape**

**lumberjack**
*Lumberjack* is a compound word made up of *lumber,* meaning trees used for wood, and *jack,* meaning "man." *Jack* originally comes from the Hebrew name for Jacob.

---

ōō b**oo**t / ou **ou**t / ŭ c**u**t / û f**u**r / hw **wh**ich / th **th**in / th **th**is / zh vi**si**on / ə **a**go, sil**e**nt, penc**i**l, lem**o**n, circ**u**s

# P

**peas·ant** (pĕz´ ənt) *adj.* Of or relating to a poor farmer or farm worker: *The couple lived a simple* **peasant** *life in the country.*

**pe·cu·liar** (pĭ kyōol´ yər) *adj.* Unusual; strange or odd: *The warm weather was* **peculiar** *for January.*

**per·sist** (pər sĭst´) *v.* To continue repeatedly to say or do something: *My sister* **persisted** *in asking me to read to her.*

**phonograph**

**pho·no·graph** (fō´ nə grăf´) *n.* An old-fashioned record player: *Jenna danced to a happy song playing on the* **phonograph**.

**pi·o·neer** (pī´ ə nîr´) *n.* A person who settles in an unknown, unclaimed region: *The* **pioneers** *made their new homes in the valley.*

**pioneer**
*Pioneer* comes from the Italian word for "foot soldier," the first kind of soldier to go into battle. Today, *pioneer* refers to the settlers of the American West or to anyone who leads the way for others.

**pitch in** (pĭch ĭn) *v.* To start working with other people to get a job done: *Everyone on the farm* **pitches in** *to finish the work.*

**plaque** (plăk) *n.* A flat piece of wood, metal, or stone with writing on it that usually honors a person or event: **Plaques** *on the sunken ship honor the people who lost their lives.*

**plat·form** (plăt´ fôrm´) *n.* A raised floor or surface, for example, by a track at a train station: *They stood on the* **platform**, *waiting for the train.*

**prai·rie** (prâr´ ē) *adj.* Of the plains, a wide area of flat or rolling land with tall grass and few trees: *The* **prairie** *winds covered everything with dust.*

**pro·test** (prə tĕst´) *or* (prō´ tĕst´) *v.* To express strong objections to something: *Many people came to* **protest** *the plan to build a new airport.*

**proud** (proud) *adj.* **1.** Thinking too highly of oneself: *The boy was* **proud** *because he thought he was better than anyone else.* **2.** Full of self-respect: *Li felt* **proud** *to be marching in the parade.*

# R

**re·mind** (rĭ mīnd´) *v.* To make someone remember something: *The song* **reminded** *him of home.*

**re·new** (rĭ nōo´) *or* (rĭ nyōo´) *v.* To make new again; to bring new life to: *Each spring the forest* **renews** *itself with green leaves.*

**re·un·ion** (rē yōon´ yən) *n.* A gathering of members of a group who have not seen each other for a while: *The school holds its yearly* **reunions** *in the gym.*

**rhythm** (rĭth´ əm) *n.* **1.** A movement, action, or condition that repeats in a regular pattern: *Everyone's walk has a special* **rhythm**. **2.** A musical pattern with a series of regularly accented beats: *We sang songs with many different* **rhythms**.

**rug·ged** (rŭg´ ĭd) *adj.* Having a rough, uneven surface: *The* **rugged** *trail was hard to climb.*

---

ă r**at** / ā p**ay** / â c**are** / ä f**ather** / ĕ p**et** / ē b**e** / ĭ p**it** / ī p**ie** / î f**ie**rce / ŏ p**ot** / ō g**o** / ô p**aw**, f**or** / oi **oil** / ŏŏ b**oo**k

# S

**satch·el** (săch´ əl) *n.* A small bag used for carrying books, clothing, or other small items: *The two **satchels** held all she owned.*

**sat·is·fac·tion** (săt´ ĭs făk´ shən) *n.* The condition of being pleased and contented: *Her **satisfaction** with her family showed in her big smile.*

**scale** (skāl) *n.* **1.** One of the small, thin, flat parts that cover a fish or reptile: *The lizard was covered with shiny green **scales**.* **2.** An instrument used for weighing: *Anton weighed a bunch of bananas on the **scale**.*

**scav·en·ger** (skăv´ ĭn jər) *n.* An animal that feeds on dead animals or plants: ***Scavengers** often eat dead fish.*

**set·tler** (sĕt´ lər) *n.* A person who settles, or makes a home, in a new region: *The **settlers** traveled west to find a better life.*

**ship·wreck** (shĭp´ rĕk´) *n.* **1.** A wrecked ship: *The* Titanic *is the most famous of all **shipwrecks**.* **2.** The destruction of a ship, in a collision or because of a storm: *A **shipwreck** may happen during a storm at sea.*

**short·stop** (shôrt´ stŏp´) *n.* The baseball player who plays the position between second and third bases.

**singe** (sĭnj) *v.* To burn slightly; scorch: *Celia saw that the fire was about to **singe** her sweater.*

**slump** (slŭmp) *v.* **1.** To sink down suddenly: *The woman **slumped** to the ground and cried.* **2.** To experience a period of poor performance, especially in a sport: *Our best hitter always **slumps** in hot weather.*

**snake** (snāk) *v.* To move like a snake: *The line of children **snaked** through the playground.*

**snow·shoe** (snō´ shoo´) *n.* A rounded wooden frame with leather strips stretched across it, attached to the shoe; used for walking on top of the snow.

**spawn** (spôn) *v.* To lay eggs and reproduce, as fish and some other water animals do: *Salmon return to **spawn** in the same river where they were born.*

**spe·cial·ize** (spĕsh´ ə līz) *v.* To be involved in a particular activity or branch of study: *This bookstore **specializes** in children's books.*

**sports·man·ship** (spôrts´ mən shĭp´) *n.* The quality of someone who acts with dignity in difficult situations, especially used with people who play sports: *It was good **sportsmanship** to clap for the other team.*

**sto·ry·tel·ler** (stôr´ ē tĕl´ ər) *n.* A person who tells stories.

**stride** (strīd) *v.* To walk with long steps: *The boy **strides** quickly down the street.*

**stu·pen·dous** (stoo pĕn´ dəs) *adj.* Amazing; marvelous: *The falling star was a **stupendous** sight.*

**scale**
*Scale* comes from the Old Norse word for "bowl," or a drinking vessel made from a shell. Scales used to have two plates or bowls to hold the objects that were being weighed.

---

ōō b**oo**t / ou **ou**t / ŭ c**u**t / û f**u**r / hw **wh**ich / th **th**in / th **th**is / zh vi**si**on / ə **a**go, sil**e**nt, penc**i**l, lem**o**n, circ**u**s

**sur·round** (sə **round´**) *v.* To put all around: *He **surrounded** his desk with pictures of his family.*

**sur·vi·vor** (sər **vī´** vər) *n.* Someone or something that has stayed alive: *The rescue ship picked up the **survivors** from the lifeboats.*

# T

**teem·ing** (tēm´ ĭng) *adj.* Full; crowded: *The parade moved through the **teeming** city streets.*

**tem·per·a·ture** (tĕm´ pər ə chər) *n.* Hotness or coldness as measured on a standard scale: *The **temperature** outside was low, so we put on our warmest clothes.*

**ther·mom·e·ter** (thər **mŏm´** ĭ tər) *n.* An instrument that measures temperature, usually by the height of a liquid that expands or contracts inside a slender glass tube.

**tim·ber** (tĭm´ bər) *n.* **1.** Trees that can be used as wood: *They used **timber** from their own land to build their house.* **2.** A long, heavy piece of wood for building; a beam: *Only a few blackened **timbers** of the barn remained after the fire.*

**tim·id** (tĭm´ ĭd) *adj.* Easily frightened; shy: *The **timid** squirrel sat still until everyone had left.*

**tire·less** (tīr´ lĭs) *adj.* Capable of working a long time without getting tired: *She was a **tireless** worker who always stayed late.*

**trou·ble·some** (trŭb´ əl səm) *adj.* Causing trouble or difficulty: *Ben felt he was in a **troublesome** situation when he couldn't find the movie tickets.*

# U

**un·sink·a·ble** (ŭn´ **sĭngk´** ə bəl) *adj.* Not capable of being sunk: *The ship was so big that people thought it was **unsinkable**.*

# V

**voy·age** (voi´ ĭj) *n.* A long journey to a distant place, usually made by ship or airplane.

# W

**weath·er·vane** (wĕth´ ər vān´) *n.* A moveable pointer that shows which way the wind is blowing: *The **weathervane** on top of the barn pointed north.*

**woods·man** (wo͝odz´ mən) *n.* A person who works or lives in the forest: *The young **woodsman** walked to the forest every day.*

**world·wide** (wûrld´ wīd´) *adj.* Extending or spreading throughout the world: *Several songs became **worldwide** hits.*

**wreck·age** (rĕk´ ĭj) *n.* The remains of something that has been damaged or destroyed: *The **wreckage** of the ship was found on the ocean floor.*

**thermometer**

*Thermometer* comes from two Greek words: *thermē,* meaning "heat," and *metron,* meaning "measure." A thermometer measures heat.

**weathervane**

ă **r**a**t** / ā **p**a**y** / â **c**a**re** / ä **f**a**ther** / ĕ **p**e**t** / ē **be** / ĭ **p**i**t** / ī **p**ie / î **fie**rce / ŏ **p**o**t** / ō **go** / ô **p**aw, **fo**r / oi **oil** / o͝o **b**oo**k**

# Acknowledgments

*Akiak: A Tale from the Iditarod*, by Robert J. Blake. Text and illustrations copyright © 1997 by Robert J. Blake. All rights reserved. Reprinted by permission of Philomel Books, a division of Penguin Putnam, Inc.

*Amelia and Eleanor Go for a Ride*, by Pam Muñoz Ryan, illustrated by Brian Selznick, published by Scholastic Press, a division of Scholastic Inc. Text copyright © 1999 by Pam Muñoz Ryan. Illustrations copyright © 1999 by Brian Selznick. Reprinted by permission.

Selection from *The Borrowers*, by Mary Norton. Copyright © 1953, 1952 by Mary Norton and renewed 1981, 1980 by Mary Norton, Beth Krush, and Joe Krush. Reprinted by permission of Harcourt, Inc.

*Boss of the Plains: The Hat That Won the West*, by Laurie Carlson, illustrated by Holly Meade. Text copyright © 1998 by Laurie Carlson. Illustrations copyright © 1998 by Holly Meade. Reprinted by permission of Dorling Kindersley Publishing, Inc.

Selection from *By the Shores of Silver Lake*, by Laura Ingalls Wilder. Copyright © 1939 by Laura Ingalls Wilder. Copyright renewed © 1967 by Roger L. MacBride. Reprinted by permission of HarperCollins Publishers.

*Cendrillon: A Caribbean Cinderella*, by Robert D. San Souci, illustrated by Brian Pinkney. Text copyright © 1998 by Robert D. San Souci. Illustrations copyright © 1998 by Brian Pinkney. All rights reserved. Reprinted by permission of Simon & Schuster Books for Young Readers, an imprint of Simon & Schuster Children's Publishing Division.

Selection from *Chester Cricket's Pigeon Ride*, by George Selden, pictures by Garth Williams. Text copyright © 1981 by George Selden. Pictures copyright © 1981 by Garth Williams. Reprinted by permission of Farrar, Straus and Giroux, LLC.

*Duke Ellington*, by Andrea Davis Pinkney, illustrated by Brian Pinkney. Text copyright © 1998 by Andrea Davis Pinkney. Illustrations copyright © 1998 by Brian Pinkney. Reprinted by permission of Hyperion Books for Children.

*Finding the Titanic*, by Robert D. Ballard, illustrated by Ken Marschall. Published by Cartwheel Books, a division of Scholastic, Inc. Copyright © 1993 by Madison Press, Ltd. Reprinted by permission of Scholastic, Inc. and Madison Press, Ltd.

*Gloria Estefan: A Real-Life Biography*, by Susan Boulais. Copyright © 1998 by Mitchell Lane Publishers, Inc. Reprinted by permission of Mitchell Lane Publishers, Inc.

*Grandfather's Journey*, by Allen Say. Copyright © 1993 by Allen Say. Reprinted by permission of Houghton Mifflin Company. All rights reserved.

*Happy Birthday, Dr. King!*, by Kathryn Jones, illustrated by Floyd Cooper. Copyright © 1994 by The Children's Museum, Boston. Published by Modern Curriculum Press, Inc., an imprint of Pearson Learning. Reprinted by permission.

*Heat Wave!*, by Helen Ketteman, illustrated by Scott Goto. Text copyright © 1998 by Helen Ketteman. Illustrations copyright © 1998 by Scott Goto. Reprinted by permission of Walker & Company. All rights reserved.

Selection from *Juan Verdades: The Man Who Couldn't Tell a Lie*, by Joe Hayes, illustrated by Joseph Daniel Fiedler, published by Orchard Books, an imprint of Scholastic Inc. Text copyright © 2001 by Joe Hayes. Illustrations copyright © 2001 by Joseph Daniel Fiedler. Reprinted by permission of Scholastic Inc.

*The Last Dragon*, by Susan Miho Nunes, illustrated by Chris K. Soentpiet. Text copyright © 1995 by Susan Miho Nunes. Illustrations copyright © 1995 by Chris K. Soentpiet. Reprinted by permission of Houghton Mifflin Company. All rights reserved.

"Lord of the Fleas," by Thomas Willke, from *MUSE* magazine, May/June 2001, Vol. 5, No. 5. Text copyright © 2001 by Thomas Willke. Reprinted by permission of *MUSE* magazine and the author.

Selection from *Lost on a Mountain in Maine*, by Donn Fendler as told to Joseph B. Egan. Copyright © 1978 by Picton Press. Reprinted by permission of Picton Press.

Selection from *Louis Braille, The Boy Who Invented Books for the Blind*, by Margaret Davidson. Text copyright © 1971 by Margaret Davidson. Reprinted by permission of Scholastic Inc.

*Lou Gehrig: The Luckiest Man*, by David A. Adler, illustrated by Terry Widener. Text copyright © 1997 by David A. Adler. Illustrations copyright © 1997 by Terry Widener. Reprinted by permission of Harcourt, Inc.

*Marven of the Great North Woods*, by Kathryn Lasky, illustrated by Kevin Hawkes. Text copyright © 1997 by Kathryn Lasky Knight. Illustrations copyright © 1997 by Kevin Hawkes. Reprinted by permission of Harcourt, Inc.

Selection from *My Name Is Maria Isabel*, by Alma Flor Ada, illustrated by K. Dyble Thompson. Text copyright © 1993 by Alma Flor Ada. Jacket illustration copyright © 1993 by K. Dyble Thompson. Reprinted by permission of Atheneum Books for Young Readers, an imprint of Simon & Schuster Children's Publishing Division. The song "The Candles of Hanukkah," by Suni Paz, that appears in this selection reprinted by permission of the author. Lyrics and music copyright © 1990 by Suni Paz. All rights reserved.

"The Parcel Post Kid," by Michael O. Tunnell, from *SPIDER* magazine, July 1997 issue, Vol. 4, No. 7. Selection copyright © 1997 by Michael O. Tunnell. Cover copyright © 1997 by Carus Publishing Company. Reprinted by permission of *SPIDER* magazine.

Selection from *Sacagawea*, by Judith St. George. Text copyright © 1997 by Judith St. George. Reprinted by permission of G.P. Putnam's Sons, a division of Penguin Young Readers Group, a member of Penguin Group (USA) Inc., and by Curtis Brown Ltd. All rights reserved.

*Salmon Summer*, written and photo-illustrated by Bruce McMillan. Copyright © 1998 by Bruce McMillan. Reprinted by permission of Houghton Mifflin Company. All rights reserved.

*Sing to the Stars*, by Mary Brigid Barrett, illustrated by Sandra Speidel, published by Little, Brown and Company. Text copyright © 1994 by Mary Brigid Barrett-Groth. Illustrations copyright © 1994 by Sandra Speidel. Text reprinted by permission of Curtis Brown, Ltd. for the author. Illustrations reprinted by permission of Sandra Speidel.

Selection from *Skylark*, by Patricia MacLachlan. Copyright © 1994 by Patricia MacLachlan. Reprinted by permission of HarperCollins Publishers.

Selection from *Stormy, Misty's Foal*, by Marguerite Henry. Copyright © 1963 by Macmillan Publishing Company. Reprinted with the permission of Aladdin Paperbacks, an imprint of Simon & Schuster Children's Publishing Division. Cover art by Steve Brennan. Cover copyright © by Steve Brenner. Cover reprinted by permission of Joseph T. Mendola Ltd., New York, New York. All rights reserved.

*The Stranger*, by Chris Van Allsburg. Copyright © 1986 by Chris Van Allsburg. Reprinted by permission of Houghton Mifflin Company. All rights reserved.

*Tanya's Reunion*, by Valerie Flournoy, illustrated by Jerry Pinkney. Text copyright © 1995 by Valerie Flournoy. Illustrations copyright © 1995 by Jerry Pinkney. Reprinted by arrangement with Dial Books for Young Readers, a division of Penguin Putnam, Inc.

*Tomás and the Library Lady*, by Pat Mora, illustrated by Raul Colón. Text copyright © 1997 by Pat Mora. Illustrations copyright © 1997 by Raul Colón. Reprinted by permission of Random House Children's Books, a division of Random House, Inc., New York, New York.

*A Very Important Day*, by Maggie Rugg Herold, illustrated by Catherine Stock. Text copyright © 1995 by Maggie Rugg Herold. Illustrations copyright © 1995 by Catherine Stock. Reprinted by permission of HarperCollins Publishers.

Selection from *The Volcano Disaster*, by Peg Kehret, cover art by Bill Schmidt. Text copyright © 1998 by Peg Kehret. Reprinted with the permission of Simon & Schuster Books for Young Readers, an imprint of Simon & Schuster Children's Publishing Division.

*Wildfires*, by Seymour Simon. Copyright © 1996 by Seymour Simon. Reprinted by permission of HarperCollins Publishers.

**Focus Selections**

"The Anteater," from *Beast Feast*, by Douglas Florian. Copyright © 1994 by Douglas Florian. Reprinted by permission of Harcourt, Inc.

"By Myself," from *Honey, I Love and Other Love Poems*, by Eloise Greenfield, pictures by Diane and Leo Dillon. Text copyright © 1978 by Eloise Greenfield. Reprinted by permission of HarperCollins Publishers.

"The Case of the Earthenware Pig," from *Encyclopedia Brown Solves Them All*, by Donald J. Sobol. Copyright © 1968 by Donald J. Sobol. Reprinted by permission of Dutton Children's Books, a division of Penguin Putnam, Inc. Cover copyright © 1968 by

*"Seal Island Kids,"* by Yva Momatiuk and John Eastcott, adapted from May 1999 *Ranger Rick.* Copyright © 1999 by the National Wildlife Federation. Reprinted by permission of the publisher, the National Wildlife Federation.

*"Snow Runners,"* by William G. Scheller from February 1999 *National Geographic World.* Copyright © 1999 by the National Geographic Society. Reprinted by permission of the National Geographic Society.

*"A Song of Greatness"* from *The Children Sing in the Far West,* by Mary Austin. Copyright 1928 by Mary Austin. Copyright © renewed 1956 by Kenneth M. Chapman & Mary C. Wheelwright. Reprinted by permission of Houghton Mifflin Company. All rights reserved.

*"Summer sky...,"* an untitled haiku by Shiki from *The Penguin Book of Zen Poetry,* edited and translated by Lucien Stryk and Takashi Ikemoto. Copyright © 1963, 1965, 1977 by Lucien Stryk and Takashi Ikemoto. Reprinted by permission of Lucien Stryk.

*"Sunflakes,"* from *Country Pie,* by Frank Asch. Copyright © 1979 by Frank Asch. Reprinted by permission of HarperCollins Publishers.

*"That's Amazing! with Chris Van Allsburg"* – The autographed bookplate illustration is from *Zathura,* by Chris Van Allsburg. Illustration copyright © 2002 by Chris Van Allsburg. Reprinted by permission of Houghton Mifflin Company.

*"This Land Is Your Land,"* words and music by Woody Guthrie. TRO © copyright 1956 (Renewed), 1958 (Renewed), 1970 (Renewed) by Ludlow Music, Inc., New York, New York. Reprinted by permission.

Special thanks to the following teachers whose students' compositions appear as Student Writing Models: Cindy Cheatwood, Florida; Diana Davis, North Carolina; Kathy Driscoll, Massachusetts; Linda Evers, Florida; Heidi Harrison, Michigan; Eileen Hoffman, Massachusetts; Julia Kraftsow, Florida; Bonnie Lewison, Florida; Kanetha McCord, Michigan.

# Credits

### Photography

**3** (t) Steve Cole/Photodisc Green/Getty Images. (m) Floyd Dean/Taxi/Getty Images. (b) © Mark Tomalty/Masterfile. **5** Steve Cole/PhotoDisc/Getty Images. **8** Hemera Technologies Inc. **11** Floyd Dean/Taxi/Getty Images. **13** © Mark Tomalty/Masterfile. **14** (t) © Jeff Vanuga/Corbis. (r) © Niall Benvie/Corbis. **16** Siede Preis/PhotoDisc Green/Getty Images. **19** © Mark Tomalty/ Masterfile. **20-1** (bkgd) © Lafi/CORBIS. **21** (m) Steve Cole/ PhotoDisc Green/Getty Images. **22, 24** Courtesy of Allen Say. **25** C Squared Studios/PhotoDisc/Getty Images. **26** (inset)©Galen Rowell/Mountain Light. **26–7** (bkgd)©Jeff Schultz/Alaska Stock. **27**(inset) ©Jeff Schultz/Alaska Stock. **28-9** (bkgd) Howard Platt/ Taxi/Getty Images. **28** Jeanne Conover. **53** (b) ©Jeff Schultz/ Alaska Stock. **54–7** Richard Nowitz/NGS Image Collection. **60** (b) ©Christie's Images Inc. **61** (tl) Archive Pictures. (tr, br) Brown Brothers. **62-3** (bkgd) © James Schwabel/Panoramic Images. **75** Houghton Mifflin Company. **76** (b) Japanese American National Museum. **80–1** The Titanic, 1911. Antonio Jacobsen (1850-1921) ©Christie's Images Inc. **82-3** (bkgd) Tsuneo Nakamua/Index Stock Imagery. **82** Illustration by Ken Marschall ©1993 from FINDING THE TITANIC, a Scholastic/Madison Press Book. **83** The Titanic, 1911. Antonio Jacobsen (1850-1921) ©Christie's Images Inc. **84** (both) Emory Kristof/NGS Image Collection. **85** Don Lynch Collection. **86** (left inset) ©Underwood & Underwood/ Corbis. (right inset) ©Ralph White/Corbis. **86–7** Illustration by Ken Marschall ©1993 from FINDING THE TITANIC, a Scholastic/Madison Press Book. **87** (left inset) ©Ralph White/ Corbis. (right inset) The Illustrated London News Picture Library. **89** Illustration by Ken Marschall ©1993 from FINDING THE TITANIC, a Scholastic/Madison Press Book. **90–1** Illustration by Ken Marschall ©1993 from FINDING THE TITANIC, a Scholastic/Madison Press Book. **92–3** The Illustrated London News Picture Library. **94** Brown Brothers. **97** (tl) Perry Thorsvik/ NGS Image Collection. (tr) Martin Bowen/Woods Hole Oceanographic Institution. (bl) ©Ralph White/Corbis. (br) Harland & Wolff Photographic Collection, ©National Museums and Galleries of Northern Ireland, Ulster Folk & Transport Museum negative no. H1455. **98** Illustration by Ken Marschall ©1993 from FINDING THE TITANIC, a Scholastic/Madison

Press Book. **99** Hulton-Deutsch Collection/Corbis. **100** Emory Kristof/NGS Image Collection. **101** (bkgd) © PhotoDisc/Getty Images. (inset) AP/Wide World/Lennox McLendon. **102** (b) Don Lynch Collection. **104–5** ©VCG/Taxi/Getty Images **105** (all) Courtesy, International Ice Patrol, U.S. Coast Guard. **107** (top) Courtesy, International Ice Patrol, U.S. Coast Guard. **108** (l) Union Pacific Museum Collection. **109** Corbis Images. **110-1** (bkgd) Water Everywhere/PhotoDisc/Getty Images. **127** (bkgd) Artville. (top)Corbis/Bettmann. (b)Jim Rimi Photography. (picture frames)Image Farm. **128** Union Pacific Railroad Museum. **130–33** (all)©Ron Cortes. **134-4A** (bkgd) © Bill Brooks/Masterfile. **134** (b) Steve Cole/PhotoDisc Green/Getty Images. **134J** (t) Gerald Sipes. (b) New Perce County Historical Society, Lewiston, Idaho. **148** (l) Hulton-Deutsch Collection/Corbis. (r)©1998 Viacom International. All Rights Reserved. **151** (m) Hemera Technologies Inc. **152–3** (bkgd) Steven McBride/Picturesque. **152–4** Courtesy of Valerie Flournoy. **156** Courtesy, Special Collections Library, University of California Riverside/Rivera Library. **157** (tl) ©Al Key. (tr) Courtesy, Southwest Texas State University. (b) Courtesy, University of California Riverside Media Services. **158-9** (bkgd) © Neil Meyerhoff/Panoramic Images. **158** (t) Courtesy, Random House. (b) Courtesy, Raúl Colon. **178** (b) Cary Wolinsky/Stock Boston. **179** Hereford Cathedral Library. Photo by Gordon W. Taylor L.R.P.S. **180** (t) Scala/Art Resource, NY. (b) Eric Lessing/Art Resource, NY. **181** Scott Goodwin Photography. "Old King Cole" Courtesy, Michael Canoso. **184** (bc) John Rubartsch for Reunions Magazine. (br) ©Ron Karten/Omni-Photo Communications, Inc. **185** (t) ©Bob Daemmrich/Stock Boston/PNI. (b) Patrick Robinson for Reunions Magazine. **186-7** (bkgd) © Royalty-Free/Corbis. **186** (t) Courtesy, Valerie Flournoy. (b) Myles Pinkney. **216–17** (b) Church of Jesus Christ of Latter-Day Saints Archives Division #C-188. **217** (t) Used by Permission, Utah State Historical Society, All Rights Reserved. Photo no. 917.81. (c) Courtesy, John B. Stetson Company. **218** (t) ©Courtesy, DK Publishing. (b) ©Bill Franson Photography. **218-9** (bkgd) © Tom Bean/The Image Bank/Getty Images. **241** (cr) Paramount Pictures/Movie Still Archives. **242** Denver Public Library no. Z332. **245** (bl) The Kansas State Historical Society, Topeka, Kansas. **246** R. Kord/H. Armstrong Roberts. **247** (t) ©Henry T. Kaiser/The Picture Cube, Inc. (bl) Corbis/Patrick Ward. (br) ©James Marshall. **248-9** (bkgd) © Richard Berenholtz/Corbis. **248** Courtesy, William Morrow. **249** Courtesy of Chris Van Allsburg. **272** (t) Courtesy, Kids Voting USA. (b) Dayton Daily News. **273–5** (bkgd) Donovan Reese/ Stone/Getty Images. **276-6A** (bkgd) © PhotoDisc/Getty Images. **276** (b) Hemera Technologies Inc. **282** The Image Bank/Getty Images. **292-3** (bkgd) © Josef Fankhauser/The Image Bank/Getty Images. **293** (m) Floyd Dean/Taxi/Getty Images. **298** (b) ©Zig Leszczynski/Animals Animals. **299** (l) ©Jose Azel/Aurora. (tr) ©Chase Smith/Corbis. (br) ©Ed Young/Corbis. **300-1** (bkgd) Darrell Gulin/The Image Bank/Getty Images. **300** (cr) Scott Goodwin Photography. (bkgd)© PhotoDisc/Getty Images.. **318** © PhotoDisc/Getty Images. **319** (tl)© PhotoDisc/Getty Images. **326** (cr) ©Jake Rajs/Stone/Getty Images. **327** (t) ©Chad Ehlers/Stone/ Getty Images. (border fish) ©Norbert Wu. (border red hibiscus) ©Amos Nachoum/Corbis. (border orange hibiscus) © PhotoDisc/ Getty Images. **328-9** (bkgd) Stuart Westmorland/Stone/Getty Images. **328** (tl) © PhotoDisc/Getty Images. (t) Dennis Gray/ Mercury Pictures. (b) Michael Tamborrino/Mercury Pictures. **355** (l) © PhotoDisc/Getty Images. (r) ©The Walt Disney Company/Courtesy, Kobal Collection. **356** (b) Culver Pictures. **357** (tl) North Wind Picture Archives. (tc) The New York Public Library for the Performing Arts (tr) ©Jack Vartoogian. **358** (banner) © PhotoDisc/Getty Images. (c) ©Charles O'Rear/Corbis. **359** ©Miro Vintoniv/Stock Boston. **360** (bkgd) © PhotoDisc/Getty Images. **360** (bkgd) © Ron Watts/Corbis. **377** (t) Courtesy, Helen Ketteman. (b) Courtesy, Scott Goto. **382-3A** (bkgd) © Craig Tuttle/CORBIS. **382** (b) Floyd Dean/Taxi/Getty Images. **382G–L** Volker Steger. **384-5** (bkgd) © Ted Horowitz/CORBIS. **385** (m) © Mark Tomalty/Masterfile. **386** (b) Michael Newman Photoedit, (t) Courtesy of Alma Flor Ada. **387** Courtesy of Alma Flor Ada. **390** (t) ©James Frank/Stock Connection/PNI. (b) ©Frank Siteman/Stock Boston/PNI. **391** (t) Bob Daemmrich/Stock Boston. (b) ©Frank Siteman/Stock Boston. **392-3** (bkgd) Dan Hallman/The Image Bank/Getty Images. **392** (t) Ann Duffy. (b) Courtesy, Melodye Rosales. **409** (l) © PhotoDisc/Getty Images. (r) Ken Karp. **410** (b) ©Coco McCoy/Rainbow/PNI. **411** (t) ©David Lees/ Corbis. (b) ©Roger Garwood & Trish Ainslie/Corbis. **412** (t) ©Minnesota Historical Society/Corbis. **413** (t) © PhotoDisc/Getty

Images. **415** (t) Photo Courtesy of Clearwater County Historical Society, Bagley, MN. (b) Minnesota Historical Society. **416** (bkgd) JH Pete Carmichael/The Image Bank/Getty Images. **443** (t) Christopher Knight (b) Courtesy, Kevin Hawkes. **446–7** Scott S. Warren/NGS Image Collection. **447** (tr)© PhotoDisc/Getty Images. (br) ©Scott S. Warren. **448** (cl) (cr) ©Scott S. Warren. (t) ©Scott S. Warren/NGS Image Collection. **449** (t) ©Tom Brakefield/Bruce Coleman Inc. NY. (b) Scott S. Warren/NGS Image Collection. **450** ©Robert Brenner/PhotoEdit. **451** (t) ©Barbara Alper/Stock Boston. (b) ©Gary A. Conner/PhotoEdit. **452-3** (bkgd) © Phil Schermeister/Corbis. **452** (t) Courtesy, Susan Miho Nunes. (b) Michael Tamborinno/Mercury Pictures. **481**© PhotoDisc/Getty Images. **482-3** ©A. Ramey/PhotoEdit. **486** (b) ©David Young-Wolff/PhotoEdit. **486–7** © PhotoDisc/Getty Images. **487(t)** ©Carol and Mike Werner/Stock Boston. (b) ©Lawrence Migdale/Stock Boston. **488-9** (bkgd) © Zane Williams/Panoramic Images. **488** (t) Mary Brigid Barrett. (b) Thor Swift/Mercury Pictures. **509** (r) © PhotoDisc/Getty Images. **510** John Bigelow Taylor/Art Resource, NY. **511** (t) Erich Lessing/Art Resource, NY. (b) Green Violinist, 1923-24, Marc Chagall. Oil on canvas. Gift, Solomon R. Guggenheim, 1937. The Solomon R. Guggenheim Museum, New York. Photograph by David Heald ©The Solomon R. Guggenheim Foundation, New York. ©2001 Artists Rights Society (ARS), New York/ADAGP, Paris **512-2A** (bkgd) © Paul Hardy/CORBIS. **512** (b) © Mark Tomalty/Masterfile. **516** © PhotoDisc/Getty Images. **517** ©James C. Amos/Photo Researchers. **520** ©Jeff Vanuga/Corbis. **521** ©Niall Benvie/ Corbis. **522** ©William A. Bake/Corbis. **523** ©Jeff Vanuga/Corbis. **524** © PhotoDisc/Getty Images. **526-7** (m) © Brett Panelli/Stone/Getty Images. **527** (bkgd) Siede Preis/Photodisc Green/Getty Images. **528** (tr) Courtesy of David Adler. (bl) Dean Berry/Index Stock Imagery. **529** (t) Corbis/Colorized by Walter Stuart. (b) Bettmann/Corbis/Colorized by Walter Stuart. **530** (t) Michael Nicholson/Corbis/Colorized by Walter Stuart. (ml) Malcolm Piers/The Image Bank/Getty Images. **532** (b) ©Bettmann/Corbis. **531** ©Bettmann/Corbis. **534-5** (bkgd) Patrick Bennett/Stone/Getty Images. **534** (t) Courtesy, Kathryn Jones. (b) Velma Cooper. **539** ©Flip Schulke/Corbis. **542** AP/Wide World. **552** (inset) AP/Wide World. (frame) Image Farm. **554** AP/Wide World. **558** (b) ©Bob Kramer. **559** (t) ©Jack Vartoogian. (bl) ©Bob Kramer. (br) ©Susan Wilson. (CD)© PhotoDisc/Getty Images. **560-1** (bkgd) Gabriel M. Covian/The Image Bank/Getty Images. **561** (t) © PhotoDisc/Getty Images.. (b)Anthony Nesye/Liaison International. **562** (t) Randy Taylor/SYGMA. (b) AP/Wide World Photos. **563** Arnaldo Magnani/Liaison International. **564** (l) Govert De Roos/Sunshine/Retna. (r) © PhotoDisc/Getty Images. **565** Gregory Kearney Lawson/Liaison International. **566** Les Stone/SYGMA. **567** (l) © PhotoDisc/Getty Images. (r) Sherry Rayn Barnett/Michael Ochs Archives/Venice CA. **568** Joe Traver/Liaison International. **569** (l) © PhotoDisc/Getty Images. (r) Murry H. Sill/Life Magazine ©Time, Inc. **570** Mitchell Gerber/CORBIS. **571** Dirck Halstead/Liaison International. **572** Ed Kennedy. **573** AP/Wide World Photos. **574** (l) Mitchell Gerber/Corbis. (r) AP/Wide World. **575** (t) Raul Demolina/SYGMA. (b) Allen Eveston/The Palm Beach Post. **576** (l) Gamma Liaison. (r) Gary Gershoff/Retna. **577** (l) Courtesy, Mitchell Lane Publishers. (r) © PhotoDisc/Getty Images.. **580** Photo by Maggie Rodriguez, Courtesy, Estefan Enterprises. **582** (t) National Baseball Hall of Fame Library, Cooperstown, NY. (b) National Baseball Hall of Fame Library, Cooperstown, NY. **582–3** (b) National Baseball Hall of Fame Library, Cooperstown, NY. **583** (b) AP/Wide World Photos. **584-5** (bkgd) © Gail Mooney/Masterfile. **603** (t) Michael Tamborrino/Mercury Pictures. (b) Paul Buck/Mercury Pictures. **604** © PhotoDisc/Getty Images. **605** Corbis/Bettmann. **607** (t) National Baseball Hall of Fame Library, Cooperstown, NY. (b) ©Bettmann/Corbis. **608-8A** (bkgd) © Chad Slattery/Stone/Getty Images. **608** (b) Siede Preis/Photodisc Green/Getty Images. **608J** (t) Clark Family Collection/Missouri Historical Society Archives, St. Louis. (m) Missouri Historical Society Archives, St. Louis. **624** © PhotoDisc/Getty Images.. (inset)©Tom Brakefield/The Stock Market. **626-7** (bkgd) © Dr. Robert Munterfering/The Image Bank/Getty Images. **627** (m) © Mark Tomalty/Masterfile. **628** (t) Courtesy of Seymour Simon, (b) Bullaty–Lomeo/Imagebank/Getty Images. **629** (tl) John Dominis/Index Stock Imagery, (tr) Nina Crews, (br) Corbis Images/Picturequest, (bl) RO–MA Stock/Index Stock Imagery. **630** (tr) William Koplitz/Index Stock Imagery Picturequest, (bl) Nina Crews, (br) John Warden/Index Stock Imagery. **631** Rich Reid/National Geographic/Getty Images. **632** (banner)© PhotoDisc/Getty Images. (t) ©Richard Cooke/CORBIS. (b) ©Wolfgang Kaehler/CORBIS. **633** (b)©Tom Bean/CORBIS. (cr) ©W. Perry Conway/CORBIS. **634-5** (bkgd) © Garry Black/Masterfile. **634** (t) John Henry Williams/Bruce Coleman, Inc. (inset) Photo by Benner McGee/©1995 Bruce McMillan. **635–43** ©Bruce McMillan. **648** © PhotoDisc/Getty Images. **649** © PhotoDisc/Getty Images. **650** (b) ©Yva Momatuik & John Eastcott. **650–1** (bkgd) © PhotoDisc/Getty Images. **651** (t) Map Courtesy of Ranger Rick™ Magazine. Copyright 1999 National Wildlife Federation. (b) ©Yva Momatuik & John Eastcott. **653–4** ©Yva Momatuik & John Eastcott. **656** ©Kevin Schafer/CORBIS. **657** ©Kevin Schafer/CORBIS. **659** (t) ©Raymond Gehman/CORBIS. (cl) ©Dennis Flaherty/Photo Researchers, Inc. (br) ©Dr. Edward S. Ross. **660-1** (bkgd) © Michael Rutherford/SuperStock. **660** © PhotoDisc/Getty Images.. (inset) Courtesy, Seymour Simon. **662** (t) © PhotoDisc/Getty Images. **663** Dan Morrison. **665** Seymour Simon. **667** Dan Morrison. **668–9** Alan and Sandy Carey. **671** Alan and Sandy Carey. **673** Alan and Sandy Carey. **675** Gary Braasch/Life. **677** Seymour Simon. **678–9** John J. Lopinot/Silver Image. **681** Alan and Sandy Carey. **682** © PhotoDisc/Getty Images. **684–5** (all) ©Dan Helms. **686** (cl) ©Kevin Schafer/CORBIS. (cr) ©W. Perry Conway/CORBIS. **686-7** (bkgd) ©David Muench/CORBIS. **687** Nebraska State Historical Society, Solomon D. Butcher Collection. **688-9** (bkgd) Stephen Simpson/Taxi/Getty Images. **688** (t) John MacLachlan. (b) Lisa Ratgeb. **705** Photofest. **708-8A** (bkgd) © Don Klumpp/The Image Bank/Getty Images. **708** (b) © Mark Tomalty/Masterfile. **708C** (tr) Associated Press Photo. **711** ©Lowell Georgia/Corbis. **712** ©Wolfgang Kaehler/Corbis. **713** ©David Young-Wolff/PhotoEdit. **714** ©Richard Hamilton Smith/Corbis. **715** ©Adam Woolfitt/Corbis. **716** © PhotoDisc/Getty Images. **717** © PhotoDisc/Getty Images. **718** © PhotoDisc/Getty Images.

## Assignment Photography
**103** (r), **279, 289, 290, 150–1, 485** (b), **581** © HMCo./Joel Benjamin; **135, 277, 383, 513, 609, 709** © HMCo./Michael Indresano Photography. **9, 278, 280–1, 284, 286, 288, 409** (r), **509** (l) © HMCo./Ken Karp; **214, 215** © HMCo./Allan Landau.

## Illustration
**23** Courtesy of Allen Say. **29** (i), **30–51** Robert Blake. **62** (i), **63–74** Allen Say. **78–79** Lark Carrier. **110** (i), Garth Williams. **111–126** Copyright, 2001 by Dorris Ettlinger.. **139–143** Michael Chesworth. **134I, 134K, 134L** Renee Graef. **136-37** Fred Lynch. **144–147** Linda S. Wingerter. **243, 244, 245** William Brinkley and Associates. **295–96** Chris Van Allsburg. **321** Pablo Torricella. **322–323** Linda Wingerter. **326** (maps) XNR Productions, Inc. **380–381** Chris Reed. **382B–F** Bruce MacPherson. **392, 394, 397–407, 408** (b) Copyright, 2001 by Melodye Benson Rosales. **489** (i), **490–507** Sandra Speidel. **512H, 512I, 512L** Steven Noble. **514-15** Karen Chandler. **519** nancy Gibson-Bash. **529–30** Walter Stuart. **580–581** Francisco Mora. **608B–F** Keith Neely. **608G–J** (bkgd) Phil Wilson. **608G** (b) Pablo Torricella. **608I** Pablo Torricella. **610-11** Lori Lohstoeter. **615–619** Krystyna Stasiak. **613–614** Craig Spearing. **620–623** Fred Lynch. **633, 658** XNR Productions, Inc. **689** (i) Marcia Sewall. **690–703** David Somon. **706–707** George Schill. **708B, 708D, 708F** Patrick Whelan. **708G–L** James Bernardin.